Rudolf Kittel, Ebenezer Brown Speirs, John Taylor, Hope W. Hogg

A History of the Hebrews

Vol. 2

Rudolf Kittel, Ebenezer Brown Speirs, John Taylor, Hope W. Hogg

A History of the Hebrews
Vol. 2

ISBN/EAN: 9783337417413

Printed in Europe, USA, Canada, Australia, Japan

Cover: Foto ©ninafisch / pixelio.de

More available books at **www.hansebooks.com**

A HISTORY
OF
THE HEBREWS

By R. KITTEL
ORDINARY PROFESSOR OF THEOLOGY IN THE UNIVERSITY OF BRESLAU

IN TWO VOLUMES

VOL. II.

SOURCES OF INFORMATION AND HISTORY OF THE
PERIOD DOWN TO THE BABYLONIAN EXILE

TRANSLATED BY

HOPE W. HOGG, B.D., AND E. B. SPEIRS, B.D.

WILLIAMS AND NORGATE
14 HENRIETTA STREET, COVENT GARDEN, LONDON
20 SOUTH FREDERICK STREET, EDINBURGH
AND 7 BROAD STREET, OXFORD
1896

Edinburgh: T. and A. CONSTABLE, Printers to Her Majesty

FROM THE PREFACE TO THE GERMAN EDITION.

I HAVE often been asked as to the historical limits of my book. My theme has been the history of the Hebrews. But this terminates amid the ruins of ancient Jerusalem, under which we may say that the ancient Hebrew people found its grave. The history of *Israel*, it is true, goes farther; it is continued in the history of the Jews, and has not yet reached its end. Perhaps I may some day find time and opportunity to follow up the History of the Hebrews with a history of the Jews, at least in its earlier portion.

The analysis of the text of the Book of Kings has been carried out on the presuppositions gained from the analysis of the Books of Judges and Samuel, of which I have given the results in the Translation of the Old Testament, edited by Kautzsch (1894). It was a satisfaction to me to see that, starting from these principles, I reached conclusions quite similar to those reached by the translator of the Book of Kings in Kautzsch's work, in which it should be noticed that the symbol 'Sa' (in 1 Kings) corresponds to my own symbol 'So.'

THE AUTHOR.

BRESLAU, *May* 1892.

₊ The quotations from the prophetical books in this volume are in accordance with the Revised Version. Where necessary, to harmonise the version with Professor Kittel's German translation, the marginal rendering has been substituted

for that in the text of R. V. The Editor desires to acknowledge the kind assistance of Professor Kittel in adding to the notes the most necessary references to recent critical literature. Some slight but interesting changes of opinion on the part of the author will also be found indicated among those additions. In constantly growing subjects like the historical criticism of the Old Testament, such evidence of a writer's progressiveness will be welcomed by all candid readers.

FURTHER ABBREVIATIONS

(Continued from Vol. i. p. x.)

Baethgen, *Beitr.*	Beiträge zur semitischen Religionsgeschichte. 1888.
Bu(dde), *RiSa.*	Die Bücher Richter und Samuel. 1890.
Corp. Inscr. Sem. (*CIS.*)	Corpus Inscriptionum Semiticarum.
Corn(ill), *Grundr.*	Grundriss der theol. Wissenschaften. Einleitung ins Alte Testament. 1891.
Driver, *Introd.*	Introduction to the Literature of the Old Testament. First Edition, 1891.
—— *Notes*	Notes on the Hebrew Text of the Books of Samuel. With an Introduction. 1890.
Kautzsch	Die heilige Schrift des Alten Testaments, in Verbindung mit Baethgen, Guthe, Kittel u. s. w., hrsgb. von E. Kautzsch, 1894.
KgSt.	Königsberger Studien.
Klost. *SaKö.*	Die Bücher Samuelis und der Könige, von A. Klostermann, 1887.
Kuen(en)	Historisch-kritische Einleitung (=Ond.²) zum AT. 2nd ed. The figures following the number of the section indicate the notes.
Mey(er), *Gesch. d. Alt.*	Geschichte des Altertums. Vol I. Ed. Meyer, 1884.
—— *Ägypt,*	Geschichte des alten Ägyptens. Ed. Meyer, 1887.
Pietschm. *Phön.*	Geschichte der Phönizier. R. Pietschmann, 1889.
Schrad(er), *KBibl.*	Keilinschriftliche Bibliothek. Edited by Eberhard Schrader. 1889 : still in progress.

FURTHER ABBREVIATIONS

Sta(de), *Gesch.*	Geschichte des Volkes Israel. B. Stade. Vol. I. 1887.
Stade²	The second impression of the same work.
Tiele, *Gesch.*	Babylonisch-assyrische Geschichte. Part I., 1886; Part II., 1888.
Wellh. *Comp.*²	Die Composition des Hexateuchs und der historischen Bücher des AT., von J. Wellhausen. 2nd ed., 1889.
—— *Nachtr.*	Nachträge, appended to the above.
—— *TBS.*	Der Text der Bücher Samuelis. 1872.

CONTENTS

BOOK II

THE PRE-MONARCHIC AGE AND THE FIRST REPRESENTATIVES OF THE MONARCHY

A.—*SOURCES FOR THIS PERIOD.*

	PAGE
§ 30. The Book of Judges	1

I. *The Stories of the Judges.*

1. The so-called Framework	2
2. The Chronology and the Minor Judges	8
3. The Hero-stories	14

II. *The Appendices.*

1. Chapters xvii. and xviii.	19
2. Chapters xix.-xxi.	21
§ 31. The Books of Samuel	22
1. Samuel and Saul: 1 Sam. i.-xv.	23
2. Saul and David: 1 Sam. xvi.-xxxi.	35
3. David in Hebron and Jerusalem: 2 Sam. ii.-xx.	45
4. The Appendix: 2 Sam. xxi.-xxiv.	48
§ 32. 1 Kings i.-xi.	49
1. The Text	49
2. Unity and Age	53

B.—*HISTORY OF THE PERIOD.*

CHAPTER I.

THE SO-CALLED AGE OF THE JUDGES.

	PAGE
§ 33. The General Situation. Israel's Task	60
§ 34. Further Wars of Conquest	68
§ 35. Inroads from without. The Tribal Monarchy of Ophrah	77
§ 36. Continuation. The Tribal Monarchy of Ophrah. Abimelech in Shechem	83
§ 37. Jephthah. Samson	89
§ 38. Civilisation and Religion in this Age	93

CHAPTER II.

SAMUEL AND SAUL.

§ 39. The Philistine Domination. Samuel	103
§ 40. Saul	111
§ 41. Continuation. Saul and David	119
§ 42. Continuation. Saul's End	131

CHAPTER III.

DAVID, KING.

§ 43. David and Eshba'al	138
§ 44. David in Jerusalem. The Philistines	150
§ 45. Further Wars. David's Army. Saul's House	160
§ 46. Family History of David. Absalom	168

CHAPTER IV.

SOLOMON.

	PAGE
§ 47. Solomon's Accession	177
§ 48. Solomon, King	183
§ 49. Solomon's Temple and Palace	189
§ 50. Civilisation and Religion of the First Period of the Monarchy	196
1. Mode of Life. Political Organisation. Literature	196
2. Morals	199
3. Religion and Belief	200

BOOK III

THE DECLINE OF NATIONALITY AND THE ADVANCE OF RELIGION

A.—*THE SOURCES FOR THIS PERIOD.*

§ 51. The Book of Kings: 1 Kings xii. and onwards	205
1. The Text	205
2. The Framework	207
3. The Annals of the Kings	208
4. The Separate Narrative-pieces as far as 2 Kings xx.	211
5. 2 Kings xxi.-xxv. and the Redaction	223
§ 52. The Book of Chronicles	224
§ 53. Information from Foreign Sources	230
1. Palestinian-Phœnician	230
2. Egyptian	231
3. Assyrio-Babylonian	232
§ 53*a*. Supplement. Chronology of the Hebrew Kings	234

B.—*THE HISTORY OF THE PERIOD.*

CHAPTER I.

REHOBOAM AND JEROBOAM AND THEIR IMMEDIATE SUCCESSORS.

	PAGE
§ 54. The Division of the Kingdom	241
§ 55. Rehoboam. Abijah. Asa	246
§ 56. Jeroboam, Nadab, Baasha, Elah, Omri	250

CHAPTER II.

THE DYNASTY OF OMRI.

§ 57. The Assyrians. Omri	257
§ 58. Elijah and the Prophecy of his time	262
§ 59. Ahab's Wars with Damascus and Assyria	270
§ 60. Ahaziah ben Ahab. Jehoram ben Ahab	274

CHAPTER III.

JEHU AND HIS DYNASTY. THE KINGDOM OF JUDAH.

§ 61. Jehu's Revolution	278
§ 62. Jehoshaphat of Judah and his sons. Athaliah	282
§ 63. Jehu and his successors until Jeroboam II.	289
§ 64. Culture and Religion in the period after Solomon	296
1. Mode of Life and Customs	296
2. Constitution and Social Organisation	299
3. Literature	302
4. Religious Life	304

CHAPTER IV.

THE INTERVENTION OF PROPHECY.

§ 65. Prophecy from the Eighth Century	312
§ 66. Amos. Hosea	320

CHAPTER V.

THE END OF THE NORTHERN KINGDOM.

§ 67. Azariah-Uzziah. Menahem	329
§ 68. The Syro-Ephraimitish War. Isaiah's first appearances	337
§ 69. Samaria's End	348

CHAPTER VI.

THE ASSYRIANS IN JUDAH. JUDAH'S END.

§ 70. Hezekiah	355
§ 71. Sennacherib in Palestine	360
§ 72. Manasseh. Amon	370
§ 73. Josiah	379
§ 74. Jeremiah; Judah's End	385

INDEX   397

BOOK II

THE PRE-MONARCHIC AGE AND THE FIRST REPRE-SENTATIVES OF THE MONARCHY.

A. SOURCES FOR THIS PERIOD.

§ 30. *The Book of Judges.*

FOR the time immediately following the entrance of Israel into Canaan the most important, and almost the only, source of information is the so-called Book of Judges.[1] As it now lies before us it reaches back in its first section even into the time of the Conquest, but it has already been shown that on this very ground the section referred to cannot originally have belonged to the Book.[2]

In its present form the Book of Judges falls into three unequal main divisions: the section just mentioned, which forms the introduction to the present book, i. 1—ii. 5; a long narrative section containing the Stories of the Judges, ii. 6—xvi. 31; and lastly, a narrative section serving as appendix to the Stories of the Judges, and treating of two independent events of the pre-monarchical

---

[1] *Cf.* in general: Studer, *Das B. d. Richt.*[2] (1842); Bertheau, *Die BB. Richt. u. Ruth*[2] (1883); Wellh. *Bl.*[4] 181 ff. *Prol.*[2] 238 ff. [Eng. Trans. 228 ff.]; Van Doorninck, *Bijdrage tot de tekst-kritiek van Richt,* i.-xvi. (1879); Kuen. *Ond.*[2] § 17-20, 27; Budde, *RiSa*; Cornill, *Grundr.* 90 ff.; Driver, *Introd.* 151 ff.; [Öttli, *Deut. Jos. u. Richt.* 1893; König, *Einleit. ins A.T.* § 51; Wildeboer, *Letterkunde des Oud. Verb.* 1893, § 9. 14.] For text, translation, and analysis of sources (apart from minor differences) see also my edition of the book in Kautzsch's translation of the O.T. (1890 ff.).

[2] On this see above, vol. i. p. 239 ff. [Eng. Transl. i. 264 ff.].

period, chaps. xvii. f., and xix.-xxi. As we have already made an independent examination of the first section, we have here to deal only with the other two.

I. THE BOOK OF THE STORIES OF THE JUDGES, ii. 6—xvi. 31.

When this section is viewed as a whole, it is at once seen to have no immediate connection either with what precedes or with what follows. It forms the kernel of the present Book of Judges, but was manifestly once an independent work. The only question that can arise is whether it still has its original beginning and its natural conclusion. The first is likely, since the section connects itself directly with the Book of Joshua :[1] the latter, most unlikely. It is beyond question, however, that the entire section had originally nothing to do with that which immediately precedes it, viz. i. 1—ii. 5, or that which follows it, viz. the two appendices to the Stories of the Judges.[2]

1. *The so-called Framework.* Even a superficial glance shows, moreover, that the great middle division of the present Book of Judges (Ju. ii. 6—xvi. 31, which contains the Stories of the Judges), is not a complete literary unity, but breaks up into diverse constituent parts. The individual Stories of the Judges are not narrated by one and the same person;[3] and none of the principal narrators can be identified with the author of the Stories of the Judges as a whole, the writer who gathered them for us into their present, or some approximately equivalent form.[4] The relation of this author to the stories is rather this, that he supplied a framework

---

[1] *Cf.* Ju. ii. 6 with Josh. xxiv. 28.
[2] *Cf.* Ju. ii. 6 ff. with i. 1*a*., ii. 1*b*. ff. Whoever wrote ii. 6 ff. cannot at the same time have written i. 1*a* and ii. 1*b* ff. It is just as clear that Ju. xvii. ff. were not compiled by the author of ii. 6—xvi. 31. *Cf.* xvii. 6; xviii. 1*a*; xix. 1*a*; xxi. 25, with viii. 23; and thereon Kuen. *Ond.*[2] § xx. 11.
[3] *Cf.* Ju. iv. and v. ; vi. f. and viii. 3 ff.
[4] The individual narratives often stand in very loose connection with the introductions that unite them. The introductions and transitions are marked off from the substance of the narratives by a spirit peculiar to them, and by independent linguistic marks; in particular, by a series of similar, often recurring formulæ.

exhibiting under general aspects the several pictures which lay practically ready-made before him. It is with perfect justice therefore that his contribution has been called the *framework* of the Book of Judges; better, of the Stories of the Judges. It will appear, however, that this designation is valid only *a potiori*, for there are several cases where the compiler has had a share in the business of the narrator himself.[1] I designate the author of the framework 'Ri,' as being the editor of an independent book, the Stories of the 'Judges' [Richter], out of which the present Book of Judges did not grow till later.[2]

For the editor of the *present* Book of Judges, the customary designation R, or (in view of the fact that he belongs, at all events, to Deuteronomist circles) R^d, may be retained.[3]

The structure and age of this framework, and of the immediately related sections of Ri, must now be more closely defined. Here we must start from the *introduction*, ii. 6—iii. 6, prefixed to the Book of Stories of the Judges. It comes, as its contents show, from the author of the book himself, for it contains a preliminary systematic survey of the events afterwards to be described. It is, in other words, the programme of the historian of the age following Joshua. Apart from small additions,[4] it is generally regarded as a unity.[5] Still, Budde may be right when he points to the fact that at the end of chap. ii. new points of view prevail, so that from here onwards R seems to have interposed.[6] Strictly

---

[1] In Ju. iii. 7 ff. at all events, and most probably also in vi. 25-32; vii. 2-8; viii. 22 f., 33-35. He probably appears also in vi. 2-7; vii. 15-22; xi. 1-11, as a reviser of older fragments, although it is not possible to indicate definite additions from his hand.

[2] To Ri I assign Ju. ii. 6-12, 14-16, 18 f.; iii. 7-11, 12-15*aa*; iv. 1-3, 23 f.; v. 31*b*; vi. 1, 2*a*, 6*b*, 25-32, 35; vii. 2-8, 12; viii. 22 f., 27*b*, 28, 33-35; x. 6 f., 8*b*, 10*a* (?), 17 f.; xiii. 1; xiv. 4*b*; xvi. 31*b*.

[3] In chaps. i-xvi. there belong to R, according to my analysis, Ju. i. 1*a*, 4*a*, 8 f.; ii. 1*b*-5*a*, 13, 17, 20-22; iii. 4-6, 31; vi. 7-10; x. 9-16 (exc. perh. 10*a*).

[4] *vv.* 13 and 17 belong to R.

[5] So espec. by Kuen. § xviii. 2.

[6] See Budde, *RiSa*, 156. His assumption, however, that *v.* 20 ff. are from E, is hardly correct. The verses do not appear to me to be old. They contain the same matter as iii. 1 ff., and are probably derived thence. In chap. ii. I regard only *v.* 23 (perh. J) as old; in iii. 1-6, only *vv.* 1-3 (which belong rather to J than

speaking then, the introduction included only ii. 6-19 (with the omission of *vv.* 13 and 17).[1]

It is specially worthy of note that this programme is governed by a very definite point of view. It gives us nothing less than the general scheme according to which the events of the period disposed themselves, in conformity with the prophetic-theocratic conceptions of the editor. The apostasy of the people immediately after the death of Joshua, is followed by the judgment of Yahvé; the punishment of Yahvé leads to amendment; the people's amendment is followed by deliverance through a Judge; and then, after a longer or shorter interval, apostasy and amendment appear again.

It is a characteristic feature of the author of this introduction, that he entertains an idea of the Judges that cannot be regarded as strictly historical. For him, they are rulers of Israel in the proper sense of the term, and in fact rulers of the whole people,— who even in times of peace exercise over Israel theocratic sway. These features of his work show that the author we have to do with was less concerned about the strictly historical establishment of facts, than he was to turn to account the theocratic and pragmatic materials furnished him by tradition, and to illustrate their religious and moral significance.

In closest connection with this introduction to the Book of Stories of the Judges stand certain sections of the book itself. They consist in the main, though not exclusively, of the connective passages by which the stories of Othniel, Ehud, Barak, Gideon, Jephthah, and Samson are bound together, and united to the rest of the narrative material that was perhaps even then received into the book. In respect of language[2] and range of ideas, they are a work of the same R to whom the introduction belongs.

to E: so in the main Meyer, *ZAW.* i. 145; *cf.* the text in my transl., where, however, the analysis is somewhat different). *Vv.* 5 f. also belong rather to R than to E (against Budde; *cf.* the nations mentioned in *v.* 5, which are to be found also in Jos. xxiv. 11*b*, and there belong to R).

[1] The section ii. 20—iii. 6 has been inserted by R to bring into prominence a point of view arising from the history of the Conquest in Ju. i.

[2] On this see Kuen. § xviii. 3. For the passages themselves see above, p. 3, notes 1 and 2.

In particular, they are based on the same conception of the Judges and their time, and of the history of Israel generally. Here also the Judges are magistrates permanently governing Israel, ruling over the whole people. Here also the religious-moral way of looking at things comes into the foreground. Sin is regarded as the first and chief ground of disaster to the people— the whole people; and the interference of Yahvé on the ground of Israel's amendment, as the first cause of relief. Here again, we recognise everywhere not so much immediate records approximately contemporary with the events, as a historical view, of the highest moral worth and interest indeed, but such as was reached only by religious-moral reflection on the events, which it partly developed and enlarged upon in an imaginative and independent way. We recognise here the historical standards of men who had absorbed the ideas of the prophets, and who regarded the national past from a purified point of view in consequence of Israel's calamity. It is not so much history as a philosophy of history. It is elucidation, estimation, adjustment of facts from the standpoint of subsequent knowledge of the consequences and goal of the historical development, rather than simple narration of the course of the events themselves; a history that is more satisfactory as a means of religious and moral improvement, than as supplying historical knowledge about the original course of events. In short, there appear here the same, or very nearly the same, phenomena as those met with above in the historical sections of Deuteronomy, assigned by us to D^2, and in the Deuteronomistic parts of the Book of Joshua.

Wellhausen[1] and Kuenen[2] accordingly regard the sections, assigned by us to the hand of Ri, as the work of a Deuteronomist redactor, and so assign them to the time of the exile or the last decades preceding it. Stade[3] and Budde[4] also regard the framework as belonging to R^d. At the same time, however, most of the scholars mentioned believe themselves able, although neither on

---

[1] *Bleek*,[4] p. 186.
[2] *Ond.*[2] § xviii. 1, 3.
[3] *ZAW.* i. p. 339 ff.
[4] *RiSa*, p. 94.

the same lines, nor to the same extent, to detect the traces of older documents that Ri followed.

But, valuable as it must ever be to detect the earliest traces of a historical phenomenon, and welcome as an older forerunner of the Deuteronomist Ri would be to us here, such traces are in the present case, so far as I am able to see, not discoverable even after diligent search, except in so far as they go back to the narrators themselves.[1] What have been represented as such traces have, for the most part, nothing to do with the framework of the Stories of the Judges, but belong to R, the redactor of the present Book of Judges. The latter seems, indeed, in part to have followed in his language other models than Ri, and in particular to have come one step nearer than Ri does to the expressions of E of the Pentateuch. In this we have the explanation of the fact, emphasised by Kuenen, that certain sections of the framework—as a matter of fact they belong entirely to R—exhibit signs of a peculiar linguistic usage not of the Deuteronomist type.[2] We have no need to make the assumption, nowhere supported by palpable facts, that a special recension in the shape of a pre-Deuteronomic edition was used by Ri.[3] Thus disappears also the ground of

---

[1] This applies especially to Wellh. who finds intimations of this pragmatism in vi. 2-6, 11, ff.; viii. 28 (*Bleek*,[4] § 92). Here, however, whatever has not been added by Ri, must have already existed in the narrative. To suppose still another hand, seems to me arbitrary, as the reference to Israel is to be found even in ix. 22. If this verse must come from some other source, we should at all events have to assign it, not to the pre-Deuteronom. redactor, but to R (*cf* also iii. 27; vii. 23). The crying to Yahvé also, and the humiliation of the enemy (p. 187), in so far as they are not due to Ri, may likewise belong to the original narrative (Cornill, *ZAW*. x. 107 E²). On this, and what follows, *cf*. my article: *Über die pent. Urkunden in den BB. Richt. u. Sam.* in *StKr.*, 1892, 44 ff. (In the translation in Kautzsch the analysis is still in parts somewhat different.)

[2] *Cf.* § xviii. 2, 3; xix. 11. Kuenen cites as examples, ii. 20 ff.; vi. 7-10; x. 6-16. From these is inferred a written work—not simple individual narratives —used by Ri. On ii. 20 ff. see above; vi. 7-10 belongs, as a matter of fact, to R. It recalls ii. 1b ff. rather than ii. 6 ff. To suppose that it belongs to E (Budde, 107 f., Cornill, *ZAW*. 1890, p. 105), on account of single expressions that are also to be found in E, will not do in the case of so late a passage (*cf.* איש נביא). Moreover על־אדות is proved to occur in later passages by Josh. xiv. 6, and Jer. iii. 8. The passage is distinctly Deuteronomistic. It is to be compared with such passages as 1 Sam. ii. 27 ff. On x. 6 ff., see note [1] on p. 7.

[3] *Cf.* also the concessions of Kuenen in § xix. 11 at the beginning, and xix. 12.

Stade's difficulty—viz. the presence of an introduction in the middle of the Book of Judges—and at the same time the somewhat fantastic hypothesis built on it, that Ju. x. 6-16 originally formed the continuation in E of Ju. iii. 13 ff.[1] The only ground that can be urged in support of the view that we have here an independent source, or that at least the redactor employed independent accounts, lies in the mention of the heathen peoples out of whose hands, according to Ju. x. 11, Yahvé had delivered Israel. Besides the Egyptians and Amorites, mention is made of the Ammonites, Philistines, Sidonians, Amalek, and Maon (Midian ?[2]). It might be argued that the writer of this sentence had, in the copy that lay before him—*i.e.* E according to Stade and Budde—an account of wars between Israel and these nations. On historical grounds, however, it is most improbable that such a narrative ever existed, and the hypothesis gains nothing in credibility from literary considerations. For if an editor had omitted the account of the wars themselves, one cannot see why he did not also omit the allusion to them in Ju. x. 11, but preserved precisely this trace of E. The enigmatical reference to such wars is explicable simply as a misunderstanding on the part of a late editor, whether the anachronism be ascribed to R himself, or be due, at least in part, to a gloss from some later hand.

[1] See Stade, *ZAW*. i. 340 ff. Budde, *RiSa* 128. In point of fact only x. 6 f. 8*b* (excluding 'by the hand of the Philistines and,' which is a gloss, or an addition, made by R) are of the nature of an introduction. It comes from Ri and presents nothing remarkable. V. 8*a* I assign to the source (*cf.* the verbs); 8*b* is an addition from the hand of Ri. V. 9 is inserted by R to describe the distress as affecting all Israel. 10*a* could, if necessary, be a further fragment of the introduction of Ri. All the rest, however, belongs to R, who has here introduced a speech quite in the manner of ii. 1*b* ff.; vi. 7 ff. The presence, in x. 6-16, of single touches in the style of E cannot claim for that writer an independent share in its production. V. 6 does not point immediately to Josh. xxiv., but in the first place to Ju. iii. 7 f. The nations were perhaps only added by R, or inserted as a gloss still later. In the same way the following verses are drawn not directly, but indirectly from E—*i.e.* R took E's book as his model. In point of fact, with the exception of the clause 16*b* (=Num. xxi. 4*b*) every single expression that can be claimed for E, appears also in Deuteronomistic passages. Even for that clause, *cf.* Job xxi. 4, Zech. xi. 8, Mic. ii. 7.

[2] *Cf.* however, the frequent mention of the Meunim in Chronicles.

2. *The Chronology and the Minor Judges.*—What value the statements of our author possess for the historical treatment of the period, is clear from what has been already said. It lies in the pragmatism of his view of history, not in the positive contribution that he offers to our knowledge of the events. In view of the relatively late origin of the additions of Ri, we cannot in general expect from him any considerable extension of our knowledge of the individual occurrences of the old time. Where such a claim is still made, there must be special grounds for believing that the author had older accounts at his command.

It is certainly in favour of our author that he aims much less at such an enlargement of our stock of knowledge of the events, than at giving an estimate of their ethical-religious value. It is therefore only occasionally that we are able to take into consideration the historical character of his contributions. There is one case, it must be granted, where this question will arouse a special interest on our part—viz. the case of the chronology contributed by him.[1] The investigation of its literary character must be combined with the investigation of the origin of the accounts that we possess of the so-called minor Judges.

The part of the present Book of Judges that exhibits the characteristics of Ri contains a continuous chronology, giving information about the length of the rule of each Judge, or of the period of rest that followed his victory over the enemy, and also of the length of the period of foreign domination that preceded. Many of these figures—viz. those relating to the so-called major Judges, with the exception of Jephthah, *i.e.* Othniel, Ehud, Barak, Gideon and Samson,[2] and to the foreign domination preceding Jephthah's appearance—belong obviously to Ri.[3] Moreover, it is

---

[1] On this *cf.* generally: Nöldeke in *Unterss. z. Krit. d. AT.*, p. 173 ff.; Köhler, *Bibl. Gesch.* ii., p. 35 ff. Wellhausen in *Bleek*,[4] p. 184 f.; *Prol.*[2] p. 239 f; Reuss, *Gesch. d. AT.* § 96, 277; Bertheau, *Richt.*[2], p. xi. ff. Riehm, *HWB.*, p. 1291 f., 1801 f.; Budde, *RiSa*, p. 134 ff.

[2] Judges iii. 8, 11, 14, 30; iv. 3; v. 31*b*; vi. 1; viii. 28; xiii. 1; xvi. 31*b*. On xv. 20 see below: as also on xii. 7.

[3] Judges x. 8*b*.

in the highest degree probable that the figures were inserted by Ri himself when he combined the stories of the Judges into a whole, and set them in the framework of his pragmatic observations, although he may have found some of them in the narrative before him. It is a decided argument in favour of this view, that in the case of these Judges the continuous chronology is to be found most frequently, not in the text of the narrative, but in the course of the observations that are characteristic of Ri,[1] and even here often in peculiar, formal turns of expression.[2] In one case, the state of the text still shows clearly enough that the chronological notice is only a later addition to the text of the original narrative.[3]

The question of the meaning and origin of this chronology becomes peculiarly difficult and involved when we observe that notes of time, pointing to a continuous chronology, are to be found not only in the framework and the parts immediately connected therewith, but also in the sections referring to the so-called *minor Judges*.[4] By this term are meant those Judges, regarding whom all that we find in the Book of Judges is their names and perhaps a few scanty notices—viz. Tola, Jair, Ibzan, Elon, and Abdon. In spite of all his summary brevity, the narrator finds room to assign a number of years to each of these five heroes, allowing them altogether seventy years of activity as Judges.

We seem to have found the key to the whole chronology lying ready to hand, when we discover that in 1 Kings vi. 1, the time from the Exodus to the fourth year of Solomon's reign, in which he began the building of the temple, is fixed at 480 years. As the 480 years are made up of twelve generations of forty years, what is more natural than to expect the chronology of the period of the Judges to agree with them, when extended proportionately forwards and backwards? The agreement is the more to be

---

[1] See the passages cited above, exc. iii. 8, 11, where Ri himself is clearly the narrator.   [2] See iii. 11, 30; v. 31; vi. 1; viii. 28; xiii. 1.
[3] Judges x. 8: 'They oppressed the children of Israel in that year for eighteen years all the children of Israel. . . .'
[4] Judges x. 1-4; xii. 7-15. On Shamgar, who is often reckoned among the 'minor' Judges, *v.* p. 13, note 2.

expected, as 1 Kings vi. 1 comes from a Deuteronomist hand, and as obviously the number forty already plays in the Book of Judges a part not to be overlooked.[1]

The hope of thus reaching a solution threatens to melt away at once, when we attempt to reckon up the figures occurring in the Book of Stories of the Judges. These yield a sum-total of 410;[2] so that only seventy years remain for the journey through the wilderness, and the time of Joshua and his generation, at the one end, and for Eli, Samuel, Saul, and David, together with the first four years of Solomon, at the other. And yet the first, third, and sixth of these items alone have each again forty years secured them.[3]

Wellhausen has hit upon an expedient of special interest to us here, since it promises at the same time some help in regard to the literary difficulty. He believes it can be computed that the twelve generations of forty years each, manifestly intended in 1 Kings vi., are obtained when we leave out of count the seventy years of the minor Judges. According to him the chronology is complete without any reference to these minor Judges. They are, as the special schematic form of the narrative shows, described by a narrator of their own, and indeed only introduced into the Book of Judges by way of addition. The writer who added them did not include in his calculation the periods of foreign domination, but only the periods of rest under the rule of a Judge.[4]

This proposal is fascinating; but it is found on closer inspection to be encumbered by so many difficulties, that we can easily understand how its own author has come to be in doubt about it. Is it likely that two hands were at work on the chronology of the period of the Judges, the second of whom had no idea that he was

---

[1] *Cf.* iii. 11, 30 ; v. 31 ; viii. 28 ; xiii. 1. Moreover, in iv. 3 ; (xv. 20) xvi. 31, the number 20. Also, the forty years of Moses, Eli, and David. (See below.)

[2] *Vide* the individual items in Berth.² p. xi. xii. The twenty years in xv. 20 and xvi. 31 must of course be only once reckoned.

[3] *Cf.* 1 Sam. iv. 18 (LXX. 20) ; yet see Field, *Hexapl.* i. 484) ; 2 Sam. v. 4.

[4] *Bleek*,[4] 184 f. Somewhat differently, *Prol.*² 239 f. [Eng. Transl. 229 f.] In the *Nachträge* to the *Composit. d. Hexat*, etc. (1889), p. 356, Wellhausen himself admits the uncertainty of this computation. On the other hand, Budde (*RiSa*, 136) has adopted it anew.

completely subverting the work of the first, although the first was supported by 1 Kings vi.? Further: if we must suppose that the chronology can be understood only on the presupposition that it requires the reader to allow for the periods of foreign domination within the periods of rest, why should this demand be made only by a later writer, and not by the real originator of the system? Does it thus become at all less strange, more easily intelligible to the reader? Or is it not the case that the reader needed to know how such chronological data are to be fitted into each other?[1] If he needed to know this in the case of a later writer, he would also need to know it in the case of Ri. If, however, this later writer wished to 'displace' the years of foreign domination by the insertion of these merely enumerated Judges,[2] why did he not rather choose as his way of dealing with those years the expedient, elsewhere not unknown to him, of striking them out?[3]

Besides, there are important literary considerations with regard to the accounts of the minor Judges themselves. As a matter of fact, these have a scheme of their own. But this very feature turns against Wellhausen, and in the following way. In the case of Samson, who belongs to the major Judges, we possess a certain chronological datum given twice over.[4] Only the second can be from Ri, closing as it does the story of the Judge after the manner of that writer.[5] The first, thrust into the middle of the story, neither occupies its right place there, nor is it in any sense a conclusion in the manner of Ri.[6] Were it the latter, it would not need to tell the reader that Samson judged *in the days of the Philistines*. This added phrase shows that the notice originally did not conclude, but rather supplied the place of, an account of

---

[1] On this see Nöldeke, *Unters.* p. 194. It is incorrect, however, to regard as Nöldeke does the periods of foreign domination as included in those of the Judges. The eighteen years of x. 8 could not possibly be included in Jephthah's six, nor the forty of xiii. 1 in Samson's twenty. They appear, however, alongside of the scheme, without any definite way of working them in. For the rest, *cf.* the computation of the 480 years, Wellh. *loc. cit.*, and Nöldeke, p. 192.

[2] So Budde, *RiSa*, p. 136.   [3] *Cf.* Budde, 134 f.

[4] Ju. xv. 20, and xvi. 31*b*.   [5] *Cf.* xvi. 31*b* with iii. 10, etc.

[6] This against Budde's attempted explanation, *RiSa*, 133.

Samson. It comes from a special source, that told of Samson only in a summary way.

Compare now with this the formula, agreeing with it word for word, used in the case of each of the minor Judges. It runs thus: 'and he judged Israel . . . years,' and is followed by a few words giving a brief survey of the history of the Judge in question.[1] It can hardly admit of doubt that these surveys once existed, not only for the minor Judges but also for all or several of the major. But if this is so, the possibility is excluded of these summary notices having been first introduced into the book after the time of Ri, by a later supplementer, possibly to complete the number twelve. For, in the case of Samson, there was no gap to be filled. We must rather suppose a number of already existing notices, which Ri was unwilling to see perish.[2]

Thus, what was *a priori* not probable, is refuted by the facts themselves. The proof is, however, considerably strengthened by another argument. Wellhausen excises seventy years for the minor Judges, regarding them as requiring to be treated independently on the ground of their own peculiar scheme. Kuenen[3] has quite justly maintained against him, that in view of this scheme the chronological data for Jephthah would also need to be set aside.[4] The seventy years thus become seventy-six, and so Wellhausen's four hundred and eighty years are reduced by six, and the resemblance between the seventy years of the minor Judges and the seventy-one of oppression disappears.[5] Kuenen's

---

[1] Ju. x. 2, 3; xii. 9b, 11-13, and especially xii. 11b, 14b. In Ri only in iii. 10. For obvious reasons xv. 20 contains only the middle part of the scheme: the clause, 'And after him arose,' is rendered superfluous by the preceding history; and the clause, 'And he died, etc.,' by that which follows.

[2] According to Budde (*RiSa* 94), the scheme of the minor Judges betrays its younger origin by its briefer form, as compared with Ri. Kuenen, § xix. 11, and Cornill, *ZAW*. 1890, p. 107 f., come to the opposite conclusion. In any case, the comparison yields no conclusive result. [3] *Ond.*[2] § xviii. 7.

[4] Ju. xii. 7; cf. v. 8 ff., x. 2 f. For the same reason as in the case of Samson, the introductory expressions are curtailed, and the conclusion omitted.

[5] In Wellhausen's calculation of these, indeed, the forty years of xiii. 1 are also ignored without reason. This would be legitimate only if we merged the times of oppression in those of rest.

proposition finds support in the fact that the seventy-six years thus obtained, supplemented by the four years of Solomon's reign before the building of the temple, once more yield the unit of forty which controls the whole computation. In this way, if the numbers for the foreign domination are set aside, the reckoning proceeds simply by generations, or half or double generations (forty, twenty, or eighty years).[1]

Our result is this. The five minor Judges, Tola, Jair, Ibzan, Elon, and Abdon,[2] do not form a group by themselves. The short account of them is connected with corresponding notices of Samson and Jephthah, as well as of Abimelech.[3] These sketches were neither written by the narrators of the present histories, nor by Ri himself, nor yet, as the chronology shows, inserted by a later hand, but worked in by Ri. They formed a distinct little document, a brief sketch of the period of the Judges, without the pragmatism of Ri, but probably already containing the characteristic idea of 'Judge.' If we search for material that Ri could make use of in addition to the Stories of the Judges themselves, we can find it most plausibly in this Little Book of Judges. To distinguish it from Ri, we may call it 'ri.'

Our inquiry as to the sources for the history of the period of the Judges and their literary structure, has thus led to a result not altogether unimportant. It appears that Ri worked on certain materials which most probably already contained, in addition to the traditional history, also a few chronological data. In view, indeed, of the system elsewhere apparent, it can hardly be accidental that the five minor Judges, with Jephthah and Solomon, have a total of eighty years assigned to them. But some, and even the majority of the numbers, are not involved in this charge of artificial structure. On the contrary, their

---

[1] See Nöldeke, *Unters.* 192.

[2] Shamgar (iii. 31) does not belong here. He remains outside of the scheme, and is perhaps loosely inserted here from v. 6, by R. *Cf.* גם הוא. The phrase ואחריו היה is due to imitation.

[3] *Cf.* x. 1. What was said of him has been cancelled by Ri. Abimelech is not regarded by him as a Judge. Hence he also reckons his three years as part of the period of foreign domination in Gideon's time.

irregularity as compared with the systematic structure of the numbers assigned to the major Judges, points much rather to old tradition. The same may be said of the intervals of oppression, which Ri may very well have found ready to hand, since they stand outside of the scheme. And even the figures for the major Judges, closely interwoven as they now are with the schematic elements of the narrative, cannot, in view of this result, be absolutely surrendered.[1] If David's forty years are most probably historical, the numbers may also elsewhere, in one case or another, rest on good tradition, although we may not be able to substantiate it in individual cases.

3. *The Hero-stories.*—When the parts of the Book of Stories of the Judges with which we have dealt are set aside, what remains consists of a number of narratives concerning heroes of the pre-monarchic time. To this belongs nearly all the material of the accounts of the so-called major Judges—that is, besides Othniel, Ehud, Barak-Deborah, Gideon, Jephthah, and Samson.

For the historian all the questions hitherto discussed culminate in this one: What can we learn of the time and place of origin of these accounts?

That they do not represent any simple unity is obvious. The song of Deborah marks itself off from the narrative as a deposit of much greater age. In the story of Gideon, and probably here and there elsewhere, we easily discern a severance and a reconnection of the thread of the narrative.

Such observations, however, are of minor importance as compared with the cardinal question, whether we can trace throughout the whole book certain main threads, or whether we must assume that each narrative stands alone, and is to be judged by itself.

It would be the simplest and most satisfactory solution of this question if we could show that the narrative books J and E, known to us from the Hexateuch, are continued in the Book of Judges.[2] We should then enjoy the advantage of being able to

---

[1] See besides, Matthes in *Theol. Tijd.* xv. 605 f., and Kuenen, § xviii. 4; also some additional particulars below.   [2] *Cf.* my article in *StKr.*, 44 ff.

take for granted here, the results already obtained there, as to the time, place, and character of these writings. Moreover, nothing is in itself more natural than to expect to find a continuation of those books on the history of the Origins of Israel, carrying the narrative through the Conquest of Canaan. If their authors described the preliminary history of the chosen people and its fortunes in the desert, why should they not have given posterity also an account of its further course? No one will regard it as a serious objection to this view, that the Priestly Writing P was not continued through the time of Joshua. It has, as a law-book, a quite special interest in the time down to Joshua, and can thus quite well occupy a place by itself. On the other hand, we must admit that the bare possibility of the existence of a continuation of E and J does not free us from the duty of finding proof. For over against it there stands a whole series of other possibilities, that in themselves possess the same degree of probability. Is it the ordinary course of things for a people to describe first of all the history of its own beginnings, or its recollections of the events lying nearer at hand? E and J belong to a time when Israel must have long been accustomed to the practice of writing, and do not represent the beginnings of their literature. A series of old songs, also the Book of Wars, and the Book of the Upright, were already in existence. Who can tell whether other attempts at literary production, in the form of popular historical narratives, may not also have preceded those comprehensive representations of the early history? This is, at all events, highly probable. And if that is so, on what materials would the annalists and chroniclers in Israel have first of all tried their hand, before they went back to the hoary distance of the primeval and patriarchal time? Surely it would be on the history of the hero-king and his wars, his unfortunate predecessor, and the glorious days of Midian under Jerubbaal, and of Moab, Canaan, and Ammon, under Ehud, Barak, and Jephthah. An old song,[1] considerably older than E and J, enumerates for us the tribes of Israel in order, according to

[1] Gen. xlix.

their character and fortunes, as they had appeared in the old heroic age. The next step in literary work was probably the filling in of sketches of this sort with flesh and blood, the formation of concrete pictures of the wars and experiences of the tribes, and groups of tribes, in the heroic age.

We do not by these considerations reach a decision on the question in hand; but we have justified our demand for conclusive proof, in confirmation of the assertion that E and J had a prominent share in the history of the time after Joshua, and our dissatisfaction with indefinite possibilities. At the same time we have indicated the principles according to which we must judge such possibilities.

In point of fact the theory we have been considering has been maintained lately[1] with great energy. After Stade[2] thought he had discovered evident traces of E, and Böhme[3] of J, in the part of the Book of Judges under consideration, Budde made the attempt to apportion nearly the whole narrative between these two main Hexateuch sources.

With reference to the results of Böhme, and especially of Stade, Kuenen[4] expressed his doubts. After fully acknowledging that a very close relationship exists between J and the two sections that were claimed for it by Böhme, Kuenen still demands convincing proof of the identity of the authors. Neither can I divest myself of certain doubts. It is true the accord with J is so obvious that if the sections stood in the Hexateuch we could not hesitate to claim at least one of them[5] for J. But the case is

---

[1] On earlier attempts based on presuppositions no longer tenable, cf. *StKr.* 1892, 45 f.

[2] See above, p. 8. *Cf.* also E. Meyer, *ZAW.* i. 143 ff. Yet in Ju. i. 1—ii. 5 and iii. 1 ff. we have fragments of J and E that have made their way here from the Hexateuch.

[3] *ZAW.* v. p. 251 ff. on the oldest representation in Ju. vi. 11-24, and xiii. 2-24.

[4] *Ond.*[2] § xix. 13. *Cf.* also before that, Bertheau, *Richt.*[2] p. xxiii.

[5] Ju. vi. 11 ff. In the case of the other, xiii. 2 ff., even in the Hexateuch the question would not be quite easy to settle. I hold Böhme's analysis as in part not sufficiently established. Moreover, the assumption of a subsequent insertion of Elohim for Yahvé in *vv.* 6, 9, 14, has its difficulties. The Jahvistic origin of the section is thus, in spite of all agreement with J, seriously called in question.

quite different when it is the very presence of J at all in the Book of Judges, that is itself to be established on this ground. For this, the proof is not sufficient in the case of chap. vi.; still less in that of chap. xiii. The affinity with J, marked as it may be, does not exclude non-Jahvistic features,[1] so that we have as much right to think of some other narrator, for reasons unknown to us closely related to J, as of J himself. The writer might quite as well be a man of the same circle and linguistic usage. We might have before us a case of imitation of the narrative style of J, or a predecessor whom J copied, if not of both of these at the same time.

Without then absolutely rejecting Böhme's results, we need not leave out of sight the necessary reservations. And this is true to an even greater degree, of the inferences that Budde[2] has drawn from them. He attributes a whole series of sections to J, in many cases not on the ground of independent criteria, but simply because of their coherence with J.[3] But the special signs of a section's belonging to J, that he urges, are not conclusive; while in so far as he appeals to general coherence,[4] his reasoning lacks, as we have said, a sufficiently sure basis. On the other hand, this argument loses in strength when we consider how seldom the Jahvistic features are to be found with this clearness, even in the two sections in chaps. vi. and xiii.; and if we grant that J is to be found in them, where are such features in the others?

The question now is, whether the case is any better for E. Stade has contented himself with ascribing a single section[5] to E in addition to those spoken of before.[6] Budde, on the contrary, claims for this source the whole of the narrative material not attributed by him to J.[7] Here also the argument seems to me

---

[1] *Cf.* on vi. 11 ff., the fuller proof in *StKr.* 1892, 57 f.
[2] *Cf. RiSa*, pp. 100, 106 ff., 122 f., 130 ff.
[3] Thus vi. 2b-6a; vii. 1-8, iii. 20 conjecturally; further, chaps. xiv.-xvi., although here also not quite decisively.
[4] Thus iii. 15 ff., 'according to the impression made'; and chap. iv., on account of its supposed close relation to chap. i. [5] iii. 15 ff. See *ZAW.* i. 343.
[6] ii. 6—iii. 6 (more exactly, ii. 20 ff.), and x. 6-16. On this, see above, p. 3 ff., 6 f. [7] *Cf. RiSa*, pp. 107, 109 f., 118 f., 122, 127.

not conclusive. Weighty reasons could certainly be urged for the derivation of some of these sections from E,[1] in the event of its having been otherwise established that E had a share in the composition of the stories of the Judges; but they are not sufficient to establish this latter point, if it is in any way in question. A number of the reasons urged by Budde in support of E's authorship admit of another explanation;[2] while, on the other hand, a number of features in the sections in question may be employed directly against Budde's view.[3] Amongst the latter I include especially the aversion to the Monarchy, adduced by Budde, as it appears in certain passages.[4] As a matter of fact, no analogous expression can be pointed to anywhere in what has any fair claim to be regarded as the text of E; indeed E's book gives undisguised expression to the proud joy over the Monarchy in Israel.[5]

This being the case, it must recommend itself to us as the safer way, in seeking the historical value of the Judge-stories for the time of their origin, not to trust to the results already won for E and J, but to try to arrive at an independent decision in the case of each individual narrative.[6]

---

[1] Especially the circumstance that the majority of these narratives point to the kingdom of Ephraim, and to a time near that of E.

[2] This applies to vi. 25-32 (p. 110). *Cf. StKr.* 1892, 59. Similarly, the possible reference to the golden calf in viii. 22 f., does not lead to any conclusion in favour of E (p. 122). J also tells of this.

[3] In view of Josh. xxiv., the history of Abimelech cannot be from E. There Shechem is Israelitish. If E inserted the fable of Jotham (Bu. 119), he is certainly also the author of Ju. ix.—but this he cannot be, on account of Shechem. Individual expressions, to which others can easily be opposed (*StKr.* 1892, 60), are no proof. In vi. 36 ff., *cf. v.* 39a, with Gen. xviii. 32 J. In view of Gen. xxii., the history of Jephthah can hardly be from E; *cf.* also ויולד in xi. 1.

[4] Esp. viii. 22 f.; acc. to Budde also in the fable of Jotham.

[5] *Cf.* Nu. xxiii. 9 ff., esp. *v.* 21 (*cf.* יי אלהיו and Bu. 110 thereon), Dt. xxxiii. 5, 17. The case is even clearer if Nu. xxiv. 7 is to be assigned to E (Kue.). See in general Cornill, *ZKWL.* 1885, p. 135. In spite of this, Cornill assigns Ju. viii. to E. He derives the present form of *v.* 23 however from E[2] (*ZAW.* x. 105); on which, see below.

[6] On this, see below, §§ 34-37.

II. THE APPENDICES.

The kernel of the Book of Judges is followed by two appendices, independent of the Judge-stories proper, and attached to them only by a reference to the time when 'there was as yet no king in Israel.' Each of these brings into view an episode of that time. They were placed together and incorporated in the Book of Judges by R, but differ much in literary structure and historical value.

1. *Chaps.* xvii. *and* xviii.—The first of these appendices relates the origin of the sanctuary of Dan. The Danites, numbering 600 men, and as yet without fixed abode, win their later settlement by an attack on the town of Laish in the far north. On their way thither they carry off an image from Mount Ephraim, and found with it their sanctuary, afterwards to become so famous.

The narrative is not a unity. Vatke remarked this, and therefore sought for two independent documents.[1] After this had been opposed by Oort,[2] Wellhausen,[3] and Kuenen,[4] who thought they could get rid of the obvious inequalities of the narrative by supposing a revision, Budde has again—following in part in the footsteps of Bertheau[5]—attempted[6] to prove the existence of two sources. His results with regard to the separation of the parts, I can accept in the main points.[7] According to this view there has been worked into the main narrative a second, having various features of a somewhat different type. In view, however, of the

---

[1] *Relig. d. AT.*, p. 268, note.   [2] *Theol. Tijdschr.* i. 285 ff.
[3] *Bleek,*[4] 198 f.   [4] *Ond.*[2] § xx. 4, especially with reference to Bertheau.
[5] *Cf. Richt.*[2] 239 ff.   [6] *RiSa*, 138 ff.
[7] To the main narrative—called N in the translation in *Kautzsch*—of this appendix I assign: xvii. 1-5 (from לו onwards) . . . 8-11a, 12aa, 13; xviii. 1b, 2aa (exc. מקצותם), 2b, 3b, (from ויאמרו)—7*, 8-10aa, 10b-14*, 15*, 16*, 17*, 18a*, 18b-29 (31?). The second narrative (N¹) exhibits several independent features (the priest is a נער), but on the whole contents itself with giving to N, by minor additions, a new and unfavourable sense. By the addition of פסל ומסכה, the sanctuary is characterised as objectionable; and according to xvii. 2-4 it is, even to begin with, of disreputable origin. This narrative would have us regard the attack on Laish, as well as that on Micah's farm, as less harmless than the other narrative suggests. N¹ is to be seen in: xvii. 2-4, 6 f. 11b, 12aβb; xviii. 1a (2aβ?), 3a (as far as שם), 7*, 10aβ, parts of 14-18 and 20 (פסל), (30?) On the text *cf.* the above-named Translation: the sources are there somewhat differently given.

tendency apparent in most, if not all¹ of the interpolated elements, it must remain doubtful whether the second rests on an independent document, or whether its compiler was not rather at the same time the reviser of the whole.

For the purpose of the historian, at all events, the first narrative, which is manifestly the older, demands special attention. Budde believes he can recognise in it E, and is not indisposed to ascribe the second to J. In view of the results we have already reached, neither of these conjectures commends itself very strongly.² The greater age of J as compared with E ought, in Budde's case, to weigh against this identification.

We may unconditionally regard the main account as one of our oldest fragments of narrative. Its great age is proved not only by the knowledge that the author has at his command, of the highly primitive state of things³ which we otherwise know actually prevailed in that pre-monarchic age, but even more by the completely artless way in which he reports it. Indeed, the original narrative is so far from finding any impropriety in the conduct of the Danites, that the naïve delight at the success of the clever enterprise favoured by Yahvé is rather allowed to appear. Possibly the narrative even originated directly in Dan itself. Perhaps many of the expressions,⁴ differing from the usage of south and middle Palestine otherwise known to us, may be explained in the same way. For all that, the narrative is neither contemporaneous with the events, nor of a time immediately following them.⁵

---

¹ Even the youth in N¹ could be accounted for by the desire to make the outrage seem greater.

² *Cf. loc. cit.* p. 144 f. *Teraphim* is no proof. If *Teraphim* were at all in use in ancient times, they might be mentioned in any ancient narrative whatever. The inoffensiveness of the mention in N stands in the way of ascribing it to E; *cf.* further ערך בגדים xvii. 10; שבט הדני, xviii. 1 (*cf.* 11); שׂכר, xviii. 4 (Gen. xxx. 16 J); יי נכח, xviii. 6; עצל, xviii. 9; נזעק, xviii. 22 f; מרי נפש, xviii. 25.

³ *Cf.* Wellh. *Bleek*,⁴ 198; Kuen. § xx. 3.

⁴ See above, note 2. Moreover, xviii. 12*b* seems to have been written at some distance from Judah.

⁵ *Cf.* xviii. 12, and Kuen. § xx. 3; also xviii. 31, yet notice פסל; the verse is generally doubtful (see Wellh. *Nachtr.* 357).

In view of the opposition to the sanctuary of Dan that the elements worked into the main account betray, we may with certainty ascribe them to the kingdom of Judah and to the time after Jeroboam I. With this, as well as with the general tone of these passages, agrees the reference to the time preceding the Monarchy.[1] The lower limit is the year 722 B.C., since after the transportation of Israel such a polemic had no longer any object. Yet we are not compelled to go so far down.[2]

2. *Chaps.* xix.-xxi.[3] This second appendix to the Book of Judges differs considerably from the first. It contains the narrative of an outrage perpetrated at Gibeah of Benjamin and the consequent extermination of the tribe of Benjamin by the whole community.

Neither are these chapters strictly homogeneous. Yet the question arises again whether we have a right to distinguish two originally independent narratives.[4] It appears to me the most probable view that we have to do simply with a revision, certainly very radical, of an older account.[5]

This older narrative appears at all events in chap. xix., but is probably continued in some measure in chaps. xx. and xxi. In the present form of the narrative, however, the reviser comes very markedly into the foreground in the last two chapters, so that, with a few exceptions, it is no longer possible to separate the older passages. Decidedly old touches, due to authentic tradition,[6] as well as a certain affinity with chap. xvii. f. in tone and

---

[1] xvii. 6; xviii. 1. Even this contains an element of reproach.

[2] xviii. 30 is, at all events as regards its last words, but perhaps generally, a gloss. Still it is historically of value.

[3] *Cf.* in addition to the commentaries: Wellh. in *Bleek*,[4] p. 199 ff.; Graetz, *Gesch. d. Jud.* i. p. 351 ff.; Güdemann, in Graetz's *Monatsschrift*, 1869, p. 357 ff.; Smend, *ZAW.* ii. p. 110 ff.; Böhme, *ZAW.* v. p. 30 ff.; Kuenen, *Ond.*[2] § 20; Budde, *RiSa*, p. 146 ff.

[4] So Bertheau, p. 260 ff., and in chap xxi. Böhme *loc. cit.*, Budde *loc. cit.* On the other hand, Kuen. § xx. 10.

[5] To this older account I assign, in addition to chap. xix., the basis of chap. xx., and in chap. xxi. the orginal stratum of verses 13-23.

[6] *Cf.* Jebus xix. 10 f.; further, the procedure known to us from 1 Sam. xi., in xix. 29 f. 'The days of Gibeah' also in Hosea (ix. 9; x. 9) can, in view of x. 9, have hardly any other reference (partly ag. Wellh. *Bleek*,[4] 203; Kuen. § xx. 6).

language,[1] lead us to assign this one account to a relatively [2] early age. To it belonged, beside the story of the outrage in chap. xvii., perhaps the account of the hostile procedure against Gibeah, and the narrative, also manifestly old, of the rape at Shiloh, xxi. 15 ff.[3]

The age to which the reviser belongs, and the method of his work, are clear from his close correspondence in language [4] and thought [5] with P and with Chronicles, as well as from his aversion to Saul and everything connected with him. We have here to do with a Judæan of exilic or post-exilic time;[6] a conclusion with which agrees the discrepancy between what he relates, and the picture of the ancient times with which we are otherwise familiar.[7]

§ 31. *The Books of Samuel.*

The contents of these books,[8] which in subject at all events are closely connected, are divisible into several sub-sections: 1 Sam. i.-xv., Samuel and Saul; 1 Sam. xvi.-xxxi.. Saul and David: 2 Sam. i.-v. 5, David in Hebron; 2 Sam. v. 6—chap. xx., David in Jerusalem; 2 Sam. xxi.-xxiv., detached appendices.

---

[1] So already Studer, *Richt.* p. 455. With this in view I have in the *Transl.* marked this account likewise N. *Cf.* also such expressions as those in xviii. 7 (read ואין מחסור כל־ד'), 10, and xix. 19, 20. See other points of contact with older passages in Budde, 149 f.

[2] More I cannot say on account of Wellh. *Bleek*,[4] p. 201 end.

[3] See Kuen. § xx. 9.   [4] See on this Wellh. in *Bleek*,[4] 202.

[5] *Cf.* Wellh. *loc. cit.*, p. 199 f.

[6] The reference to the monarchy (xix. 1; xxi. 25) is here hardly from the same hand as in chap. xvii. f. In this second appendix it is not at all in its right place, since the punishment of the misdeed certainly leaves nothing to be desired. It is here therefore probably an interpolation by R after the example of xvii. 6; xviii. 1. Kuen. (§ xx. 9) takes a different view.

[7] *Cf.* the compact unity of Israel, the enormous numbers, etc.

[8] *Cf.* in gen. Thenius, *Die BB. Sam.*[2] (1864); Keil, *Die BB. Sam.*[2] (1875); Wellh. *TBS.*, *Bl.*[4] p. 206 ff., *Prol.*[2] 256 ff.; Kuen. *Ond.*[2] §§ 17, 21-23, 27; Klost, *Sa Kö*; Driver, *Notes*, and *Introd.* 162 ff.; Budde, *RiSa*; Cornill, *Grundr.*, p. 104 ff. Special investigations: Gaupp, *Zur Gesch. des Königs David* (*Progr.* 1886); Bonk, *De Davide rege* (1891); [König, *Einleit*, § 52; Wildeboer, *Letterk.* § 9, 14]. On text, translation, and analysis of sources, see also my treatment of the books in Kautzsch's *AT.* [and now, on the text and analysis: Budde, *The Books of Samuel*, in P. Haupt's *Sacred Books of O. T.*, 1894].

1. *Samuel and Saul:* 1 Sam. i.-xv. The early history of Samuel (chaps. i.-iii.) is followed by a description of the fall of the house of Eli (chaps. iv.-vi.). Samuel becomes Judge in place of Eli (chap. vii.). The people, however, are determined to have a king at their head instead of Samuel and his degenerate sons. Samuel, although against his will, gives them a king in the person of Saul (chaps. viii.-x.). Saul defeats the Ammonites and Philistines; but is, after his victory over Amalek, rejected by Samuel (chaps. xi.-xv.).

We can without difficulty distinguish, within this mass of narrative, certain more closely connected groups of passages that are clearly marked off from the rest. The discussion of these will begin best with *Saul's election as king.*

A. There can be no doubt that we possess two *parallel narratives* of this event. In the one, Samuel is the head of the people and holds sway in God's stead over the whole of Israel. The Monarchy is a heathenish institution. Samuel recognises in the people's demand for a king, a sinful pretension infringing Yahvé's rights as king. It is only with reluctance, and not without depicting before the eyes of the people the consequences of their action, that he yields to their importunity.[1] According to the other source, on the other hand, Samuel is a seer, and probably also a priest, if not of a single place, yet of a relatively narrow district in mid-Israel. The distress of his people weighs on his heart; but in the sure consciousness that in so doing he is effecting the will of Yahvé, he voluntarily looks for some one to wear the crown as king in Israel. He believes he has found the right man for them in Saul, the son of Kish, with whom he accidentally becomes acquainted.[2]

The fact that we have here two distinct representations of one and the same event, is palpable.[3] The only question, therefore, that can arise, is whether—and if so, where—each of them is connected with what precedes or what follows; and then, whether it

---

[1] viii. 1-22; x. 17-24. [2] ix. 1-27 (exc. *v.* 9); x. 1-16 (exc. *v.* 8).
[3] On this see Wellh. *Bl.*[4] § 104; Cornill, *ZKWL.* 1885, p. 114 ff. Kuen. § xxi. 7; Budde, *RiSa,* p. 169 ff.

is possible to assign to each narrative, and whatever may be connected with it, a definite origin and date.

Here we begin with chap. xi. Manifestly the second of the narratives just described has this chapter in view when it represents Samuel as pointing Saul to an opportunity of public action that would offer itself.[1] In the present text of the chapter, on the other hand, the victory over Ammon is made an occasion for the people expressing their allegiance to Saul, in a way that presupposes the events described in the first-mentioned source, especially the election of Saul, not by Samuel's prophetic vision, but by the sacred lot.[2] Hence the two sources seem again to be fused together, and it is here we can best observe their artificial combination.[3] On the other hand, the second of the above-mentioned accounts cannot possibly find its continuation, or its attachment to what goes before, in chap. xii. or chap. vii. respectively. In both chapters it is a Judge over all Israel, and not the Seer Samuel, that we have to deal with. In chap. xii. he formally retires, having through the people's wish for a king become superfluous; in chap. vii.[4] Samuel establishes his sway as Judge by a brilliant victory over the Philistines, which brings about a condition of affairs of which the account in chap. ix. knows nothing.[5] The only question, therefore, to be considered with reference to these two chapters, is whether they belong to the account in chap. viii.

If, however, we look closer, it becomes evident that these two chapters have, in respect of language and contents, a character of their own, so that they cannot without further proof be assigned to the same source as chaps. vii., x. 17 ff. In chap. vii. Samuel

---

[1] x. 7. *Cf.* also the connection of xi. 1 with x. 16, according to the emended text of xi. 1 (see on the reading Wellh. *TBS.*, and my translation).

[2] See xi. 14. The 'renewing' of the kingdom agrees only with the previous proclamation in x. 17 ff.

[3] This appears in x. 25-27; xi. 12-14. On this see esp. Budde, *RiSa*, 174 ff., where likewise proof is produced of the independence of the two narratives. See there also against Cornill, *ZAW*. 1890, 97 ff. Likewise Stade,[2] 212. *Cf.* also below, p. 29, note 1.

[4] Exc. *v.* 1, which belongs to what goes before.   [5] *Cf.* vii. 11 ff., with ix. 16.

is a Judge in the technical sense of the Book of Judges: in chap. viii. he is not.[1] In chap. vii. the chronology is carried through quite in the manner of the Book of Judges.[2] Elsewhere also, here and in chap. xii., there appear remarkable points of contact with the framework of the Book of Judges and the passages most nearly allied to it.[3] We shall therefore not go wrong in assuming that the thread of the old Book of 'Stories of the Judges,' somewhat abruptly broken off in our present Book of Judges, was once continued here.[4] The age of these fragments agrees with this view. Cornill has made it probable, against Wellhausen and Kuenen, that Jeremiah knew the contents of chap. vii.[5] We have already[6] arrived at a relatively late date for Ri, near that of Deuteronomy: we can now say more exactly that the writer of these passages was a contemporary of Jeremiah's, who wrote between 622 and 588. Apparently, however, as many traces seem to suggest,[7] the two chapters under consideration underwent a further Deuteronomistic editing at the time of their transference from the Book of Stories of the Judges to their present position.

If there is thus clearly a certain dissimilarity between the pieces, chaps. vii. and xii. on the one hand, and chaps viii., x. 17 ff.

---

[1] vii. 6-15 ff.—שפטים has a more general sense in viii. 1 f., cf. viii. 5, 6. Were this not the case, we should have to assume with Corn. that viii. 1-3 belong to chap. vii. According to Budde, p. 208, Samuel is in M [i.e. 1 Sam. viii., x. 17 ff., etc., Tr.] a God-ordained priest, prophet, and Judge. This is too much for any one writer. No Judge is elsewhere a priest.

[2] vii. 2. The beginning of v. 1 belongs to R.

[3] vii. 8, 13 (נבנע הושע זעק); xii. 8 ff. (זעק), מכר, שכח י׳. See further, Graf, Gesch. BB. 9 ff.; Kuen. § xix. 10; xxii. 6. The expressions urged in favour of E by Budde, RiSa, 180 f., 182 f., are not to be relied on, since dependence on the language of E is quite common in Deuteronomist writers. One would have as much right to claim Dt. i.-iv., or similar passages, for E. On Ju. vi. 7 ff., and x. 6 ff., see above, p. 5 ff. To say without more ado that chaps. vii. and xii. belong to the same whole as viii., x. 17 ff., is, in spite of Budde (p. 179), not correct. Cf. inter alia, xii. 2 (no knowledge of the wickedness of Samuel's sons); xii. 3, 4 (משיהו)? also above, note 1.

[4] Cf. Graf, Gesch. BB., p. 97 f.; Kuen. § xix. 10; Cornill, ZAW. 1890, p. 106 f.

[5] ZKWL. 1885, 138 f.   [6] See above, p. 5 f.

[7] See the unevenness in vii. 2 (v. 2a Rd.); cf. vii. 3 ff., with Ju. x. 10 ff.; moreover, the lack of acquaintance with the age of the Judges in xii. 9 ff. (שמו in v. 11 is an unjustifiable correction; see Wellh. TBS.; Driver, Notes). For the rest cf. Budde, RiSa, 186.

on the other, Wellhausen and Kuenen appear to be wrong in supposing that they all belong together. These critics assign them all to an exilic or post-exilic Deuteronomist.[1] But chaps. viii., x. 17 ff., are hardly so late. Forms of expression belonging to Deuteronomy are to be found in them only exceptionally,[2] and the attitude of Samuel towards the people hardly presupposes the existence of the law about the king in Dt. xvii.[3] Were this the case Samuel must have appealed to it. It rather appears that, conversely, the law resulted from this passage.

In chap. xv. the case stands somewhat differently. The estrangement of Samuel from Saul there described must have been related, in one form or another, also in the continuation of chap. ix., for it is to be received unconditionally as historical. But the present chap. xv., with its formal rejection of Saul through the prophet Samuel, can hardly have been inserted here otherwise than as a continuation of chaps. vii., viii., x. 17 ff., xii. Nevertheless, there rings through it a different tone from that of the other members of this group. It stands, as Wellhausen rightly saw, one step nearer than they to the narrative of chap. ix.[4]

B. Before attempting to trace the narrative further, the question of the sources requires yet more detailed discussion. Cornill has the merit of having emphatically called attention anew[5] to some remarkable relations between one of these series of narratives—viz. chaps. vii., viii., x. 17 ff.; xii., xv.; and the Hexateuch source E. He believes he can draw the conclusion that E was their author.[6] Since, however, in their present form there is—as Cornill rightly recognises—much in them that conflicts with the recognised character of E, Cornill supposes that the aversion of Samuel to the Monarchy, and other individual features of the narrative in chaps. viii., x. 17 ff., as well as chaps. vii.

---

[1] *Bl.*[4] § 104; Kuen. § xxii. 6.   [2] *Cf.* the list in Kuen. § xxii. 6.
[3] See Budde, *RiSa*, 183 f.
[4] *Bleek,*[4] 215. *Cf.* also Cornill, *ZKWL.* 1885, p. 120 ff., 123. Budde, *RiSa*, 189. Whether we are entitled to conclude from xv. 1, that the anointing was here *related* (Corn. Bu.), is to my mind not certain.
[5] On earlier emphasising of the same point, see *StKr.* 1892, 45 f., and also Wellh. *Bl.*[4] 216.   [6] *ZKWL.* 1885, 134 ff.

and xii., were first added to the original text of E by a later editor.¹ Yet even this later editor must, according to Cornill's present view,² belong to the school of E. He therefore calls him E²—'a secondary Elohistic editing' of the work of the Hexateuchal E.

Budde followed him, or rather developed Cornill's earlier representations, according to which the secondary editing of E had been ascribed to a Deuteronomist writer, so that now Cornill allots these passages also to E, as E². On the other hand, Budde decidedly rejected both Cornill's separation of older and younger parts in chaps. viii., x. 17 ff., and his separation of these passages from chaps. vii. and xii.—in the former case with justice, in the latter wrongly.³ When he, nevertheless, accepts Cornill's separation of E(¹) and E², it is not in the same sense as Cornill. Budde's theory⁴ is, that chap. xv. belongs to E¹, and that this passage is independent of the whole remaining series of narratives. These form a complete uniform whole, which Budde thinks himself entitled to call E². He regards E² as the Hexateuch writer himself, and E¹ as an isolated forerunner⁵ of E², who is however, now and then, merged again in the genuine E.

In considering this hypothesis, I may first of all refer to the general considerations for and against, already adduced on this point, as also to what was said of Böhme's assumption of the presence of the Hexateuch J in the Book of Judges.⁶ In fact, there is here in some passages, especially in chap. xv., an affinity⁷ with the Hexateuch E, of about the same degree of clearness as that between J and Ju. vi. and xiii. We saw in that case that there was a possibility—nay, a preponderating probability—that that connection is to be explained by ascribing the work to a writer akin in spirit to J, but not by ascribing it to J himself. The case may be similar here.

---

¹ *ZKWL.* 1885, 126 ff., 138.
² *ZAW.* x. 104 f. *Cf.* now also *Grundr.* 109.
³ *ZAW.* viii. 223 ff.; *RiSa,* 177 ff. Occupying an intermediate position, Cornill, *ZAW.* x. 96 ff. ⁴ *RiSa,* 189. ⁵ *RiSa,* 190.
⁶ See above, p. 15 ff. See further my discussions in *StKr.* 1892, 61 ff.
⁷ See the proof in Corn. *ZKWL.* 1885, 134, and Budde, *RiSa,* 181 f., 190.

Cornill's separation of two layers within chap. viii. can hardly be maintained: the violence, objected to by Budde, of the subsidiary hypotheses needed to support this assumption, will, I imagine, have long ago raised doubts in the minds of others besides myself.[1] We can all the more heartily accept what Cornill says[2] of E's relation to the Monarchy. Here Budde is wrong.[3] Hence follows our own view of the main question itself.

We could very well agree with Cornill if, from the undeniable presence in the passages in question of points of contact with E, he simply drew the conclusion that their author, although diverging from E in some essential points—as *e.g.* in his representation of the Monarchy—was a man nearly related to E, a continuer of the book of E, of like mind and like views, who might therefore be called E^2. But this is not his idea; for, according to him, E^2 is only the secondary editor (who, as a matter of fact, has really in this sense no existence at all), while the kernel of the section, according to his view, comes from E himself. I can only regard this as a somewhat hasty assumption of identity where there is really only affinity. To prove a writer to be somewhat nearly related to E in language and thought, is one thing, and to prove him to be E himself is another. To assume the former of these is the furthest we can go consistently with the duty of scientific caution.

The same may be said of Budde's view. If his E^2 had been a kindred spirit to the Hexateuch E, and his E^1 an otherwise unknown man of the same circle, his scheme might with a few modifications be accepted. But his E^1 and E^2 continually tend[4] to become simply identified with E. To avoid this misunderstanding, I give up altogether the use of E as a designation of

---

[1] See Budde, *RiSa*, 178.

[2] *ZKWL.* 1885, 135. See also the details above, p. 17 f. That Cornill's correct perception of this is of no use to him, is recognised by Budde, *RiSa*, 178 below. The aversion to the Monarchy—and with it a main argument *against* E —is left in viii. 11-20.

[3] *RiSa*, 184. It is remarkable that here also (*cf. loc. cit.* p. 119), Budde does not so much as make the attempt to prove E's aversion to the Monarchy.

[4] See Cornill, *ZKWL.* 1885, 134: 'the same pen,' and the reference to it in Budde, *RiSa*, 190, 180.

this source, and call it, as a book treating with equal interest of Samuel and Saul, the Samuel-Saul History (SS). I do not question that its author, even if not E himself, yet stands in close relationship to him. If it were desired to add a new name to the critical apparatus, already unwieldy enough, we should have to call him an 'Elohistic.' We must, however, keep in mind that the two main portions of SS with which we have so far become acquainted—viz.: chaps. viii., x. 17 ff., and chap. xv.—are not exactly of the same character. The conclusion may be drawn from this that the writing SS has resulted from the uniting of various sources.

C. Returning now to that other representation of the rise of Saul, which is to be found in ix. 1—x. 16, we find that, as was shown above, it has its immediate continuation in chap. xi.[1] But we can trace it also beyond chap. xi. The description following, in chaps. xiii. and xiv., of Saul's victorious wars with the Philistines, is at all events not in agreement with SS, as a comparison with chaps. viii., x. 17 ff., xv., clearly shows. All probability therefore is in favour of these chapters having stood in the source we are now dealing with.[2] But a relation of parts must be granted here similar to that within SS. For the same writer that in chap. ix. represents Saul as an obviously youthful son of Kish, still living in his father's house, cannot well have ascribed to him here, in chaps. xiii. f., a grown-up son of martial age.[3]

Importance attaches to the question as to the *conclusion* of chap. xiv. We seem to have here clearly the conclusion of a life of Saul, for it tells in a compendious way of his deeds.[4] Many have accordingly expressed the opinion that the history of Saul lying before us in ix. 1—x. 16, xi., xiii. f.—for brevity I call it S—is here concluded.[5] But two cogent objections may be urged

---

[1] It is to be supposed that there stood in SS an account of the Ammonite war analogous to chap. xi., which was suppressed in favour of the present chap. xi. when the two sources were united.   [2] Wellh. *Bl.*[4] 213; Budde, *RiSa*, 204 f.

[3] Wellh. *Bl.*[4] 213; Budde, *RiSa*, 205.

[4] xiv. 47-51. *V.* 52 begins something new : see below.

[5] Wellh. *Bl.*[4] 214 ; Cornill, *ZKWL.* 1885, 117, and *KgSt.* i. 52 ; probably also Kuen. § xxi. 1.

against this view. In the first place, it is certainly not probable that a history of Saul that begins with so much detail as S, can have suddenly broken off so shortly and summarily. If, therefore, in the further course of the Book of Samuel, passages should appear that seem in other respects to belong to S, the existence of this 'conclusion' could be no objection to our assigning them to S. If, on the other hand, such passages should not be found, that would not prove that the source reached here its real conclusion. But then, in the second place, S is a source of high historical value. The piece xiv. 47-51, on the other hand, is indeed hardly characterised aright by a charge of unjustifiable partiality for Saul. It may rather be regarded as coming from a writer who either did not know, or did not care much about, the facts of his history. We might think of R. But he had no inducement to make the history of Saul end here, since he immediately continues it; and to ascribe the piece to him would not agree with the circumstance that most probably v. 52 represents a transition to the further history of Saul from his hand.[1] But v. 52 excludes the preceding verses. I conjecture therefore that xiv. 47-51 was found by R in an independent, though late source, and inserted here.[2]

A further difficulty is presented by the section in S on Saul's rejection: xiii. 7^b-15^a. Although prepared for, as it seems, by an earlier notice,[3] this piece has something perplexing about its form and contents. In its present position it interrupts the connection, and is even in itself hardly intelligible.[4] As it now reads it can hardly be original. Since the rejection of Saul is accounted for in detail in chap. xv., although on different grounds, we have here a parallel account. It is certain that S, as well as SS, must somewhere or other have given reasons for Saul's early fall and

---

[1] See below, p. 44.
[2] Similarly Budde, 208, 210. On the ground of individual words in v. 47 f. (רִישׁ‎י, for which read, יִישׁ‎י, שְׁסהוּ) one might think of Ri; *cf.* also Budde, 206. But the idea of a history of Saul in Ri (so still in *Kautzsch*) is too unnatural.
[3] x. 8. This verse also belongs probably to R.
[4] On this see Wellh. *Bl.*[4] 215; Cornill, *ZKWL*. 1885, 117 f.; Kuen. § xxi. 8; Budde, *RiSa*, 191 f.

his rupture with Samuel. But we can hardly hope ever to know what it contained.

Our source S is regarded by Budde,[1] though certainly 'with all reserve,' as a continuation of J analogous to E. Few positive grounds can be urged for this view. If the further course of our source does not in some way justify the identification, we may be allowed to abandon it.

D. After what we have ascertained, there still remain, as a constituent part of the whole section with which we are dealing, chaps. i.-vi., to which vii. 1 belongs. Here, in the first place, it is beyond doubt that the piece, chaps. i.-iii.,[2] has been written with its continuation iv.-vi. in view. For the sudden fall of Eli and his sons is narrated in chap. iv. and prepared for in i.-iii. On the other hand, it is less clear whether the other section, chaps. iv.-vi., has likewise been written with reference to what now precedes it.[3] It is in the highest degree remarkable that in the whole section iv.-vi., Samuel, who up to this point has been the chief figure, is not once mentioned.[4]

If we look now at the relation of chaps. i.-vi. to chaps. vii.-xv., it is clear at once that the story of Samuel's youth in i.-iii. cannot possibly stand alone, but must have been written as an introduction to the subsequent history of that hero. It has therefore the double object of preparing for Samuel's rise and for Eli's fall. This amounts to saying that its continuation must be sought, not only in iv.-vi., but also in vii.-xv. In deciding the question, which of the series in vii.-xv. is introduced by i.-iii., we have our choice between S and SS. Here we shall decide unconditionally in favour of SS. For the Samuel of chaps. i.-iii., the divinely ordained priest and prophet, stands decidedly nearer to the Samuel

---

[1] *RiSa*, 203. See now also Corn. *Grundr.* 109 f. (yet *cf.* above, p. 16 f.).

[2] As later additions are to be distinguished: ii. 1-10, a Psalm of unknown origin, and ii. 27-36, a Deuteronomistic, but still pre-exilic, interpolation. See Wellh. *Bl.*[4] 207; Kuen. § xxii. 5; Oort, *Theol. Tijdschr.* xviii. 309 ff.; Baudissin, *Gesch. d. AT. Prestert.* 195 ff. Budde (*RiSa*, 199) thinks of E along with Rd.

[3] Wellh. *Bl.*[4] 208; Kuen. § xxii. 11.

[4] iv. 18*b* is at all events an addition, either of Ri, or perhaps rather of R. For Eli is not elsewhere a Judge in the sense in which that term is used by Ri.

of SS than to the Seer of S. If we ask, conversely, whether S or
SS refers back to i.-iii., the answer will again be in favour of SS.
For chap. viii. introduces Samuel as an old man in a way that
leads one to expect, at least, the necessary information about his
past to be supplied. Chap. ix., on the other hand, presupposes
indeed the unhappy situation of Israel,[1] but introduces Samuel in
a way that leads one to conclude positively that hitherto nothing
has been said of him. This does not preclude the possibility that
i.-iii. was nevertheless written as an introduction to S by an
editor or sub-editor;[2] but the probability is decidedly in favour
of its belonging to SS, since otherwise a second introductory
history of Samuel must be presupposed, preceding viii. 1 ff.

If this be so, then iv.-vi., vii. 1 must also have stood in SS,
since i.-iii. presupposes it. Against this no objection can be
raised if we suppose that the rest of chap. vii., as has elsewhere
appeared, does not belong to this source, but was interpolated at a
later date:[3] iv.-vi., vii. 1 is therefore not from the same hand
as i.-iii.

Very naturally Cornill and Budde, in accordance with their
previous assumption, are inclined[4] to ascribe this section also to
E. On this point, considering the close connection of i.-iii. with
viii., x. 17 ff., we must pass the same judgment as on the relation
of those parts of SS to E. There is affinity with E, but no proof
of identity. Since iv.-vi., vii. 1 belongs to another and older
author, Budde resorts to E[1] as against E[2]. iv.-vii. 1 would thus
be brought into connection with chap. xv., for which there is no
ground. iv.-vi. is so independent of the other sections that we
must assume that it has been inserted by the author of SS from

---

[1] It is to be assumed that there once stood in S an account of the fight at Ebenezer and its consequences, analogous to chaps. iv.-vi., but its place is now taken by chap. vii. See Wellh. *Bl.*[4] 210; *cf.* also Stade,[2] 202 f.

[2] So Stade,[2] 199.

[3] With his assumption of a close connection between chaps. vii. and viii., Budde falls into the difficulty of having to admit the battle of Ebenezer twice into one and the same source. This is impossible, and the difficulty is not removed by assuming an E[1] and E[2]. There is hardly any ground, however, for assuming the work of R (Budde, 187). [4] *ZKWL.* 1885, 136; *RiSa,* 198 f.

an Ephraimite source, of which we otherwise know nothing.[1] Every consideration therefore recommends our contenting ourselves here also with the result, certainly less complete but safer, that SS—*i.e.* the sections i.-iii.; iv.-vii. 1; viii.; x. 17 ff. ... xv.—represented a book resulting from the fusing of several elements of tradition more or less nearly related to E. In the blank space there must have stood a version of what is related in chap. xi., as well as probably a short description of Saul's Philistine wars, which cannot have been altogether passed over. One might most plausibly assume that the compiler of the book was at the same time the writer of i.-iii. and viii., x.; while iv.-vi. and xv. appear to be inserted from older sources.

E. We have still to determine the age and place of origin of the individual sections.

Nearest to the events in point of time stand the narratives in S; first of all, chaps. xi., xiii. f., then ix. 1—x. 16. But even the former is not contemporaneous with the events, though it appears to be not far removed from them. In coming to this conclusion, I am influenced not so much by some traces of later style in the section in its present form, which might very easily be interpolations of a different hand,[2] nor yet by the grounds adduced by Wellhausen and Kuenen,[3] but rather by the lack of complete perspicuity in the narrative, which, in spite of all its faithfulness of reproduction, gives rise to many questions.[4] Somewhat younger than this section is the other, ix. 1—x. 16. Here the figure of Saul no longer stands quite in the light of history.[5] Hence, even if we might assume that xi., xiii. f. were written while Saul or

---

[1] The remarkable interchange of divine names,—Yahvé in i.-iii., Elohim in iv.-vi.—does not argue strongly for the ascription of both sections to E, however far we are from being justified in drawing from it otherwise any positive conclusions. *Cf.* Wellh. 209.

[2] Here belong xi. 8*b* (*cf.* xiii. 2, 15); xiii. 1 (R); xiii. 19-22 (*v. Bl.*[4]). On xiii. 7*b*-15*a* see above, p. 30; on xi. 12-14 see p. 24, note 3.

[3] § xxii. 10.

[4] *Cf.* esp. xiii. 2 ff., where, apart from the condition of the text, much is obscure. See fuller details below, in § 40.

[5] *Cf.* esp. ix. 1 ff., where one gets an impression of Saul as an 'immature lad' (Wellh.), with chap. xiii., where he himself has a grown-up son.

David was still alive, the source S as a whole, would demand a somewhat later date. If we might conclude from the great partiality for Saul that appears in chap. ix., that the northern kingdom was the native soil of S, the conjecture that this source is to be attributed to Saul's own tribe of Benjamin,[1] would be attractive. We should then have to assume for S, in view of the point just touched on, a date somewhere about the time of Jeroboam I.

Within SS the priority is to be given to the section on the loss and the return of the ark. The remark of Kuenen[2] is certainly correct, that the conception of the ark represented by the narrative, as actually identified with Yahvé himself, can hardly date from any time later than the eighth century, though it may belong to a considerably earlier time, all the more that the expression 'ark of the Covenant' is foreign to the original text.[3] In other respects also the account has the colouring of naïve antiquity.[4] There is no reason why we should not assign it to the ninth century.

The second place is occupied by chap. xv. It cannot be older than E. With this agrees the position of Samuel, who stands midway between prophets like Elijah and Elisha, and such as Amos and Hosea.[5] This points to the time between Elijah and Hosea, yet nearer to the latter than to the former.[6] We may perhaps think of the beginning or middle of the reign of Jeroboam II.

We are thus left with a somewhat later date for the author of i.-iii., viii., x. ff., who is apparently the same person as the author of SS in general. His conception of Samuel, as well as of the Monarchy, agrees with this view. The latter consideration points to a contemporary or imitator of Hosea,[7] and there is much

---

[1] So Stade, *Gesch.* 209.   [2] § xxii. 11. *Cf.* also Wellh. *Bl.*[4] 208.
[3] *V.* Wellh. *TBS.*; Driver, *Notes, ad loc.*
[4] *Cf.* the numbers, at least in iv. 2.
[5] Wellh. *Bl.*[4] 215. On the relation to the Hexateuch E, *v. StKr.* 1892, 67 f.
[6] It is hardly necessary to come down later than Hosea on account of xv. 23 (*cf.* Hos. iii. 4): the idea that Hosea approves of Ephod and Teraphim is a myth. *Cf.* iii. 4a with xiii. 10.
[7] *V.* esp. Hos. xiii. 10 f. On the other hand, on viii. 4 and ix. 9, *v.* below § 68 towards the end.

else in favour of this time.[1] Perhaps Kuenen is right when he refers us somewhat more definitely to the reign of Hezekiah, after the year 722.[2] The distinctly pre-Deuteronomic conception of the cultus and priesthood,[3] shows that we cannot come down any further.

2. *Saul and David*: 1 Sam. xvi.-xxxi.—Our first care must be to answer the question whether S and SS, the main writings we have so far discovered, are continued here. The sections put together in this division do not, as will immediately appear, come from one and the same hand: on the contrary, two parallel series of narratives are clearly marked off from each other. We easily recognise that one of these carries on the thread of SS, and indeed in a way that seems to point to the same writer. With reference to the other, the case is not so clear.

A. The double thread of narrative appears at once from the way in which David, who now comes forward, is introduced to Saul. In ch. xvi. 14-23 Saul's men seek for some one able to dispel the king's melancholy, and find him in David, who is known to them at the same time as a valiant warrior.[4] This narrative has not the same author as xvii. 1-xviii. 5. In the latter place David is a youth, still unknown to the king, not yet intrusted with the bearing of arms, who comes to the army on his father's errands, and there slays the Philistine Goliath. It is only in consequence of this deed that he becomes known to the king and is introduced by him to the court. The latter narrative will prove to be a continuation of SS; the other, as the beginning of a history of David, I provisionally designate 'Da.'

The disagreement between the two narratives seems certainly less harsh, although it is not removed,[5] if instead of the Massoretic

---

[1] *Cf.* in general, Wellh. *Bl.*[4] 213. Cornill, *KySt.* i. 25. Budde, *RiSa*, 184 f.

[2] *Ond.*[2] § xxii. 11; Kuenen's argument applies only to i.-iii.

[3] Samuel not a Levite; sleeps beside the ark; the feast and offering; the priestly dues.

[4] Yet he is still (*v.* 19) under the *potestas patria*, whence the possibility of his being his father's shepherd. So, with Kamphausen in *Theol. Arb. aus d. rhein. Pred.-Ver.* vii. 10, against Stade 224, Budde 211.

[5] *Cf.* xvi. 18 and xvii. 38 ff. LXX.

text of xvii. 1–xviii. 5, we take that of the Cod. Vatic. of the LXX. as basis.[1] Hence it is natural to suppose that the LXX. has here made use of 'harmonistic criticism' and removed the worst discrepancies. Certainly it would have to be admitted, at the same time, that it has only imperfectly attained this object. Hence the possibility must remain open, that the additional matter of the Hebrew text is due to an independent recension of the history. Still I regard this as less probable.[2] The same kind of thing is seen in the course of chap. xviii. Budde finds here also harmonistic efforts on the part of the LXX., on the score that both cases must be judged alike. If this is really so, this passage would determine our view of the other passage also, in spite of what has been said above. For here we have plainly an independent recension alongside of the LXX.[3] But it is in my opinion not impossible that both things are present at the same time. In fact, certain traces seem even to indicate that in chap. xviii. itself both are to be found side by side.[4]

If the view here represented is correct, we have to take the Massoretic text for basis in chap. xvii. 1–xviii. 5, and the LXX., for the most part,[5] in xviii. 6 ff. However, this need not involve a later origin for the Hebrew text of chap. xviii. 6 ff. than for the Greek. At any rate, the portions which the Hebrew text has,

---

[1] On this question, v. Wellh. *TBS. ad loc.*; *Bleek*,[4] § 106 f.; Kamph. *Rhein. Arb.* vii. 1 ff.; Gaupp, *David*, 7 ff.; Kuen. § xxiii. 7; Cornill, *KgSt.* i. 25 ff.; Klost. *SaKö, ad loc.*; Stade,[2] 226 f.; Budde, *RiSa*, 212 ff.; Dillmann in *Sitz.-Ber. d. Berl. Akad.* 1890, 1372; [W. R. Smith, *OTJC*,[2] p. 431 ff.; F. H. Woods, *Studia Biblica*, i. 99].

[2] The chief ground with me is that chap. xvii. (LXX.) provides no satisfactory connection (against Cornill, 32 f.) with chap. xv. It is thus probably not an independent conception. See also later, p. 37 f.

[3] *Cf.* Wellh. *Bl.*[4] 218. Chap. xviii. (LXX.) is a connected unity, and *v.* 12*a* is not likely to have been left by a harmoniser. The proof would be still clearer if Corn. (27 f.) were justified in declaring that there is an uninterrupted connection in the additional matter of the Hebrew text. But *cf.* on the other hand *v.* 6*a*, and especially 21*b*.

[4] xviii. 1-5 I do not regard as original (see against Corn. p. 26, below on p. 38); but probably *vv.* 9-11, 21*b*, and the additional matter in *v.* 26 ff. On the other hand, *vv.* 6*a*, 8*aa* seem to have been purposely omitted. With regard to 17-19 this is, at all events, very possible.

[5] *V.* the preceding note.

but not the LXX., need not be regarded as additions introduced into the text subsequently to the date of that version.[1] The Greek translator may have had before him simply another and shorter recension of the story of David. This would indicate that the shorter recension was that which first obtained recognition, whereas the more elaborate form did not make its way into the Canon till later. Upon this theory the Hebrew text would have to be regarded as younger than the LXX., not in respect of its formation, but only in respect of its recognition as canonical.

If now we compare chap. xviii. LXX. with the preceding, it is clear that xviii. 12a, 'Saul was afraid of David,' forms the conclusion of a narrative accounting for this fear. The narrative itself tells of the song of the women that disparaged Saul in favour of David. The contents, as well as the express connection with what precedes, appear to mark this section as a continuation of the Goliath story. But its suitability for this purpose, whether in point of contents or of connection, is only apparent. 'If David has slain his tens of thousands, he is not the unknown shepherd lad, but the leader of Israel alongside of Saul.'[2] Moreover, v. 6 is crowded at the beginning, and thus betrays its artificial attachment to the Goliath story.[3] Vv. 6-8 thus belongs to xvi. 14 ff., yet do not form its direct continuation, but presuppose certain military exploits through which David distinguished himself. It is not necessary to suppose that the section once stood at some other point in Da.[4]

In obvious agreement with this section, is the love of Michal for David, which provided a still stronger ground for Saul's fear, and which, contrary to Saul's wish, led to marriage (xviii. 20-29ᵃ). This account knows nothing of an obligation on the part of Saul to give David his daughter, on the ground of a previously given promise. On the contrary, the love of his daughter for David has first to be reported to Saul. Only v. 21ᵇ, which is lacking in the

---

[1] Against Budde, 213.   [2] Wellh. *Bl.*⁴ 218.
[3] *V.* Budde, 218. For the rest, it is most probable that the first two words of *v.* 6 stood in Da ; the rest to את־הפלשתי, and also *v.* 8aa, in R.
[4] So Corn. *KySt.* 35.

LXX., refers to that promise, as also the last words of *v*. 26.¹ Here also we have Da. Between these two passages from Da, there now stands in the LXX. the account in *v*. 13-16 of the conferring of a military office on David. This passage does not suit Da, less for the reason given by Cornill,² than because, in that source (*v*. 6 ff.), David already has a command. It agrees well however with SS, at least in xvii. 1–xviii. 5 LXX. It was perhaps a 'doublet' in SS, and one of the grounds for the omission of xviii. 1-5 in the LXX.³

If we look now at the extra matter in the M. T. of the section under consideration (xviii. 6 ff.), the two passages *vv*. 9-11 and 17-19 also claim our notice. The former is the direct continuation of *vv*. 6 ff. in Da. Whether it did not make its way into Da till later, or was for some unknown reasons lacking in the recension used by the LXX. translator, we cannot say. Even xix. 9 f. was no reason for omitting it. The second passage, 17-19, clearly belongs to SS, from whose premises it starts, while on the other hand it cannot belong to *v*. 20 ff. In this case we may see in the hiatus between *v*. 19 and 20 ff., a ground for the omission.

Before leaving chaps. xvi.-xviii., however, we must mention another account of the circumstances of David's appearance on the stage of history, which we have as yet passed over. This is to be found in xvi. 1-13. That it does not belong to Da is evident at once, for in this new narrative David is a shepherd-lad and Jesse's youngest son. One might be tempted, simply for this reason, to connect it with chap. xvii. and so with SS. In reality, however, neither is this admissible.⁴ We have here a later passage interpolated by R.

B. Chaps. xix. and xx. form a second section by themselves. Saul's suspicion of David has become open hate, which he reveals to Jonathan. The latter, by reminding Saul of David's exploit, succeeds in pacifying him. David is even able to return once more

---
¹ On וימלאום למלך in *v*. 27, *v*. Corn. *KgSt*. 27.   ² *KgSt*. 35 f.
³ The ascription of it to this source is confirmed by xix. 1 ff.
⁴ *V*. Wellh. *Bl*.⁴ 217; also Corn. *KgSt*. 52; Bu. 216.

to Saul's presence (xix. 1-7). Hardly, however, has David achieved new successes in the Philistine war, than one day Saul hurls his spear at him, so that it is with the greatest difficulty that David escapes (8-10). By night Saul has David's house watched to have him slain next day. Through Michal's clever management David is enabled to escape (11-17). Here 1-7 [1] belongs to SS; only *v.* 3 is to be excluded as an addition [2] from the hand of R. To the same source belong also *vv.* 8-10, since they quite naturally connect themselves with it, and moreover have already their counterpart in Da, in xviii. 10 f. On the other hand, the passage 11-17 presents difficulty.[3] It is generally regarded as an independent piece: so still by Cornill, who takes objection to the teraphim in *vv.* 13, 16, on account of xv. 23. It is true that the teraphim can have been mentioned here by the author of xv. 23, only if he had the additional object of casting blame on Michal, as the daughter of Saul. If one may read this between the lines, the passage may belong to SS; otherwise it is (with Wellhausen, Stade, and Cornill) to be regarded as a fragment from some other source unknown to us.[4] The close of the chapter, on the other hand, which narrates David's flight to Ramah, xix. 18-24 (also xx. 1ᵃ), is hardly original. It belongs to the same category as xvi. 1 ff.[5]

If there is thus no trace of the source Da to be found in chap. xix., on the other hand almost the whole of chap. xx. belongs to it. There is here no knowledge of David's flight. He is still in Gibeah, in the company of Saul, along with the crown prince and the leader of the forces—*i.e.* in the position in which we found him (xvi. 14 ff.), and left him (chap. xviii.) in Da.[6] His flight is only

---

[1] *Cf.* esp. *v.* 4 with chap xvii., and *v.* 7 with xviii. 13.
[2] *V.* Budde, 221. Corn. (37 ff., 47) wishes to omit *vv.* 2 and 3.
[3] On the text in *v.* 11 *v.* my translation.
[4] The other reasons I regard (with Budde) as not decisive—at all events not for the literary view of the question. Even xviii. 17 ff. will hardly exclude our passage.
[5] *V.* Wellh. *Bl.*[4] 219; Corn. *KySt.* 53; Budde, 223. Perhaps we are to think (Corn.) of an insertion from the hand of D² (Dt. Rd.).
[6] *V.* Corn. 51.

now explained. The passage is, however, considerably worked over, or supplied with extraneous additions.[1]

C. In chaps. xxi. and xxii. we have a continuation of the narrative of SS. David has fled from Gibeah after Saul's attempt at his life.[2] We learn that he went first to Nob, and are told what befell him there.[3] Then we learn that for a time he found shelter in the stronghold of Adullam, and there gathered around himself a band of adventurers. On the other hand, Saul's fury raged against the priesthood of Nob, because their head had assisted David in his flight. The connection with SS is undeniable: 'everything here hangs upon the sword of Goliath.'[4] We have a later addition to this section in xxi. 11-16, the narrative of David's stay with Achish at Gath. This is hardly to be regarded as an independent source, as Cornill supposes.[5] On the other hand, it may be questioned whether Wellhausen is right in separating also *vv.* 8-10 from the context. I see no serious discrepancy between these verses and xxii. 9.[6] It is thus also shown to be unnecessary to assign xxii. 6-23 to another source.[7] Nor is there any sufficient reason for excising xxii. 3, 4,[8] or xxiii. 5.[9]

D. Chaps. xxiii.-xxvii. There follows now a longer section taken from Da, chaps. xxiii.-xxvii. We left David, in this source, as he was betaking himself to flight. He is now fled from Gibeah (although the account of this has not been preserved for us in Da), and is fighting for Keilah against the Philistines, obviously at the head of his band. Saul prepares to attack him in Keilah, whereupon he leaves the town. But Saul pursues him into the territory of the Ziphites, and it is only by a sudden attack of the Philistines that he is rescued from destruction; wherefore he goes

---

[1] *V.* below, § 40. [2] xix. 10 or xix. 17.
[3] xxi. 2-10 [*vv.* 1-9 in E.V.] (*v.* 1 [Heb. text] belongs to the preceding, thus to Da.) [4] Cornill, *KgSt.* 31.
[5] *V.* Cornill, *KgSt.* 54; Kuen. § xxii. 13. Klosterm. wrongly alters the text in *v.* 12.
[6] *V.* Cornill, *KgSt.* 30 f.; *cf.* Kamphausen, *Rh. Arb.* vii. 9.
[7] So Budde, *RiSa*, 226.
[8] *V.* Budde, 227; Kamph. *ZAW.* vi. 67. [9] *V.* Cornill, *KgSt.* 41.

in the direction of Engedi (xxiii. 1-13; xxiii. 19; xxiv. 1). Between the first and the second of these statements there has been inserted a passage taken from SS. Cornill rightly ascribes it to the source E, whereas Wellhausen and Stade suppose a redactional addition.[1] xxiii. 6, on the other hand, belongs to R, provided that it is not simply a gloss.[2]

Chap. xxiv. is a continuation of the same narrative. Saul follows David to the wilderness of Engedi, and the latter has here an opportunity of showing his magnanimity. He betakes himself hence to the steppe of Maon where, according to chap. xxv., he falls in with Nabal of Carmel, and this leads to his marriage with Abigail.[3] In these two chapters only individual verses can be cut out as later additions.[4] All the rest forms a well-connected whole. In immediate connection with this there stands, in chap. xxvi., a second proof of David's magnanimity. This is obviously parallel to xxiii. 19 ff., xxiv. 2 ff., and must therefore belong to the other source, SS. With this statement Budde would agree,[5] for he believes he has established the traces of E in chap. xxv., and of J in chap. xxiv.; while Cornill, on the contrary, assigns xxiii. 19 ff. chap. xxiv. to E. Cornill's chief reason seems to be that chap. xxvi. manifestly contains the older form of the anecdote.[6] Yet this reason is not conclusive. More important for our purpose than the decision of this point, is the observation that within Da chap. xxv. merits a decidedly higher rank, in respect of originality

---

[1] V. Wellh. *TBS.* 128; also Stade, 245 (15-18 later, 14 in part); on the other hand, Corn. 45. It is possible that v. 14a belongs to v. 19. So Budde, 230. The analysis in the trans. in Kautzsch is different.

[2] V. Cornill, *KgSt.* 45.

[3] For the rest, it is quite possible that the original text of Da had chap. xxv. *before* xxiv. So Budde, 230 f. The affair at Carmel would then fall in the time of Saul's expedition against the Philistines, v. xxiv. 2.

[4] xxiv. 14 is a gloss. In the case of xxiv. 21-23 there is no more need of this assumption than in that of xxv. 28-31 (on this v. Budde, 231). xxv. 1a is clearly from R (cf. xxviii. 3a). xxv. 44 is original: see against Wellh. and Stade, Corn. 48 f. On the correct order of the portions in xxiv. 5-8, see Gaupp, *Zur Gesch. Dav.* 17 and Corn. 47. [5] *RiSa,* 228 f.

[6] Wellh. *TBS.* 137; Corn. *KgSt.* 43 ff. At all events, to found a claim in favour of a definite source on the phrase הסך את־רגליו (Corn. 48) is more than daring.

of narrative than its immediate context, whether that is to be sought in chap. xxiv. or xxvi.

Chap. xxvii. forms a natural continuation both for chap. xxiv. and chap. xxvi. David, tired of the continued persecution, goes over to Philistine soil. In itself this incident may well have stood in either of the sources. Yet we must decide here for Da, since, as we have hitherto found, the redactor favours this source more than the other. Wellhausen is not justified in proposing to cancel verses 7-12.[1]

E. The crisis: 1 Sam. xxviii.—2 Sam. i. Here it is at once apparent, and it is therefore undisputed, that xxviii. 1, 2 forms the immediate continuation of chap. xxvii. The going over to Achish is followed at once by the dangerous consequences of this step. Chaps. xxix.-xxxi., which carry on the course of events, belong likewise to xxvii.; xxviii. 1, 2.[2] Here, therefore, at all events we have Da. With regard to xxviii. 3 ff., on the other hand, it is not so easy to decide. It is commonly assumed that the source of chap. xv., in our view SS, has here left the surest trace of its continuation. So especially Wellhausen. Cornill accordingly ascribes the section to E, and agrees with Wellhausen in the view that the natural continuation of xxviii. 1, 2 is not to be found till xxix.-xxxi.[3] The chief reason urged is the relation of the positions assigned to the Philistine army in the two passages,[4] as also the affinity of xxviii. 3 ff. with chap. xv.

This whole view of xxviii. 3 ff. has been contested by Budde.[5] We must admit that there is no trace here of the specific features of the figure of Samuel as portrayed in SS, and that Samuel may just as well represent the Seer of S, to whom Saul would once more, and for the last time, apply for advice. If we suppose with Budde that the passage is out of its place, and stood originally

---

[1] *V. Bleek*,[4] 220. On the other side, especially Kamph. *ZAW*. vi. 85 ff.; also Corn. 49, Budde, 232.

[2] On xxix. 5 *v*. Corn. 49; on xxx. 10 *v*. Stade, 256.

[3] *Cf*. Wellh. *Bl*.[4] 220; *Prol*.[2] 271 ff.; Corn. *KgSt*. 42 f.; also Stade, 254 f.; Kuen. § xxii. 7.

[4] *Cf*. xxviii. 4 with xxix. 1, 11; xxxi. 1.   [5] *V. RiSa*, 233 ff.

after chap. xxx., and also that it has received certain additions[1] from the hand of R, a strong case would be made out for his hypothesis, and we should in that case have to assign xxviii. 4-16, 19ab-25 likewise to Da. What makes one doubtful, however, is not only that Budde is unable to assign a reason for this transposition,[2] but still more, that on the other supposition the insertion of the passage at an unsuitable place is easily explained. If, in editing the Book of Samuel, R found this passage in another source (SS) than that which, on the whole, controls the narrative here, the otherwise unimportant misplacement is easily understood. If he drew from one and the same source (Da), it is inexplicable.

With the concluding chapters of the first Book, 2 Sam. i. stands in the closest connection. The whole of the first chapter is often regarded as their continuation.[3] We should in this case have to assign that chapter to Da. But Wellhausen called attention to certain doubts raised by the narrative of the Amalekite.[4] The assumption that he told an untruth is not sufficient, since, according to iv. 10, David himself knew nothing of the actual or supposed death of Saul at his hand.[5] Budde[6] therefore rightly assigns i. 6-16 to the other source, our SS, whereas i. 1-4 may very well belong to Da. With i. 17 the chief narrator, Da, once more appears, in order to introduce the song taken from the *Sepher ha-Yāshār*.[7]

Before proceeding further we must determine how we are to conceive the relation of the sources SS and Da in 1 Sam. xvi. ff. to SS and S in i.-xv. As the nomenclature itself indicates, I suppose SS to be the direct continuation of the history of Samuel and

---

[1] To R would belong, in this case, xxviii. 3 and 17-19*aa*,—the latter as a link of connection with chap. xv. So in the main, still in my trans.; *cf.* further, Wellh. in *TBS.* on *v.* 19.

[2] So already Stade,[2] 255; *cf.* on the other hand Budde, 236, note 3.

[3] So Cornill, *KgSt.* 54 f.; at all events for 1-16. Klosterm. *ad loc.*

[4] *Bleek*,[4] 221; *v.* also Kuen. § xxi. 9.

[5] If iv. 10 presupposed i. 7 ff. the antithesis in the former passage would be not between harmless bearing of tidings and slaying, but between slaying by request and assassination. [6] *RiSa*, 237 f.

[7] *V.* 5 is probably from R. We must suppose a continuation of the narrative of Da in harmony with iv. 10.

Saul, begun in i.-xv. Even if it may be disputed whether individual pieces belong to this source, we must recognise, in the narratives assigned to SS, a distinctly coherent group. The first piece in SS, chap. xvii., connects itself with chap. xv. without any forcing. On the rejection of Saul, it introduces his successor, and it introduces him just as in the case of Samuel (1 Sam. i. ff.), not as a man ready for his work, but as in the making, gradually coming to the front over the head of his divinely rejected predecessor. But with chap. xvii., and the Goliath story, most of the parts of SS in chaps. xvi. ff. are directly or indirectly connected. Besides, the affinity with E in several sections, remarked by Cornill and Budde,[1] confirms the impression that we have here the continuation of that source. This view is also supported by the fact that, from Saul's death onwards, as we shall see, there is nothing to suggest the presence of SS. With Saul's disappearance from the scene, this source has run its course. We have a right to call it after both Samuel and Saul, because it is most probably this source that, after Samuel has long been dead, makes him rise up once more before the reader.

The other source I have provisionally called Da, because at all events it has David as its central figure. This becomes clear from its being continued, in contrast with SS, beyond the death of Saul. There can be no doubt that it stands in close relation with S in 1 Sam. ix. ff. Budde pronounces it actually the continuation [2] of S. In fact, xiv. 52 seems to justify this. For the verse has the evident object of making the transition from the history of Saul to that of David.[3] This conclusion, however, is decisive only if xiv. 52 is original.[4] But, from its immediate context, it is rather to be conjectured that the verse is from R. In this case, though effecting the transition, it will not at all prove the identity of the writers who compiled the histories of Saul and David that R combined. Hence I prefer to designate the two by independent symbols. In view, however, of the close affinity of S and Da, I do

---

[1] V. Corn. *KgSt.* 30 ff. ; Budde, *RiSa*, 215, 228, 230, 238.
[2] *RiSa*, 215.   [3] V. Wellh. *Bl.*[4] 214, 220.   [4] So Budde, 208.

not exclude the possibility that their author was one and the same man, resuming with xvi. 14 the thread he had dropped at xiv. 46, either directly, or at a later stage in the history.[1]

On the equation SS=E, as supported by Cornill and Budde, and Da=J, also supported by Budde, no elaborate statement is needed after what we have already ascertained. The grounds for E—the identity of S and Da not having been established, J is even more doubtful here than in 1 Sam. ix. ff.—are in this section in no respect new and conclusive. Whether we decide for or against the above identification, we have to do simply with the application of the results already attained, to the continuation of the earlier sections in this division. The affinity of SS and E, which we have not disputed, may even occasionally be of use in distinguishing the sources.

What we can gather from this section before us with regard to the age of SS, agrees with our former results. In general this source exhibits here, just as in i.-xv., the younger layer of narrative. Yet even it contains elements relatively old and good. To these must be reckoned especially xxviii. 3 ff., which we can best take with chap. xv. But the Goliath story also (chap. xvii.), and what is directly connected with it, is at all events pre-exilic.[2] These sections suit best the time of 1 Sam. i.-iii. (v. above, p. 34 f.).

Da also, so far as we now know this source, agrees in general with the date assigned to S. To the best and oldest sections belong 1 Sam. xxvii. ff., xxv., xx. Even these were written, at the earliest, in the last days of David, or under Solomon.[3] The younger elements, to which *e.g.* xxiii. 19 ff.; xxiv. belong, need scarcely be assigned to a later date than Rehoboam or his successor.

3. *David in Hebron and Jerusalem*: 2 Sam. ii.-xx.—The narrative of Da finds here its immediate continuation: the consequence of Saul's fall is David's rise as king in Hebron, 2 Sam. ii. 1-7.[4] We

---

[1] Still it should be considered (v. above, p. 34) whether S is not North-Israelitish, or Benjamitish; whereas Da, at all events, is of Judæan origin.

[2] V. Kamph. *Rh. Arb.* vii. 9.

[3] V. *e.g.* xxv. 28, 30; xx. 31 (cf. 2 Sam. i. 10, iii. 9 ff., v. 2; 1 Sam. xxvi. 25).

[4] There is at least no literary ground for removing *vv.* 4b-7 (Mey.).

expect likewise information about Saul's house (ii. 8-12). Only the chronology betrays here another hand.[1] To v. 12 is attached easily and naturally, instead of a formal account of the war, the narrative of a leading episode in it (ii. 13-32). Budde finds at the beginning an addition from elsewhere.[2] Yet this supposition is not absolutely necessary. We may also reckon chaps. iii. and iv. to Da. Only iii. 2-5 breaks the connection, and must belong elsewhere.[3] So also iv. 4: whereas iv. 2b, 3 may very well belong to the text.[4]

Chaps. v. and vi. are to be examined together. The former recounts the choice of David as king over all Israel, the conquest of Jebus, and David's wars with the Philistines; the latter, the transference of the ark to Zion. Even this summary of contents shows that chap. vi. is most akin to the middle portion of chap. v. Wellhausen perceived[5] that these two sections do not belong to the preceding context (Da), and that chap. vi. is to be connected with chap. ix. ff. It is very natural to infer that the conquest of Jerusalem belongs to the same connection. To Da belong, at all events, the choice of David at the beginning of the chapter, and the Philistine war (vv. 17-25), which was immediately connected therewith. Since however v. 3, alongside of vv. 1 f., is a doublet, only v. 3 is to be reckoned to Da. Wellhausen rightly removes 4-16[6]; but only the chronological notices in vv. 4 f., belong to R; the rest belongs at all events to an old source. The verses 6-16[7] are most naturally regarded as the continuation—even if not the direct continuation—of vv. 1 f., and as continued in turn by chap. vi. The source, the beginning of which we here recognise, I designate 'Je,' as the history of David in Jerusalem.

Chap. vii. seems also to have belonged to this source. For the natural sequence of subjects is: Jerusalem, ark, temple. But the

---

[1] Vv. 10a and 11 have been inserted by R; v. Wellh. Bl.[4] 222.
[2] In 13b-17. V. RiSa, 240.
[3] So Wellh., Cornill, and Budde. V. 30 also will be better assigned, with Wellh., to R.
[4] On this see Budde, 241.
    Bleek,[4] 222.
[6] Disputed by Cornill, KgSt. 55.
[7] Or perhaps more accurately simply 6-12, as Budde (p. 243) supposes. Vv. 13-16, like iii. 2-5, agree better with chap. viii. See next two pages.

chapter as it now reads is the result of a thorough revision. Wellhausen and Kuenen regard the whole chapter as Deuteronomistic. Budde supposes a precursor of Deuteronomy. This might hold as regards the reviser; but the kernel of the passage seems to me to be older.[1]

The continuation of Je is to be found in David's family history, 2 Sam. ix.-xx., to which 1 Kings i. ii. belong.[2] As Wellhausen has shown (against Thenius), this forms a coherent whole,[3] with only unimportant later additions.[4] The section is at the same time a historical source of the first rank: 'with all its partiality for David and Solomon it recounts the course of events with obvious objectivity and with great interest in the details of the story.'[5] The only question here is whether the section is composed of contemporary records, or whether we must ascribe its contents to a date later than the reign of David. The latter alternative is not only demanded by 1 Kings i. ii., but also suggested by the general contents.[6] It almost seems that the narrator knows the secession of Israel from the house of David, and the conditions of the time of Rehoboam generally, from personal observation.[7] However, we are on no account to descend later than the reign of Rehoboam, for there is no trace as yet of any idealising of the figure of David.

Finally, chap. viii. offers special difficulty. As the section is connected externally by v. 1 with v. 25, we might be inclined to assign it to the source Da. By its contents, on the other hand,

---

[1] See below, § 44, end.   [2] *Cf.* also *StKr.* 1892, 68 f.

[3] *V. Bleek,*[4] 224 f. ; Kuen. § xxii. 9. Budde, 247 ff.

[4] The only larger addition is to be found in xii. 10-12 (Wellh.); lesser additions, *e.g.* in xiv. 26 ; xv. 24, 27 (read הראש) and xviii. 18 (*v.* 18*aβ* is a gloss ; *cf.* xiv. 27). For the rest *cf.* Wellh. 226 f. ; Kuen. § xxii. 9.

[5] Wellh. *Bl.*[4] 227.

[6] That the narrator stood at a certain distance from the events, may be inferred from the free use of direct speech (*e.g.* in xi. 21); also from xiii. 18 read (מעיב); xviii. 18 ('unto this day'); xii. 20 ('house of Yahvé').

[7] *V.* Wellh. 227 f.; and, moreover, xii. 8 (Israel and Judah). It is not so much the individual points themselves that are decisive, as the coincidence of many points of this kind.

the chapter shows itself to be an extract from the continuation of the history of David, whence it cannot belong to Je. Since fragments of this sort, obviously related to chap. viii., are found interspersed elsewhere[1] in the text of Da, it appears to me the most natural thing to suppose that chap. viii. belongs, in fact, to Da. This writer would in that case have had as his object to describe the history of David only as far as his ascension of the throne of all Israel. After having given his narrative in detail, he only cursorily alludes, in *v.* 3, to the conquest of Jerusalem, recounts further in *v.* 17 ff., the Philistine victory, and then concludes his book, in chap. viii., with a survey of David's further deeds, partly extracted from Je.[2] Our former conclusion that Da is somewhat, though not much, younger than Je, is thus confirmed.

4. *The Appendix*: 2 Sam. xxi.-xxiv.[3]—Here we find brought together, at the end of the Book of Samuel, a number of heterogeneous fragments, the relation of which to the rest of the Book it is not very easy to determine.[4] Since the first piece, xxi. 1-14, still treats of Saul, we might at first be tempted to assign it at once to the book SS, if we look for traces of the sources already known to us. Cornill[5] accordingly points to E. But against this is its close affinity[6] with the last piece, chap. xxiv., which would not suit SS. The question, therefore, to which source the two pieces belonged, must remain unanswered. Judged by their contents, they are old; still, younger[7] than Je: they stand on about the same level as Da.

One can with more confidence count on general assent in the attempt to connect the second piece, xxi. 15-22, with the sources

---

[1] iii. 2-5; v. 13-16. (The analysis given in my translation is still somewhat different.)

[2] *V.* another solution of the difficulty in Budde, 249 ff.; *v.* 11 f. is a later addition (*v.* Budde, 246). [3] On this see esp. Budde, *RiSa*, 255 ff.

[4] See an interesting attempt in Budde, 255 f.

[5] *KgSt.* 57 f. Budde, on the other hand, points to J. Moreover, xxi. 2 probably belongs to R.

[6] *Cf.* esp. xxiv. 1 with xxi. 1; xxiv. 25 with xxi. 14, and Kuen. § xxii. 13.

[7] On the distinction see the valuable observations of Wellh. *Bl.*[4] 228

known to us. As it is not only connected with *v.* 25,¹ but also agrees in its contents and its whole character with chap. viii., it probably stood originally in the same source—*i.e.* Da. In that case xxiii. 8 ff., the piece about David's heroes, would probably belong to it also.²

None of the sources hitherto identified by us can be recognised in the two songs, chap. xxii. and xxiii. 1-7. We cannot say whence the redactor took them, if it was he himself that inserted them here. Nay, the fact that they separate the two passages, xxi. 15 ff. and xxiii. 8 ff., taken from Da, suggests a doubt whether it was R himself that introduced them. A similar separation, indeed, is found in xxi. 1 ff. and xxiv; but those pieces are at least not inseparably connected by the nature of their contents. There has been much discussion on the question of the Davidic origin of the two songs. It can hardly be proved in the case of xxiii. 1-7; and hardly conclusively in the case of chap. xxii., at least in its present form. If an older kernel can be proved to exist in chap. vii., there would thus be created at least a prejudice in favour of the age of xxiii. 1-7.³

§ 32. 1 *Kings* i.-xi.

Only this first section of the Book of Kings⁴ belongs to our period. It deals with the history of Solomon.

1. In investigating the character and date of the accounts contained in these chapters, we must first of all examine a remarkable divergence in the traditional texts, if we wish to get to the bottom of the matter.⁵ The Alexandrine recension varies from our Hebrew Masoretic text to no slight extent, without its being

---

¹ *Cf.* and *v.* 22.
² transl. in Kautzsch. ³ *V.* xxiii. 5.
⁴ ... the Book of Kings in general: Thenius, *Die BB. der Könige*² (1873); Keil, a.o.² (1876); Wellh. *Bl.*⁴ 231 ff.; *Prol.*² 285 ff.; Kuen. *Ond.*² § xvii. 24-27; Klost. *SaKö.*; Cornill, *Grundr.* 120 ff.; Driver, *Introd.* 175 ff.; [König, *Einl.* § 53; Wildeboer, *Letterk.* § 14; now also, Farrar, *The First Book of Kings*, 1894. On the text of the LXX. *cf.* the excellent article of Silberstein in *ZAW.* 1893, 1 ff., 1894, 1 ff.]
⁵ *Cf.* in general, Wellh. *Bl.*⁴ 231 ff., and Klost. *ad loc.*; also Kuen. § xxvi. 10.

possible to say at once that the one or the other is throughout in the right.

For chaps. vi. and vii. I refer to Stade's thorough discussion,[1] for which I can, for the present at least, substitute nothing better. Moreover, I shall pass over a great number of minor differences between the two texts, since for our purpose they have no importance, and shall confine myself to the main points of divergence.

The section that forms chap. ii. of our present Hebrew text has in the Greek text of the LXX. a considerably different form. Verse 35 of the M.T. is immediately followed in the LXX. by a section composed of elements of the M.T. to be found at other points of the history of Solomon. This is followed by a longer section on Solomon's works, buildings, and offerings. To this succeeds a repetition of the verses ii. 8-9, with a new introductory formula. Thus is effected the transition back to the M.T., the continuation of which (ii. 36 ff.) agrees in the main with the further narrative of the LXX. up to the end of the chapter in the M.T. (ii. 46).[2] Then, however, it is only after supplying a lengthy passage on the might and wealth of Solomon, and on his chief officers,[3] that the text of the LXX. again joins the M.T. Yet while this is so, the latter contains in iii. 1 a short passage that is not, at least in this form and at this point, to be found in the LXX.—although it may be noted here at once that this is not, strictly speaking, a case of an addition on the part of the M.T.[4] Not till iii. 2 do the two narratives again run parallel.

The question arises whether the additional matter of the LXX. is to be traced to an old narrator, and may thus as valuable material deserve to be received into the text. This is not, however we look at it, very likely. The tangled confusion that prevails in the narrative of the LXX. shows that the original

---

[1] *ZAW.* iii. 129 ff.; *The text of the accounts of Solomon's buildings.*
[2] ii. 46b is to be found in the LXX. at v. 35.
[3] *Cf.* on the latter subject the doublet in iv. 2 ff.
[4] The main substance of the verse is to be found in the LXX. several times: after ii. 35; ix. 9; v. 14 (M.T.). At this last place it seems to be relevant.

narrator could not possibly have narrated things in this order. The additions of the LXX. relating to Solomon's wisdom, might, and greatness, are manifestly out of place in the account of his ascending the throne. Moreover, in respect of their contents, they contribute little or nothing that was not known from the M.T. What does vary from the text otherwise known, as *e.g.* some names in the list of officers, has no claim to originality.[1] We have rather, according to all appearances, very late additions to the older text that have, moreover, been inserted in most unsuitable places. The original position of the first of the above additions I am not prepared to indicate: the second probably once stood before chap. iv.

We may perhaps gain one advantage, however, from this amplification of the text. The doublet to ii. 8 f., at the end of the first additional section, sounds as if it were the original reading, and had stood at this point. With this agrees the position that ii. 46^b of the M.T. occupies in the LXX. It is therefore probable that chap. ii. originally observed the following order: *vv.* 1-35, 46^b of the M.T.; [the second form of] 8, 9, of the LXX.; 36-46 [of the M.T.].[2]

A second case of important divergence between the two recensions is to be found in chaps. iv. v. Ignoring minor variations (among which is the changed position of *v.* 17 of the M.T.=*v.* 19 of the LXX.), chap. iv. of the M.T. runs parallel with the LXX. as far as *v.* 19. On the other hand, *v.* 20 is wanting in the LXX. in this connection: so also v. 1.[3] But even after removal of this additional matter the LXX. does not, as one might expect, go on with v. 2, but connects v. 7 f. immediately with iv. 19. Then follow v. 2-4, 9-14 of the M.T., and these are succeeded by iii. 1; ix. 16 M.T. Not till this point do the two recensions again meet, with

---

[1] See on this below, § 48.

[2] [This no longer appears to me quite certain. It is at least a doubtful proceeding to detach and insert here a fragment of Theod. Perhaps also *v.* 46^b suits better in iii. 1.]

[3] [Note that in Eng. Ver. ch. iv. includes also the first 14 verses of ch. v. of the Heb. Text: hence v. 1 M.T.=iv. 21 Eng. Ver., and so on.—*Tr.*]

v. 15 M.T. = v. 1 LXX.; while v. 5, 6 M.T. again are wanting in the original LXX.

Here the LXX. seems to be decidedly in the right. The enumeration of the overseers of Solomon, common to both texts, is not so appropriately followed by a digression on Solomon's greatness and glory, as by a notice of the work of those overseers. When there is appended to this an account of the supplies for Solomon's table, and this is followed (v. 9 ff. M.T.) by a section on Solomon's wisdom, we are supplied with the key to the growth of such later accretions of the same kind as lie before us in iv. 20; v. 1 f., 5 f. M.T.[1] Even this is certainly not a perfectly appropriate place for iii. 1^b; ix. 16 M.T. But the fact that they stand together here in the LXX., and have a better position than in the M.T., shows that they are in a relatively correct position as a part of the section we are dealing with.

Chapter viii. again has been treated in a most interesting way by Wellhausen,[2] who shows that at several points in its first section (vv. 1-10) the text of the LXX. is not only shorter, but also better. Even more instructive is the comparison instituted by the same scholar between the two texts in viii. 11 ff. The prayer of Solomon in viii. 12 f. is mutilated in the M.T., whereas the LXX. has preserved it intact, though at a quite different place—after viii. 53. The reason of this displacement, although not difficult to guess, is a secondary matter as compared with the vital importance of the fact that we are able to recover the exact words of the utterance. The gain here accruing from the LXX. is obvious.

It is very difficult to pronounce judgment on the relation of the two texts in ix. 15-25 (M.T.) and x. 22 ff. (LXX.). In the LXX. of chap. ix., v. 14 is immediately followed by v. 26. On this point it seems to be in the right, as against the M.T. For by the insertion of vv. 15-25 where they stand in the M.T., the details concerning Hiram are disconnected in a confusing manner. The way in which the LXX. provide a place for these verses, certainly does not at all convey the impression of originality. Still the LXX.

---

[1] V. 6 might also have been lost through pure accident. [2] *Loc. cit.* p. 234 ff.

is to be preferred to the M.T., were it only for the reason that it has not, like the M.T., admitted the whole section 15-25 with its confused medley of statements, but only vv. 15, 17 ff., 20-22. Some of the specially disturbing features are thus removed. But the state of affairs is not much cleared up. Still, the form and position of this passage as it stands in the LXX. is preferable.[1]

Of little consequence are several transpositions at the beginning of chap. xi., as well as the omission of v. 38ᶜ and 39 in the LXX. But several verses in the middle of the chapter merit consideration.[2] The narrative about Hadad breaks off abruptly in the M.T. with verse 22, while the LXX. completes it. On the other hand, almost as a compensation for this curtailment, the M.T. offers us, in 23-25, the story of Rezon, which is foreign to the LXX. Can this have fallen out of the LXX. by pure accident? Considering it on its own merits, one would not be disinclined to regard it as a genuine old fragment. But the circumstance that $v.$ 25ᵇ is in fact the missing end of the story of Hadad,[3] and thus coincides with the LXX., bids us hesitate. It seems almost as if the whole story had grown out of a *lapsus calami*: Aram for Edom. Were the error once committed, the names Damascus and Rezon are not hard to account for.

2. If the text is thus settled, at least in general outline, the further question arises here also as to the unity and age of the text thus won.

Looking first of all at the section 1 Kings i.-xi. as a whole, we are struck in the first place with the peculiar relation of chaps. i. and ii. to what follows. The chapters are indispensable in the story of Solomon, for they describe the circumstances of his accession, and what immediately succeeded it. And yet by their characteristic features they belong rather to the preceding group of narratives. If we ignore some Deuteronomist additions,[4] they

---

[1] On ix. 16 M.T. see above, p. 51 f.; on ix. 24 M.T. *cf.* iii. 1 M.T.; vii. 8; ix. 9 LXX., and above, p. 50, note 4.

[2] On the conclusion of the chapter see below, § 51.

[3] Read וְאֵת הָרָעָה = αὕτη ἡ κακία.

[4] ii. 2-4, 27; perhaps also 10-12. On ii. 5-9 see below, § 47; on the place of v. 8 f., see above, p. 51.

belong, from a literary point of view, to Da of the books of Samuel.¹ Moreover, they narrate not simply the beginning of Solomon's career, but, at the same time, the end of David's. This shows that they occupy a double place. They refer just as much forwards as backwards, and thus form the link of connection between the history of David and that of Solomon. This is an important result. It shows us either that both the histories—that of David and that of Solomon—come from the same author, or else that the arrangement of these stories in their later form, and therefore the editing of the Books of Samuel and Kings in their present form, belongs to one and the same hand. Which of these alternatives we are to choose will appear immediately.

What remains, chaps. iii.-xi., describes the history of Solomon after his accession. The arrangement of the material is evidently controlled by the thought of Solomon's wisdom, might, and greatness. As a most striking proof of this, Solomon's building of the temple and the edifices connected therewith, is set in the centre of the account. Not till the close of the whole history of Solomon, are some points unfavourable to him gathered together, so as to 'add a little shade'² to the picture—but certainly not such alone as belonged chronologically to the end of his life.

Here clearly is method. Ill arranged as the material may be in its details, even after our attempted restoration of the text, the grouping of the larger sections is undertaken with a sure hand and perfectly clear points of view. Nor is it simply the course of the history that is the determinative principle, individual points being simply added at the end in the form of appendices, if for some reason they could not be dealt with chronologically. That was the method of the Books of Judges and Samuel. But here the material is arranged from definite points of view not immediately dependent on the historical course of events, and thus in accordance with an independent literary plan. If I am not mistaken, we have here the *first example* in the Old Testament of the writing of *history*, in distinction from bare annalistic records of

---

¹ See esp. Wellh. *Bl.*⁴ 225 f. ; Budde, *RiSa*, 261 ff.   ² Wellh. *Bl.*⁴ 239.

facts. And so it is not accidental that it is here, in the history of Solomon, that the collector of our information for the first time finds occasion to refer to a book of history lying before him, a 'history of Solomon.'[1] That these two facts coincided is far from being accidental. They are two analogous symptoms of the awakening of the historical sense.

To what date may we assign this 'History of Solomon'? That its pragmatism does not belong to the Deuteronomistic redaction, has hitherto indeed been assumed, but not yet proved. I go back to the dilemma propounded a short time ago with regard to the relation of the history of David to that of Solomon. Granted that the second alternative is actual fact, that therefore the Books of Samuel and Kings were drawn up by the same hand, this assumption is intelligible only if 1 Kings iii.-xi. was already in existence in its present arrangement. For it would not be conceivable why the editor should, in the case of Solomon, have deviated so essentially from his usual custom of letting the facts tell their own story, and only supplying them with his own characteristic additions. The history of David, at least, was not lacking in phases that would readily lend themselves to pragmatic treatment. Conversely: if the arrangement of 1 Kings iii.-xi. is relatively old, the redaction of the present Books of Samuel and Kings may come from the same hand; otherwise it is impossible. But this is in itself in the highest degree probable, and so Kuenen (§ 27) for other reasons, arrives at the same conclusion. Two important results are thus gained: the establishment of the relative antiquity of the view of history in 1 Kings iii.-xi., and the corroboration of the decision sought above, on the question of the present narrator's independence with respect to the narrator of the history of David.

This, it is true, does not yet give us the absolute age of the history of Solomon. But we have come one step nearer it.

Here also what we are in search of would be reached at once,

---

[1] 1 Kings xi. 41. Older references to books of songs are not to be compared with this.

could we succeed in showing that what we have is only a constituent part of the *documents* of the *Hexateuch*. As was to be expected, Cornill has lately attempted the proof of this also. Apart from the additions of Rd, he cuts out two layers in our history of Solomon: an older, which he is inclined to identify with J, and a younger, which supplies legendary additions to it.[1]

In the light of what we have found with regard to the whole plan of the pre-Deuteronomic history of Solomon, this supposition seems to have many considerations against it. Above all: the real author of this history of Solomon is not the first but the second writer. If one of the two is to be identified with J, it must, in view of our results, be the second.

In point of fact, what we have is not a case of later additions to an earlier narrative, but of a combining of elements of earlier narratives by a later hand. The earlier elements have throughout the character of annals. The stringing together of events by a clumsy 'then,' which seems to me more frequent here than elsewhere, itself points to this.[2] Affinity of any importance with the Yahvist will here be looked for in vain. Even the tracing back of the words of Solomon at the dedication of the temple to the *Sepher ha-Yāshār*, were it certain, and not merely quite possible, would make no difference. It is much more natural to suppose old records, quite or nearly contemporaneous with what they relate, at all events considerably pre-Yahvistic. If the office of court annalist is once proved to be historical, and we possess here annals or fragments of narrative, of the oldest type, we see really no reason why these notices might not be traced directly, or at least indirectly, back to that *Sôphēr*.[3]

The only question is, how much of our history of Solomon we may in this way trace back to his *Court-annals*, the work of

---

[1] *Grundr.* 120 ff.   [2] *Cf.* viii. 1, 12; ix. 11; xi. 7.
[3] [In the German text I wrote *Mazkîr* instead of *Sôphēr*. But it is more probable (*cf.* also below, pp. 198, 208) that the *Mazkîr*, 'he who brings to remembrance,' was not an officer for carrying out literary works, but a counsellor by word of mouth—the *grand vizier*. *Cf.* also Kautzsch, *Die Heil. Schr. des AT*, *Beilagen*, p. 171.]

his *Sōphēr*—I call it A. Perhaps the fresh start of the narrative in iv. 1 may serve as a guide. Here a narrator begins who is not acquainted with the preceding narratives. There follows an enumeration of Solomon's chief officers, quite after the supposed manner of A. This continues as far as iv. 6, and is then in *vv.* 7-19 [1] succeeded in turn by a similar list which mentions Solomon's overseers.[2] It is unintelligible to me how any one can here think of J: clearly we have A. The same is true of the continuation in chap. v. of the M.T.[3] in the order v. 7 f., 2 f.[4] *V.* 6 may also perhaps belong here, as well as the statements in iii. 1 and ix. 16 of the M.T., the original position of which we have considered above, and iii. 4, to which belong perhaps the main contents of iii. 5 ff. From this point A proceeded to the description of Solomon's buildings, especially his temple. This is preceded by some statements regarding the negotiations with Ḥiram. Perhaps the pronunciation Ḥirôm gives us here the clew. At least v. 24 f., 31 f. belong to A. To this was added the oldest account in chap. vi. f., as Stade (certainly in the main rightly) saw, as also the substance of chap. viii. after removal of the additions of Rd and the LXX., and incorporating *v.* 53 f. of the LXX. The conclusion consisted of statements such as ix. 11; x. 16-20 (22?); ix. 17 f. (19?) 24, 25 (?) 26-28, perhaps also xi. 7. The substance of x. 1-10 may also belong to A: still it is safer to relegate the Queen of Sheba to the next layer of tradition. I conjecture that we have before us in A the *oldest* historical records to a certain extent connected, to be found in the Old Testament.

A further stage in the development is represented by the *History of Solomon* described above. I designate it 'So.' To it belongs iii. 5-13, in which at most some additions by D[2] are to be found, but which rests in the main on old tradition.[5] This is

---

[1] On *v.* 20 see above, p. 51 f.
[2] On these *cf.* Kuen. § xxv. 2, 3; and below, § 48.
[3] v. 1 ff. of the Heb. represent iv. 21 ff. of Eng. Ver. [*Tr.*].
[4] On this see above, p. 51 f. *V.* 4 is a later addition, *cf.* Kuen. § xxv. 2: xxvi. 4.
[5] D[2] first appears at *v.* 14: notice, in particular, מִשְׁפָּט (*v.* 11), in the judicial, not the legal sense (*cf. v.* 9 מִשְׁפָּט and the narrative in iii. 16 ff., esp. *v.* 28).

followed by the narrative of Solomon's judicial sentence in iii. 16-28. Both sections illustrate the king's accession to the throne. To the history of his buildings So adds v. 15 f., 20-23, 27 f., if the last two verses do not already belong to A. The conclusion then consists of some pieces of So in chaps. ix. ff., especially xi. 12 f.; x. 1 ff., 11 f.; xi. 14-22, 23-25,[1] 26-32, 37-40.

The standpoint of this writer has much in common with Je and Da of the history of David. That he did not stand in immediate proximity to the events, appears from many indications,[2] not least from direct references to the past.[3] It is not necessary to determine whether we must assign him a date appreciably later than that of those books, because of his more artistic arrangement. This may have been due to personal preferences on the part of the writer. It must be noted that the impulse to historical writing was awakened in Israel, as elsewhere, not so much by the lapse of time, as by the greatness of events. If we are asked to find traces of affinity with J or E, my view of the nature of So does not present any serious obstacle, although such traces do not present themselves to me sufficiently clearly.[4] Perhaps So was that very history of Solomon that our compiler mentions among his sources (xi. 41). Still he might have in view a later and considerably enlarged edition of So, much of which he found occasion to omit.

If A and So are taken out of 1 Kings iii.-xi. all that remains will be seen pretty plainly to belong to the Deuteronomistic editing (D[2]; in Kautzsch, Dt; Kuenen, Rd). Proof of this can without difficulty be found in the language and conceptions characteristic of these sections.[5] Yet even here many features

---

[1] Provided that these verses are original; v. above, p. 53.

[2] On these see espec. Kuen. § xxv. 3.   [3] Cf. 1 Kings ix. 13; x. 12.

[4] In iii. 5 ff. some points accord with E, whereas in iii. 16 ff. we rather detect the tone of J. Yet little can be built on this. On the other hand, cf. expressions like גבור חיל xi. 28 (never in the Hexateuch, but here and there from Judges vi. 12; xi. 1 onwards).

[5] To this group belong iii. 2, 3, 14, 15 (cf. v. 15 with 4); v. 9-14, 18 f., 26, 29 f. (on iv. 20, v. 1-8, see above, p. 51 f.); considerable parts of chap. vi. f. cf. ZAW. iii. 129 f.; the revising of viii. 1-11; viii. 14-66; ix. 1-9; parts of ix. 15-25 M.T.; and some things in chap. x.; xi. 1-6, 8-13, 33-36, 38 f., 41-43. Cf. Wellh., and Kuen. § xxv. 2.

show that the first editing of the royal history beginning with Solomon's time (Kuen. Rd¹) was followed by a second, the later editor being the author of the Book of Kings in its present form (R; Kuen. Rd²).[1] The former belonged to the pre-exilic age,[2] whereas the latter presupposes the Babylonian-Persian age.[3] That many other influences in addition to these have had a share in the development of the text, has appeared from the criticism of the text prefixed to this paragraph. It has also appeared, however, how fluctuating is the boundary between criticism of the text and of the sources.

[1] He is nearly related to the author or authors of the Books of Judges and Samuel. Most probably all three books are, in their present form, his work (on this *cf.* also above, p. 55).

[2] *Vide* viii. 8 ; ix. 21 ('unto this day').

[3] See espec. v. 4 ('beyond the river').

B. HISTORY OF THE PERIOD.

CHAPTER I.

THE SO-CALLED AGE OF THE JUDGES.

§ 33. *The general situation. Israel's task.*

To how small an extent Palestine was really in the possession of the people of Israel in the period that we call the age of the Judges—*i.e.* after Joshua had died and about a generation had elapsed since the beginning of the real war of conquest—appears from the history of the Judges we are about to trace, as well as from the details given about the conquest. In reality, little more was achieved towards the conquest and occupation of the land than the first beginnings, although these were full of promise. The people had set a firm foot in the land, and that at several points, and were doubtless determined not to suffer themselves to be forced without good reason from the positions they had won. Everything else, however, was left to the future.

As matters stood, it was a slow work that devolved on Israel, a work involving even centuries of effort, though there was not lacking the prospect of final success. This appears from a glance at the situation in Palestine, as described in the Book of Judges, and presupposed in the history of the monarchy.[1] The light shed by the history of the neighbouring peoples, and especially by the recently found Tell-el-Amarna tablets, will afford us some help. The descriptions which the latter give us of the relations in

---

[1] On this *cf.* Meyer, *Gesch. d. Alt.* i. p. 349 ff. Pietschmann, *Gesch. d. Phön.*, p. 264 ff.

Palestine,[1] refer indeed to a considerably earlier time, that of the close of the 15th century B.C. But there is no doubt that those descriptions are in many points applicable also to our period. Only it must not be forgotten that the supremacy of Egypt, under which at that time the whole of Syria unquestionably lay, had now, with the progressive decline of the empire of the Pharaohs, ceased to be maintained.[2] Neither at the actual time of conquest, nor in the period before us, can the slightest traces of Egyptian supremacy over Palestine be detected in our documents. Not even the remembrance of it seems to have remained to later times.

The Canaanites from early times formed a series of independent communities. Indeed, a certain tendency to separatism seems to have been inherent in the blood of this branch of the Semitic stock.[3] Accordingly they do not, in ordinary times, seem to have formed a real confederacy of states or cities. Commonly their relation to each other was rather that of isolated city-republics or city-kingdoms, often in a state of conflict.[4] But they well knew how to bind themselves more closely together for special ends, and where they succeeded in working together they were a source of danger to Israel.

They had long since taken to agriculture, and, to a large extent, to city life. They practised the former in the fruitful plains and the fields of the low country, while through their cities lay the most important trade routes.[5] They had thus reached a relatively

---

[1] On this see espec. Zimmern in *ZDPV*. 1891, 133 ff. ; *Z. f. Assyr.* vi. 245 ff. [further : Jastrow on Palestine and Assyr. in the days of Josh. in *Z. Assyr.* 1892, 1 ff. ; Halévy, *L'état de Palest. avant l'Exode*, in the *Verhh. d. Stockh. Orient. Congr.* ii. 141 ff. ; also Aubert, in *Rev. de théol. et phil.* 1894, 326 ff.].

[2] *Cf.* Pietschmann, *loc. cit.* p. 260 ff., and espec. Meyer, *Gesch. d. alten Aegypt.* 278 ff., 304 ff. The question might be raised whether Ramses III. did not exaggerate his achievements.

[3] See Pietschmann, *loc. cit.* p. 96. This may be connected with the deep ravines dissecting the country.

[4] The Hittites alone form an exception (according to Amenhotep IV.). On the relations already existing under Thothmes III., *cf.* Meyer, *Gesch. d. Alt.* 235. Quite similar relations are presupposed by the wars of Ramses II. and Ramses III.

[5] See Meyer, *Gesch. Ägypt.* 228 f.

high degree of civilisation;[1] but in their cities voluptuousness and dissolute morals prevailed.[2]

In the art of war they were more than a match for the still nomadic Hebrews. They were in possession of war-chariots,[3] never alluded to by the Hebrews without horror, as well as of strong walled cities,[4] the special mention of which leads one to surmise that they were quite familiar with the art of fortification. Israel had little military art to bring against them, though it had indeed the unbroken vigour of a primitive people still in its youth, and the unsubdued temper of the fresh, defiant son of the desert. The Canaanite, on the other hand, had, through centuries of subjection to Egypt, long become disused to freedom.

What Israel had reached up to this point can be determined better negatively than positively. We possess lists, probably substantially complete, of the districts that were not conquered and occupied in the first period.[5] These were, in the first place, the strong maritime cities of the Philistines [6] and the Phœnicians.[7] On the latter, so far as we know, no attack was ever ventured; while if, in individual cases, attacks were undertaken against the former, they were at all events not subdued. Israel met with the same experience also in regard to the strong cities of the interior. If those maritime cities served to preserve the shores of the Mediterranean, especially the fruitful maritime plain, in the possession of their former lords, the cities of inner Palestine

---

[1] *Cf.* the utensils and garments on the well-known tablet of Ḥui at Thebes, which presuppose a high degree of skill in art (in Meyer, *Ägypt.*, opposite p. 242).

[2] *Cf.* espec. the description in Gen. xviii. f.

[3] Ju. i. 19. *Cf.* Perrot and Chipiez, *Hist. de l'Art*, iii. 716 f.

[4] Num. xiii. 28, Josh. vi., and elsewhere. For a Hittite city of the time of Ramses II. (Dapur), see Meyer, *Ägypt*; opposite p. 290.

[5] Ju. i. espec. *v.* 27 ff. and the parallel passages; on which see vol. i. p. 243 f. [Eng. Trans. i. 269 f.] Also Ju. iii. 1 ff. (on which see above, p. 3, note 6).

[6] Ju. iii. 3. It is possible that even these were originally in the possession of the Canaanite-Phœnicians, and only passed to the Philistines by conquest in our period (Meyer, *Gesch. d. Alt.* 319 f.).

[7] Ju. i. 31. Canaanite and Phœnician are here for brevity treated as equivalent; by the latter therefore being understood simply the Canaanites that settled on the coast. On the more exact relationship *cf.* Pietschm., *Phön.* 87 ff.

served to secure to them their most important trade route, and the inland plain richest in corn, the valley of the Kishon. The route referred to led through this plain, and in it, encircling the plain like an iron girdle, lay a number of strongholds, impregnable for the present—*e.g.* Taanach, Megiddo, Beth-shean.[1] Moreover, the extensive plain afforded the Canaanite war-chariots the space they needed. Thus the Canaanites were for the present the unquestioned masters of the plain.

The position of Israel was still further threatened by the fact that this plain, inaccessible to its hosts, separated Mount Ephraim and the chief tribes of the central district, from the tribes settled farther north—viz. Asher, Naphtali, Zebulon, and Issachar. These tribes themselves, again, were not in unquestioned possession of the northern districts on the slopes of Lebanon and Hermon. They shared them with the Phœnicians, the other Canaanites, and the Hittites.[2]

While the chief tribes of the central land were thus divided from their brother tribes towards the north by a deep indentation, that we may suppose to have reached from Carmel to the Jordan, it was the same towards the south. Here also the Canaanitish territory penetrated far into the interior of Israel. The cities of Shaalbim, Aijalon, Gezer, Har-Heres,[3] and Jebus, with which according to others also Gibeon[4] with its district would be included, mark out the line.[5] Of this group of cities, Jebus, which was considered impregnable,[6] would form the central point. Judah-Simeon were in this way almost completely cut off from the other tribes. They went their own way, and, unless we have lost important constituent parts of our narratives, were for some time as good as lost, so far as the history of Israel was concerned.

We thus see that if much was done, even under Joshua and in

---

[1] Ju. i. 27.
[2] Ju. i. 31 ff., iii. 3. (Read החתי Meyer, *ZAW*. i. 126.)
[3] On this see Budde, *RiSa*, 17.
[4] See above, Eng. Trans. vol. i. p. 300 f.
[5] Ju. i. 34 + Josh. xiv. 47 LXX. (see above, i. 244 [Eng. Trans. p. 270]). Further, i. 21, 29, 35; and above, i. 241 f., 271 f. [Eng. Trans. p. 266 f., p. 300 f.].
[6] 2 Sam. v. 6.

his generation, towards gaining possession of the land, much also remained for the following generations to achieve. What was won, in addition to the first conquered district east of the Jordan, was substantially the Jordan valley and the wooded hill country of the central district, as far as the border of the maritime plain in the west. Besides this, Israel possessed two strips of land, ever indeed becoming narrower, to the north and south respectively of the two groups of Canaanite cities that lay on the Kishon and in the neighbourhood of Jebus. One of these strips reached up to the district of the sea of Merom, while the other sent out its last spurs into the wilderness. As Israel's most important points of support, are mentioned the cities of Jericho, Ai, Bethel, and Hebron —few enough for the task that lay before them.

The policy of Israel was, from the nature of the case, not uniform in the various districts where it succeeded, in whole or in part, in gaining a firm footing. In not a few cases complete extermination seems to have been resorted to.[1] Religious considerations rather encouraged than checked such a course. Revolting as the barbarity of this policy of massacre may seem to our feelings, there is something that commands respect in its pitiless thoroughness at the bidding of religion, and its unselfishness as compared with the common raid of depredation.[2] Yet the extermination was not consistently carried through. There often appears in its stead simple subjugation, or even amicable alliance by covenant and intermarriage. Probably the case was something like this. Where means and strength were forthcoming, the enemy, after being decisively subdued beyond the possibility of further resistance, were pitilessly 'banned,' exterminated 'with the edge of the sword.' Any one who would live must seek safety in flight. Cases, however, would not be rare, where neither side had decidedly gained the upper hand, but both maintained an equal right of possession. It was necessary in such circumstances to come to terms. Both parties settled down side by side, and this

---

[1] e.g. in Ju. i. 17, 25; Josh. xix. 47 LXX.; Ju. xviii. 27, 28; Heb. חרם; on which see Driver, *Notes*, 100 f.   [2] See Cornill, *ZKWL*. 1885, p. 121 f.

state of things continued until in some way in the course of time one of the parties gained the upper hand, and as soon as it felt itself in a position to do so, displaced the other or enslaved it. Such a proceeding is related of Israel several times in the words: 'when Israel was waxen strong they put the Canaanites to task-work;'[1] but the same thing could also happen to them at the hands of their adversaries.[2] If finally this process failed to lead to subjugation, or if from the first it seemed hopeless, they could at an early stage enter into friendly alliance. Here and there also, especially in the hill country, the Canaanites would easily make up their minds to a surrender of land, so as to set at rest the intruders, and free themselves from what was a burdensome menace to their right of possession. Even in the plain and the cities, Israelitish colonies early found it possible to settle down beside the ancient inhabitants. The relations in Shechem during the period under consideration[3] are a typical example of this. From peaceable residence in the same place there followed, as a matter of course, intermarriage and a gradual general blending.[4] Hence the historians of a later age find fault with this very procedure, and not unjustly; for there lay in it an unmistakable danger for Israel's religion and national individuality. Besides being found in Shechem, and probably also in Jebus, this kind of relation seems gradually to have established itself, especially in the northern tribes which occupied the *hinterland* of the great Phœnician cities. Active relations of trade were here doubtless soon developed, and the two peoples learned to live side by side in peace.[5]

The whole period between the death of Joshua and the rise of the monarchy under Saul, we call, according to a traditionary conception, the age of the 'Judges.' Whether our documents

---

[1] Especially Ju. i. 27 ff.
[2] So in Ju. i. 35. This is clearly the meaning also of the words about Issachar in Gen. xlix. 14 f. : 'and he bowed the shoulder and became a servant under task-work.'   [3] *Cf.* Gen. xxxiv. ; Ju. ix.
[4] Ju. iii. 6 (probably a redactional sentence, but resting on reminiscences of fact); Gen. xxxiv. 9, 21.   [5] See Stade, *Gesch. Israels*, i. 141 f.

already used the term 'Judge' to indicate the leading agents of this heroic age of Israel, need not be determined here.[1] It is at least not till we reach the later strata of the material supplied by tradition, that we find associated with it the idea of men who exercised a magisterial sway over the whole of Israel, and even, as a rule, for some length of time. This representation of the so-called Judges, as theocratic precursors of the monarchy, life-long rulers over all Israel, is quite opposed to the old tradition. So is the other representation, closely connected with it, that they formed a continuous series, beginning with Othniel and Ehud, and closing with Eli and Samuel, each delivering over to his successor in unbroken line, authority and supreme dominion over Israel. The fact is, that these leaders of the age of the Judges are war-captains, that advance at the head of their tribes—sometimes here, sometimes there, wherever need calls them and danger makes them heroes. Each tribe or clan, for the most part, goes its own way, caring little for the weal or woe of the others, content to defend itself against the foe. And so the Judges were ordinarily nothing but petty princes, heads of tribes, generally of noble blood, who gathered the warriors of the tribe and marched with them against any foe that might break into the land for plunder or war. Only more rarely, when perhaps the need was specially great, or the chief succeeded in awakening in his own and the adjoining districts a feeling of community of interest, did other tribes unite themselves with the one first affected, and the 'people' gathered together for common action. This occurred but rarely, and was soon over. We see it at its best in the incident of Deborah.

What the task was that awaited the tribes of Israel during the first period after their entrance into Canaan may easily be inferred from what has been said. It was necessary, above all, to secure permanent possession of those districts in which Israel

---

[1] See above, p. 13, p. 3 f. Perhaps an example of the older designation has been preserved for us still in קצין (Ju. xi. 6 [Isa. i. 10]). With the Hebrew שפטים is to be compared the Carthaginian *suffetae* and the Phœnician שפט. *Cf. Corp. Inscr. Sem.*, 47, 118, 143. Here the word means, governor of the city. On the Assyrian *shiptu-shâpitu* = leader of a band, see Jensen, *Z. f. Assyr.* iv. 279 f.

had already gained a firm footing—a task often enough by no means light, in face of the ever-renewed onward pressure of foes; a task in which Israel was, in fact, here and there defeated. But it was also necessary to strengthen the position once won, and at the same time meet the need of room to spread out in the land, by striving to push on and effect a settlement where this had not as yet been accomplished. If the maritime districts of Philistia and Phœnicia were entirely, or for the most part, out of reach, Israel had to regard as the ultimate goal of its aims at least the whole interior, from the slopes of Lebanon to the Judæan south-country. The strong Canaanite cities in the midst of Israel must have been a thorn in the flesh. The fruitful plains, so long as they remained in the possession of strangers, must have been an eyesore. The barriers between the tribes and groups of tribes had to be broken through, and the possibility of a combination, at least for definite ends, to be striven for. Finally, as the realisation of these aims necessarily involved a coming to terms with the original inhabitants of the land, it was needful, even if this were brought about by warlike means, but still more if by peaceable means, to give heed that Israel's nationality and religious individuality suffered no loss—a task that was much more difficult to achieve than the gradual appropriation of land and people.

In facing these tasks Israel was certainly not unhampered by hindrances. Thus we understand why at the beginning Israel did not get beyond the effort to achieve them, and for a long time met with, in general, only partial success in the attempt. Two powerful and dangerous enemies of every normal development of a feeling of common interest, stood in Israel's way, retarding it at every step—internal want of union, and attacks from without. As is so often the case, the two went hand in hand. Internal strife on the part of the tribes, and the tendency to break up into small parties, under the scattering force of private interests, provided occasion for hostile attacks, and made them more dangerous. In this respect also Israel showed itself akin to the Canaanites. At last there remained for the Israelitish tribes only one way of securing undisturbed possession of land and nationality. The appearance here and there of individual heroic figures no longer sufficed. These might give some temporary help, but they could not keep what had been gained. A unification of the tribes must take place through the rise of some strong central power. Only then could Moses' legacy to his nation seem attainable in politics and in religion. For not till then could the idea, that he had bequeathed to the Israelitish tribes, of a real and independent national existence and individuality, be realised. And not till then could the unity of the nation find its complement, and at the same time its support, in the unity of God. For in Israel, if anywhere, the soul of the nation was its religion, its God.

Thus, even amid division and separatism, everything made for unity. And whoever in this epoch was able to get at all at the soul of the nation and surmise its destiny, must have perceived this tendency. In reality, what we call the age of the Judges was a period of conflict and opposing elements. Even the few fragments of narratives that remain to us, enable us to see clearly that we stand in a time of struggle with great tasks, which were recognised by only a few individuals, and to which even they were not equal. But it was enough at the outset to be conscious of the task. After a series of fruitless efforts, after going astray more than once in the sphere of politics and religion, a people of such original strength and so lofty a destiny must eventually find its way to its high goal.

§ 34. *Further Wars of Conquest.*

We are not able to offer a coherent account of the progress of the wars of conquest any more than of the other events of the period of the Judges. This is due to the fragmentariness of the material supplied us by tradition, and the entire absence of any continuous chronological reckoning. Several attempts have, it is true, been made to attain the latter. Indeed, the present Book of Judges is even set in a complete and rounded chronological scheme. But this belongs, in its present form, to the latest of the constituent parts of the book. The attempt has, however, been made above[1] to show that it does not rest, as has often been supposed, on the pure invention of later times. It is rather, according to all appearances, to be traced to older chronological notes belonging to the documents themselves. Especially do the numbers for the so-called minor Judges, and those for Jephthah and the times of oppression, appear in part to rest on older tradition. But even if they have in individual cases a certain value, they do not suffice to lead us to a continuous chronology. It remains, therefore, necessary to determine in every case the chronological order of events by the help of internal marks. In this the arrangement of the Judge-narratives will give us a certain amount of help.

It is self-evident, on a consideration of the general situation, that the wars of conquest continued even when the Israelitish tribes had planted themselves firmly in the land, individual tribes going forth here and there, sword in hand, to extend their possessions. Our information, little though it be, is enough to enable us to discover, from certain typical cases, how we must conceive the course of these wars. Many other such struggles doubtless occurred, although no record of them has been preserved for us.

At a time when an Israelitish colony, though small in numbers, had got a footing in Shechem,[2] the attempt to gain possession of this important city by force of arms, doubtless with a view to settling in its territory, was made by the tribes of Simeon and Levi. The latter, the tribe of Moses, is not mentioned in the earlier wars of conquest, and so it had probably not yet won for itself any territory.[3] Simeon on the other hand may, like Dan, not have been able to maintain itself in its territory, which bordered on that of Judah on the south.

---

[1] *Cf.* p. 13 f.

[2] Shechem ben Ḥamōr had an intrigue with Jacob's daughter Dinah—*i.e.* a branch of Israel settled in Shechem.

[3] According to Wellh. *Comp.*[2] *Nachtr.*, p. 354, it had with Simeon joined itself to Judah.

The attack of these two tribes, which perhaps thought they could rely on the help of the Israelitish minority in Shechem, was felt by the other Israelitish tribes to be base treachery. It disturbed the compact between Israel and the Canaanites, and provoked the latter to retaliation in other places. So Simeon and Levi, though hard pressed by the Canaanites, were not aided by Israel. The result was their complete extirpation.[1] Henceforth Simeon disappears from history. At most, some traces of its former stay in the south have been preserved in that district.[2] Levi is scattered among the several tribes, so that from this time onwards only single families were to be found here and there in the territories of the other tribes. But these did not forget their tribal connection with Levi. As Moses' tribe, it betook itself from this time onwards more to priestly duties[3]—either following ancient custom, or inventing in its need a new usage.

The land east of the Jordan, too, although in its southern parts it was Israel's first-won possession, was still for long, probably beyond the times of the Judges, a scene of violent feuds. The tribe of Reuben was not able to maintain its territory. This is proved not only by the success of Eglon of Moab, but also by the circumstance that the heroic song preserved to us from that old time, uses every occasion to throw contempt on Reuben.[4] Gad succeeded much better in maintaining itself against the pressure of the neighbouring peoples.[5] It seems in time to have actually taken the place and played the part of Reuben.

A specially interesting example, however, of such wars of conquest has been preserved for us in the story of the tribe of *Dan*. Dan had originally established itself on the western slopes of Mount Ephraim. It was soon, however, driven by

---

[1] The representation is taken from Gen. xxxiv., with which Gen. xlix. 5, 7, is to be compared. On Gen. xxxiv. see above, vol. i. p. 141 [Eng. Trans. i. 156 f.] and recently, Wellh. *Comp*². *Nachtr.* 353 f., and Cornill, *ZAW*. xi. 1 ff.

[2] See Graf, *Der Stamm Simeon* (Meissen, 1866).

[3] See Graf, *Zur Gesch. des Stammes Levi*, in Merx's *Archiv.* i. ; Kautzsch in Ersch and Gruber's *Encykl.*, Art. Levi ; Baudissin, *Gesch. des isr. Priestert.*, 67 ff.

[4] Ju. v. 16 ; Gen. xlix. 3 f. ; *cf.* Dt. xxxiii. 6.

[5] Gen. xlix. 19 ; Dt. xxxiii. 21.

the Amorite[1] inhabitants of this region back towards the east, and finally so weakened that nothing remained for it but to yield to superior force and seek for itself a home elsewhere.[2] We have in Ju. xvii. f. an account of the way in which the tribe came into possession of its new home, which is equally important from the point of view of ordinary history and of the special history of civilisation.[3] According to this account the Danites, after gathering information about the condition of affairs through spies, set out from their strong cantonment at Kiriath-jearim, to the number of six hundred men capable of bearing arms, along with their wives and children, and wend their way northwards. In the region of the sources of the Jordan, they come upon a city called Laish, inhabited by a small peaceable community. The people live a life of quiet security, far removed from the Phœnicians to whom they belong, and without any dealings with the Aramæans[4]— hence alike unprotected and unmolested. After seizing an idol on their way, in Mount Ephraim, and carrying off its priest also, the Danites fall on this city, burning it and pitilessly slaying its inhabitants. In its stead they build a new city, called by their own name—the Dan that was afterwards so well known. In consequence of this daring *coup de main*, the tribe of Dan long led an independent existence, respected by all, here at the northern boundary of Israel.[5] In the time of David it still passed for a genuine model of an Israelitish tribe—nay, a storehouse for good old customs.[6]

It was, however, hardly the whole tribe of Dan that was concerned in this episode. The song of Deborah,[7] and, even more, the story of Samson, points to the probability that a

[1] It should be noticed that the Philistines are not (yet?) mentioned as adversaries.
[2] See Ju. i. 34 f.; Josh. xix. 47 LXX.; on the latter passage, Dillm. in his Comment. [3] On this see above, p. 19 ff.
[4] So according to LXX., xviii. 7, 28. See my transl. in Kautzsch.
[5] *Cf.* Gen. xlix. 16 ff.; Dt. xxxiii. 22.
[6] 2 Sam. xx. 18 LXX. (Wellh. *TBS.* 207 f.).
[7] In Ju. v. 17, אניות is doubtful, since it is not probable that Dan, even if Ju. v. refers to the southern Dan, was a seafaring tribe.

part of the old tribe, perhaps relying on the 'camp of Dan,' succeeded after all in maintaining itself in the old home. The narrative we are discussing seems itself to point to this.[1] At least we cannot infer from it the contrary, as this narrative, though of the greatest value in regard to its general features, is not so accurately informed in regard to the details.[2]

But the last decisive battle with the old occupiers of the land was still to come. It brought about the glorious union of the tribes of Israel under Barak and Deborah, for the repulse of the Canaanites under Sisera.

Two accounts of the event are at our command, a poem and a narrative in prose.[3] Wherever they may not agree, the former is entitled to the preference. This is the song of Deborah, hardly to be attributed to that heroine herself,[4] yet at all events to a contemporary of the events sung about—a gem of old Hebrew literature, a pearl among the poetry of all ages.[5] The song is a genuine heroic lay, whose poetry consists not simply in word, but in deed and force—a fire kindled at the holy flame of ardent enthusiasm for Israel, and purest, most fervent love for Yahvé and his people.

Sisera, the king of the northern Canaanites (Haroseth), had done violence to the Israelitish tribes of the middle and north of the land. In league with the still Canaanite cities of the valley of the Kishon, it could not be a difficult undertaking for him, if the tribes of Israel to the north and south of that valley did not hold fast together, to subdue them one by one or in small groups, and thus to keep them all in check. What had failed in the days of Joshua he might expect to bring to a happier issue now. United, and with the help of superior military skill and strong

[1] Ju. xviii. 11 : six hundred men of the tribe of the Danites.
[2] Cf. Ju. xviii. 1b with i. 34 + Josh. xix. 47 ; also xviii. 12.
[3] Ju. iv. 4-22, and v. 2-30 (31a?). On the share of Ri in the two chaps. see above, page 3, note 2. On the relation of the two accounts see Wellh. Bl.[4] 187 ff. ; Kuen. § xix. 3 ; Budde, RiSa, 101 ff. In the song, Sisera himself is the hostile king, whereas the prose narrative mistakenly makes him simply the general of Jabin the King of Hazor (Josh. xi.). Deborah appears, according to v. 15, to have belonged like Barak to the tribe of Issachar, not to Ephraim.
[4] On מקמי v. 7 f. see Wellh. Bl.[4] 190 ; Nachtr. 256 ; also Budde, RiSa, 103.
[5] On the song see my transl. and A. Müller in KySt. i. 1 ff. ; Budde, loc. cit.

fortresses, the Canaanites hoped even now to become masters of the intruders.

The chief part of the work seemed already done. Severe oppression, long continued, had already succeeded in making the Israelitish peasant tired of resistance, and bringing him to lay aside his arms in despondency. 'There was neither shield nor spear to be seen amongst 40,000 in Israel.' And if the courage of Israel showed signs of reviving, threatening attacks, undertaken now here and now there, were sufficient quickly to lay it low again. Trade and communication was menaced, roads were no longer sure, and the point was not far off when the tribes of Israel, weary of the burden, would prefer to retreat or to become tributary.

'In the days of Shamgar ben Anath,'[1]

so says the song,

> 'In the days of Jael, the paths rested,
> And they that went by the ways, went by crooked paths.
> The peasants (?) of Israel were idle, they were idle
> Till thou stoodest up, Deborah,
> Stoodest up, a mother in Israel!'

Deborah came on the scene, and with her, deliverance. A prophetic woman,[2] a Seer somewhat like what Samuel was in later times, not content to give direction to the people for pay, she carried in her breast faith in Yahvé and his helping hand. The distress of the people went to her heart. It was at the same time a dishonour to Yahvé. Therefore help must be given, and deliverance must be at hand. The thought that the tribes belonged to one another, that they were Yahvé's tribes—yea, that they must become Yahvé's nation—lived in her. Though to a great extent dead among a multitude which was disheartened, and by this time tired of the obligation of nationality, it still certainly lived here and there in

---

[1] Shamgar is thus proved to be a historical person belonging to the time shortly before Deborah, and playing a certain part in it. As the context shows, he was not a deliverer of Israel. Ju. iii. 31 is from R. See above, page 3, note 3; 13, note 2.

[2] This item is taken from chap. iv.

individuals. They flock together round this God-inspired woman. The watchword: 'Israel and Yahvé belong to each other; Israel's tribes are Yahvé's tribes, a nation, a unity,' stirs them up to common action. 'My heart is toward the leaders of Israel, you that showed yourselves willing among the people: praise Yahvé!' The chiefs of the tribes follow the impulse, carrying their tribes along with them. Enthusiasm fires the masses. The victory is theirs.

Ephraim, Benjamin, Machir-Manasseh, Zebulon, Naphtali, Issachar, send forth their troops, the tribal chiefs at their head. The whole host of Israel is commanded by Barak ben Abinoam. Personal injury that he had suffered, whets his sword.[1] Only a few tribes hold back. Wrathful scorn is the reward of Reuben's indolent irresolution, Gilead's lazy indifference, Dan and Asher's base avarice; wild curses are the reward of the cowardly selfishness of the neighbouring Meroz. By the Kishon, in the plain where the war-chariots could deploy and the cities afford shelter, Sisera gathers his host.

'Kings came and fought.
There fought the kings of Canaan,
At Taanach by the waters of Megiddo:
Booty of silver took they none.
From the heavens fought the stars,
From their courses fought they with Sisera,
The stream Kishon swept them away,
A stream of battles is the stream Kishon.'

Even wilder and more passionate than its beginning is the end of the drama. The enemies are scattered before the hosts of Israel. Sisera flees. A woman's hand deals the dread one his death-blow.

'Praised above women be Jael,
The wife of Heber the Kenite,
Above women in the tent be she praised.
For water he asked, milk did she give,
In a lordly dish presented she cream.

---

[1] Translate in v. 12, with Luther, 'lead thy captors captive' (שְׁבְיֶךָ) Wellh.

> Her hand stretched she forth after the peg,
> And her right hand after the workman's hammer,
> And with the hammer struck she Sisera, battered his head,
> Shattered and pierced his temples.
> At her feet he gave way, he fell down:
> Where he gave way, there did he lie, stricken dead.'

It is hardly possible to estimate too highly the value of Deborah's feat. In this time of Israel's sorest dismemberment, at the moment of greatest danger to the national sentiment, the knowledge of Israel as One and as Yahvé's People, that lived in the heart of this woman, stirred the soul of the masses.[1] The dying spark burst forth, at least once in this time of trouble and gloom, into bright flame. The spirit of Moses appears to have revived. And even if the darkness closes again after Deborah, the fire that she kindled must long have been reflected in the memory and heart of the tribes. Even those who basely held back must have been touched in heart and conscience by Deborah's deed and song.

At the same time, the process of the amalgamation of the Canaanites with the newly strengthened Israel, certainly now received a fresh impulse. The last attempt at united action that we hear of, on the part of the former lords of the land, had now been made. Its failure, brought about by Israel's strength and united action, must have had far-reaching consequences. The power of Canaan was finally broken. One fragment crumbled away after another, and was absorbed by Israel. Even the strongholds of the plain of Jezreel maintained themselves no longer. For, when at a later date, the Philistines made themselves masters of the land, although the Canaanites had not indeed disappeared—Jebus, Gibeon, and Gezer still belonged to them—they had no longer sufficient strength and footing to work into the hands of the Philistines. It would have required little, in league with the Philistines, to annihilate Israel; but that little was wanting. The truth is, they had become merged in Israel.

---

[1] The words of the song do not indeed expressly say this, yet certainly the spirit of them implies it. See Baethgen, *Beitr. z. sem. Religionsgesch.* 204 f.

Accordingly, after the days of Barak and Deborah, there can have taken place at the most, only isolated battles with the former lords of the land. The chief thing was that individual tribes were encouraged by the signal success of the Israelitish arms to press farther forward into regions till now closed against Israel. This is probably the explanation of the fact that our Book of Judges, in the further course of its narrative,[1] adds several supplementary names of heroes, who apparently had their part in the wars of conquest—the so-called 'minor Judges.' They are generally regarded as simply *heroes eponymi* of their tribes, and so quite unhistorical.[2] But the fact that only their names and a few meagre notices of them have reached us, does not prove this. Indeed, Jephthah once belonged to their number, and the numbers of years assigned to them are older than the rest of the chronology of the Book of Judges,[3] facts which rather favour another view, viz. that they were historical tribal heroes, who at different times, perhaps also some of them contemporaneously, made themselves a name in the war of conquest. But Elon, as being *eponymos* of Aijalon, and Tola (since this is also a clan name[4]) may be in part, yet cannot be altogether fabulous figures. There is no ground for a similar assumption in the case of Jair, Ibzan, or Abdon.

We have information elsewhere of one of these—viz. Jair—in connection with matters that likewise point to the time under consideration. He would appear to have gone across the Jordan, in common with the Manassite families of Machir and Nobah, and to have taken parts of Gilead from the Amorites who were settled there.[5] Since the enterprise originated west of the Jordan, it can

---

[1] Ju. x. 1-4 ; xii. 8 ff.
[2] So Nöldeke, *Unters.* 181 ff. ; Meyer, *Gesch. d. Alt.* 359 ; Budde, *RiSa*, 96 f.
[3] See above, pp. 8 ff., 13 f.
[4] See Gen. xlvi. 13 ; Num. xxvi. 23 ; Gen. xlvi. 14 ; Num. xxvi. 26. Yet it is also possible that these passages only reflect the later conception of P. See also Budde, p. 100, on Ehud and Shimei ; and *cf.* Shamgar ben Anat, who, although his father bears the name of a god (Baethgen, *Beitr.* 52, 141), is a historical person.
[5] Num. xxxii. 39 ff. On Dt. iii. 14, see Stade, *Gesch.* 150.

have taken place only after the time of Joshua.[1] Jair became the founder of the Havvoth Jair—*i.e.* the villages of Jair—a designation that offers no occasion to stamp the bearer of the original name as an unhistorical *eponymos*.

§ 35. *Inroads from without. The Tribal Monarchy of Ophrah.*

The victory of Deborah brought to an end the natural resistance of the Canaanites, attacked and driven from their inherited land by the Israelitish invaders. The time, however, was not yet come for Israel to enjoy unenvied and undisturbed possession of its newly-won land. It is the ancient custom of the restless, wandering Bedouin tribes of the desert, to look with jealousy from time to time on the comfortable life of their neighbours, settled within the boundary of the cultivated land. The pride of the nomad is in his free, unimpeded right to roam in boundless space. He looks down with pity and disdain on the peasantry bound to the soil. But ever and anon the charm of the comfortable, secure, and at the same time richer, life in the cultivated land succeeds in throwing its spell even on him, in spite of his old instinct for freedom. This was for centuries the experience of Egypt. Time and again did the Semitic nomads from the north seek to gain admission and possession, sometimes peaceably, sometimes by force. The Israelitish tribes themselves, as nomads, before their entrance into Canaan, were under the influence of this impulse. Now it turned against them. Hardly had Israel got some relief from the powerful resistance of Canaan, than from all sides nomadic neighbours came forward to contest its newly-won possession. Some of these were tribes nearly related to Israel. What Israel had achieved, they thought themselves entitled to imitate.

Perhaps this struggle had begun before the last decisive battle with Canaan took place. Already in those days, Othniel, the son of Kenaz, a Judæan hero of the time of Joshua, is said to have

---

[1] See also Wellh. *Abriss.* p. 17.

waged victorious warfare with hostile intruders.[1] The bold exploit of the Benjamite Ehud ben Gera, although likewise resting on notices of later date, stands much clearer in the light of history. Treacherously he slays the Moabite king Eglon, who had broken into the territory of Israel, perhaps in league with Ammon and Amalek,[2] conquered Jericho, and for twelve years laid the tribes adjoining Moab, perhaps especially Benjamin, under heavy tribute. Ehud calls out the army of Israel from Mount Ephraim, and delivers part of the tribes of Israel from unworthy bondage.[3] It is historically quite probable that after Moab recovered from the hardships of the time of Moses, it bethought itself of recovering its old position. The weakness and early decline of Reuben, which in the time of Moses had taken Moab's place, would only stand it in good stead.

Special danger, however, threatened the central district, east and west of the Jordan, from the populous eastern desert tribe of *Midian*. This tribe, which was closely related to the Kenites, was in the time of Moses settled wholly or in part in the region of Sinai. Doubtless under the influence of the migration of Israel, it seems, either at the same time or shortly afterwards, to have made its way to the north. It probably availed itself of the old friendship to win by the side of Israel, somewhere in Gilead, a share of the fruitful cultivated soil. Still this conjecture is not

---

[1] Ju. iii. 7-11. I cannot regard the figure of Othniel as unhistorical. But nothing beyond his name, and the fact of battles, is to be learned from the late narrative which has been preserved for us only by Ri. In particular, we can hardly now discover from the words כושן רשעתים מלך ארם נהרים who his adversary was. I regard it as probable that we have, in this incident, a faint reminiscence of the wars that disturbed Palestine under Ramses III. of Egypt and Tiglath Pileser I. of Assyria. Jewish families might very well ascribe to themselves some sort of share in these wars. See Meyer, *Gesch. Ägypt.* 314 ff.; Hommel, *Gesch. Ass.* 531 f.

[2] So v. 13; but not certainly belonging to the sources.

[3] Ju. iii. 12-30. This narrative is in its present form likewise young (Ri). Apart from this, however, there is not the slightest ground against accepting it as historical. Indeed, its contents are altogether in favour of it. We have here therefore probably old tradition in a younger form. Most recent scholars accordingly assume that the compiler used an older document, and that this would have to begin with v. 15b or 15aβ. See, moreover, Budde, *RiSa*, 99. With regard to its age I do not venture to pass any judgment.

necessary; for the Arab never needs to await an excuse for a raid on fruitful land. Our document[1] tells how, suddenly, in dense crowds, like swarms of locusts, the Midianites, along with Amalek and the (other) children of the east, overflowed the land. Year after year, shortly before harvest, they swept in on their camels, destroying the harvest, and driving off the cattle.[2]

It is impossible to say how long may have been the time between these events and the days of Barak and Deborah, but we must not assume too short an interval. For there is little trace to be found of such a spirit of lofty sentiment and national unity as then animated the tribes. Though that elevation of sentiment may for a while have continued to work—and as long as it did so it would certainly preserve Israel from threatening attacks—the lofty thoughts of a better time were lost in the ease that comes from possession, and in care for tribal interests. The loose cohesion among the tribes, along with the lack of strong personalities to take the lead, begat the feeling of weakness, and a condition of lethargy. Manasseh and Ephraim, along with the neighbouring tribes, though they had done many a daring deed, could not muster the courage to make a stand against the Bedouin hordes. On occasion of such an incursion they could do nothing better than abandon the open country to the marauders, and withdraw the population for safety to the mountains. Thither the

---

[1] Ju. vi. 2-6a. The mention of the allies in H (see below) is indeed only from the redactor, but appears to be derived from H¹ (viii. 10).

[2] The story of Gideon is to be found in Ju. vi.-viii. For analysis of sources see above, pp. 3 f., 6, 14 ff.; also Studer, *Richter*, 212 ff.; Wellh. *Bl.*⁴ 190 ff.; Stade, *Gesch. Isr.* 181 ff.; Budde, *RiSa*, 107 ff. The narrative runs in two clearly distinguishable accounts, which have been united by the hand of a redactor (Ri: according to Budde, JE). The combination can be seen most clearly in vii. 25b, and in viii. 10, from כל־הנותרים onwards. There are also additions by R. The chief accounts can hardly have existed independently; at least one of them was connected with other older hero-stories. If we call them H and H¹, there will belong to H, vi. 2-6a (excluding 'and the Amalekites and the children of the east'), 11-24, 33 f., 36-40; vii. 1, 9-11, 13-25 (15-22 worked over); viii. 1-3, 24-27a (29-32?); to H¹, viii. 4-21. H¹ has throughout the indications of age and originality, and stands at least on a level with chap. ix. H, inserted here in place of the lost beginning of H¹ shows easily recognisable traces of later style, but still stands in close relationship with such sections as chaps. ix., xvii.

bands of horsemen could not penetrate; and if it came to the worst, fast rock strongholds, or barricaded caverns, could provide shelter.[1]

A Manassite family-chief of the clan of Abiezer, Jerubbaal or Gideon by name, of Ophrah,[2] ventured finally to oppose the insolent brigands. A renewed attack of the Midianites, in which they pressed onwards, plundering and slaughtering, as far as Mount Tabor in the north of Palestine, furnished him the occasion.[3] Among the slain were Gideon's brothers. The sacred duty of blood-revenge, combined in his case with the indignation of the patriot. Gideon called out the fighting force of his family of Abiezer, three hundred armed men in number. The bands of the enemy, returning from Tabor, pitched in the plain of Jezreel; Gideon with his men, not far off by the spring Harod.[4] Reliance on the help of Yahvé, and the ominous dream of one of the enemy which, on stealing by night into the enemy's camp, he overheard, inspired him with courage for his little band. A daring stratagem, undertaken forthwith under shelter of the night, was successful. The enemy's host, startled by the sudden glare of torchlight and the wild battle-cry, fell into confusion and disorganised flight.[5] As they fled eastwards they had to cross the Jordan. But the hastily summoned army of Ephraim barred the way of the fugitives to the fords and slew two hostile chiefs, Oreb and Zeeb, while, at the same time, the tribes of Naphtali, Asher, and Manasseh, opposed the enemy in their way farther north.[6]

[1] Ju. vi. 2. *Cf.* 1 Sam. xiii. 6.

[2] Its site is not yet certainly ascertained, but is probably to be sought not far from Shechem : most plausibly, with Fischer and Guthe, *Handk.*, Far'ata.

[3] See viii. 18. Budde (p. 114) supposes another Tabor, but without sufficient ground.

[4] Ju. vi. 33 f. ; vii. 1. vi. 35 and vii. 2-8 (which is connected with it) are later additions. That the valley of Kishon was still in Canaanitish occupation cannot be assumed (Stade, p. 190) without proof.

[5] Ju. vii. 9-22 (excluding *v.* 12). *V.* 15 ff. shows traces of revision (see Berth., Kuen., Budde) but is not therefore to be rejected.

[6] Ju. vii. 23-25*a* (25*b* is due to an editorial attempt at harmonising). Whether H originally intended here a final conquest and destruction of the enemy, depends on the answers to the questions raised on p. 81, note 1. I regard viii. 1-3 as an imitation of xii. 1 ff.

A part of the fugitives had already won the Jordan before Ephraim's interposition in the contest. These are pursued farther by Gideon himself with his band. The cities of Succoth and Penuel, lying east of the Jordan, intimidated by the many surprises they had suffered, and long unaccustomed to hold together with Israel, refuse bread to his exhausted bands. Left in the lurch by them, Gideon hurries farther eastwards on the caravan road. He overtakes the enemy and captures their two chieftains, Zebah and Zalmunnah. The haughty sons of the desert confess to their murder of Gideon's brothers. Haughty and bold even in bonds, they disdain to meet their destined death at the hands of boys. The hero himself, and no other, must strike the death-blow, for 'as the man is, so is his strength.' Returning home, Gideon takes severe vengeance on Succoth and Penuel. The cowardice and insult that they had shown towards their countrymen, they expiated at terrible cost.[1]

Crowned with victory and laden with rich booty, Gideon returns at the head of his followers to Ophrah. Although he was at the head of but a small band, it was not for himself and his family alone that Gideon had taken the field. What he accomplished benefited the equally suffering tribes, and was certainly also undertaken with a reference to them. The peaceable peasant was protected from the marauding nomad: Israel became again master of its own land. It was once more proved how much could be achieved, not by Israel as a whole, but by even a small portion of that vigorous nation, if it would only arouse itself to earnest

---

[1] In the text above, the attempt has been made to combine H and H¹, not with the idea that the combination offers the only possible solution, but only in opposition to the one-sided preference for H¹ favoured by some (Wellh., Stade). H too contains certainly historical traits, as even Isa. x. 26 shows. (On this, see now also Budde, *RiSa*, 115.) I had much rather suppose that there was a second, perhaps an earlier, event alongside of that of H¹, so that Gideon would really appear twice as a hero, than attribute a purely legendary character to H. If H¹ contained the second feat of Gideon, this would explain the designation 'children of a king' in viii. 19. Or shall we suppose that Gideon and Jerubbaal were once two persons answering to the two narratives? Since the two accounts have too much in common, I prefer to regard them as parts of two narratives of the same event (*cf.* also ררד viii. 4 ff.; Kuen. § xix. 4).

purpose and become conscious of its strength. And the man who taught his own family and the house of Joseph this lesson was, for that reason alone, a hero, worthy of honour in his own and after ages.

It is intelligible enough that Gideon was rewarded with honour and power, that the people took care to enjoy also in the future the strong arm and protection of the victorious deliverer. Manasseh, and probably Ephraim, offered him the kingship; and, though he may perhaps have hesitated a while in view of Yahvé's kingship over Israel, he certainly did not finally refuse it.[1] So, not indeed all Israel, but certainly the house of Joseph, the centre of the older Israel, had now a king. With the rich share of booty that fell to his lot, he erected, like other kings after him, a royal sanctuary for himself at Ophrah.[2] The object of worship in it was certainly Yahvé: but not the Yahvé of Moses. In this matter also the age of the Judges went its own way. The place of the invisible, imageless one was taken by an image of Yahvé, in the shape of an ephod[3] covered with gold. No wonder, therefore, that the later editor of our narrative sees in this a grievous defection on the part of Gideon and his contemporaries.[4] In fact, whether those concerned in it were conscious of it or not, it was a dangerous relapse in the direction of the Canaanitish nature-worship.

[1] In the present form of the passage, verses viii. 22 f., at all events, are later (Ri), as ix. 2 and even the name Abimelech (=my father is king) show. But some sentence in H must have served as foundation. Whether the same source contained also the original refusal, cannot from the context be either proved or disproved. The decision depends on general considerations regarding the age of the theocratic conception. Yet *cf.* the judgment on the kingdom in ix. 8 ff. and Kuen. § xix. 5.

[2] It is noteworthy that in Porphyry mention is made of a priest of the god Ἰευώ, named Ἱερόμβαλος. This doubtless refers to our Jerubbaal; but from this no conclusion can be drawn as to the historical value of the passage. See Ewald, *Phönik. Ansicht. v. d. Weltschöpf.*, p. 52; Baudissin, *Studien*, i. 25.

[3] On this see Siegfried and Stade in their Lexicon. Differently, Berth.² 164 (there further reff.). König, *Hauptprobl.* 59 ff. Characteristically, Lagarde, *Gött. Gel. Nachr.* 1890, 15 f.

[4] viii. 27*b* (from ויהי onwards).

§ 36. *Continuation. The Tribal Monarchy of Ophrah. Abimelech in Shechem.*

The family of Gideon, however, was not long to enjoy its newly-won dominion. After his death it came quickly to ruin. We possess an account of its fall that is one of the most precious historical documents in the Old Testament.[1] The ruin of Gideon's dominion is to be traced to his harem. Among his wives, who were so many that he is said to have had seventy sons,[2] he had a distinguished Canaanite woman of Shechem. In this town the old Canaanite noble family of the benê Hamôr[3] lived in peaceful association with Israelite intruders.[4] Their god, who had his temple amongst them, was El berîth, also called Ba'al berîth, the Lord of the Covenant—perhaps the protector of this very compact between Canaanites and Israelites. The reception of the Canaanitess into Gideon's harem was doubtless intended to bind the only half-Israelite Shechem to his kingdom.

On Gideon's death it appeared that his rule was regarded as a legitimate kingship, at all events over Manasseh and Ephraim. There happened here what appears in the case of none of the other 'Judges.' Every one took it for granted that Gideon's crown would pass to his family as hereditary right. It was probably destined for the first-born; though possibly nothing had been settled, and so a contest for the inheritance on the part of the brothers was to be feared.

It is in this light at least that Abimelech plans the death of Jerubbaal. This man, the hero of the important historical fragment relating to the time we are now considering, preserved for us in Judges ix., was the son of the already-mentioned Shechemite in Gideon's harem. His overtures to the Canaanitish Shechemites made a decided impression. 'Which is better for

[1] Ju. ix. *Cf.* esp. Wellh. *Bl.*[4] 194; Kuen. § xix. 5. The narrative may date from the earliest days of the monarchy (ix. 2).

[2] Ju. viii. 29; ix. 2. Compare, however, ix. 5; where seventy sons are mentioned in addition to Abimelech and Jotham.

[3] Called also *ba'alê Shechem*, as the lawful possessors of Shechem.

[4] On this see at the same time above, p. 65 (*cf.* p. 69 f.).

you,' he said, 'that seventy men, all the sons of Jerubba'al, should bear rule over you, or one man? Moreover, consider that I am your flesh and bone.'[1] They prefer a ruler of Canaanitish blood to the legitimate sons of Gideon, and deliver the city to Abimelech. With the treasure out of the temple of Ba'al berîth, he hires a troop, goes with them to Ophrah, and murders his seventy brothers 'upon one stone.'[2] Abimelech is thus lord not only of Shechem, but of the whole dominion which Gideon had united under his hand. The narrator even calls him, in so many words, ruler 'over Israel.'[3] Hence, from this time onwards, he does not regard Shechem as the main point. On the contrary, turning his back on it, he resides at another place, and contents himself with leaving Shechem to its civic chief, Zebul, who, without doubt, plays the part of an adherent of Abimelech.[4]

We can hardly be wrong in assuming that this and nothing else was the cause of the rupture between Shechem and Abimelech. Shechem, as Abimelech's home, had a claim to special favour. Instead of this, although he was of Canaanitish blood on one side, Abimelech left the half-Canaanitish city during all the three years of his rule, and sought an Israelitish residence. So Shechem, the very place where Abimelech, had he been prudent and mindful of his own interests, might have had the firmest support, became the centre of an evidently deep-seated movement against him, to which he eventually succumbed.

Various circumstances combined further to foster the dissatisfaction, the germ of which was thus laid through Abimelech's lack of discernment.

Jotham, Gideon's youngest son, escaped the massacre at Ophrah. Probably soon after the installation of Abimelech, yet not before the latter had left Shechem to take possession of the

---

[1] Ju. ix. 2.

[2] Can it be that a sacrifice is intended? הרג (ix. 5) does not favour this.

[3] Yet Beer, *e.g.* seems to be excepted (ix. 21), although we do not elsewhere find it mentioned as a non-Israelitish town. The narrator is thus conscious of the inaccuracy.

[4] This governor of Shechem (שר העיר *v.* 30) need not have been Abimelech's steward in the strict sense (*v.* 28). Wellh. *Nachtr.* 353 f.

rest of his father's kingdom, Jotham gathered the citizens on Mount Gerizim.¹ There, standing on the brow of a cliff, he reproached them for their outrage on the house of Gideon, making use of an ingeniously constructed fable. For their ingratitude toward Jerubba'al, who had delivered them also from Midian, and for the murder of his sons in which they had taken part with Abimelech, the vengeance of Yahvé is declared against Shechem as well as against Abimelech. Their anger at his daring words Jotham evades by speedy flight, but the sting had gone to their hearts. It would be felt all the more keenly, the harsher Jotham's words sounded. For, indeed, he added to reproach and threatening the taunt that in accepting Abimelech they had made the son of a maid, a despised concubine, their king, simply because he was near of kin. Nay, the taunt of Abimelech's origin formed the key-note of the whole fable.

These words might sound strange if regarded as flung in the face of the Canaanite Shechemites.² They lose this character when one considers that there lived in Shechem, alongside of the Canaanites, a considerable number of Israelites. If directed at these, Jotham's speech is a well-conceived attempt to drive a wedge into the unity of the two parties. The Israelitish party in Shechem could certainly not be wholly inaccessible to such reflections as Jotham's speech gave rise to. They lay in the nature of the case, especially if Abimelech was neglecting Shechem itself.

Thus both parties, which were probably originally at one in adhering to Abimelech, had reason enough to be discontented with him. Hardly had three years elapsed since Abimelech's usurpation, when the alienation of Shechem reached so high a point that it led to a breach hardly any longer concealed, if not at once to declared desertion. 'There came an evil spirit from Elohim

---

[1] On the locality cf. Furrer, *B. Lex.* ii. 330, and *Wanderungen*, 244 f.

[2] This is probably the chief ground that can be urged against Jotham's action being historical. If it is given up, the others have little convincing power. The author does not say, nor even imply, that Jotham shouted to the city from the summit of the hill eight hundred feet in height (Kuen. § xix. 5), but only that he called a meeting there. For the rest, see on the fable, Reuss, *Gesch. d. A T.*² p. 131.

between Abimelech and the Shechemites, so that they deserted Abimelech.' Without troubling themselves about Abimelech and the rest of his dominion, they began to plunder and waylay, and attacked the passing caravans from the heights around Shechem, as much to their own profit as to the injury of Abimelech's rule. Abimelech would have reason to exercise special forbearance towards his native place; he had nothing to gain by further alienating this kindred people.

There was now only one step more to open revolt. Up to this point the alienation and partial withdrawal of Shechem from Abimelech was certainly in great measure the work of the Israelitish half of the population. They were doubtless in league with the rest of the house of Joseph. Jotham also would hardly be idle in this matter. What he proclaimed from the mountain at Shechem, he may have preached from the housetops at Thebez, Beer, and other places. Thus a general reaction was preparing against the half-Canaanite usurper, which it was cleverly devised should first show itself at Shechem. Were Abimelech deprived of all further support there, that would be the end of his tyranny.

It was therefore well planned that now, after the Canaanitish *Ba'ale Shechem* had been prejudiced against Abimelech, the party hostile to him should be suddenly strengthened by a powerful reinforcement from without. The governor Zebul being still at least in name attached to Abimelech, and ready with his followers to defend his cause, some counterpoise had yet to be found against him in Shechem itself. So it was skilfully arranged, though it bore the appearance of chance, that an Israelitish band consisting of Ga'al ben Joba'al[1] 'and his brethren,' gaining the confidence of the inhabitants of Shechem, were received into the town.

---

[1] *i.e.* 'Yahvé is lord.' So according to the LXX., instead of *ben 'ebed*, which is an intentional alteration. Yet see Hollenberg in *Theol. LZtg.* 1891, col. 371. [Also Nestle, *Israel. Eigennamen*, p. 122. I am myself not so sure about this name as I was when I wrote the German text; yet it is still quite possible that Ἰωβηλ (Cod. Alex. Ἀβεδ) originated from עֶבֶד simply by a slip of the pen—although the prefixing of the Iota is still, in spite of what Nestle has said *loc. cit.*, to be noted.]

It must soon appear for what purpose Ga'al has come. At the festival of the vintage, the Shechemites are seated in the temple of their 'Baal of the Covenant' in merry feasting and revelry. As they had doubtless done on many previous occasions, they curse Abimelech. Losing their usual reserve under the influence of the wine, they give free vent to their displeasure against the faithless usurper. Ga'al seizes the opportunity to fan the fire already breaking into flame, and by taunts to force Zebul to a decision. 'Who is Abimelech,' he calls out, 'and who is the son of Jerubba'al, that we should serve him? Is he not a Shechemite, and Zebul his agent? If he, and with him all the company of Hamor the father of Shechem, serve Abimelech, why should *we* be his slaves?'[1] The 'we' was certainly spoken with emphasis. Ga'al speaks as an Israelite, with the applause of the Israelitish party who formed the majority. He could not otherwise have allowed himself to use such words. They seem, however, to have made a profound impression. Zebul, the governor of Shechem representing Abimelech, seems, throughout the whole affair, to have played a very ambiguous part, now even more than at first. The temper of the town having visibly turned against Abimelech, Zebul seems to have made the best of a bad case, and to have joined Ga'al as a friend, when the latter arrived and took in hand the movement against Abimelech. At the festival of Hillulim, when every one was cursing the king, Zebul appears to have heartily joined the rest.[2] Subsequently, however, playing a double game, he secretly[3] sent word to Abimelech, summoning him to make a sudden attack on the city.

On receipt of this news, Abimelech marched by night against Shechem, and lay in ambush. Zebul, even yet playing the part of

---

[1] [ix. 28.] On this verse see Wellh. *TBS.* xiii.; Rob. Smith, *Theol. Tijd.* xx. 195 ff.; Kautzsch, *ZAW.* x. 299 f.

[2] It is only thus we can explain his remaining unmolested in the city at all, still more the friendly understanding between him and Ga'al; and, above all, the fact that he afterwards proceeded with Ga'al to the gate of the city. He played the part of friend till Ga'al returned defeated.

[3] Only so is בתרמה (ix. 31) to be understood.

friend of Ga'al and his party, informs Ga'al of what has happened.[1] Both march with their bands to the city gate to repulse the attack. Abimelech appears on the horizon with his troops. Zebul artfully induces Ga'al to make a sally. Ga'al's anxiety on account of the size of the enemy's force he dissipates by ironically referring to the latter's speech at the Hillul feast. No doubt he makes as if he would himself defend the city and protect the rear. So Ga'al makes a sally at the head of the citizens, while Zebul remains behind in the town. Ga'al is routed by Abimelech, and returns conquered and enfeebled into the city. Zebul now throws away the mask, shows himself as Abimelech's partisan, and drives Ga'al out of the city. Abimelech, however, not trusting the friendship of Zebul, does not venture to make any attack. But Zebul himself now falls a victim to the vengeance of the citizens. They will have nothing to do with Abimelech, and put an end to Zebul's double play.[2] Not till the following day, after Zebul, who knows his plan, has been put out of the way, does Abimelech succeed in taking the city.[3] It is destroyed, not to be built again for some time.[4]

This being once accomplished, it was an easy matter for him to become complete master of the citadel. It seems to have lain outside of the city. On learning that the city had surrendered, its inhabitants fled to the upper story of the temple of their 'God of the Covenant.' Without consideration for the holy place, to which he owed the basis on which his dominion rested, Abimelech set fire to the temple, and a thousand men and women met their death in the flames.

The rising was now suppressed in Shechem itself, but it was

[1] Thus alone can we understand how Ga'al marched out even before Abimelech appeared (v. 35).

[2] Zebul cannot have been surprised by Abimelech on the occasion of the pursuit of Ga'al, since according to v. 32 f. it was Zebul himself that occasioned Abimelech's manœuvre. (Against Wellh. *Nachtr.* 354.) He did not fall in battle against Abimelech, but perished at the hands of the populace. Hence in v. 42 simply העם, without Zebul.

[3] This is the explanation of vv. 42-45. (Against Meyer, *Gesch. d. Alt.* 357.)

[4] See 1 Kings xii.

not thereby put an end to: on the contrary, it spread further. Before the next city which Abimelech sought to chastise in a similar way, however, his rule reached its end. Thebez, a place distant several leagues from Shechem, which he attacked immediately after the fall of Shechem, fell, indeed, like it into his hands, but here also the citadel stood out. Men and women fled thither. Abimelech adopted the plan which had succeeded in the case of Shechem, of taking the tower by fire. As he stood before the barricaded door, he was hit by a millstone which a woman flung on his head from above. He made his armour-bearer put him to death, that he might not be said to have died at the hand of a woman.

§ 37. *Jephthah. Samson.*

The Manassite tribal kingdom of Gideon, and with it the first attempt at the establishment to kingly rule in Israel of which we have any knowledge, thus reached a sudden end. At least we do not know who the heir to the kingly power of Abimelech was, and it is to be presumed that Jotham, or whoever else may have survived of the house of Gideon, did not step into his place. We should otherwise surely have had some account of it. But the fact is, the fate of Israel from the death of Abimelech to the days of Eli and Samuel, is almost completely enveloped in darkness—a clear proof that the history of Israel from this time onwards breaks up once more into inglorious and inactive tribal life.

Only two figures stand out with some distinctness in the hazy twilight that envelops the time following Gideon and Abimelech— viz. Jephthah and Samson. But neither of them comes so distinctly and fully into the light of history as to shed a clear and decided ray on his surroundings. This is specially true of Samson.

The personality of Jephthah is, in our present records, clearly encompassed with legend. The narrator of the history has no certain knowledge of his origin and his fortunes.[1] It is easy

---

[1] See Ju. xi. 1 f. He is represented as a son of Gilead: *cf.* the late word יִלּוֹד. Besides, it is remarkable that xi. 12-29 interrupts the connection, and with

enough, therefore, to understand how the figure of Jephthah has been relegated to the sphere of inventive legend,[1] or even of absolute myth.[2] The offering of his daughter made such a treatment of the story natural. But we find in Jephthah some traits that so clearly suit the character of his age, and what actually happened in it, that we must consider seriously before we reject them as unhistorical, simply because of the later literary dress in which they are clad. Such are his victory over Ammon who so often figures as the enemy of Israel; and, at an earlier stage, his compulsory flight, his wandering life in the steppe which reminds us of the freebooter's life of David, and the way in which at the moment of danger he was summoned by his tribesmen as their only helper in distress.

Even Jephthah's affray with the tribe of Ephraim, which from envy at his success tried to pick a quarrel with him, has so much in it that is characteristic, and it is, especially by the Shibboleth incident (imitated in the 'Sicilian Vespers'), so ensured against the suspicion of being an invention under the influence of a 'tendency,' that even the exorbitant number of forty-two thousand Ephraimites, who are made to fall victims to the Shibboleth, is not sufficient to discredit it. Still less is any discredit thrown upon it by the parallel in the history of Gideon. If either of the episodes has a legendary origin, it is rather that of Gideon than that here recorded of Jephthah.[3]

Least of all, however, should we be inclined to give up the claim of Jephthah's strange vow and offering to historical character. The Persephone myth was, as far as our knowledge goes, quite unknown to Israel. Barbarous customs and rough manners are, on

---

respect to its contents seems to be a compilation from the Pentateuch, that is rather irrelevant. Moreover, xii. 1-6 is not in its right place: *cf.* xi. 34, 39. xii. 7 makes a fresh beginning (ri); see above, p. 12 ff. Jephthah's home in xi. 34 is also remarkable as compared with xi. 3. *Cf.* in general, Wellh. *Bl.*[4] 194 f.; Kuen. § xix. 6; Budde, *RiSa*, 125 ff. There is also, in the last-mentioned work, an attempt to restore the original setting of xi. 1 ff.

[1] So Wellh. *loc. cit.*; Meyer, *Gesch. d. Alt.* 356.
[2] So Goldziher, *Der Mythos bei den Hebräern*, 113 ff.
[3] See also above, p. 81 f.

the other hand, quite natural to the time of Jephthah, especially in a rude chieftain of the steppes, although even he was not lacking in feeling and sense of duty.[1]

Hence, although Jephthah's origin and personality are obscure, and the exact occasion and course of his war with Ammon unknown, and even the time of his appearance only to be inferred with a certain amount of probability from his place in our Book of Judges,[2] yet we know the following facts about him. Summoned from the steppe by Gilead, and elected leader, he defeated the Ammonites, wreaked bloody vengeance on Ephraim for its contentiousness by a cleverly devised stratagem, and finally, returning home victorious, plunged himself and his only child in distress and ruin through a rash vow which he had made. 'The rough warrior rent his garments and kept his word.' A feast, yearly celebrated by the maidens of Gilead, reminded Israel in after ages of Jephthah's glory and misfortune.

The second figure of this age, that of Samson, is of a considerably different type. If in Jephthah we are confronted with a historical phenomenon having a background of legend, in the case of Samson, on the other hand, the story moves uncertainly amid myth and legend and history. It belongs to none of them wholly; each claims a share in it.

The purely mythical interpretation of Samson (Heb. Shimshôn), has been specially dealt with by Steinthal, and more recently by Wietzke.[3] It cannot be denied that such an interpretation is suggested by Samson's name, as well as that of his mistress Delîlah.[4] Moreover, the hero's long hair, as the source of his strength, naturally reminds one of the rays of Helios. But many other points, that have been explained by similar references, are

---

[1] *Cf.* Reuss, *Gesch. d. AT.*[2] 132; also Kuen. and Budde, *loc. cit.* On the attempt to give a new interpretation to the sacrifice, see the Commentaries, and König, *Hauptprobl.* 74; Köhler, ii. 1, 100.

[2] With which the relatively later occupation of Gilead by Israel agrees.

[3] *Zeitschr. f. Völkerpsych.* ii. 129 ff.; Wietzke, *Der bibl. Simson*, 1888. [*Cf.* now also G. A. Smith, *Historical Geography*, p. 220 ff., and especially, Doorninck, *de Simsonsagen*, in *T. Tijdschr.* 1894, 14 ff.].

[4] Shimshôn = Sun-man; Delîlah, connected with לִיל, night.

explicable much more naturally and simply as local legend, and even as naïve popular tale.¹

At the same time, we must take into account the fact that the story of Samson, viewed from a literary point of view, dates from a relatively early age,² even if it is not, as Budde in particular thinks he can prove,³ to be attributed to the Jahvist of the Pentateuch; and also that it is capable of a quite satisfactory historical explanation at the place assigned it by the redactor of the Stories of the Judges. It is intrinsically improbable that the whole tribe of Dan was involved in the expedition to Laish,⁴ and there are traces elsewhere of the gradual growth in strength of the Philistines, who had immigrated into the maritime districts. If this is so, collisions with the nearest tribes of Israel in the time immediately preceding Saul, are in themselves quite probable, and there is no ground for regarding Samson as simply the shadow of Saul cast back into the time of the Judges.⁵

Further than this we can hardly venture to go. To a popular hero of the tribe of Dan, belonging to the time of the first collisions between Israel and the Philistines, concerning whom there circulated among the people many a tale of valour, there gradually became attached a motley mushroom-growth of legend concerning *ruse* and wrong of every kind, such as were or were said to have been perpetrated here and there on the Philistines. In time, a native religious and foreign mythological element were mingled with this. The hero was brought into connection with a solar myth that had been introduced from abroad, but was little understood. It seems to have even given him his name. As a counterpoise, he was credited with the characteristics of the national Israelitish Nazirite.

¹ See espec. Wellh. *Bl.*⁴ 196 f. There is no trace in the text of twelve labours, corresponding to those of Hercules (Ewald, *Gesch. Isr.*³ ii. 559; [Engl. trans. ii. 396]). For the rest *cf.* also Baethgen, *Studien z. sem. Religionsgesch.* 161 ff.

² xiv. 4b is a later addition. On xv. 20, xvi. 31b, see above, p. 11 and p. 3, note 2. On chap. xiv. *cf.* Stade, *ZAW.* iv. 250 ff.

³ See *RiSa*, 132, and above, p. 16 ff. I regard chap. xiii. in particular as a later imitation of J.

⁴ See above, p. 71 f. ⁵ Wellh. 197. *Cf.* also below, p. 104.

§ 38. *Civilisation and Religion in this Age.*[1]

Through the entrance into the land of Canaan and the consequent transition to agriculture and settled life, Israel's whole mode of living naturally underwent a transformation. Dwelling in villages and towns took the place of roaming over the boundless desert. Hut and house more and more took the place of tent. The wandering cattle-owner became a peasant and farmer. Ancient Israel was a genuine peasant people. It produced corn, wine, oil and figs, and from its herds, milk and flesh. Whatever of these Israel produced in greater abundance than its own wants demanded, found ready purchasers in the Phœnician dealers that were to be met everywhere throughout the land. These offered in exchange the products of Tyrian and Sidonian industry, as well as foreign produce imported from all directions.[2]

The change in mode of life and occupation, moreover, did not leave the hereditary popular organisation quite intact. To begin with, the admission of Canaanite, or, speaking generally, foreign elements into the community of Israel, which was becoming increasingly common, would necessarily in the course of time break down the old tribal polity. There were soon individual persons and family groups in abundance, that belonged to none of the old Israelite tribes. But still more did living in villages and towns, and clinging to the soil, demand new forms. So, ere long, there existed alongside of the old nomadic patriarchal tribal organisation, in which the tribal head ruled and directed his kinsmen, also an oligarchic organisation, in which a number of noble families or their representatives, directed the affairs of the community. The latter organisation seems to have, more and more, supplanted the former. We find the former expressly mentioned only in case of

---

[1] [On this subject *cf.* now also the corresponding sections, in the works of Nowack and Benzinger on Archæology, and in Smend's *A. Tliche Religionsgeschichte.*]

[2] On this see above, p. 62, note 1, and the interesting examples of Phœnician-Canaanitish industry, difficult indeed to fix chronologically, given in Perrot et Chipiez, *Hist. de l'Art,* iii. chap. x. Besides, on art and industry amongst the Phœnicians, Meyer, *Gesch. d. Alt.* i. 238 f.

urgency, when an individual tribal head set himself up as chief or Judge[1] over a tribe, or group of tribes, as a rule only to retire again forthwith from his higher dignity after performing his task. This shows, no doubt, that the ancient order was passing away. Already, in the time under consideration, the new order of things that was destined to bear within it the germ of a complete transformation of the organisation of ancient Israel, had fairly established itself. Especially in towns, but no doubt also in whole districts, there ruled in place of a single *sheikh*, a number of men, the nobility of the tribe or district. It is these that are referred to as 'men' (*be'ālim*),[2] and we have a kind of selection from these ruling families, in the elders of a district or town (*zeqēnîm*), who were in turn represented by a city magistrate, or several such (*sar hā-'îr*).[3] Such was the condition of things in Shechem, in Succoth and Penuel, and in Gilead.[4] The Phœnician[5] and Philistine cities, and still better, the story of Jerubbaal and Abimelech, show that this form of organisation really constituted only the transition to 'Tyranny' and monarchy, possibly also temporarily to a regular oligarchy.

Living close together, and often enough associating in a peaceable way with the former possessors of the land, could not fail to exert its influence also on Israel's moral and intellectual life. Israel entered on the inheritance of a much richer and more advanced civilisation than that which it had itself as yet commanded. The industrial art and the discoveries of Phœnicia, still more perhaps the art and civilisation of the Euphrates and Egypt that Phœnicia had borrowed,[6] were, through the active trade relations subsisting, soon the property of Israel. Its horizon was

---

[1] *Qāṣin* or *Shôfēṭ*. How far the latter is an ancient name is discussed above, p. 65 f. (*cf.* also p. 3 f. and 13); for the former see Ju. xi. 6.

[2] Ju. ix. 2, 18, 23 f., 26, 47 f. *Cf.* the word *marina* occurring in Egyptian inscriptions.

[3] = Mayor and Alderman. Ju. viii. 14; ix. 30.

[4] See, in addition to the places just mentioned, Ju. xi. 5 ff.

[5] See also Pietschmann, *Gesch. d. Phön.* 237 f.

[6] On the various things borrowed by Phœnicia from Babylonia and Egypt (glass, purple, etc.), see Pietschm. *loc. cit.* 239 ff.

widened; knowledge and interests, but with them also needs and enjoyments, that had up to this time remained unknown to this rough desert people, were made accessible to them. Even though Israel protested against certain abuses, and looked with contempt on the voluptuousness and wickedness of the Canaanite cities [1]— still, in the main, those who conquered with the sword may, as has so often happened, soon enough have lain at the feet of the vanquished, in the moral and intellectual sphere.

Alongside, however, of a slowly advancing refinement of life and custom, the rude, unpolished manners befitting the iron age, remained still, in general, characteristic of Israel. War and feud occupied most of the time. Predatory excursions, marauding expeditions, even when they fell on the unsuspecting and the innocent and at times injured fellow-countrymen, hardly met with serious censure.[2] Crafty injury of the enemy was hardly felt to be blameworthy.[3] Rape in one's own land was considered in special cases an act of lawful self-defence.[4] Only open treachery and gross violation of the usages of hospitality and recognised custom, were strongly detested.[5] In general, the right of the strongest prevailed, and notions of law were based on the custom of blood-revenge. In the case of an enemy, even assassination was lawful: in the case of Ehud and Jael it is highly extolled. Men did not shrink even from human sacrifice, to honour a vow once made.

The discovery of the art of writing is, beyond doubt, the most important triumph of civilisation. When and in what form this art reached Israel, we cannot say. If, as I believe, Moses was a historical personage and had been in Egypt, he would most likely have adopted the Egyptian mode of writing. But we know at the same time that there was early used in Palestine a new way of writing[6]—the alphabetic, or, strictly speaking, consonantal script, in

---

[1] *Cf.* Gen. xviii.; Gen. xv. 16; ix. 22 ff.; Ju. xix. ff.
[2] Ju. xvii. f. See above, p. 70 ff.   [3] Samson; Jacob in Genesis.
[4] Ju. xxi. 13 ff. See above, p. 21 f.
[5] Gen. xxxiv.; Ju. xix. ff.; Ju. ix. 7 ff., etc.
[6] The oldest monument is still the stone of Mesha. It proves, however, long previous practice in the use of a script.

which the phonetic principle, already known to the Egyptians, though not carried out by them, was recognised in its immeasurable importance. This script originated as a consonantal script in Semitic soil, and was thence adopted by the Græco-Roman civilised world—with results incalculably great for it and for our civilisation. We are told that Jerubbaal-Gideon had written down for him by a young man [1] of Succoth, casually picked up, the seventy-seven names of the aldermen and council of the town. If the statement is credible, this fact alone shows such a general spread of the art of writing as was possible only by the help of the extraordinary simplification produced in that art, in its older form so complicated, by writing the consonants alone. If this new way of writing is not, as most have hitherto been inclined to believe, to be regarded as having been invented in Syria,[2] but as pointing back to the oldest Arabia,[3] it will still remain more probable that it was thence introduced by the Canaanites,[4] and transmitted by them to the Israelites, than that the reverse process is to be assumed.

The consequence of the introduction of the new script was the beginning of real literature. Now, the first heroic lays[5] and the oldest laws referred to Moses,[6] perhaps also, even several hero stories, such as those of Jerubbaal and Abimelech, were reduced to writing—promising beginning of a rich literature that has outlived the centuries.

---

[1] It is hardly a 'boy' that is meant: *v.* נער מאנשי, Ju. viii. 14. On the other hand, nothing is to be concluded, as to the character of the script at all events, from the name Kiriath Sepher in Ju. i.

[2] So still Ed. Meyer, *Gesch. d. Alt.* 237. See, however, Wellh. *Bl.*[4] 631 ; at least in so far as concerns invention by the Phœnicians. On derivation from Egypt, *v.* Lagarde, *Symmicta*, i. 111 ff.

[3] *V.* Ed. Glaser, *Skizze der Geogr. u. Gesch. des ältest. Arab.* 1889; and Prætorius thereon, in the *Litt. Centr.-Bl.* 1889, col. 1540.

[4] *When* this must have happened, can to a certain extent be determined from the Amarna Tablets, since in them the Babylonian cuneiform script is still in use. It merits special notice that even Hebrew-Canaanitish expressions that are interspersed as explanatory glosses, are likewise given not in Canaanite, but in Babylonian script. *V.* Zimmern and Winckler, in *Z. f. Assyr.* vi. 154 ff., 145.

[5] At all events, Ju. v. ; perhaps Gen. xlix. and others.

[6] Especially Ex. xx ff. (Decalogue and Book of the Covenant).

The question of greatest importance, however, for us at present is whether Israel, the conqueror of Canaan, became the conquered, also in respect of its *religious*[1] life and thought. We must answer the question in the affirmative and in the negative at the same time.

So far as we can see, Israel held fast to the God brought them by Moses. The song of Deborah is an enthusiastic hymn to Yahvé as the God in whose name, and for whose people and cause, the tribes of Israel had gone to war, and who had therefore helped his hosts to victory.[2] Jerubbaal-Gideon, Jephthah, Samson, are worshippers of Yahvé; the Danites find on Mount Ephraim a sanctuary of Yahvé, and transplant it as that of their own God to Laish. Even in the half-Canaanitish Shechem, at least the Israelites living there, were worshippers of Yahvé.[3] We find in really old accounts no single case of a formal defection on any considerable scale to alien gods, or of an express disavowal of Yahvé.[4]

The more recent strata, indeed, of the book under consideration, especially the redactors, Ri and R, working under the influence of Deuteronomy, tell of an oft-repeated general apostasy of Israel in favour of the Canaanite deities.[5] But it is noteworthy that the statements are confined exclusively to these late narrators. Accordingly there are remarkably few concrete facts adduced in support of them. The idea is therefore suggested that these Deuteronomistic statements represent the way in which the spirit of the later times estimated certain phenomena actually existent in the age of the Judges, which did not, indeed, signify a formal defection from Yahvé, but yet certainly in no way corresponded to the ideal of pure Yahvé-worship.

---

[1] [Cf. *La relig. des Hébr. à l'époque des Juges*, in the *Rev. de l'Histoire Rel.* 1893, 1 ff.]

[2] *V.* especially Baethgen, *Beiträge*, 204 f.   [3] *Cf.* the name Gaal ben Jobaal.

[4] In the passage, Ju. v. 8, cited by Baethgen, *Beitr.* 186 f., the text and translation are too uncertain for us to found any argument on it. From the single name, Shamgar ben 'Anat, we cannot at any rate draw any more general conclusions.

[5] Ju. ii. 11 ff. ; iii. 5 f. ; x. 6 ff. ; viii. 33 (*v.* above, p. 3, notes 2 and 3). *Cf.* Jer. ii. 1 ff., 7 f. ; Ez. xvi. 16 ff. ; xx. 28 ff. ; xxiii. 37.

So far as we can form an idea of the worship really characteristic of the age, it was of the kind described above. Yahvé was Israel's God—at least the leading men appear to have adhered to his worship—and we may assume the same of the people in general. Yet close contact with the Canaanites could not fail to have its influence also in this sphere. The chief god of the Canaanites was Ba‘al, the 'lord' of the land, of the people, of the individual district and township;[1] the chief female deity was ‘Ashtart. In addition to these there existed a number of inferior gods, such as Dagon, ‘Anāt, Resheph,[2] and others. It is very noteworthy indeed that we find no mention in any old source of a formal desertion of Israel on a large scale to these gods, and even allusions to them in Israelitish names occur only very exceptionally.[3] On the other hand, the fact that allusions to Baal do play a part in the proper names and the worship of Israel, sheds all the clearer light on the religious conditions of the age under consideration.[4] The later historical treatment of this period indeed recognised in this latter circumstance a formal apostasy to Baal, and therefore either removed such names or explained them away.[5] If this was a mistake—at all events the practice in question implied a friendly, neighbourly approach to the Canaanite worship. The name Jôbaal[6] is typical of the whole relation. People worshipped Yahvé—he was certainly the God of Israel—but they did not see so great a distinction between him and the chief god of their neighbours, till now the god of the land in which they dwelt, that they could not in the main identify them and call Yahvé Israel's Baal. Israel thus did not get beyond the limits of henotheism;

[1] *V.* the article, 'Baal,' by Ed. Meyer in Roscher's *Wörterbuch der griech.-röm. Mythologie*, col. 2867 ff.

[2] On this, as also on this whole subject, *v.* the instructive section in Pietschmann, *Gesch. d. Phön.*, p. 152 ff.

[3] So ‘Anāt. Names like Gad and Asher, if they are to be explained in this way, belong to an earlier period.

[4] *Cf.* Jerubbaal, Jobaal, Baalberith: later Meribaal (Mephibosheth) and Eshbaal (Ishbosheth); also Baaljada‘ (1 Chr. xiv. 7; 2 Sam. v. 17).

[5] *V.* the passages from Judges cited above, p. 97, note 4. Further, Dillmann in *Sitz.-Ber. d. Berl. Akad. d. Wiss.*, 1881 (Ba‘al with fem. article).

[6] [Yet *cf.* the remark on p. 87, note 1, end.]

but it accomplished a union between Yahvé and Baal that brought it to the boundary of Nature-religion.

The consequences could not fail to appear.[1] The Canaanites had long worshipped their gods on eminences (*bāmóth*), which as being places nearer the deity were considered holy. Israel, having come into possession of the land, and soon learned to bring its Yahvé into connection with the Canaanite Baal, did not shrink from also becoming heir to these holy places. Bethel, Beersheba, Shechem, Hebron, Gilgal, Penuel, Ramah, Mizpeh, and many other places became soon just as holy for Israel as they had once been for the Canaanites. To a number of them the patriarch legends became attached, a clear proof that already at an early date these legends had found acceptance in Israel, and been quite appropriated to the service of Yahvé-worship. Sacred trees, to be found in the neighbourhood of the high-place or in the open field, standing alone, or in groups, were added;[2] and in particular the Canaanite high-places were frequently associated with the so-called *Maççebas*, originally, large exposed stones, which were 'erected'—*i.e.* set with the pointed end upwards—and honoured as seats of the deity with oil, and blood of sacrifice. Later, they appear to have been artificially wrought pillars, that probably stood in the proximity of an altar.[3] Beside the *Maççeba* stands often also the *Ashēra*, originally perhaps the simple trunk of a tree or a pole (as symbol of 'Ashtart the goddess of fruitfulness) fixed in the earth in her honour beside her altar.[4] All these parts of the old Canaanite

---

[1] *V.* on this Pietschmann, *loc. cit.*; Stade, *Gesch. Isr.* i. 466 ff.; Baethgen, *Beitr.* 213 ff.; Baudissin, *Studien*, ii. p. 143 ff.

[2] Such a tree, the 'terebinth of the oracle,' stood *e.g.* at Shechem, Gen. xii. 6; Ju. ix. 6, 37; Gen. xxxv. 4; Josh. xxiv. 26; Deut. xi. 30. *Cf.* Ju. iv. 5. On sacred trees in general *cf.* Baudissin, *Studien*, ii. 184 ff.

[3] *V. Corp. Inscr. Sem.* i. 42, 44, 46, 57, 58, 59, 60; Gen. xxviii. 18, 22; xxxi. 13; xxxiii. 20 (read מצבה) xxxv. 14, 20; xlv. 51 f.; Hos. iii. 4. *Cf.* Stade, 459 (there also an illustration). Baethg. 215 ff.; Pietschm. 212.

[4] *V.* the inscription of *Ma'ṣûb*, and Hoffmann, *Phön. Inschr.* 26; perhaps also *Corp. Inscr. Sem.* i. 13 (*cf.* Stade, *ZAW.* i. 344); Ex. xxxiv. 13; Ju. iii. 7; vi. 35 ff. (Ri). Further, in the Amarna tablets, *cf.* Winckler, *Sitz.- Ber. d. Berl. Akad.* 1888, 583 ff., 1341 ff., esp. 1357 and *Z. f. Ägypt.* 1889, 42 ff. (No. 114 [115]: *abd[u] as-ra-tum*=עבד־אשרה). On the question whether Ashera was a deity (Ju. iii. 7), *cf.* Stade, *ZAW.* i. 345 (iii. 1 ff.; iv. 291 ff.);

worship were taken over by Israel with the exception of the last mentioned.¹ But here also Israel preserved its independence. The worship at the *bamôth* and *Maṣṣebas* was from the very beginning regarded as offered to Yahvé.² Even when the outward forms employed were closely allied to those of the Canaanite cultus—for along with the places, important usages were also adopted by Israel—even when an effort was made to identify Yahvé and Baal as much as possible, it was still Yahvé that Israel worshipped. The great mass of the people would not allow themselves to be robbed of him.

A number of examples of the mode of worship of this time have been supplied us, and they confirm the general picture just given. In Shechem Israelites and Canaanites had entered into a treaty to dwell together in peace. When a certain *Ba'al-berith* (lord of the covenant) is found to have been an object of worship there at that time, we are justified in conjecturing that he was the guardian and protector of the treaty.³ Whether this god was Yahvé or the Phœnician Baal is not said. Nor is this unintentional; for in fact he represented both. By the Canaanite half of Shechem he would be regarded as their Baal; with the Israelites he was indeed called Baal, but was in fact Yahvé. This involved no conscious renunciation of Yahvé.

Jerubbaal, although he bore the name of that other god, was a faithful worshipper of Yahvé. For Yahvé he drew the sword, and to Yahvé he erected a sanctuary in his native city of Ophrah. But the Canaanitish custom of erecting in the sanctuary images of the deity artificially wrought and covered with precious metal, exerted a powerful influence over him. He could not resist it,

---

Schrader, *Z. f. Assyr.* iii. 363 ff.; also *Acad.* 1889, No. 919 (Cheyne), 917 f. (Sayce). See what is probably a representation of one in Stade, 461; perhaps also on the *stele* from Lilybæum, *Corp. Inscr. Sem.* i. Pl. xxix. 138 (otherwise Meyer, Art. *Baal*). *Cf.* besides Pietschm. 213.

[1] At least we learn nothing of them in older times. If they were connected with phallus-worship (Baethgen, 219 ; Collins, *Proc. Soc. B. Arch.* 1889, 291 ff.), this would be explained.

[2] Even Moses erected such *Maṣṣebas* (Ex. xxiv. 4), naturally to Yahvé.

[3] Ju. chap. ix., and on it above, p. 83.

and departed from the custom hitherto prevailing in Israel, of worshipping the deity without image. The later editor of his history is fully aware, and rightly, that a dangerous innovation was thus introduced into Israel. What Jerubbaal did, although it was not apostasy from Yahvé, was still apostasy from the imageless, spiritual worship of Yahvé.[1]

When a man like Jerubbaal found nothing to object to in this, we need not wonder that the custom approved by him naturalised itself here and there amongst the people. The Danites on their expedition to Laish found by the way in Mount Ephraim, a sanctuary of Yahvé quite like that of Jerubbaal. The deity worshipped at it was Yahvé.[2] His priest was at first the son of the owner of the sanctuary, but soon a travelling Levite, who was passing by, was appointed a welcome substitute for the ordinary lay priest. The object of the Yahvé-worship consisted of *Ephod* and *Teraphim*—an image of Yahvé of the same kind as that at Ophrah, and an image probably representing the dead ancestor of the family. That he may leave us in no doubt as to the character of these images, the editor appends untiringly the explanatory words, that they were graven and molten images (*pesel u-massēka*)—that is to say, there were now images in place of the imageless worship.[3] But even he knows that they were not images of Baal or 'Ashtart, but emblems belonging to the worship of Yahvé. Carried off by the Danites along with the priest, these images were transferred to Dan, and were the origin of a long celebrated Yahvé sanctuary, the Levitical priests of which traced themselves back to Moses.[4]

Beside all this, we find at Shiloh, at the transition from the time of the Judges to that of the Monarchy, a sanctuary[5] with the ancient Yahvé-ark, and a Levitical[6] priesthood reaching back to

---

[1] See above, p. 82.

[2] *Cf.* Ju. xvii. 13; xviii. 6 in N; just so in N¹.

[3] See above, p. 19, note 7. See further on Ephod and Teraphim below, § 50, 3.   [4] Ju. xviii. 30.

[5] See a (later) representation of a temple of this kind in Pietschm. 200.

[6] See 1 Sam. ii. 27 ff., as well as the incident narrated above, and below, p. 107, note 1.

the time of Moses. In it there is no trace of image, but simply the ark. Shiloh appears to have retained the traditions of the age of Moses in their greatest purity. If it formed already in the time of the Judges the nucleus of a Yahvé-worship, without image[1] and less affected by Canaanitish elements, this would explain whence Samuel got the impulse to his later efforts towards this end.

[1] For proof that imageless worship was not without examples in Phœnicia, cf. Pietschm. 204 (Herakles in Gades).

CHAPTER II.

SAMUEL AND SAUL.

§ 39. *The Philistine Domination. Samuel.*

SOME time after the fall of Abimelech—it may have been between the second third, and the middle, of the eleventh century B.C.—Israel fell into new distress. The menace was not, as so often before, from the predatory nomadic tribes of the desert, but from a maritime people, the warlike Philistines. The latter had some time previously [1] occupied not only the Mediterranean coast, but also the fruitful plain lying farther inland, to the west of the mountain district of Israel—the plain of Sharon west of Ephraim, and the Shephelah west of Judah. They were protected by a line of fortified cities from the onward pressure of the Israelites, and we may suppose that the two peoples lived on for a long time in peace. The Philistines rejoiced in the possession of their fruitful plain by the sea, while the adjoining Israelite tribes of Judah, Dan, and Ephraim were satisfied with the mountain districts and their modest harvests. At last, however, Dan was seized with a desire to extend itself, and this longing, doomed to disappointment, cost a part of the tribe the loss of its old home.[2]

It may have been due to the superiority of which the tribes of Joseph were conscious, thanks to the closer union they had attained under Jerubbaal and Abimelech, that in Israel people refused to be content any longer with their meagre lot. After

---

[1] When this happened we cannot say. *Cf.* the conjecture above, p. 62, note 6.
[2] See above, p. 70 ff.

the misfortune that befell Dan, a fresh effort to press forward into the plain in the west seems to have been made by Ephraim, probably also by Judah.[1] Thus there arose between the two parties a struggle that lasted years and even decades. It was carried on with varying success: neither of the opponents was able to gain decided supremacy over the other. It is to this time that the popular stories and legends, with which the Book of Judges magnifies the name of Samson, point. These afford us to a certain extent an insight into the conditions that then prevailed.[2] It was a time of long-continued skirmishing here and there; not continuous organised military expeditions, but rather sudden blows, inflicted on the enemy whenever occasion offered. There may also have been regularly planned campaigns and real battles, but they led to no decisive issue; the aimless skirmishing and manœuvring continued as before.

At last the Philistines succeeded in dealing a decisive blow, and with this event the whole struggle comes at last more clearly into the light of history. By the victory of the Philistines the struggle became the occasion of Israel's recovering its strength, through the establishment of a monarchy in the person of Saul. From the plain of Sharon the Philistines undertook an important advance towards the north. If they could only win the chain of hills that lay between the maritime plain and the plain of Jezreel, they could gain access to the latter and also to Mount Ephraim. The tribes of Israel that were most closely concerned, seem in the moment of danger to have combined and called out a considerable army; but it appears to have been wanting in unity of command, if it did not lack proper coherence altogether.

The Philistines encamped at Aphek, at the north end of the plain of Sharon, towards the hills; while Israel occupied a strong position not far distant, at Eben ha-'ezer, probably in the mountains.

---

[1] It is also possible, however, that the Philistines themselves, encouraged by the success they had achieved in the case of Dan, made a further attack on Israel. So Wellh. *Abriss.* 19 f. [Eng. Trans.[3] p. 39 f.]; Cornill, *Entsteh. d. V. Isr.* 23. Still, the example of Dan suggests rather the other view.

[2] See above, p. 92.

Twice did they meet in battle.¹ The first shock resulted unfavourably to Israel: four thousand slain covered the field of battle, and Israel had to withdraw hastily to its strong camp in the mountains. With a view to giving a decisive blow they brought the ark from Shiloh. They were sure victory could not fail if Yahvé was in the midst of His host. But this hope proved vain. Israel's army sustained a worse defeat the second time than the first, and thirty thousand warriors met their death at the hand of the enemy. The rest were thrown into confusion and fled in wild disorder, 'every man to his tent.' The ark of Yahvé, the sacred palladium of Israel, was captured by the enemy, and its bearers, the priests Hophni and Phinehas, were slain. Israel's army and shrine were lost to the enemy, and with them country, honour, and freedom. The way was now open northwards and westwards, to the fruitful plain of Jezreel, and to Mount Ephraim; and the Philistines, using their advantage, pressed onwards. The temple of Shiloh in Mount Ephraim was destroyed,² and apparently the whole land occupied. Henceforth a Philistine governor³ resided at Gibeah, considerably farther south than Shiloh. He would certainly not be the only such officer. In short, what had never yet occurred, in spite of the many calamities of later times, now came to pass: Israel became in its own land the vassal of a foreign despot. Even its very arms are said to have been taken away, and the smiths carried off from the land.⁴

Intelligent men in Israel would have little difficulty in seeing what the cause of this disaster was. It could not have occurred if all the tribes and clans that acknowledged themselves to be

---

¹ See 1 Sam. iv., and the discussion of the sources above, p. 31 ff., 34.

² This is not, indeed, specially related, but it is presupposed. A longer account of the advance of the Philistines seems to have dropped out. See Wellh. *Bl.*⁴ 210.

³ 1 Sam. xiii. 3 (*cf.* x. 5). Perhaps, however, we are to understand נְצִיב as a pillar of victory. (*Corp. Inscr. Sem.* i. 123, 194 f., 380, etc.)

⁴ This is stated in 1 Sam. xiii. 19 ff. Yet the repeated mention of the army of Israel in the intervening chapters is enough to suggest reasonable doubts with regard to this passage. Klosterm. *ad loc.* attempts to remove the difficulty by amending the text.

sons of Israel, had set themselves in a body against the danger. Nay, had there only prevailed as much union as Jerubbaal and Abimelech for a time produced, and had the proper man stood at their head, the misfortune could hardly have become so great and far-reaching as it was. It is significant that our account has not preserved the name of any leader. The army can hardly have been united in the hands of one man, for had it been, there would be something unintelligible, even after a severe defeat, about the wild precipitate flight, the sudden disorganisation, and the unconditional surrender, without another stroke, of the whole hill country, easily defensible as it was.

The memory of what Deborah and Gideon had done was enough to indicate the course to be pursued, and it did so now. Israel needed to be united and led by one man. But this unification would not suffice if achieved in only one or two of its chief tribes—these were no longer adequate to meet the distress of the hour: it must include the whole people. Nor was it enough that provision should be made for this hour of danger, it must be permanent. The people must feel themselves once more to be a nation, and determine to remain a nation. They must intrust themselves to a king who would call out his army and lead it to battle. It was only in a monarchy, which should comprise all the people really belonging to Israel, that deliverance lay. Intelligent men, indeed, might have recognised this long ago. But the question was whether the nation would prove to have sufficient strength and union in action for such a step, and would at the same time succeed in finding the right man to carry it through.

It succeeded in both these respects, but not at once. We do not know how long the disgrace of bondage lasted; at all events, for a long time.[1] It was an aged seer, Samuel, that pointed out the way of escape.

He had come in his early youth to Shiloh, the temple of which

---

[1] If the accounts in 1 Sam. i. ff. and chap. iv. represent the real relations of events as to time, the Philistine domination must have lasted at any rate about sixty years.

was still standing. This was not very long before the battle of Aphek [still it must have been from ten to twenty years before it]. Samuel was admitted by Eli, the priest[1] of the ark at Shiloh, as temple servant, and was introduced into the priesthood,[2] although he was of the tribe of Ephraim by birth.[3] After the disastrous day of Aphek and the destruction of the sanctuary at Shiloh, we lose sight of him along with the rest of Israel. It is not till he is an old man, towards the close of the period of oppression, that he appears once more. He seems to have betaken himself to his home at Ramah.[4] Here he laboured as priest and seer. The two offices are not opposed, but rather most closely connected. For if as seer he stood in special communication with Yahvé, he would by this very fact be the appropriate man for priest. Moreover, there stood at Ramah a high-place, at which no sacrifice was performed without his presence.

That Samuel's activity was not connected with the ark of God where his labours had begun, is something of a mystery, yet not more so than the fate of the shrine itself. Lost in battle with the Philistines, it had wandered to the temple of Dagon.[5] When disaster came on them in many forms affecting both god and people, the Philistines recognised the avenging hand of Yahvé. They sent the ark of Yahvé solemnly back to Israel. But the

---

[1] Eli himself was a Levite: we need not determine whether he was considered an Aaronite. On this, see *ThStW*. iii. 295 ff.; Baudissin, *Priestert*. 193 ff.

[2] On the age of 1 Sam. i.-iii., see above, p. 31 ff., 34 f. The chapters are among the younger parts of SS. This does not, however, preclude the existence of a historical kernel in the narrative (against Wellh. *Bl.*[4] 208).

[3] On the text of 1 Sam. i. 1, see Wellh. *TBS*. and Driver, *Notes, ad loc.* Klosterm., on account of 1 Chron. vi. 7 ff., assumes that he was of Levitical descent; so also Köhler. This is hardly justified; see Ewald, *Gesch. Isr.* ii.[3] 594 [Eng. Trans.[4] ii. 421]; Driv. 4.

[4] Ramah in Zuph (1 Sam. i. 1) is identical with the abode of Samuel in ix. 1 ff. (against Köhl. ii. 1, 93, 135; Klost. 27, and Budde, *RiSa*, 171). For Samuel does not seem in chap. ix. to have come from some other place, but to be staying at his own home (*cf.* vers. 12, 24). The abode of Samuel in chap. ix. (ver. 4) is in Zuph, as is the Ramah of i. 1. To distinguish two places is not practicable. The site of the Ramah of Samuel is indicated by *Beit Rîmâ*, not by *er-Râm*, as we may see from the route of Saul's journey in ix. 1 ff. (Wellh. *TBS*. 70.)

[5] On the significance and origin of this Philistine deity, see Pietschmann, *Gesch. d. Phön.* 145.

whole people, as well as Samuel and Saul, held aloof from the famous shrine of their fathers. It remained in Kiriath-Jearim till the time of David, laid aside and half forgotten. Did its misfortune seem to have robbed it of its power, or had it been defiled by its stay with the enemy, that people hardly remembered it any longer? Or did they regard it as inseparably connected with the sanctuary of Shiloh, now lying in ruins, while perhaps the Philistines prevented the rebuilding of the latter, hoping thus to deprive Yahvé of His sanctuary and seat, and Israel of its strength? I should be inclined to regard the latter explanation as the most probable.[1]

Samuel, however, although removed from the ark, perhaps by force, would doubtless not stand idly by during the long time of disgrace and bondage that ensued. If we find him in his old age a patriot, the distress of whose people has gone to his heart, and who cannot rest till he has found the right man, we are warranted in thinking of the man in his prime as in no way different. From Ramah, as a centre, he must certainly have exerted a far-reaching influence during that time of distress and shattered hopes. What was wanted was to arouse again Israel's self-confidence and trust in God, which must have fallen very low. A work done in quiet was needed to awaken an idealism in the people, and to promote a purer worship of Yahvé in face of such a manifold blending with heathenish elements as was manifestly to be found in the age of the Judges, and as was made natural by the Philistine domination. Perhaps Samuel was guided by the traditions of Shiloh.[2] An intimation of some activity of this kind is still to be found in 1 Sam. vii., although it has certainly been preserved to us only in a tradition of very late date, and has therefore been modified in several points. The section in its present form is undoubtedly unhistorical,[3] for a thorough conquest of the Philistines by Samuel

---

[1] [Cf. however, now in this connection the interesting article of Kosters on the fate of the ark in *T. Tijdschr.* 1893, 301 ff. He supposes that the riddle is to be solved by the hypothesis that the ark was not recovered from the Philistines till the time of David.]   [2] See above, p. 101 f.

[3] On the chapter cf. above, p. 24 f. It belongs to Ri and D².

is historically out of the question. By such a defeat the kingship of Saul, and the whole subsequent development of events, would be deprived of all foundation. But there appears to remain this basis of fact for the incidents here related, that Samuel held at Mizpah[1] a conference with the heads of clans of Israel. The question was, what could be done to escape the Philistine oppression. The idea of the monarchy must have then suggested itself to Samuel and the elders of the people. At the same time, however, Samuel, the priest and seer of Yahvé, who had passed his youth by the ark at Shiloh, must have seen the surest escape from the present distress in a return to Yahvé, and to a mode of divine worship less tainted by foreign elements than that practised in these latter days. There is no ground for attributing this idea in its simple form only to later authors.

We obtain a similar view of Samuel's position by considering his relation to the *prophetic guilds*. The narrative concerning Samuel that has reached us, quite recognised that he was not what a later age called *nābî*, 'prophet.' It designates him not a prophet, but a 'seer,' and calls attention to the fact that the latter is the old name, and the former the more recent name, for the same thing.[2] It implies thereby that, with all their distinctness, there is yet a very close connection between the two. The prophets of later times were an outgrowth of just such seers as Samuel. The latter were the historical basis. But Samuel himself stands in a close relation to the transition from the older to the newer form. Not only is this change of name connected with his person, but he seems also to have been closely connected, at least in their first beginnings, with the establishment of special prophetic guilds, of which we learn in later times.

These societies appear to be the natural basis from which prophecy arose in Israel, vivified by the spirit of the religion of Yahvé, and guided by such men as Samuel, and afterwards Elijah.

---

[1] On Mizpah, see Kamphausen in *StKr.* 1889, 197, and Budde, *RiSa*, 185, as against Wellh. *Bl.*[4] 203; *Prol.*[2] 268 [Eng. Trans. p. 256]. See also Renan, *Hist. du p. Isr.* i. 374 [Eng. Trans. p. 301 f.].   [2] *Cf.* 1 Sam. ix. 9.

Bands of ecstatic men, singing and dancing, carrying all before them in wild frenzy, rush like madmen through the land. They are religious fanatics, filled with holy ardour for their God; but it is certainly not only religious fanaticism that impels them; religion and patriotism are united. For Israel is Yahvé's people. God, people, and land are inseparably bound together. The weight of the Philistine yoke that rests on Yahvé's land and people has called forth these madmen, and in holy zeal for Yahvé and His cause, they roam over the land. We meet here in Israel with a character something like the Eastern dervish of to-day, who, in times of religious and political excitement, unfurls the banner of the prophet and preaches a holy war. Bands of wild, excited dervishes scoured the land, enlisting recruits everywhere for Yahvé and the liberation of His land.[1]

It is, to begin with, not credible that Samuel should have stood in no connection with these men. In fact, it would seem to be no accident that it was in his home of Ramah that they had their seat, and that it was just after Saul had his important interview with Samuel that they encountered him. There could not have been in Israel such a time of ferment as there actually was, nor could the Philistine yoke have been in the minds of the people a burden so oppressive and disgraceful as it was, without Samuel and the ecstatic national prophets appearing, and without Samuel's effort to clear away the turbulent and boisterous element of their character, and enlist the movement in the service of the religion of Yahvé.

It is decidedly incorrect to attempt to ascribe to Samuel a simply local importance. If he was the man who took counsel with the heads of the people at Mizpah regarding Israel's weal and woe, and if he had relations, none the less important that they were kept in the background, with the ecstatic *nebiim*, then he was not an unknown seer, spoken of only in a corner of Benjamin, with no other importance in Israel. But even if he is not to be credited

---

[1] This description is drawn from 1 Sam. ix. (especially ver. 9), and x. 1 ff., in combination with 1 Sam. x. 10 ff. and kindred passages.

with any such importance, the monarchy established in the person of Saul was, at all events, a matter with which he was most closely connected. If, however, he was the man that gave Israel its king, his importance and influence extended beyond Ramah and its immediate neighbourhood. Whatever may have been the precise way in which the events came about, this at least is certain, that Samuel exerted an influence on the establishment of the monarchy. Hence he must, both before and after that event, have occupied a position the influence of which reached far beyond the walls of Ramah. It will fall to the history of Saul to set this in its proper light.

§ 40. *Saul.*

It was Samuel who discovered the right man to make king. This man was Saul, the son of Kish, the head of a Benjamite family, of Gibeah in Benjamin.

The way in which Saul became king is enveloped in darkness, and will remain so. Only one thing is certain, namely, that Samuel had in some special way a hand in the matter. The attempt has been made to determine the part played by Samuel in regard to Saul and the monarchy, by following that one of our accounts which is manifestly the older, and simply setting the other aside, as offering a later view of the course of events.[1] According to this theory, Samuel, having at heart the distress of the people, accidentally meets with Saul and discerns in him the right man—the man he has long been seeking. Animating him with a sense of the people's distress, Samuel sends him home, confident that he will recognise the right moment to act. Saul does as he is directed, and a cry for help from Jabesh in Gilead gives him the opportunity of setting himself at the head of the army. On this view everything else, not only the election of Saul, but also Samuel's original attitude of reluctance towards the monarchy, must be held to rest on later invention.[2]

---

[1] The later account is SS; the older, S. On these, see above, pp. 23 ff., 26 ff.
[2] So especially Stade, 213, with Wellhausen and Kuenen.

I cannot accept this view without qualification. The representation just given may indeed substantially correspond to the actual facts of the case; but certain features of the additional narrative preserved in the younger source, appear likewise to be genuine and original.[1] Among such I include especially the mention of negotiations about the monarchy, supposed to have taken place between Samuel and the elders of the people. An absolutely unhistorical feature has been found here by some, and especially in Samuel's holding aloof at first from the proposal to found a monarchy. Such an idea, it is said, could originate only in later times, when there was no king, or when men were disgusted with the monarchy.

But Samuel's attitude is not in point of fact so surprising as it might at first sight appear. Doubts with regard to the monarchy might really arise very readily in the mind of a far-seeing patriot of those days. Monarchs and monarchic systems were indeed not unknown to Israel. 'All the nations round about,'[2] Egypt, Assyria, Edom, Moab, Ammon, the Canaanitish and Philistine cities, had long had kings. Even Israel had made their acquaintance in Gideon and Abimelech. Obvious as the outward advantages of a monarchy certainly were, people could not fail to notice also the disadvantage of such an innovation as Israel was striving after, for a community that had till now been constituted rather on a republican basis. Moreover, Israel's most glorious memories were against the change. Moses had made Israel a nation and yet had not become king. Least of all could the experiences of the age of the Judges give any encouragement. These showed how, behind

---

[1] SS is decidedly younger than S, and is strongly permeated, especially in its conception and reproduction of the facts, by the ideas of the time of Hosea. But this source is not so young that it cannot have retained real reminiscences of the actual course of events. On the other hand, although S is older and, on the whole, more accurately informed, it is by no means a document contemporaneous with the events it describes (see above, p. 34). And this reservation applies especially to chap. ix., x. 1 ff. This is enough to show that it is not permissible simply to declare S historical (Cornill, *ZKWL.* 85, 116), and SS unhistorical. Our duty is rather to make a cautious use of both these documents, endeavouring to determine by internal evidence what the real facts probably were.

[2] *Cf.* 1 Sam. viii. 5.

such a monarchic constitution as ancient 'Tyranny' there ever stood the danger of violence and despotism.

There is in fact nothing more conceivable than that Samuel, and probably many another along with him, at first expressed grave doubts before giving consent to the establishment of the kingly power.[1] If he resisted and overcame his scruples, he only did what many another in his position had already done. Even such naïve joy over the monarchy as shines through the literary productions of the earlier period of the monarchy,[2] in no way conflicts with the existence of hesitancy for a time. But our sources themselves tell us that these scruples did not exist everywhere, and especially not among the people and their leaders. And it is obvious that if the monarchy, once in existence, led Israel to an undreamed-of height, as it actually did under David and Solomon, it would easily win men's hearts.

The attitude of Samuel is thus described in our sources with substantial accuracy. It is a very different question, however, whether we are entitled to say the same of the election of Saul.[3] I regard it as inadmissible. If Saul was chosen king by Samuel, and if, as I am inclined to suppose, the latter had selected Saul in full agreement with the elders of the people, there was no room left for an election, or rather a destination, by lot. Such a proceeding would, indeed, have been only an empty formality, on the supposition that the individual had been chosen.

The first thing Saul did was to chastise the Ammonites. It came about in this way. Jabesh in Gilead, an Israelitish city east of the Jordan, insolently threatened by the Ammonite King Nahash, sent messengers across the Jordan imploring succour from the other tribes. The messengers came in due course—certainly not by accident[4]—to Gibeah. Saul was in the field, and the people of Gibeah had only their sympathy and regrets to offer

---

[1] Whether the objections were of a purely religious nature ('Yahvè is your king') is indeed doubtful, as such an idea cannot be proved to exist, before the time of Hosea. But the very name *Malk* for a Phœnician deity made it plausible.

[2] *Cf.* Num. xxiii. 21; xxiv. 24; Dt. xxxiii. 4 f.

[3] 1 Sam. x. 17 ff.   [4] So Wellh. *Bl.*[4] 211; Stade, 212.

their countrymen across the Jordan; they lacked the courage to go to their aid. As Saul returned from the field, following his oxen, he heard what had happened. His decision was quickly come to. Seizing a pair of oxen, he slew them on the spot, and cut them up. Then he bade the messengers take the pieces of flesh and go through all Israel, summoning the people to the holy war with the threat: 'Whosoever cometh not after Saul and Samuel,[1] so shall it be done unto his oxen.'[2]

It was a bold impetuous act, and a startling word, that the messengers were able to publish in Israel. Nor did it fail to do its work. Saul had acted as a man and a hero, already encircled with the lustre of his destined crown. He was not to suffer for his chivalrous daring and his chivalrous trust in the tribes. His summons found an echo in people's hearts; he succeeded in gathering an army; and Jabesh was relieved. Saul had now earned his crown by his own achievements. He was conducted by the people in triumph to Gilgal and there offered the throne.[3]

Saul's work was not over. Rather, the time had now fully come for him to act. The yoke of the Philistines still lay on Israel, and was felt to be a greater disgrace and oppression than anything Ammon had inflicted. Here then was Saul's opportunity, 'what his hand should find.' What Samuel had whispered to him, though enigmatical, was intelligible enough.[4] A representative[5] of the Philistine oppressors of Israel had his seat in Gibeah itself, Saul's home and present residence. It was probably immediately after the return from Gilead that this man was slain by Jonathan, Saul's son. The signal for the rising was thus given. As the army appears to have been already entirely, or for the most

---

[1] The reference to Samuel is generally struck out as a gloss. I do not, however, regard a reference to him as impossible.

[2] Cf. 1 Sam. xi.; and above, pp. 24, 29, 33 f. The section is generally accepted as historical.

[3] On xi. 12-14 see above, p. 24, note 3. A passage of somewhat different form must have stood in S instead of what we now read. At least, נחדש in v. 14 does not agree with S (against Klost. 36). [4] 1 Sam. x. 7.

[5] For another possible interpretation see above, p. 105, note 3. 'The Philistines heard of it,' in xiii. 3, agrees very well with that explanation.

part disbanded, Saul collected again hastily what force he could [1]—six hundred men. They encamped at Gibeah; the Philistines, opposite to them, at Michmash. Here, at the ascent to Mount Ephraim, is the well-known pass that forms the southern key to the mountain district. It seemed as if Saul with his company would here be cut off from the rest of Israel. Hence it appeared an easy matter for the superior force of the Philistines to crush the little band.

Michmash and Gibeah are separated by a ravine. Descending on both sides in rugged precipices, it seemed a natural and insurmountable barrier between the two camps.[2] A Philistine picket was indeed stationed as watch on the brink of the gorge. But it felt it to be unnecessary to be on its guard. Who would climb the perpendicular cliff? Jonathan, however, with reckless daring succeeds, along with his armour-bearer, in climbing the cliff. The unwatchful picket is surprised; Jonathan strikes down all who come in his way; while the attendant following behind gives the death-blow. The rest of the picket, imagining that the two foolhardy men are followed by a company, flee in terror and carry sudden panic into the camp. Consternation and wild disorder ensue.[3]

Saul's watch on the Gibeah side observe the confusion in the Philistine camp and report it to Saul. When Saul gathers his men, Jonathan and his attendant are missing. It is clear at once what has happened, and what ought to be done. Saul seizes the

---

[1] *Cf.* 1 Sam. xiii. 1-6. We must not however conceal from ourselves that there is much here also that remains obscure. If Saul had some plan of action against the Philistines, why did he disband the army (xiii. 2)? Why did the Philistines come to Michmash if Saul was stationed there (xiii. 2)? Is the situation of xiii. 2 ff. (espec. *v.* 6, the fear of the Hebrews) conceivable, immediately after the victory over Ammon? and so on. It is thus a question whether much more of xiii. 1-6 is original than *v.* 3. (On the text see my trans. in Kautzsch.) In that case we should have to suppose that immediately after his return, Saul proceeded with his six hundred men against the Philistines, or that, to keep up appearances, he retained or summoned afresh these six hundred men and no more, out of the whole army. This latter is the view taken in the text. On xiii. 7*b*-15*a*, see above, p. 30.

[2] On the locality see Furrer, in Schenkel's *BL.* iv. 216.

[3] 1 Sam. xiv. 1-15.

opportunity to make a sudden swift attack. The Philistines flee in wild confusion. Such as had deserted to them now return to Israel, and such as had hidden in caves and caverns come out to share in the pursuit. During the pursuit, however, Jonathan, not knowing of the prohibition issued by his father, tastes some food, and almost falls a victim to the latter's blind zeal. Indeed, it is only the intercession of the people that saves the life of the hero of the day. Possibly some one else was sacrificed as a victim to the superstitious fanaticism of the king.[1]

We do not know how great and lasting Saul's success was; but we shall do well in any case not to suppose it to have been too great. There was no real victory won; the Philistines, seized by panic, apparently did not wait for an engagement to take place, and must thus have brought home in safety the principal part of their army. Yet a moral victory had been won for Saul and Israel; and in point of fact, the territory of Benjamin, at all events, and probably Judah as well, was cleared of Philistines. The Philistine wars were not indeed at an end.[2] On the contrary they continued, as one writer[3] expressly declares, throughout Saul's whole life. The feud may have been prosecuted with varying success until it finally cost Saul his throne and his life.

The defectiveness of our traditional sources makes itself felt here painfully. Only once again before his removal by death from the scene of action, is Saul introduced to us as occupying himself with foreign affairs. Even this expedition is probably

---

[1] 1 Sam. xiv. 16-46. On chap. xiv. in general, see above, pp. 29 f., 33 f. Wellh. is wrong in removing xiv. 36-45. When we consider the spirit of the age (*cf.* 2 Sam. xxi. 1 ff.) we shall not regard redemption by the offering of a human sacrifice, probably some prisoner of war, as inconceivable. See esp. Ewald, *Gesch. Isr.*[3] iii. 51 [Eng. Trans.[2] iii. 36]. Yet, as the redemption of a human being through the substitution of something of less value is to be found in the oldest laws (Ex. xxxiv. 20, *cf.* xiii. 13; xxi. 8), the reference may very well be to an ox or a gift to the sanctuary. So Driver, *Notes*, p. 91, and most writers. Klostermann's emendation of the text is quite unwarranted.

[2] On 1 Sam. xiv. 47-51 see above, p. 29 f. The statement in *v.* 47 cannot (*cf. v.* 52) correspond to the real course of events.

[3] *Cf.* xiv. 52. The writer is R, but his statement represents a perfectly just view of the state of affairs. On this verse, see above, pp. 30, 44.

related only because with it was connected the estrangement between him and Samuel, an estrangement which had such weighty consequences, and which probably contributed more than anything else to drive Saul's spirit into fatal madness.

If Saul established his supremacy first of all in the east by the war against Ammon, then in Israel proper, at least in Benjamin, Ephraim, and Judah, by the expulsion of the Philistines, it would seem natural that he should turn to the south of Judah and undertake to quiet, once for all, the rapacious Amalekites, ever eager for an attack. What the special occasion was, we do not know.[1] The enmity, however, between Israel and Amalek was old enough, and there was no need for any fresh incitement to war.[2] Saul attacked the enemy and achieved a brilliant success. Such Amalekites as were taken captive were, in accordance with long-honoured usage in war, put to death, while King Agag and a part of the captured cattle were kept alive. Samuel, not satisfied with this, slew Agag with his own hands 'before Yahvé in Gilgal,'[3] and announced to Saul that Yahvé repented of having made him king. Thereupon Samuel returned to Ramah, and Saul to Gibeah. 'And Samuel saw Saul no more till the day of his death.'[4]

A serious and calamitous breach was thus brought about in the relations between the two men. We have no ground for calling in question its historicity. In fact, Saul's rejection by Samuel, and his feeling that the Seer of Yahvé who had procured for him his crown was now against him, are the only satisfactory explanation of the unhappy state of mind that now came over Saul. What the real ground of the unfortunate rupture was, however, we do not learn. The difference of opinion with regard to Agag and the spoil, may have brought matters to a crisis, but cannot have been the only reason. The fact that our sources seek for further

---

[1] See, however, the mention of Agag's deeds in 1 Sam. xv. 33.

[2] Hence the mention of Amalek's old offence (1 Sam. xv. 2 f.).

[3] It is unnecessary to assign a sacrificial meaning to Samuel's slaying Agag (Wellh. *Bl.*[4] 216; Cornill, *ZKWL.* 1885, 123, etc.), since it was merely the carrying through of the *ḥerem*.

[4] 1 Samuel xv. On the chap. generally see above, pp. 26, 34. It is, at all events, one of the older sections in SS.

grounds,[1] shows that many things had occurred to disturb the relation, delicate enough from the beginning, that existed between King and Seer. Of what nature they were, however, we are not told. The source—perhaps Benjamite,[2] certainly favourably inclined to Saul—to which we are indebted for the first history of Saul, has withheld them from us. Perhaps it omitted, out of consideration for Saul, many matters that were little creditable to him. This may also be the reason why our information about Saul's doings in general is so meagre.

In the war against the Philistines, the course of events would not always be as favourable as Israel might wish. The Philistines were, after all, their superiors, from long practice in war, and from being accustomed to prevail. Moreover, this would lead the tribes of Israel to submit less unreservedly to the sceptre of Saul, for although they readily submitted to him as a conqueror, they had not forgotten their old independence. Saul's position, thus already hard enough, must have been absolutely intolerable when, in addition to all this, the bond that united him to Samuel the Seer threatened to break. According to all appearance Saul was an impetuous sanguine spirit, buoyed up by success, depressed by misfortune. No wonder if the unenviable position he was in proved too much for his strength. 'An evil spirit from Yahvé' came over him.[3] Deep melancholy wrapped his spirit in gloom and plunged him into hopeless dejection. This was soon to be further intensified by the torture of jealousy, and Saul to be driven to wild outbreaks of frenzy.

[1] *Cf.* 1 Sam. xiii. 7*b*-15*a*, and above, p. 30. The passage, as it now stands, is from R. But it must have been based on a narrative belonging to S (in connection with which source this passage stands), which likewise told of a rupture between Samuel and Saul, on the occasion of a sacrifice at Gilgal.

[2] See above, p. 34.   [3] 1 Sam. xvi. 14.

§ 41. *Continuation. Saul and David.*[1]

A young man[2] came to the court of Saul, David ben Jesse by name. He was of Bethlehem-Judah,—a good soldier, master of the lute, handsome in appearance and fluent in speech. He was brought in the hope that his playing would drive away the king's melancholy. He was still a shepherd in the service of his father,[3] but Saul's attendants had discovered him and recommended him to the king. The young David became Saul's page. The latter at once took a fancy to the attractive and clever young man, who soon became his armour-bearer. Thus, when David had proved himself and 'found grace with Saul,' the relation between them became, at his master's special request, a lasting one. The soothing power of this attractive man, who was able to play so skilfully on the lute and to speak and recite[4] so agreeably, had a most salutary influence on Saul.[5]

But Saul was not to enjoy his new friend. After he had broken with Samuel, or the latter with him, it was as if disaster had conspired against him; he felt himself forsaken by God, and could find no more pleasure in existence. He saw spectres everywhere which brewed disaster; and, tragically enough for him, the very man in whose hands he had put himself, in the hope that he might be able to chase away the evil spirit from his mind, was the means of awaking it to fresh and more fearful activity.

David was one of those divinely favoured natures that irresistibly attract every one they touch, and whose charm no one is able to withstand. Hardly had he joined the court of Saul, when he

---

[1] [On the life of David, *cf.* W. R. Smith, art. 'David' in *Encyclopædia Britannica*; and Cheyne, *Aids to the Study of Criticism*, 1892, Part I., 'The David Narratives.']

[2] David was about twenty-five years old, and therefore on the borderland between youth and manhood.

[3] The statement in question, at the end of 1 Sam. xvi. 19, is generally struck out as a gloss. See, however, above, p. 35, note 4.

[4] This is probably implied in 1 Sam. xvi. 18.

[5] 1 Sam. xvi. 14-23. On this see above, p. 35; and on the source Da, to which the narrative belongs, p. 44 f. On the passage, xvi. 1-13, which we have passed over, *cf.* p. 38 and the references there.

won to himself in succession first the king, then his subjects, court, son, and daughter. This, however, was too much for Saul's suspicious nature. He began to fear for his throne, and David's royal patron soon became his most bitter and deadly enemy.

Meanwhile, the Philistine wars continued. Collisions occurred from time to time—now here, now there. Hence we find Saul sometimes at home in Gibeah, sometimes with the army in camp. David, his intimate companion and armour-bearer, was with him wherever he went. In one of the wars David slew a Philistine giant. Legend has identified the latter with Goliath of Gath, whom one of David's heroes, Elḥanan of Bethlehem, slew at a later stage, and whose 'spear was as a weaver's beam.'[1] David won further laurels[2] of all kinds in the war with the Philistines, which seems to have been the chief task of Saul, and he was in consequence honoured by Saul with an important post in the army.[3] In this position, also, he succeeded in whatever he undertook, and it did not really need the song of the women, 'Saul hath slain his thousands, but David his ten thousands,'[4] to enable Saul to perceive that the youthful minstrel and hero was in fact about to cast the king himself into the shade.[5]

---

[1] On 1 Sam. xvii. generally, and its relation to xvi. 14 ff., see above, p. 35 ff. It appears from what is said there that, even according to the LXX. text of chap. xvii., the two narratives do not agree. There is also to be taken into consideration the statement in 2 Sam. xxi. 19, according to which Goliath was slain by one of David's heroes, Elḥanan of Bethlehem. On the text of this passage and its relation to that of 1 Chr. xx. 5, see especially the admirable discussions in Driver, *Notes*, 272, and Kuen. § xxi. 10. Klost. (*SaKö.* 238), like Grätz and others, does violence to the text. Nevertheless, a real exploit of David's may lie at the basis of the Goliath story. [*Cf.* also Cheyne, *Aids to the Study of Criticism*, pp. 125-128.]

[2] 1 Sam. xviii. 6-8 was once (perhaps with a somewhat different text) the continuation of xvi. 14 ff. in Da, and in that case presupposed certain exploits of David's, to which the slaying of a Philistine hero may have belonged. See above, p. 37.

[3] This is presupposed in xviii. 6-8 (Da), and related, although in another connection, in xviii. 13-16 (SS).

[4] That the song is historical is beyond doubt. It may be questioned, however, whether it was sung at so early a stage (Cornill, *KgSt.* 35).

[5] On xviii. 9 f., 17-19, see above, p. 36, note 4; and Kamphausen, *ZAW.* vi. 19 ff. Chap. xviii. in its present form is a completely unintelligible collection of all that was known about the origin of the quarrel between Saul and David. It

A sound man seated on Saul's throne could only have rejoiced over David and his successes. But that is just what Saul was not. His mind was fatally clouded, and what another would have seen with pride and joy, and made use of for his own good and the good of his kingdom, appeared to him, seeing as he did disaster everywhere, only as a threatening danger, and awakened in him gloomy suspicions.

When finally David won the sympathy of the people and the court, the friendship of Jonathan the chivalrous son of the king— nay, even at last, to complete his happiness and success, the love of Saul's daughter Michal,[1] the measure of Saul's secret suspicion was also filled. One development after another occurred to excite Saul's jealousy afresh.[2] At last the turbulent ferment of passion broke forth into wild frenzy. Saul has no longer any doubt: the armour-bearer, whom he had promoted to be leader of his forces, is not satisfied with casting into the shade the king's name and martial glory; his aim is higher; he wishes to become the friend of the king's son, the king's son-in-law—the traitor wishes to become the king's successor before his death. Henceforth Saul's decision is immovable: the traitor is doomed to death. Saul seeks to carry out his decision, however and whenever he can. The victim of his suspicion having escaped his murderous steel, he goes forth expressly to seek him. With the tenacity peculiar to one haunted by an illusion, he devotes himself henceforth almost exclusively to his purpose of avenging himself on his supposed mortal enemy and persecutor. We may confidently assert that this thought, which never again left the unfortunate man, finally wasted him away.

Whether David was or was not guilty of what Saul reproached him with, will hardly be seriously discussed.[3] David may have

was therefore abridged, even by the Alexandrian translator (see above, p. 36 f.). An attempt is made in the text above to indicate to some extent the original course of events.

[1] See 1 Sam. xviii. 7, 16, 1, 20. Although the order is disturbed, we have here at all events facts.

[2] *Cf.* the gradation in 1 Sam. xviii. 12, 15, 29a, 29b.

[3] As against Duncker, see esp. Kamph. *ZAW.* vi. 76.

been so far human that, having risen almost too suddenly, he prided himself more than was wise in his good fortune and splendour. It may have afforded him a satisfaction, which we can well understand although it was dangerous, that public opinion preferred him and his deeds to the king himself and his achievements. But that David was striving after the throne is neither proved nor credible. Even his friendship with Jonathan the legitimate heir, which is surely authentic, is decidedly against such an idea. Had any such suspicion existed anywhere else than in the morbidly excited brain of Saul, and perhaps in the circle of David's envious rivals at the court of Saul—for such would certainly not be wanting—Jonathan himself would surely have been the first to turn away from David with disgust. Moreover, if David looked at what he had attained, he might well be satisfied with his lot. As the king's son-in-law he would, at all events after Saul's death, be the nearest to the throne, and so long as the latter lived he was the first man in the kingdom after Jonathan.

That Saul gave to David in marriage his daughter Michal, who had fallen in love with him, is beyond a doubt. It is even not impossible that his destination to be the king's son-in-law may have fallen in the time of Saul's undisturbed goodwill towards him.[1] On the other hand, according to a narrative bearing in many points the impress of credibility,[2] we should have to connect with this very event the first attempt of Saul to get rid of David, who had suddenly become hateful to him as a supposed rival. Confirmed in such a suspicion, already probably entertained in secret by learning of the love of Michal for David, Saul hoped to turn it into a weapon for David's destruction. He promised him his daughter, but at a price which he thought David could

---

[1] In itself this would be the more natural supposition. It is reflected also in chap. xvii. In this case xviii. 21 must once have stood in another connection.

[2] 1 Sam. xviii. 20-29a. Kamphausen, *Rhein. theol. Arb.* vii. 21, regards this account of the course of events as unhistorical. See, however, the following note. At all events, grounds of taste and propriety are not decisive against the historicity of the narrative. *Cf.* 2 Sam. iii. 14; also Brugsch, *Gesch. Ägypt.* 575 f. [Eng. Trans.² ii. 126 f.]; Meyer, *Gesch. d. Alt.* 312.

not pay without exposing his life to great danger. He was to deliver over to Saul, as a dowry for Michal, the foreskins of a hundred Philistines to be slain by himself[1]—a striking illustration of the rudeness of those wild warlike times. Contrary to expectation, David passed through the trial without meeting any harm. He even brought home double the required number of the strange trophies. Saul had pledged his royal word to David: the king's daughter was his.

The first plot had thus failed. But Saul's wild hate would be only the more intent on David's destruction, the nearer the latter had now been brought to him as his own son-in-law.[2] One day, when David returned safe from a victorious expedition against the Philistines, Saul was suffering from a new attack of his melancholy. As David played for him on the lute, Saul unexpectedly hurled his spear at him. By a dexterous movement David escaped with his life.[3] But to stay any longer in the palace was out of the question, and he hastened home. There was some hope that through Michal's interposition it might be possible to allay the king's rage and suspicion. But Saul sent messengers after him to watch the house by night and seize him next morning. Michal, informed of this, urged David to speedy flight. When the officers came, they were told by Michal that David was lying sick in bed. Saul commanded him to be brought before him in his bed. The attendants came once more, and made their way to the bed, only to find lying there not David but his wife's Taraph.[4] I see no reason to contest the historicity of this narrative on the ground of its contents.[5] On the other hand, we

[1] Since, surely, only opponents slain by his own hand can be meant, the objection of Kamphausen that David, as commander in the army, could have chosen his own position in battle, is not to the point.

[2] 1 Sam. xix. 1-7 relates a reconciliation on the part of Saul, brought about by Jonathan. It must at all events have been quite temporary. V. 3 belongs to R. The passage is probably a parallel in SS to chap. xx.

[3] xix. 8-10 (SS). This passage is here in a better place than its parallel in Da, xviii. 10 f.   [4] xix. 11-17; cf. above, p. 39.

[5] Otherwise Wellh.; Stade, 234 f.; Cornill, KySt. 41; also Gaupp. Zur Gesch. Davids. Saul's fit of madness was not enough to prove that he had further designs. This appeared first from the sending of the officers. On xix. 18-24; xx. 1a, cf. above, p. 39.

must admit that it seems to conflict with another account of the mode of David's flight from Saul. The fragmentary and often confused condition of our accounts, makes it really impossible to reach a clear idea of the real occasion of this event. According to the other representation, David had good ground to suppose from the king's behaviour that he was cherishing suspicion against him, and was aiming at his life. He confided in Jonathan, who promised to put an end to his uncertainty on the subject. David, as the king's son-in-law and armour-bearer, ate daily, when not on the field, at Saul's table along with Jonathan and Abner, the commander of the forces. This suggested a plan. David absented himself from table, and hid himself in the field. This would lead to the king's showing what his feeling towards him was, and by an appointed sign the result would be made known to David. Jonathan was to go into the field where David was hiding behind a heap of stones, and shoot an arrow. If he called to the boy, 'Fetch the arrow and come here,' David could return without danger; if he told the boy to go away, David must flee. In point of fact Saul did miss David from table, at least on the second day. Jonathan made excuse for him on the score that he had left in haste for Bethlehem to attend a sacrificial feast of his family. Saul fell into a rage against his own son for daring to plead the traitor's cause, and brandished his spear threateningly against him. Jonathan now knew all that was necessary, and in the manner agreed upon with David made known to him the king's feeling.[1]

The breach with Saul was complete: David must flee. Whither to flee, David could be in no doubt. Home and the ties of kinship called him south; the mountain-land of Judah offered him the best chance of protection and concealment; the

---

[1] There is nothing about this narrative, apart from the manifestly wrong position (xx. 1, after David's flight) it now occupies, thanks to the redactor, that seriously calls its historicity in question. However, vv. 5, 12, 19 f. and everything connected with them, are later interpolations; cf. v. 5, 'evening,' v. 35, 'morning'; in v. 12 f. Jonathan sends (secret word) to David; v. 18, he gives the signal with the arrow. In v. 12 to morrow (evening), in v. 24 ff. on the third day. See my analysis in Kautzsch. The rest belongs to Da.

Canaanites and Edomites, who adjoined Israel here on the west and the south, lived on tolerably peaceable terms with Israel, so that he had not much to fear from them if he were ever to cross into their territory; and he had nothing to fear from the hand of Saul, which did not reach so far.

His way to the south led him past Nob, a small town a little to the north of Jerusalem. The priests of the house of Eli had, it seems, after the destruction of their sanctuary at Shiloh, established themselves here at a new sanctuary, although they no longer possessed the ark of Yahvé. At their head was Ahimelech. As David arrived here alone and without arms, he alleged in explanation a secret commission of Saul's calling for great haste. Instead of common bread and a sword, which were not at hand, the priest gave him at his own request sacred bread and the sword of the giant whom he had slain, which had been deposited as a votive offering beside the ephod.[1]

David hurried farther south and hid himself in the mountain fastness[2] of Adullam. It is not clear to whom this belonged, and how it came into David's possession. The most natural supposition seems to be that the castle was still in the possession of the Canaanites,[3] and that these were glad to receive amongst themselves the famed—and doubtless also feared—favourite and warrior of Saul. His family, dreading the revenge of Saul, fled to him here, and formed the kernel of a small band which David gathered round himself in defensive and offensive alliance, as a protection against an unexpected attack from Saul. In addition to these, dissatisfied and discontented persons of all kinds collected around him, so that his troop reached the number of four hundred men.[4]

Saul could not fail to observe that David had fled, and that he had here found a safe refuge. Leaning on his spear, surrounded by his attendants, he held council with the heads of clans of

---

[1] 1 Sam. xxi. 1b-10 (SS). I see no ground for the rejection of *vv.* 8-10 (Wellh., Stade). On xxi. 11 ff. see above, p. 40, and Kamph. *ZAW.* vi. 71.

[2] 1 Sam. xxii. 1. Read מְצֻדַת.

[3] *Cf.* Gen. xxxviii. 1 ff.

[4] 1 Sam. xxii. 1-5 (SS). See above, p. 40.

Benjamin. He detailed to them in stirring words what he had done for his tribe; yet, he complained, they allowed his son to enter into a compact against him with the Judæan David, without bringing him word of it. This complaint was heard by Doeg the Edomite, who had been at Nob at the same time as David, and was accidentally now staying at Gibeah. He informed the king of what he had seen at Nob. Saul in his anger summoned the whole priesthood before him. No assertion of innocence, no reference to David's being the king's son-in-law and most trusted servant, no protestation on the part of Ahimelech that he had had no misgiving when he inquired of Yahvé for David, as he had so often done before, could produce any effect on the furious king. The matter was clear in his mind: the whole priesthood were at one with David and Jonathan in seeking to remove the infirm king and set another—whether Jonathan or David—in his place. They must expiate their offence with their death. The bodyguard, however, refused to lay a hand on the priests of Yahvé, and so Doeg himself accomplished the king's bloody command— eighty-five priests were cut down. Moreover, Saul vowed the destruction of their city, Nob. Their relatives, man, woman, and child, together with the cattle, were given to the sword. Only a son of Ahimelech's, Abiathar by name, escaped the frightful massacre, and fled to David to become his priest.[1]

What David and such in Israel as sided with him had to expect of Saul, could be seen from the fate of Nob. No doubt it was Saul's intention to leave no one in uncertainty about the matter. In point of fact, he had made an example that would deter any one in Israel from incurring such suspicion as had befallen Nob and its priests.

David seems to have lived for some time on Judæan soil,[2] but so hidden that Saul could not easily make himself master of him. There was reason enough why he should now look for some other

---

[1] 1 Sam. xxii. 6 ff. (SS). See above, p. 40.
[2] *Cf.* xxiii. 3. If this be so, David must have left Adullam again; yet it is also quite possible that the narrator (Da) simply reckoned Adullam to Judah.

place. His fears would be not so much for himself—although his men at least would not be free from such fears—as for his Judæan fellow-countrymen. Moreover, he saw an opportunity of making himself useful in the neighbourhood. The city of Keilah,[1] which probably lay between Judah and the Philistines, and was therefore still Canaanitish, was being threatened by the Philistines. David attacked them, took from them rich spoil, delivered Keilah, and settled there.[2] Saul heard the news with joy. If his enemy were once in a city, even were it walled, he could beleaguer him and must eventually get him into his hands. Accordingly he summoned the army of Israel, and determined to lay siege to Keilah. David, however, had reason to fear being delivered up to Saul by the inhabitants, and so, following an oracle of Yahvé, he left the city with his troop, now six hundred strong. He preferred to move about here and there in the mountains as hitherto. The wandering life of an adventurer afforded him much better protection from Saul's troops than staying in one place.[3]

The mountain country around Hebron, abounding as it did in dens and caverns, seems now to have become his special abode.[4] It is not impossible that Jonathan once paid him here a secret visit, with the view of encouraging his friend and 'strengthening his hand in God.'[5]

From this point onwards we lose almost all trace of David's doings and movements. It is not that we have no statements referring to this time, but that there are too many of them. Here, in the immediate neighbourhood of his home, inventive legend was probably specially active; it delighted to magnify the heroic figure of David with adventurous and wonderful incidents and experiences of all kinds, the historical basis of which we can now only partly discover. Thus it is to this time and place that an

---

[1] On the age of this place, *vide* Sayce, *Acad.* 1889, 19 Jan.
[2] 1 Sam. xxiii. 1-5. Ver. 6 is from R; see above, p. 40 f. On the credibility of this and the following story, see especially Kamph. *ZAW.* vi. 74 ff.
[3] 1 Sam. xxiii. 6-13. [4] 1 Sam. xxiii. 19 ff.
[5] 1 Sam. xxiii. 14-18. On this, *cf.* p. 41. Yet, even if the passage is documentary (SS), it is not to be denied that its contents awaken certain suspicions. *Cf.* Stade,[2] 247.

incident displaying David's magnanimity in sparing Saul's life, seems to belong. But the detailed account of the incident is to be found in our documents in two different versions,[1] and we have in at least one of them the result of the free elaboration of the affair in the mouth of the people, while it is probable that this is to be seen in both of them.

On the other hand, we stand once more on firm historical ground when we pass to another incident of this time. In the neighbourhood of Hebron, as the history of the conquest has already taught us, the tribe of Caleb had its seat. A wealthy man of this tribe who lived in Maon, Nabal by name, was, as David learned, celebrating with his men the feast of sheep-shearing at Carmel, a little town south-east of Hebron, towards the Dead Sea.[2] Nabal possessed three thousand sheep and one thousand goats. David, who had his camp in the wilderness of Maon, had naturally to find sustenance for his troop, now grown to six hundred men. He had to trust to such booty as he could gather from predatory nomads who might overrun the Negeb of Judah, and to what he could exact from the cattle-owners of the Negeb, whose natural protector he was. Thus he had a right to demand of the wealthy Nabal a share for himself and his people of the feast that was being kept.

He sent messengers reminding Nabal of the protection he had been to him, and asking for his reward. Nabal answered them roughly and brusquely: there were servants in abundance escaped from their masters; was he to prepare for such his bread, his wine,[3] and his cattle? David resolved to avenge the insult. He took four hundred of his men with him to chastise Nabal, while two hundred remained behind in the camp. Nabal's wife, Abigail, recognising how much her husband had been benefited by David, and fearing David's vengeance, went out with rich presents to meet him. She succeeded in appeasing his rage. When Nabal,

---

[1] 1 Sam. xxiv. (Da) and xxvi. (SS). See above, p. 41 f.
[2] On Carmel, *cf.* Bädek.[2] 179 [Eng. Trans. (1894), p. 144].
[3] So, according to LXX., in 1 Sam. xxv. 11.

who had gone to some excess at the feast, was struck with apoplexy and died a few days later, David sought the hand of his clever and beautiful wife. Not only did Nabal's considerable possessions thus come into his hands, but what was of much more importance to David, by marrying into one of the wealthiest and most influential families of Caleb he established himself in that tribe, which was in great part Israelitish, and, where not Israelitish, at all events nearly related to Israel.[1]

Perhaps this very circumstance occasioned him new troubles from Saul. Not only would Saul feel himself touched in the honour of his family by David's new alliance,[2] but, what is more to the point, the fact that a homeless freebooter had become a rich *sheikh* of the tribe of Caleb, would give him cause for actual anxiety. It is a fact that David, who had probably remained some time in this neighbourhood, no longer felt himself safe here. Driven first of all from the south-west, now from the south-east, and thus reduced to the last extremities, David seemed to have no choice but to take a final and desperate step. He went over with his six hundred men to the territory of the Philistine king of Gath, Achish ben Maoch. At his own request, as he did not care to remain long at the royal residence, a country town called Ziklag[3] was given him in fief by Achish. David would, for reasons easily imagined, feel himself safer from suspicion and strife at some distance from the court than in the capital.[4]

This was something unprecedented that had happened. David, the patriot, the most popular man in Israel, their most successful and celebrated champion against the Philistines, had actually gone over to this hereditary foe of Israel. Not long before—it can hardly have been more than a year—after being pursued to death by Saul, he had let his old passion, the Philistine war, revive once more, and snatched Keilah from the hands of the enemy. Now

---

[1] 1 Sam. xxv. 1-43 (Da), one of our best narratives.
[2] *Cf.* 1 Sam. xxv. 44, and also above, p. 41, note 4.
[3] On its position, see Mühlau in Richm's *HWB*.
[4] 1 Sam. xxvii. 1 ff. See also above, p. 42, and especially Kamph. *ZAW.* vi. 85 ff.

he was one of them. How is such a change conceivable? How could the Philistines bring themselves to receive him?

This is, however, not the only case in history of two that have before been at variance, uniting in common hatred of a third, and so forgetting what has hitherto kept them apart. It is not even necessary to suppose an old understanding, according to which David had even before this time agreed to spare Philistine territory,[1] although such a supposition is not excluded. The approximation may, I believe, very well have been brought about suddenly and independently. David was, whenever he might come, a valuable ally for the Philistines. He had been, as long as he remained in the service of Saul, their most dangerous enemy; and who could say whether Saul might not, after all, if the Philistines pressed upon him hard enough, some time recognise his own interest and become reconciled to David? Or, what would happen if the feeble king should die, and Jonathan should lead back in triumph his long-persecuted friend? In short, it would be good for the Philistines, in any case, to have David on their side. For then, it seemed, he would become for ever harmless as a fighter for Israel against Philistia.

David's step, however, naturally presupposes that definite arrangements were now made between David and Achish. If David wished to be regarded as a friend of the Philistines, and maintain himself as such, he must of necessity offer certain guarantees of the loyalty of his intentions. He must pledge himself to military service with Achish in the event of a war with Saul;[2] nay, he must even now bring proofs that he had really become Saul's foe, and the Philistines' friend. David's ingenuity and shrewdness achieved even this, without his being actually reduced to the position of taking the field against Israel. From his new abode at Ziklag—and now we understand better why the capital seemed to him an uncomfortable residence—he often undertook expeditions, from which he returned home laden with booty.

[1] So Kamph. *loc. cit.*, pp. 82, 89.
[2] See 1 Sam. xxviii. 1, and Kamph. *loc. cit.*, p. 84.

These were directed apparently and ostensibly against Judah, but in reality against the desert tribes of Arabs. As a protection against discovery in these secret proceedings, all were put to death wherever he went—men, women, and probably even children.[1]

It was indeed a desperate step that David had taken. Only the courage of despair could have enabled him to carry his policy through. If he did not wish indeed to become a traitor to his people, if he wished to be better than he pretended to Achish to be, he had no choice left but dissimulation, falsehood, deceit, and even cruel murder. It was a dangerous game that David was playing, all the more daring that he could never, after all, be sure how long duplicity and deceit would succeed in deceiving Achish. An accident might any day bring about discovery, and with it his certain and ignominious destruction. Only deliverance from this unbearable and unworthy situation could now save him. It was David's good fortune that he was soon delivered from it, although the hardest trial of all yet awaited him.

§ 42. *Continuation. Saul's End.*

The consequences of David's going over to Achish, and alliance with him, were not long in showing themselves. The Philistines felt themselves now sufficiently strong to undertake once more a decisive attack on Israel: they hoped for a return of the times of Eli and Samuel. Achish gathered his army. David, being now a Philistine vassal, was simply reminded by Achish of his duty, and promised to do it. Like others before him, this Philistine king was unable to withstand the captivating power of David's personality: he trusted him unconditionally, and even appointed him one of his own bodyguard.[2] His fellow-kings, who probably had no knowledge of David from personal intercourse, and saw in him only the former champion of their enemies, the favourite of Saul and the friend of Jonathan, thought otherwise.

---

[1] On the credibility of this narrative (1 Sam. xxvii. 8-12), see Kamph. *loc. cit.*, p. 85 ff., as against Duncker, Wellhausen, and Stade.

[2] 1 Sam. xxviii. 1, 2.

As they had done a few decades before, the forces of the Philistines now set forth northwards, with the view of advancing against Israel from the plain of Jezreel.[1] As Saul's kingdom does not seem to have reached any farther north, they were protected in the rear. Thus far David had gone with them loyally: now, matters must be decided. The collision of the forces was at hand; what should become of him?

It is hard to say what David could possibly have done if Achish had insisted on his right to make use of his services, and had actually taken him with him into battle against Saul and Israel. Would he—as Duncker and others believe he was capable of doing[2]—have unhesitatingly wielded the sword against his people? Or would he, at the last moment, have refused to serve Achish—a step which would have been certain death? Or, finally, would the shrewdness that never failed him have found even now a means of relieving him from the painful necessity of playing the traitor, either on this side or on that? The situation was so critical that probably many others would not have been able to endure the inner conflict so long. Not so David. He advanced with the host to Aphek, certainly with no light heart, but doubtless leaving his cause even now to his God whom he had ever trusted.[3]

In point of fact, at the last hour the deliverance did come. The chiefs accompanying Achish, not convinced by their suzerain's confidence in David, imperiously demanded his withdrawal from the army. It was enough for them that David did not fight against them; anything more they did not expect of him. We cannot regard them as wrong; any other prudent commander, less full of confidence than Achish, would have acted as they desired. Human nature is not to be counted on. Who can say whether, had Achish carried out his will, the result might not have proved those men right, at least if circumstances had so turned

---

[1] 1 Sam. xxix. 1 ff. The passage forms the continuation of xxviii. 1, 2. See above, p. 42 f.

[2] Against Duncker, and also Wellh. and Stade, see espec. Kamph. *ZAW.* vi. 86 f.   [3] *Cf.* his conduct at Nob, Keilah, and later at Ziklag.

out that David's interference could still have been of any considerable use to Israel?

It was only another demonstration of David's often-proved shrewdness, that he indignantly repelled as an insult to his honour, what he certainly in his heart ardently desired. It was with reluctance that Achish yielded, and he tried to excuse himself to David. But David was now free.[1] He returned to Ziklag. Arriving there on the third day, he found the city empty and reduced to a heap of ashes. The Amalekites, no doubt taking their revenge for raids undertaken by David from Ziklag, had made an attack during his absence, burnt and plundered the city, and carried away wives and children. David's men broke into loud lament. There threatened to be a mutiny against himself, for it was on him that his men laid the responsibility for the disaster. They would recall his cruel conduct against the Bedouins of the desert. David, quickly making up his mind, inquired of Yahvé, and determined to pursue the enemy. Two hundred of his men, who were worn out, he left behind at the Wadi esh-Sheri'a: the other four hundred went on southwards. A man whom they found half-dead by the way and brought back to life, pointed out the track. He was the Egyptian slave of an Amalekite who had taken part in the expedition. Thus David was able to make a sudden attack. The men who did not escape were slain, and the spoil they had taken from Ziklag, people and cattle, besides other rich booty, was recovered.[2]

Meanwhile, in the plain of Kishon, the fate of Saul and his followers had been speedily determined. Like Israel in the days of Eli, Saul did not wait for the Philistines to establish themselves in the plain of Jezreel and thence force their way on into the middle of the land. He proceeded himself against them there. Once more the battle was to be fought in the plain of Jezreel or its neighbourhood. Before Saul had called out his army, the Philistines had already become masters of the plain, and were encamped at its eastern end at Shunem. Saul assembled his

[1] 1 Sam. xxix. [2] 1 Sam. xxx.

army on Mount Gilboa.¹ It was here the battle had to be fought.

As he had done on previous occasions, Saul now sought an intimation of Yahvé's will before advancing to the decisive battle. Evil dreams had cast into a deeper gloom the already clouded mind of the unhappy ruler. The oracular decision of the sacred lot and the prophetic judgment which he procured, did not seem to him to be auspicious.² His gloomy spirit was filled with anxious forebodings. Anguish of mind drove the unhappy man to the last means of procuring the desired communication, a means the use of which had been forbidden by himself. His misfortune was connected with the name of Samuel. Since the latter had forsaken him, Saul had been forsaken by God. Samuel was indeed long since dead; but in this hour of mortal peril Saul felt he must see him once again to ask his counsel. He stole away by night in disguise, accompanied by only a few trusted attendants, to Endor, where dwelt a woman who practised necromancy. Even apart from this he was not free of superstition;³ but in union with Samuel, and no doubt at the latter's instigation, he had forbidden the black arts associated with it to be used in Israel. Now, in his despair, he was inconsistent with himself. The shrewd woman quickly perceived who was consulting her. It would indeed not be hard to discover, from the nature and connection of the questions, who the questioner was. Samuel, whom the woman brought up to speak to him, gave him little encouragement. Deeply affected, already bowed down by care, and exhausted unto death, Saul returned again by night to his camp.⁴ Next morning the battle began.

The cause of Saul was lost before a single blow had been

---

[1] 1 Sam. xxviii. 4. The passage xxviii. 3-25 (SS cf. p. 42 f.) properly follows chap. xxix. f. There is no need to assume (Stade,¹ 255) a previous battle in the plain in consequence of which Israel was driven back into Gilboa.

[2] It is thus we are to understand v. 6. He probably received an answer, but such as did not satisfy him.   [3] Cf. chap. xiv.

[4] The story is (against Stade,¹ 255) to be regarded as historical. The character of SS admits, and internal grounds do not forbid, the belief that the narrative xxviii. 3-25 rests on a real incident.

struck for it, for energy deserts an army when its leader is hopeless. Saul's forces were defeated and fled, and his three elder sons, Jonathan, Abinadab, and Melchishua fell. He himself was hard beset by the Philistine archers, and when his armour-bearer refused his request to smite him to death, he threw himself on his own sword to escape the foeman's hand.

The pursuers gave no thought as yet to the slain; over their bodies they passed in search of the survivors, till night fell, mercifully concealing the battlefield and its royal dead. Not till morning, when the victors returned to plunder the slain, did they find among the rest the body of Saul. Cutting off his head, they sent it along with his armour as a trophy to their own land. The body they hung up, as an insult to Israel, on the wall of Bethshean. The citizens of Jabesh Gilead (the place where Saul had achieved his first military success) loyally and gratefully remembered their former deliverer. They came in haste to Bethshean, carried away the body by night, and gave it an honourable burial at their own city of Jabesh.[1]

With the fall of Saul Israel lost a hero who had begun his career with brilliance and great promise. He seemed to be called to do great things. A very talented nature, richly gifted, quick to decide, firm of hand, bold to venture, valiant in battle, animated with zeal for the greatness of Israel, and devoutly attached to Yahvé, he stopped suddenly short in his course, paralysed by a mysterious power. He suddenly showed himself unequal to the task that his nation and his crown imposed upon him, without our being able to say wherein exactly his weakness or his fault lay. His relation to Samuel had certainly something to do with it. But what was it that Samuel required of him, or he of Samuel? Why was the thought of the distress of their native land, and of all they had in common, not enough to overcome what divided them? That the difference was of a religious nature, is

---

[1] 1 Sam. xxxi. (Da). On the duration of Saul's reign see Kamphausen, *Chronologie der hebr. Könige*, p. 16. He supposes twenty years. On Saul's age at the time of his accession (1 Sam. xiii. 1) see Kamph. in *Rhein. Gem.-Blatt*, 1884, No. 6 ff.; and Driver, *Notes*, 74 f. On the chronology see below, § 53a.

hardly to be doubted. Perhaps the fact that during his whole career Saul never once thought of the ancient shrine, the ark of Yahvé, is not without significance.[1] It must have lain close to Samuel's heart from the days of Shiloh onwards. Moreover, it is hardly accidental that the note of irritation against the monarchy which our younger source discloses, was connected with the person and monarchy of Saul, and that it sees in the latter a rejection of Yahvé, and a monarchy after the manner of the heathen. This aversion may apply to Saul not simply as first representative of the monarchy. We shall rather be disposed to derive from it the impression that, with all his patriotic zeal,[2] Saul was yet deficient in the deeper understanding of Israel's peculiar religious character and special task. An estrangement between him and Samuel was thus inevitable.

But even did we know more facts than the imperfect tradition has preserved for us, the fate of Saul would not lose for us its deep mysteriousness. The veil which envelops every genuinely tragical form in human history, would still obscure his inner being and the cause of his fate. From the very beginning there slumbered in his nature, so rich in noble capacities, darker as well as brighter influences and tendencies. With a noble enthusiasm and a mysterious capacity of prophetic ecstasy[3] there were associated in him, even in happier days, blind zeal, wild fanaticism, and terrifying superstition.[4] His temperament, half-sanguine, half-choleric, was precisely that which is so apt to lead on to a dangerous melancholy. But all these germs and indications are insufficient really to explain the calamitous crisis in his inner consciousness and in his fortunes. The tragedy in his life consisted in this, that a dark overpowering fate, the cause of which we do not clearly understand, compelled the infatuated man to ruin himself by fatal broodings, all his energy paralysed, himself alienated from his duty, and sinking deeper and deeper in mental

---

[1] [Yet cf. the note, on p. 108, on Kosters' view.]
[2] See especially 2 Sam. xxi. 1 ff.
[3] Cf. the saying, 'Is Saul among the prophets?'
[4] Cf. especially 1 Sam. xiv.

gloom. It is very significant that Saul fell finally by his own hand: ever since his star began to decline, it was his fate to consume his own energies through suspicion and blind passion, and in his delusion to be the artificer of his own ruin. That in spite of all this, Saul's noble nature, and the place he occupied in Israel in his better days, and his achievements for his country, were not forgotten, is shown by the generous deed of the citizens of Jabesh, and by the elegy that David sang over him, speaking as he did for the hearts of mourning Israel.[1]

[1] 2 Sam. i. 17 ff. The story is undoubtedly genuine; yet *cf.* Budde, *RiSa*, 238 f.

CHAPTER III.

DAVID, KING.

§ 43. *David and Eshba'al.*

THE position produced by the fall of Saul and his comrades was very critical. Under him, even if its measure of success had been variable, Israel had continued to fight with the Philistines, and had at last kept them off fairly well. Now, however, war was no longer to be thought of. Israel's forces were scattered or annihilated, and their leaders fallen. The enemy lost no time in improving their victory to the full. The plain of the Kishon, not only as far as Gilboa, but even on to Bethshean, and the cities of the Jordan valley on both sides of the stream, fell at once into their hands.[1] Who could prevent them from getting possession, as before, of the mountains of Ephraim, and installing their representative in Gibeah of Saul?

For the present the way thither was open to the Philistines. If they did not avail themselves of it, it was probably policy that warned them to be moderate. They knew the energies that slumbered in Israel; and although Saul's army had been this time defeated and even destroyed, the men of Israel had learned and practised the art of war under him and his heroes; it was not expedient to exasperate them to the utmost. Moreover, Saul's dynasty was not extinct, and Abner, the leader of his forces, was still alive; these would have to be reckoned with.

We are not told how Abner escaped from the battle of Gilboa, although it is quite probable that he was present at it, nor how

---

[1] 1 Sam. xxxi. 7.

much of Saul's army he succeeded in rescuing. There would hardly be enough to permit of Abner's continuing the war against the Philistines. It is much more probable that Abner and Eshba'al (Ishbosheth[1])—the surviving son of Saul, in whose behalf he acted, and to whom by right of succession the throne of David passed—submitted to a peace which allowed Saul's dynasty to reign over Israel at least in name. It is, however, significant enough that Eshba'al's residence was no longer at Gibeah, the royal city of Saul, nor even in Benjamin at all, or anywhere west of the Jordan, but in the long famous Mahanaim on the Jabbok. It was certainly not of their own free will that Eshba'al and Abner transferred the centre of sovereignty to the east of the Jordan, where there were always narrower limits to the freedom of Israel's development. We must rather see in this, for the Philistines, one of the fruits of their victory, and for Eshba'al, one of the humiliating conditions of the peace and of his reign. In other words, as Kamphausen acutely saw and successfully proved,[2] Israel was tolerated as a kingdom at all, only as a vassal state of the Philistines. It was tributary and compelled to seek its centre of gravity in the east, so as to be farther from the Philistines, and thus not exposed to such immediate danger. Nay, it is not impossible that it was also only by paying tribute to the Moabites and Ammonites, whom his father had conquered, that Eshba'al secured the friendliness even of these neighbours.[3] In any case, the kingdom of Saul played a most ignoble part under the intellectually insignificant Eshba'al and the violent Abner—although it is rather of his words than of his deeds that we hear.

It could only be to the interest of the Philistines to increase the unsubstantiality of Eshba'al's authority. Hence they must have been eager to avail themselves of every opportunity by

---

[1] We have still a trace of the original form and pronunciation of the name in the Εἰσβααλ of the LXX. (see Holmes and Parsons, Cod. 93, Aqu. Symm. Theod.); also in the Eshba'al of 1 Chron. viii. 33, ix. 39. It is interesting that in 1 Sam. xiv. 49, a son of Saul's is called Jishwî [Ishvi] (=Ishjô=Eshba'al).

[2] In the article, 'The Philistines and the Hebrews in the time of David,' in ZAW. vi. 43 ff. On the opposing view of Ewald, Köhler, Orelli, Wellh., and others, see *ibid.* p. 46 f.   [3] Kamphausen, *loc. cit.* p. 68 f.

which new difficulties could be created for the insignificant and inactive vassal state, by which any desire to recover itself would be nipped in the bud once for all. Such considerations enable us to understand how David had no difficulties of any kind put in his way by the Philistines, who were to a certain extent now masters of the situation throughout the whole of Saul's kingdom, although David's plans might, if circumstances favoured, become very dangerous even to them.

We must not forget that at this time David was a vassal of the Philistines at Ziklag, and was bound to them in military service. As he had entered into this relationship of his own free will, he could doubtless dissolve it at any time; but yet in view of the position that he had hitherto occupied towards the Philistines, especially in view of their present predominant influence, he could undertake nothing in that region which was not agreeable to them. We left David at Ziklag as he had returned laden with booty from his pursuit of the Amalekites. It cannot have been more than a few days before the news of what had happened during the interval of his absence reached him. On the third day after his return he received the first tidings through an Amalekite, who brought him Saul's royal insignia, perhaps on the pretence that he had at Saul's request himself dealt him his death-blow.[1] One cannot see why this whole narrative should be regarded as a pure fiction.[2] It is enough to suppose that the bearer of the tidings, hoping to win a substantial reward from David, lied as to his own conduct. There was abundant opportunity for despoiling Saul's body on the night after his death, during which it lay on the field of battle. Moreover it was not unnatural to see in David, if not the future king of Israel, at least the person who on the death of Saul and Jonathan could think of securing for himself a share of the inheritance.

[1] 2 Sam. i. 1-16.

[2] So Stade (258 f.) and others; i. 6-16 belongs to SS (see above, p. 43), but on account of iv. 10 there must have stood a parallel in Da. Only there was there no account of the slaying of Saul. All the rest is unobjectionable.

How easily, on the other hand, similar thoughts would occur to David himself, and so probably to others also, is shown by the circumstance that David employed part of the booty which he had just brought with him from his raid against Amalek, in sending presents to the tribal chiefs in Judah.[1] We have every right to assume that this measure of David's, since his predatory expedition and the death of Saul were so closely connected in time, took place not before but after the arrival of the disastrous news about Saul and Jonathan. What else could the presents signify than that they were to support David's candidature for the sovereignty in Judah, and to make the tribal chiefs favourable to him? They had the same meaning as the congratulations offered shortly afterwards to Jabesh in Gilead, in recognition of the noble spirit it had shown towards Saul.[2] What David in this latter case directly expressed—that their lawful king was dead, and they might now look to him—he would doubtless not withhold from the nobles of Judah on the occasion of sending the presents in question.

These nobles likewise could have no doubt, on a little reflection, what they ought to do. Here in Judah, if anywhere, the discontent with Saul's rule would find expression. The persecution of David must have been keenly felt by his tribe. Moreover, after the overthrow of the army, the land was open to the Philistines. Abner and Eshba'al were not in a position to offer protection. What wonder if the south, lying as it did nearest to the enemy, should seek to secure itself as far as it could? Nothing could present a better opportunity for this than David's offer. He was not only a fellow-tribesman of Judah, and since the death of Nabal a rich landowner there; not only a leader against the Philistines long crowned with victory, and honour; he was also now a vassal and tributary of the Philistines. So long as he continued in this position (and there must have been negotiations on this subject beforehand with Achish, as well as with the nobles of Judah),

---

[1] 1 Sam. xxx. 26 ff.
[2] 2 Sam. ii. 5 ff. Klosterm. (*SaKö*) supposes presents to have been sent.

Judah could be at rest with regard to invasion from the Philistines. If, however, at any time this relation should be dissolved, David, the approved champion against the Philistines, would be the best man for Judah and Israel to have at their head.

We have already seen what the considerations may have been which led the Philistines to allow David to go his own way, without seriously inquiring whether they would not afterwards have to regret bitterly having given their consent to what was now happening. Their consent to his plans naturally presupposed David's assurance that he would be willing to remain their vassal as before. In view of this, two kings in Israel instead of one, would be quite welcome to the Philistines. They could hope that each in turn would be held in check by the other. If they overlooked the extraordinary personality of David, they could in fact count on being able to make use of the one to hold within bounds any possible encroachments on the part of the other. But David had ere this defeated many shrewd calculations.

Thus David, as he was favoured also by Yahvé and his oracle, became king over Judah. He took up his abode, at the command of Yahvé, at Hebron, the ancient capital of the district. Here he was also anointed in due form as king over the house of Judah.[1] For seven and a half years, according to the statement of our documents, he ruled over this kingdom.[2] There is no ground for calling in question the correctness of this chronology. This was a modest beginning if David already meditated reigning over an individual and independent Israel. But as compared with the danger that had for years threatened him, and with the fate which had brought him in these last months to the brink of destruction, it was a promising turn of events. Moreover, David was the man to bide his time in patience. If he had learned anything in the storms and battles of his time of flight, it must have been patience and prudent self-restraint.

How David's step was regarded at Mahanaim where Eshba'al,

---

[1] 2 Sam. ii. 1-4.
[2] 2 Sam. ii. 11; cf. Kamphausen, *Chronologie der hebr. Könige*, p. 16.

or rather Abner in his name, was reigning, may be imagined. It must have been regarded as an attack on the house of Saul, and its legitimate rule. Hence the whole time that David was at Hebron—*i.e.* the time preceding Eshbaʻal's death—was occupied with a civil war between Judah and the North.[1] Only, as Kamphausen has rightly emphasised,[2] we must be on our guard against forming too large notions as to the extent of this war. David had in fact no interest in pushing forward the war with special energy. It was otherwise than by force of arms that he had to reach his goal. Eshbaʻal, indeed, remained in a state of war with David throughout the whole of his reign of seven and a half years. But David seems to have confined himself substantially to defensive measures, while his opponent lacked, not indeed the will, but the needful strength, for a vigorous prosecution of the struggle. Among the people at large also, a domestic war would find little sympathy, and what sympathy ever existed[3] became less and less. For time only served to force, even on the Northern tribes, a clearer perception of the fact, that the star of Saul's house was sinking, and that David was the rising star in Israel, to whom the future belonged. If it was in itself a misfortune that Eshbaʻal, whether of age or not,[4] disappeared entirely behind the figure of his general Abner, the latter was himself far from being in a position to bear comparison with David. Personally brave, and, so long as Eshbaʻal allowed him to do as he pleased, faithfully devoted to the house of Saul, he yet did not in any respect achieve anything extraordinary. Hence, of necessity, the sympathy of Israel as a whole turned more and more to David. There was no hope of any one but David being adequate to the task under which the house of Saul had succumbed, and was daily succumbing further. Thus we can see David's power growing visibly,

---

[1] 2 Sam. iii. 1, 6.   [2] *ZAW.* vi. 72.

[3] So Meyer, *Gesch. d. Alt.* § 306.

[4] The one is assumed by Kamphausen, the other by Stade. Eshbaʻal appears, at all events, to have been young. The number 40 in 2 Sam. ii. 10 (see above, p. 46) for Eshbaʻal's age, is just as impossible as the two years there assumed for Eshbaʻal's reign. The latter, like David in Hebron, must have reigned seven and a half years. On this last point see Kamph. *ZAW.* vi. 44 f.

almost from day to day, while Eshba'al's throne was gradually becoming weaker and weaker.[1] Meanwhile, David's cleverness and moderation achieved more than one triumph.

Meagre as the information is that has reached us concerning individual events of the war which filled the seven and a half years of the reign of Eshba'al, we are not left absolutely in the dark. We have no right to declare what little has reached us purely unhistorical, although legendary elements have attached themselves to it. A battle took place at Gibeon, which turned out unfavourably for Abner and his army. On David's side fought Joab and his two brothers, Abishai and Asahel. The latter, 'swift of foot as one of the gazelles of the field,'[2] outstripped the rest in pursuit of the flying foe. He would not desist from following Abner, though the latter, fearing the revenge of Joab, warned him to do so. So Abner slew him, thereby sealing his own fate.[3]

This encounter between the forces of David and Eshba'al was certainly not the only one that there was to report. But the narrator may have desired as far as possible to efface the memory of the times of this inglorious civil war. Such further contests as there might be to relate, would hardly be unfavourable to David:[4] but his military reputation was too firmly established to need to be set in a clearer light at the cost of the house of Saul. On the other hand, how indefensible the position of Eshba'al as against David became in the course of time, appears of itself, without any further description of the events of the war.

David, indeed, had certainly done his best to win sympathy for himself in the domain of Eshba'al as far as it went. In his message to Jabesh in Gilead, he had notified the city that Judah had anointed him king in Hebron, and, adroitly recognising their noble conduct toward Saul, had pointed out to the citizens that,

---

[1] 2 Sam. iii. 1.   [2] 2 Sam. ii. 18.
[3] 2 Sam. ii. 12-32. The passage *vv.* 13-16 seems to be an etymological legend (Stade, Kamph. *ZAW*. vi. 71); but the battle itself, in view of the later events which cannot possibly be an invention, is certainly historical.
[4] *Cf.* 2 Sam. iii. 1.

with the death of the latter their obligations to his house were at an end.[1] This message was certainly not the only one of its kind. David was not the man to neglect his advantage. All that could be done quietly, without raising the suspicion of the Philistines, and without incurring the displeasure of the northern tribes, he did. But what helped him most was the incapacity of Eshba'al himself, the fruits of which David could watch quietly coming to maturity. A comparison between him and his rival would, even in the territory of Eshba'al, result more and more in favour of David.

Hence we cannot wonder that in course of time a party was formed, among the nobles of Israel themselves, that took a decided stand on David's side, and believed that Israel's future depended on his ruling over the whole nation. Moreover, in consequence of Eshba'al's incapacity, the Philistine yoke must have become ever more oppressive, and the longing for a deliverer—a champion against the Philistines, such as Saul had once been—ever more burning.[2] The time had thus come for David to act, in accordance with the divine call of which he had probably long been conscious.[3] But now also he was spared the necessity of reaching his goal by force. His God whom he trusted had appointed that the ripe fruit should fall into his hands.

Up to this point Abner had faithfully held to Eshba'al. Saul's house was also his own.[4] The crown of Benjamin was the pride of his tribe and family. The ambition and lust of power which were united in his character, found sufficient food in the prominent position that he had acquired at the side of Eshba'al. Everything was made dependent on his person and his personal feelings. His king might have reason enough for jealousy and dissatisfaction. But he would not allow such feelings to appear in the case of one who had become indispensable to him. On one occasion matters culminated in a rather serious outburst. Abner was believed to

---

[1] See above, p. 140 f.   [2] *Cf.* 2 Sam. iii. 17.
[3] *Cf.* 2 Sam. iii. 18. Abner's speech to Eshba'al (iii. 9 f.) can hardly have been spoken as here given.
[4] He was Saul's cousin (Kamph. 64), hardly his uncle.

have taken to himself a concubine of Saul's. In accordance with the ideas of the age this aroused in Eshba'al serious suspicions of Abner's loyalty. He became afraid that Abner was striving for his throne. With this, Abner's adherence to his cause was at an end. It was probably less fear of Eshba'al that influenced him, than other considerations; for the quarrel could easily have been settled had he so wished. It was rather a welcome occasion, enabling Abner with some show of right to turn to the rising star.[1]

Abner immediately entered into negotiations with David. He offered not only to go over to him himself, but also to bring over all Israel.[2] We must therefore assume that he not only knew the temper of Israel, but had also taken steps to secure it. Secret arrangements, such as our documents mention,[3] between Abner and the elders of Israel, and even the nobles of Benjamin, had already doubtless taken place before Abner's breach with Eshba'al. Israel wanted David as their king because it was in him alone that they saw a deliverer from the Philistines. Abner had placed himself at the disposal of this current, and doubtless actually sought the breach with Eshba'al.

David did not accept the offer without conditions. The situation did not yet seem to him so far advanced that he could expect to set himself on the throne of Saul, without fear of opposition and a prolongation of the dissension. For this purpose the bond must first be restored that once united him to the house of Saul, and would give him some right to think of succeeding him. He demanded back his wife Michal, Saul's daughter, whom Saul had taken from him.[4]

To obtain her he must have the help of Abner. Moreover, Abner was still his master's counsellor, and if the quarrel between them had already occurred, there would be the more likelihood of Eshba'al's hoping to pacify his angry general again by humouring him in this matter. For David, everything depended on getting

---

[1] 2 Sam. iii. 7 ff. On the text, especially in *v.* 7, *cf.* Wellh. *TBS.*; Driver, *Notes*; Klosterm. *SaKö*; and my translation.
[2] 2 Sam. iii. 12.   [3] 2 Sam. iii. 17-19.   [4] 2 Sam. iii. 13.

possession of his wife, not by force, but by way of right. If this were once accomplished, everything else would come about of itself. He would make Abner welcome, and it would hardly be any longer necessary to set Eshba'al aside; in any case this would not be difficult to manage if Abner no longer supported him. David could confidently leave to Abner all care about him. It is thus that we are to understand David's going directly to Eshba'al for his wife,[1] which, after Abner's offer, might seem strange, and, what is even more astonishing, Eshba'al's showing himself ready to grant David's wish.[2] This cannot possibly have happened spontaneously. Eshba'al acted under pressure of Abner's dictation. David's superior strength was probably so well known, that if Abner likewise threw his weight into the scale, it would seem advisable to Eshba'al to oblige him in this matter. Indeed, he was so entirely in Abner's hands that Abner was able to bring it about, that he himself should be selected to convey the daughter of Saul to David.

At the head of an embassy of twenty of Eshba'al's followers, Abner conducted Michal to Hebron. At the feast which David gave in their honour, Abner renewed for himself and all Israel the offer to go over from Eshba'al to David. What David had demanded, he had done; the king's daughter had been brought back to David as his lawful wife; David could now come forward, in place of the incapable Eshba'al, as heir to the crown of Saul. David now accepted the offer, and the arrangement doubtless provided that, immediately after his return, Abner should proceed to fulfil his promise.[3] Abner thus became a traitor to his lord, and David accessory to and an abettor of a long and regularly prepared, and probably well thought out, conspiracy against Eshba'al. We have no ground or right to extenuate what David did. A reasonable judgment, however, must, at the same time, acknowledge that, in so far as we can see, David did not originate

---

[1] 2 Sam. iii. 14. David, doubtless, did this in concert with Abner.
[2] 2 Sam. iii. 15. He had Michal brought, first of all, by Abner to Mahanaim (Klosterm.).   [3] 2 Sam. iii. 20 f.

the conspiracy, but only accepted its fruits. As matters stood David's course was the only possible one. If Eshba'al was once recognised as incapable of accomplishing for Israel the task that devolved on the successor of Saul, David, who had long felt in himself Yahvé's call to be Israel's king and deliverer, had a right to bid Israel welcome if they voluntarily came over to him. He could leave it to Abner to bear the responsibility of his own acts; to hinder him was not in his province.

Yet Abner was not to live to complete his work. His fate overtook him while he was still in Hebron. Joab, David's ambitious and violent captain, as Abner had slain Asahel, was necessarily his mortal enemy. Moreover, if Joab knew of Abner's plans, personal jealousy might also come into play. David had taken the precaution of having Joab at a distance from Hebron. Returning before the time, however, Joab was able to get Abner into his hands, and, acting in an illegal way as avenger[1] of his brother Asahel, he slew him in the gate of Hebron.[2] David had every reason to be angry with Joab, and sincerely to mourn over Abner. Not only did his plans with Abner seem to have come to nothing, but the shadow of ignominious treachery might only too easily fall from Joab on to David himself. For, at least in the eyes of the uninitiated, there had fallen with Abner the one support of Eshba'al's throne. And yet, as we know, there was not the slightest motive for David's getting Abner out of the way.

But Eshba'al's fate also hastened to its accomplishment. He was treacherously slain by two Benjamite chieftains. At noontide, while the portress was asleep, and Eshba'al himself was taking his mid-day rest on his couch, they broke into the palace and slew him.[3] Did David know of this, or have a hand in it? Hardly in any other way than that he knew of Abner's project, in which the assassination of Eshba'al may have played a part. It is therefore credible that when the murderers, expecting his thanks,

---

[1] See 1 Kings ii. 5, and Klosterm. *SaKö, ad loc.*   [2] 2 Sam. iii. 23 ff.
[3] 2 Sam. iv. On the text, especially in *v.* 6, see my translation.

brought him Eshbaʻal's head, he rewarded them just as he formerly rewarded the Amalekite who told him of the death of Saul.¹ For he could do this without making himself guilty of hypocrisy. What possible interest had David in Eshbaʻal's death, above all, as, after the assassination of Abner, 'his hands had become weak'?² Especially now that Abner was gone, but even before that, he had sufficient strength, and he did not lack opportunities, to get Eshbaʻal out of the way in open war if he had wished to do so. Moreover, Abner's death had caused him embarrassment enough. Doubtless, in the understanding come to between Abner and his associates, the fate of Eshbaʻal was involved. Now, however, on Abner's sudden death, his party was without a leader, and such as had been initiated into Abner's plans regarded his and their cause as lost. The thing to be done now was to act with double promptitude before Abner's plans should be betrayed to Eshbaʻal. If the latter were once removed, all danger would be obviated, and the murderers would be sure of David's royal thanks. But if David had not occasioned the conspiracy, he had also no reason to spare the murderers who forced themselves on him in so repulsive a way.

The last obstacle to David's extension of his rule over all Israel was thus removed. It is nowhere stated that any other son survived Saul besides Eshbaʻal. Moreover, of the three sons that fell with Saul, the two younger appear to have died childless, or, at all events, without male offspring. They were doubtless still of youthful age like Eshbaʻal himself. Jonathan alone left behind him a son, Meribaʻal, called by the later editors of our text Mephibosheth.³ At the time of his father's death he was five years of age. He was therefore now in his twelfth or thirteenth

---

¹ 2 Sam. iv. 8 ff.   ² 2 Sam. iv. 1.

³ See the correct form of the name in 1 Chron. ix. 40 (viii. 34) and LXX., Luc.; thereon Driver, *Notes*, 195 f. Meribaʻal, like Eshbaʻal, means 'man of Baʻal,'—*i.e.* of Yahvé. From aversion to the name Baʻal, later editors turned both the above names into 'man of shame.' Mephibosheth, instead of Meribosheth, is then a further malformation—if the process was not (*cf.* Luc. Μεμφιβααλ) completed in the stages Meribaʻal—Mephibaʻal—Mephibosheth (1 Chr. viii. 34; Ju. vi. 32; and Baudissin, *Studien*, i. 108).

year, and had not yet at all events any claim to the throne. Moreover, this one grandson of Saul's was a cripple. His nurse, on hearing the terrible news of the death of Saul and Jonathan, had let him fall in her flight.[1] Hence in no case could there be any question of his succeeding to the throne. There still remained of Saul's posterity two sons of his concubine Rizpah;[2] but these also were at all events still young. Israel was now, if ever, in need of a true man.

§ 44. *David in Jerusalem. The Philistines.*

It was only to David that the eyes of Israel could turn. All the tribes, represented by their nobles, came to David to Hebron and said, 'Behold, we are thy flesh and bone. In times past when Saul was still our king, it was thou that leddest out and broughtest in Israel. Yahvé also said to thee, "Thou shalt feed my people Israel, and thou shalt be prince over Israel."' Thereupon the elders of Israel anointed David king before Yahvé in Hebron.[3] Nothing brings out more clearly than these words of our narrator's, the idea that animated all Israel in calling David to the throne of Saul. It was as an illustrious leader in the Philistine wars, that he still lived in their memory. And the more inglorious and oppressive the present, the more vivid would this memory of the time of Saul necessarily be. Saul having perished in the Philistine war, it would be easy enough for any one to say that his and Israel's lot would have been better had he not wantonly driven from him the best of his heroes.

David could therefore be at no loss as to his first task as newly elected king of all Israel. What was to be done was clearly enough pointed out to him. Israel must again be made free, the Philistines must again be driven back to their coast-land. This was what the tribes meant when they asked that David in

---

[1] 2 Sam. iv. 4. The notice is in a wrong place, but is certainly authentic.
[2] 2 Sam. xxi. 1 ff.
[3] In 2 Sam. v. 1-3, *v.* 1 f. and 3 are doublets. Perhaps *v.* 3 gives the more original account. See above, p. 46.

particular should be their leader. Thus alone could David, like Saul, ensure the continuance of the confidence with which the tribes had met him when they anointed him king.

In the land of the Philistines, too, there was a quick comprehension of the occurrence at Hebron. There was doubtless no need of many words and messages to give notice of the termination of the vassalage in which David had hitherto stood to Philistia. Saul's crown having passed to David, the relations of the latter to the Philistines, as regards the rights of Israel, were precisely the same as those of Saul had been. Nevertheless, David appears to have suffered an attack from the enemy even earlier than he could have expected it. Immediately on learning the news of the anointing of David at Hebron, the Philistines broke into Judah. David was to be surprised, and Israel's attempt to become, through him, once more independent, to be nipped in the bud. Bethlehem, David's home, was quickly taken possession of, and Hebron threatened. David was promptly informed; but he had not time to call together his forces. He was compelled to withdraw in all haste to the stronghold of Adullam,[1] once so familiar to him. Here he seems to have tarried some time, till his forces were assembled. Finally, however, he succeeded in inflicting a decided blow on the Philistines, who had their camp in the valley of the giants, the so-called plain of Rephaim, north of Jebus, toward Gibeon.[2]

The Philistines were certainly not yet annihilated, nor even effectually checked, by this defeat. Hostilities were resumed at a later date—on the occasion of another attack on Judah.[3] In obedience to the oracle of Yahvé, David made his way round the

---

[1] It is this place alone that can be meant in 2 Sam. v. 17, as well. This appears from xxiii. 13, where instead of מערת we must, according to v. 14, read מץ (cf. also וירד there and here).

[2] This account of the course of events is obtained by combining 2 Sam. v. 17 ff. and 2 Sam. xxiii. 13 ff. v. 17 connects itself immediately with v. 3 (see above, p. 46). xxiii. 13 ff. belongs chronologically between v. 17 and v. 18-21. The situation in v. 17 ff. is only explained by xxiii. 13 ff. The site of the valley of the giants is defined by Gibeon and Gezer (v. 22 ff. So already the *Onom.*, against Josephus). [3] 2 Sam. v. 22 ff.

army of the Philistines, encamped once again in the valley of the giants, and attacked them from the north, thus falling upon their rear. He routed them from Gibeon to Gezer.[1]

For the present the Philistines seem to have been brought to a halt by these two defeats, inflicted on them in rapid succession by David. But their strength was not yet broken. A series of battles may have followed, both at this time and later.[2] Yet, strange to say, the traditions that have reached us concerning David, which are in parts so copious, have almost entirely passed over these events. And this, although they determined David's position in Israel, and Israel's position in Syria, and are therefore of critical importance for the history of Israel. It will always be a mystery, what can have led the collector of our information concerning that age, after providing us with such copious accounts of David's wars with Saul, and his struggle for the crown at Hebron and Jebus, to inform the ages to come only in a meagre way of the very achievements of David, which for the most part made good his position in history.[3]

It is a fact, at all events, that before Israel could get rest from the Philistines, David had to engage in many, and doubtless serious, battles. Many a memory of David and his heroes, many a daring exploit of his brave band, that survived to after ages, is to be referred to these wars.[4] On one such occasion, David's own life was at stake;[5] on another, Goliath of Gath was slain—the warrior who lent his name to the unknown Philistine giant, slain by David himself at an earlier date.[6] At last, by a decisive blow, David succeeded in subduing the capital of the Philistines, and with it

---

[1] It is thus we must read in v. 72, with the LXX. On Gezer, see *HWB*.

[2] *Cf.* אחרי־כן, 2 Sam. viii. 1.

[3] We may perhaps conjecture that there once existed a special book—a kind of 'Book of the Wars of Yahvé'—that told of these wars. Our author would take it for granted as well known, and therefore abstain from giving larger extracts from it.

[4] See 2 Sam. xxi. 15 ff.; xxiii. 8 ff.

[5] 2 Sam. xxi. 16 f.

[6] 2 Sam. xxi. 19. See also above, p. 120; also Kamph. *St. Kr.* 1882, 117 f.; Kuenen, *T. Tijdschr.* viii. 279; also Böttcher, *Neue Ahrenlese*, No. 402.

their whole land.¹ The power of the Philistines was henceforth broken. They do not appear again [for a long time] as enemies of Israel. It was allotted to David to subdue this adversary that had committed so many outrages on Israel, and had more than once brought its existence into question. The Philistines were no longer Israel's enemies. From David's time Israel's relation to Philistia was substantially peaceable. Notwithstanding his victories, David had not really subjugated Philistia or destroyed its nationality. He was satisfied with having again made good Israel's position, and compelled the adversary to keep peace with them. The way seemed thus to have been prepared for even a tolerably friendly relation henceforth between the two. The Philistines, giving up the hope of being able to prevail by force against David, appear, like the Canaanites at an earlier date, to have set themselves more and more to come to terms with Israel as neighbours, in peace and friendliness. They were soon so little felt to be the hereditary foe of Israel, that David selected or supplemented his bodyguard from them.²

David was, however, not content with what he had so far achieved. Had he only accomplished the one thing to which he had been in the first place called—the deliverance of Israel from the yoke of the Philistines—he would still be the greatest man that Israel had produced since Moses. He had thereby restored Israel to its true position. But his aim was still higher. Israel must not only be free: it must also be able to use its freedom. This can, in any circumstances, only be the case when a nation's freedom is accompanied by national unity and strength. Israel must be united, and must be raised to an honourable position among the neighbouring states of Syria. Step by step did David approach this goal. He taught the tribes to give expression to their unity anew, and better than they had ever been able to do it

---

¹ 2 Sam. viii. 1. On אמה cf. *Bab. and Orient. Rec.*, Feb. 1890, p. 69 ff.; *Acad.* 1890, No. 929.

² The *Krethi* and *Plethi*, who have rightly been taken to be Cretans and Philistines—*i.e.* a Philistine band. See espec. 2 Sam. xv. 18 ff.; 1 Kings i. 8, 10, 38, and below, p. 164 f.

before; he qualified them, in their estimation, to control their own destinies—nay, Israel had him to thank, that for a while it was given to it to join in speaking a decisive word in the counsels of the nations of Asia west of the Euphrates. No wonder therefore that Israel knew of no greater king than David, and that his name was for all ages the expression of the greatest glory and splendour imaginable in Israel. David was the greatest man in Israel's history next to Moses, and he was at the same time the most popular.

That the tribes of Israel felt themselves to be a unity, a nation, that they also for a time gave practical proof of being a united people, was not the result of the work of David. Moses, and again at a later time Saul, for a part of the tribes also Deborah, had given expression to this ideal unity, and actually realised it in a transitory way. The tribes must now for long have known that they were members of a nation. But there was always lacking, even as far down as Saul, the power to maintain what was transiently gained. There was lacking in particular, even where freedom had really been won, a national centre round which the life of the people, political as well as religious, might gather. Only if this could be found would the unification become really complete, and the freedom that had been won by the sword be guaranteed in peace for some length of time. With inexplicable short-sightedness Saul had done practically nothing towards this end. The national sanctuary, lost and then recovered again, he had allowed to remain unnoticed in a corner of Israel, and had fixed his seat as king, just as he did as farmer, at his Benjamite home of Gibeah, a place that had neither a past nor a future—the best proof that Saul lacked the genius of the king.[1] David saw deeper than Saul. If Saul was an able warrior, who when he had put back his sword into its sheath returned to his oxen at Gibeah, David was a born ruler. He knew that religion and national life needed a centre, unity a point of support, national strength a rallying-place—in short, that the land, if it was to maintain its

[1] See Cornill, *Entstehung des V. Isr.*, p. 26.

unity and its freedom, needed a capital that would be worthy of the monarchy and would guarantee its stability.

Immediately after bringing to an end at least the first conflicts with the Philistines, David proceeded to the accomplishment of this object.[1] His choice proved him to be possessed of the insight of genius. Hebron, situated at the southern end of the land, constituting moreover the old capital of David's tribe, was neither by position nor in view of its tribal connection, fitted to form the centre of the new kingdom, which was to be lifted above the ancient tribal distinctions. Saul's residence at Gibeah was on similar grounds unsuited, in addition to being probably strategically unimportant. On the other hand, the stronghold of Jebus met the requirements of David as no other place in Israel did. Equipped by nature as an almost impregnable stronghold, Jebus was strategically one of the most important points in the land. In the centre of communication between the Mediterranean and the East, as well as Syria and Egypt, it was a natural centre for trade and intercourse in general. As it was still in the possession of the Canaanites, it was not involved in the contest as to the relative predominance of the tribes, and was fitted to remain so. And yet again, being situated tolerably near David's home, Jebus provided for the maintenance of the connection of David's throne with the tribe of Judah, a connection that was within certain limits indispensable. In fact, David's constituting Jebus — henceforth in the Old Testament called Jerusalem[2]—the capital of his kingdom, was an act of incalculably far-reaching importance. It is quite impossible to say what would

---

[1] 2 Sam. v. 4-16 or 6-16 is not in its right place. The passage belongs between v. 21 and v. 22.

[2] The meaning of the name is obscure. On this v. Grill, *ZAW.* iv. 134 ff. Hitherto it has been assumed that Jebus was the old name of the city, and Jerusalem a name conferred on it by Israel. This assumption is overthrown by the fact, observed by Sayce, that Jerusalem occurs as Uru-salim also in the Tell-el-Amarna tablets. We must accordingly suppose that Israel only restored to the city the name that from ancient times had belonged to it. Perhaps a new light thus falls also on Ju. i. 7 f. *V.* Sayce, *Acad.* 1890, April 19, 26; 1891, Feb. 7; Zimmern, *ZDPV.* 1891, 138 ff., *Z. Assyr.* 1891, 245 ff.

have become of Judah and David's throne, in the centuries after the death of Solomon, if it had not possessed Jerusalem. What share, however, Jerusalem had in the fortunes of Israel before and after the Exile, is familiar to every one who is acquainted with those fortunes. Prophets and poets soon enough recognised its importance. Judah, and even Israel, is soon hardly conceivable without Jerusalem. Its fate determined the condition of the people, and on two occasions its fall sealed also the fall of the nation. If David's successfully conducted war of deliverance against the Philistines was the first jewel that he set in his newly acquired royal crown, Jerusalem, now won and promoted to be the royal city of Israel, was the second.

Jebus was a remnant of a greater district—a strip of land belonging to the Canaanites that extended, not only in the times of the conquest but also considerably later, into the territory of Israel itself, and included such places as Gibeon, Beeroth, Kiriath Jearim, and Chephirah. Most of this district, after remaining long separate from Israel, was doubtless in the course of time absorbed. Saul had at last set himself to accomplish this by force.[1] Only Jebus, with its strong rocky fortress of Zion,[2] had obstinately resisted all attacks. Its possessors seem to have formed a separate Canaanitish tribe, called after their city, the Jebusites.

David's attempt to win the Jebusites and their city for Israel by friendly means failed.[3] Their castle seemed to the Jebusites so strong that lame and blind men appeared sufficient to defend it.[4] Not disconcerted by their contempt, David proceeded to use force, and stormed town and citadel. The citadel he took as his own possession and called it David's citadel ('the city of David'), after

---

[1] 2 Sam. xxi. 1 ff.

[2] On the position of the hill of Zion, *v.* Furrer in Schenkel's *BL.* iii. 214 ff.; von Alten and Klaiber, in *ZDPV.* iii. 116 ff., 189 ff.; iv. 18 ff.; xi. 1 ff. Also the physical maps of Zimmermann, in *Karten u. Pläne zur Topographie des alten Jerusalem,* reproduced in Rhiem's *HWB.* and in Stade,[2] 269.

[3] We must, according to v. 6, suppose such an attempt.

[4] David's answer (v. 8) to their scornful speech is now no longer intelligible. On Ṣinnôr see *Pal. Expl. Fund,* 1890, 200 ff.

he had modified it to suit himself.¹ Hiram of Tyre, to whom the friendship of his powerful neighbour must have been a matter of some importance, is said to have given him a helping hand in this work with cedar-wood and workmen.² The former possessors of the city appear not to have been treated by David according to the usages of war, but to have been spared, just as the Philistines were afterwards. At least, there were Jebusites in later times living along with Israel in Jerusalem.

The conquest of Jerusalem by David, and the designation of that city as capital of the land, had a still deeper significance. A royal seat and capital must necessarily possess also a royal sanctuary. Religion in Israel was a national affair. No event which touched the nation could dispense with it. If the national capital, the focus of the life of the people, was to answer its purpose, it must be the centre likewise of the religious life of the people. Jerusalem could attain the position it was entitled to as capital, the position too that David was, in point of fact, to give it in Israel, only by becoming the centre of the worship of Yahvé.

It is an additional proof of the greatness of David that he perceived this likewise. It is the man who understands the spirit of his age and his nation, and is able to come forward promptly and energetically in compliance with it, that makes history. David perceived that the spirit of his people and its vocation demanded a close connection between national life and religious life. He had an eye for the secret inner nature of

¹ On the site of David's citadel see the articles of Klaiber, mentioned on p. 156, note 2, and especially also Guthe's account of his excavations, in *ZDPV.* v.; above all pp. 314 ff., 330 ff.

² 2 Sam. v. 9, 11. Hiram, by the Phœnicians probably called Ḥirôm (*cf.* Εἰρῶμος; Ass. Ḥirummu), reigned altogether, according to Josephus, *Ant.* viii. v. 3 = *c. Ap.* i. 18, for thirty-four years (commonly = 969-936; see Meyer, *Gesch. d. Alt.* 345 f.). As Hiram was also a contemporary of Solomon's, this accords only with the last part of David's reign, while the building must have fallen in the earlier period. (See Riehm, in *HWB.* Artic. Ḥiram.) Hence either Josephus' numbers, taken from Menander, are inexact, or we have in our account a confusion with what Ḥiram did for Solomon. Perhaps it was really Hiram's father Abibaʻal that helped David. With reference to him, see Pietschm. *Gesch. d. Phön.* 294.

his nation, which pointed it out as the people of religion, the people of God. Thus he became not only the national but also the religious hero of Israel, and the two aspects were inseparably connected. It is not necessary to ignore David's weaknesses and despotic moods, or to make the primitive hero into a tender-hearted saint, in order to be able to appreciate his deep religious character and his importance for the religion of Israel. As Moses sheds a lustre on Israel's past, so does David on Israel's future; and in troublous days it was his name that revived Israel's dying hope and its faith in God. Yahvé, the God of Israel, became through him at once the supreme dweller in Jerusalem; the neighbour, almost the fellow-inmate—nay, the host and father, of Israel's king. Jerusalem, the city of the king, became at the same time the city of God, the holy city. David's family was Yahvé's dynasty, and its members Yahvé's sons. And even the hero of the latter age, who shall deliver Israel and the world from all troubles, could soon be hardly otherwise thought of than as a second David, as the counterpart, the great son of the glorious founder of the holy city.

The ancient shrine of the Mosaic age, the ark of God, had been almost forgotten ever since the disastrous day when it fell into the hands of the enemy. The Philistines, indeed, had felt a religious horror of it and had restored it again to Israel. But neither Saul, nor the priests of Nob, the successors of those of Shiloh, nor any one else in Israel, had shown any interest in it. It may have seemed profaned by its stay in the enemy's land. Moreover, the indifferent military success that it had brought the hosts of Israel at Aphek had probably shaken their faith in it.[1]

It was otherwise with David. He was not alarmed by the superstitious scruples of Saul and his age. He saw in the ark what it really was, and what he himself needed: the ancient shrine of Israel, which had guaranteed the presence of Yahvé in the wilderness, and with which great memories were connected. It would, in his view, be only a further reason for restoring it to

[1] See above, pp. 107 f., 136.

honour, that it had for long—perhaps from the beginning—had its seat in the tribe of Joseph. It was just the northern group of tribes that he regarded it a matter of vital importance to win over to himself and to Jerusalem.

This being so, the ark was brought in solemn procession from Ba'al Jehûda,[1] where it had stood in the house of a private individual. It was an important occasion, and the whole nation participated in the ceremony. On the way, however, an accident befell the driver of the waggon on which the ark was being carried. This disconcerted David. The delusion with which he thought he had broken, that Yahvé's hand was withdrawn from the ark, seemed after all to be based on truth. He did not dare to bring the ark to Zion. It was not till Obed-Edom[2] of Gath, in whose house the ark was now left for three months, had found it a source of blessing to himself—stranger as he was—that David ventured to carry out his design. The people escorted Yahvé up to Zion with joyful shout and sound of trumpet. David himself, dressed in the linen garments of a priest, took part in the procession, dancing[3] before the ark; and, as highest in rank, discharged the duties of the priestly office before Yahvé in Zion. Michal, Saul's proud daughter, was ashamed of her husband for thus demeaning himself before his young men and maidens. But David's pride was in being honoured of God. His was a true religious nature, that did not hesitate to approach what even in that age seemed religious eccentricity.[4]

It must appear in the highest degree surprising that David built no temple for the ark; when he had brought it into his capital and to his palace, the idea must have occurred to him of erecting there a worthy abode for Yahvé. As he did not do so,

---

[1] According to 1 Chron. xiii. 6, Josh. xv. 9 ff., 60, xviii. 14, this was the same place as Kiriath Jearim. Perhaps the place received its name from the stay of the ark. On the text, see Driver, *Notes*, 203.

[2] On the name, see *CIS*. 295; also Baethgen, *Beitr.* 10; Wellh. *Reste altarab. Heident.* 2.

[3] *Cf.* Exod. xxxii. 19; 1 Kings xviii. 26, and the name Βαλμαρκως, *Corp. Inscr. Graec.* 4536 (*cf.* Meyer in Roscher, col. 2868; Baethgen, *Beitr.* 25).

[4] 2 Sam. vi. 1-23.

he must have been influenced by special reasons and considerations. If, moreover, it is true, as the history of Samuel suggests,[1] that the ark had already had a proper temple at Shiloh, we need have no hesitation in affirming that nothing short of a divine oracle could have withheld David from building a real temple. Without such a definite declaration of Yahvé's will, it would have been culpable indifference, and sacrilegious contempt for the majesty of Yahvé, had David built no temple. There is therefore, in point of fact, no ground for calling in question as a later invention the intention of David, obviously attributed to him by the tradition, to build on Zion a temple to Yahvé, and its abandonment in obedience to a prophetic oracle. The somewhat late origin of the passage in question cannot invalidate such overpowering internal evidence as there is in favour of the fact. Nay, it is even conceivable that, on this occasion, the prospect of a stable dynasty was also presented to David by prophetic message.[2]

§ 45. *Further Wars. David's Army. Saul's House.*

David was not to be allowed to enjoy in peace what he had won. It could scarcely be otherwise, and David himself would hardly have desired it otherwise. If Israel was to be supreme in Syria, if its boundaries were to be ensured, its independence

---

[1] *Cf.* 1 Sam. i. 24, iii. 3; Jer. vii. 14. The later representation (D^2) in 2 Sam. vii. 6 is somewhat different.

[2] 2 Sam. vii. It depends on the age and literary structure of this important chapter. On this question, see Wellh. *Bl.*[4] 223; Kuen. § xxii. 5; Budde, *RiSa*, 244 f. I regard it as proved, that the chapter as we now read it comes from circles closely related to D. It is not, however, simply to be regarded as Deuteronomic; for (*a*) ver. 13 is an interpolation which breaks the connection (Wellhausen), and only after its removal do vers. 11-17 give a satisfactory sense. Why should Solomon be called 'son of God,' and not David, if ver. 14 must refer to an individual? *Cf.* also ver. 16 and ver. 19, where it is clearly the *dynasty* that is meant. (*b*) Ver. 13 is a *Deuteronomic* interpolation, meant to bring special honour to the temple of Jerusalem. (*c*) It having been proved in one case that a writer closely related to D revised the passage, the other traces of Deuteronomic style would also point, not to the original author, but to this reviser. *Cf.* the tedious speech and the overcrowding in ver. 7 ff. The incident itself might thus very well be old and historical; at the same time, we know that from the time of Josiah the idea here represented received new life and new literary treatment.

which had been so often contested by its neighbours, to be rendered undisputed, it must come to an understanding with its other neighbours. It was, therefore, impossible that David should content himself with acquiring the crown over all Israel and overthrowing the Philistines. The occasion, however, came from without—from Ammon—although, as we have seen, it was not unwelcome to David. The different Aramaic peoples soon joined the Ammonites, so that when David subdued them, he was lord of the whole territory adjoining Israel on the north and east.

The king of the Ammonites insulted the ambassadors sent by David to congratulate him on his accession to the throne. This conduct would seem to us unintelligible, were it not that we must certainly take it for granted that the neighbours also regarded a settlement with David as inevitable. They had every reason to regard David's strong position with suspicion, and to fear for their own safety. If, moreover, it is true, as we are entitled to conjecture, that Eshba'al had been able to maintain his independence even of his eastern neighbours only by paying them tribute, the whole affair becomes still clearer. With David's accession the payment of tribute had come to an end. Ammon and Moab must seek to maintain their position. If their own forces were not sufficient for the attempt, it must be made with help from without. Ammon accordingly opened hostilities in a defiant manner, and Moab would hardly remain behind.[1]

In fact, the Ammonites were immediately joined by the Aramæans of Zobah, as well as those of Beth Reḥôb, Ishṭôb, and Ma'achah.[2] We have here, therefore, nothing short of a coalition of the neighbouring kingdoms lying to the east and north-east, having as its object to weaken the dominant position won by Israel under David, which seemed to threaten their integrity.[3]

Joab, the commander of David's army, marched against the enemy. When he arrived in the territory of the Ammonites, the

[1] See Kamph. *Z.l W.* vi. 68.
[2] On these kingdoms, see Meyer, *Gesch. d. Alt.* § 287, 300. The view that Beth Reḥôb was not properly a kingdom (Meyer, p. 364) is not a probable one.
[3] 2 Sam. x. 1-6.

enemies had already united their forces. They unexpectedly got the start of him; and while the Ammonites, sallying forth from their capital, encountered him in open battle, their allies sought to fall on him in the rear. A quick decision during the battle relieved Joab's dangerous position. He commands half of his force, under his brother Abishai, to engage the Ammonites in front, and throws himself with the rest on the Aramæans attacking him in the rear. The latter having been driven back by Joab, the Ammonites also fell into confusion before Abishai, and fled into their city.[1]

The city itself, however, Rabbath Ammon, was not conquered. The expedition was only broken off. The Aramæans also appeared again the following year, with Hadadezer,[2] the king of the powerful kingdom of Zobah, at their head. This time David himself took the field and defeated them. Hadadezer's kingdom appears, at least in part, to have fallen into David's hands. The smaller kings in his neighbourhood also submitted themselves to David.[3] In the following year, Joab succeeded in reducing Rabbath Ammon to extremities. He took the so-called City of Waters, leaving it to David himself to complete the conquest. The spoil was abundant, including as it did the golden crown of the Ammonite god Milcom, which weighed a talent, and was richly adorned with jewels.[4] The prisoners were harshly treated, yet perhaps not so cruelly as the present text would lead one to suppose.[5] The Moabites were probably also defeated and cruelly punished at this time.[6]

Whether the Ammonites were thus permanently subdued is very doubtful. At a later time, at all events, their country did

---

[1] 2 Sam. x. 7-14.
[2] *Cf.* the Hebrew names, Eli'ezer, 'Azarja (Azariah).   [3] 2 Sam. x. 15-19.
[4] 2 Sam. xi. 1, 17; xii. 26-30.
[5] 2 Sam. xii. 31. On this verse, see (amongst others) Hoffmann in *ZAW.* ii. 66 ff.; Kamphausen in *Rhein. Gem. Bl.* 1884, No. 9; Herderscheê in *Theol. Tijdschr.* 1891, 127 ff. On the other hand, *cf. e.g.* Steiner in *Theol. Z. a. d. Schweiz*, 1885, 303 ff.
[6] Their being mentioned in the first place in 2 Sam. viii. 2 seems to point to this; yet see what follows.

not belong to Israel; although it probably did under David. In any case, for the present these predatory tribes of the east, that so often threatened Israel, had been quelled. The eastern boundary of David's kingdom was now secured against invasion as far as the desert. Towards the north, David's rule reached as far as Lebanon and Hermon. Even the rulers of the districts lying farther north and east sought his friendship. Amongst these was To'i, king of Ḥamath on the Orontes, who was in a continual state of feud with Hadadezer, and so would be only too grateful to David for defeating him.[1] Another of them was Talmai, the king of Geshûr, a district near Hermon, south-west of Damascus. A daughter of his was among David's wives—the mother of Absalom.[2]

The Phœnicians had still more reason than these northern neighbours to cultivate friendly relations with David. Their commerce could only gain from the existence in the Palestinian 'hinterland' of a powerful and organised state such as David aimed at. Their king, Ḥiram of Tyre, concluded with David a friendly alliance, that continued to subsist under Solomon.[3]

Israel's position was thus secured towards the north and east. From the time when the Philistines were finally conquered, there had been no adversary to fear from the west. It was therefore only from the south and south-east that disturbances could now arise. Amalek, Edom, and Moab had all of them now and then given Israel trouble. These also were added to David's conquests, partly as early as the time of the battles with Ammon and the Aramæans,[4] partly not till a later occasion.[5] Moab was not able to maintain its ground, and became tributary to David. Amalek, the Bedouin tribe, skilful in war and ever greedy for spoil, with which Israel had so many tough fights, disappeared from history, apparently utterly destroyed by David. Edom was subdued, its

---

[1] 2 Sam. viii. 9 f.

[2] *Cf.* 2 Sam. iii. 3; xiii. 37. The subjugation of Damascus mentioned in 2 Sam. viii. 5 f. is improbable; *vide* Meyer, *Gesch. d. Alt.* 364. On the literary character of chap. viii. see above, p. 47 f., and Budde, *RiSa*, 249 f.

[3] See however above, p. 157, note 2.

[4] See above, p. 162 f.   [5] 2 Sam. viii. 11 ff.; *cf.* Num. xxiv. 17 ff.

land being henceforth administered by agents sent by David; and the approach to the Red Sea, along with the seaport towns of Eziongeber and Elath, fell into David's hands. A later notice[1] tells us that long and bloody battles were needed ere Edom submitted. The consequence of this obstinacy was a murderous massacre, which itself became the source of later complications.

David's kingdom thus reached from the Red Sea to Lebanon. It was the dominant power in Syria; its position was undisputed. It had no longer any adversary to fear. Next to David himself, his general Joab had the greatest share in these successes, especially as in later times David appears to have ceased, as a rule, to take the field in person. Joab remained from first to last faithfully devoted to David, through all storms and vicissitudes of fortune, never wavering. A warrior whose keen sword fortune never failed, he was also a man of brutal violence and ungovernable selfishness, to whom no tie seemed sacred and no means illegitimate.

It is obvious that for such wars as David had to conduct in all directions, he needed a carefully equipped and well-trained army. The basis of his army was a sort of guard in which he could place implicit confidence. This consisted of those six hundred men who had gathered around him in the days of his flight from Saul, and had held by him faithfully during the time of his persecution. When David became king, they naturally remained near him. They formed henceforth his bodyguard, and bore the name of *gibbôrîm*, 'the heroes.' It is self-evident that special undertakings would devolve upon them in war.[2] The gaps produced in the ranks of this select corps by David's numerous wars were filled up, after his victories over the Philistines, chiefly with foreigners, especially Philistines, and Cretan mercenaries akin to them—a proceeding the reason for which is to be found in the later designation of the corps to be a bodyguard

---

[1] 1 Kings xi. 14 ff. On this, see below, in § 48.
[2] For deeds of some of them, see 2 Sam. xxiii. 8 ff., and above, p. 152.

for the king. Hence the whole corps soon went by the name of Cretans and Philistines.[1]

Important as this select corps would always be for David, it could not possibly suffice for his greater expeditions. According to ancient custom all Israel[2] was called out for service when an enemy threatened from without. It was the men of Israel, capable of bearing arms, that formed the national army of Israel. The greater the cohesion of the tribes, the more numerous the muster; while, on the other hand, the fewer the tribes that seriously professed to belong to Israel, the lighter the muster that resulted. Moreover, the farther a tribe lay from the immediate danger, the more sluggishly would its men gather round the banner of Israel. This provision also seems in the long-run not to have sufficed David for his wars. His power, and the whole position of Israel as created by him, rested on his sword. If it was to be maintained, his sword had to be ever ready. David perceived that for such wars as he had to wage, it was necessary that Israel should possess, even in times of peace, a fixed and permanent military organisation. Its troops could thus be supervised even during peace, and no tribe could shirk its duty on the outbreak of war. As a step towards this object, a census of the nation was undertaken by Joab, David's general. It was meant to provide an estimate of the number of men in Israel capable of bearing arms, and afford a basis for the proposed organisation. He was engaged on it for three-quarters of a year, extending his tour as far as Kadesh on the Orontes, the capital of the kingdom of the Hittites, formerly so powerful. This must, therefore, if our notice be correct,[3] have been likewise subdued by David. Soon after this census, Israel was overtaken by a devastating pestilence. David perceived in this the chastising hand of Yahvé.[4] We have,

---

[1] See above, p. 153, note 2.

[2] *Cf.* the expression 'the people'=the army, or 'the man,' 'the men of Israel,' in the wars of Saul, and elsewhere.

[3] It rests on LXX. Luc. 2 Sam. xxiv. 6 (see Hitzig, *ZDMG.* ix. 763 f.; Wellh. *TBS.* 221). However, it might also have made its way into the LXX. through mere conjecture.

[4] 2 Sam. xxiv., on which see above, p. 48 f. For the text, *cf.* Wellh. *TBS.*, and Driver, *Notes.*

however, reason to suppose that it was not on the basis of his new military system, that David achieved his successes in war against the surrounding nations. It seems to have been rather on the ground of the practical appearance gained in these wars, that the work of organisation was taken in hand, as a measure that would bear fruit in later times.[1]

Two episodes relating to David's conduct towards the few still surviving members of the family of his predecessor Saul, may conclude the history of David, in so far as that is not controlled by the well-known occurrences in his family. These episodes belong apparently to the time before David's foreign wars. In our narrative, however, they stand out of all historical connection, so that it is difficult to fix their date.[2] The second of these must be judged in the light of the first.

The first is as follows. Doubtless some time after the whole kingdom of Saul had come into his hands and he had established himself in Zion,[3] David felt the necessity of showing his goodwill to any of the posterity of Saul that might still be living. He did this in memory of the friendship that had bound him to Jonathan, Saul's son. As a result of his investigation it appeared that there was still living a son of Jonathan's named Meriba'al. He had been lame from childhood, and was living apparently in retirement at Lô-debār,[4] probably from fear of David's revenge. David had him brought before him, and presented him with his grandfather's property. Hence it would appear that this had been, in the meanwhile, confiscated by David. Meriba'al was, however, to make his residence in Jerusalem, and Ziba, Saul's steward, was to attend to the estate at Gibeah in his stead. In this arrangement

---

[1] The position of the narrative in 1 Chron. xxi. is in favour of this, as also the expedition east of Jordan and in the far north. [2] See, however, the next note.

[3] Yet not too soon after that, as may be inferred from 2 Sam. iv. 4, in combination with ix. 12. If, at the death of Saul, Meriba'al was five years old, and so at the time of David's accession to the throne of all Israel, twelve to thirteen years old; and if he now had a young son, some ten years may have elapsed since Eshba'al's death. We cannot speak more definitely.

[4] This place must have lain somewhere in the neighbourhood of Maḥanaim. *Cf.* 2 Sam. xvii. 27.

David combined generosity and policy. He generously spared Meriba'al, who might suppose his life forfeited, and endowed him besides in royal fashion. But he did not fail to remove the prince from his family, and from Saul's royal seat, and to retain him under his own eye at Jerusalem. He was determined that Meriba'al and the nobles of Benjamin should be kept away from everything that might remind them of the rights of the house of Saul.[1]

If in this case David showed generosity in a way that no one could reasonably expect of him, it is not likely that in another case, of which an account has been preserved—the second of the episodes referred to above—he aimed at exterminating the house of Saul. 'In his zeal for Israel' Saul had done violence to Gibeon, a place that had had its individuality as a Canaanitish city assured to it by ancient treaty. We must suppose that he made an attack on it and devoted a part of its Canaanitish population to death. In consequence of this breach of faith there lay on Saul and Israel a charge of blood-guiltiness which must be wiped out. Once, during the reign of David, some time after the incident just described,[2] the land was visited for a period of three years by drought and famine. David inquired of Yahvé, and was told that the reason was to be found in the blood-guiltiness that rested on Saul's house, and therefore on Israel—for the king represented the people. The citizens of Gibeon, who had suffered the wrong, were to assign the form of expiation. They demanded blood for blood. Seven males of the race of Saul were delivered over to the Gibeonites, and 'hung up' by them 'before Yahvé.'[3] These were two sons of Saul by Rizpah, the concubine who had been the means of the quarrel between Abner and Eshba'al, and five grandsons of Saul, sons of Merab[4] by her marriage with Adriel, the son of Barzillai[5] of Abel Meḥolah. David remembered his covenant

---

[1] 2 Sam. ix. [2] *Cf.* ver. 7.

[3] This took place at Gibeon itself, 'on the hill of Yahvé,' ver. 6. See LXX. and Driver, *Notes*, 269 f. That they had previously been slain is presupposed. The aggravation of the punishment consisted in leaving the bodies unburied. On the word, see Dillm. on Num. xxv. 4.

[4] We must read thus in ver. 8 (LXX. Luc. Pesh.) instead of Michal.

[5] [See Nestle, *ZDPV.* 1892, 257.]

with Jonathan, and spared his son Meriba'al. It is an affecting picture of maternal love that we have in the unhappy Rizpah keeping watch over her dead sons, driving away wild beasts and birds of prey from their dead bodies, till at last rain fell, indicating that the anger of Yahvé was past. The bodies might now be buried. David had their bones gathered,[1] and interred in the family burying-place of Kish at Gibeah. The house of Saul had fallen a victim, hardly by the will of David, to the religious belief of the age.[2]

§ 46. *Family history of David. Absalom.*

David had gloriously subdued the enemies of Israel, but he was not able to control his own unruly passions. The same man who had the strength and skill to lead his people on from step to step, had not enough firmness of will to train his sons to virtue and honour. The bitter fruits of such weakness could not fail to appear. Our document relates them with a simple objectivity, an unsparing impartiality, and a loftiness of moral tone, that are seldom to be matched.

While Joab was with the army in front of Rabbath Ammon, David sinned with the wife of a captain who had gone to the war.[3] The consequences, which did not fail to appear, induced David to summon home the husband Uriah, with tidings of the state of the war. Ostensibly from a feeling of military duty, probably in reality because he knew what had taken place, Uriah refused to see his wife, and hastened back to the army. There remained only one way of hiding the king's disgrace. He gave Uriah a letter to Joab, which should dispose of the possible troublesome accuser. Joab was to assign him a dangerous post in the battle, and leave him to his fate. The plot was successful. Uriah's wife, Bathsheba, mourned for her husband as in duty bound, and then became the wife of her seducer.[4]

---

[1] *V.* 13 f. according to LXX. [2] 2 Sam. xxi. 1-14.

[3] The narrative furnishes interesting evidence that other houses stood on Zion in addition to the palace of David, probably those of his military staff.

[4] 2 Sam. xi. 2-27. On the whole section, chaps. ix.-xx., see above, p. 47 f.

When Bathsheba gave birth to a child, what Uriah had suspected or discovered could be hid from no one. The prophet Nathan undertook to represent the public conscience. First by a parable, and then point blank, he made known to David the judgment of Yahvé. Instead of becoming angry with Nathan, David showed his true greatness, and confessed his fault. The child fell ill and died, notwithstanding David's prayers, after seven days.[1] David recognised in this the judgment of Yahvé for his own sin, but he could not prevent his example from speedily bearing evil fruit in the lives of his grown-up sons.

Amnon, his first-born, was inflamed with a passion for his half-sister Tamar. Following the advice of an unscrupulous court favourite, he succeeded in getting her into his power by craft. By feigning sickness he found a pretext for receiving a visit from her. After accomplishing his purpose, he drove away the dishonoured maiden with rude and heartless violence, thus proving that it was ungoverned desire and not love that had moved him.[2]

When we hear the narrator describe the way in which this evil deed produced evil fruit in David's household, it is as though we were witnessing a Greek tragedy enacted before our eyes. Crime was heaped on crime, as if in obedience to an awful destiny. The father had begun with open adultery, and had then endeavoured to veil his guilt with hypocrisy and to cover it with blood. He need not be surprised if his children did not shrink from rape, if not incest, and were led on to murder and insurrection.

After what David had done himself, he did not dare to punish Amnon's misdeed otherwise than with words.[3] Accordingly another of his sons, Absalom, Tamar's full brother, constituted himself the avenger of his sister's disgrace.[4] But he could await his opportunity. Two years after the incident had occurred, he invited the royal court to a feast at his estate at Ba'al Hazor: it

---

[1] 2 Sam. xii. 1-9, 13-25 : vv. 10-12 have apparently been added by R.
[2] 2 Sam. xiii. 1-19.
[3] 2 Sam. xiii. 21, according to LXX. See my translation.
[4] 2 Sam. xiii. 20-22. On the site of Ba'al Hazor, v. Wellh. *TBS.* on v. 34.

was the feast of sheep-shearing. Amnon and the other princes presented themselves. In the course of the feast the former was suddenly slain by Absalom's men. The rest fled home, Absalom himself fleeing to Geshûr, to his grandfather Talmai.[1] He stayed there in exile for three years, until he succeeded, through a stratagem of Joab's, in reconciling the king. He was now at liberty to return to Jerusalem; but for two years more he was forbidden to appear in the king's presence. At last he succeeded, through a second intervention of Joab's, in obtaining the king's full pardon.[2]

David did not consult his own good in receiving Absalom into favour. To the ambition and haughtiness of Absalom's character were now added defiance and thirst for revenge for the wrong that he thought, or affected to think, had been done to him. Invested with the rights of successor to the throne, he availed himself of his newly won position to steal the hearts of the people from his father, who was now growing old. And not content with the prospect of becoming, after a longer or shorter time, the legitimate successor to his father, he formed a treacherous plot to remove him before his time.[3]

He was probably engaged for four[4] years in making preparations in secret for the step he meant to take, winning the people to himself by a display of royal splendour and condescending graciousness, and endeavouring to gain confidants and accomplices for his treacherous plans. Having thoroughly equipped himself, he proceeded to proclaim open revolt against the unsuspecting king.

With the king's permission, he was to celebrate a sacrifice at the ancient sacred city of Hebron, the superseded and therefore discontented capital of Judah. At the same time as he left Jerusalem, messengers also left it to publish throughout all Israel his approaching accession to the throne. At Hebron, supported by the chiefs of the clans of Judah, Absalom unfurled the flag of

---

[1] 2 Sam. xiii. 23-39. On Geshûr v. *ZDPV* xiii. 198 f. and 285 f.
[2] 2 Sam. xiv.   [3] 2 Sam. xv. 1-6.
[4] According to an emended reading in 2 Sam. xv. 7.

revolt. Soon a considerable part of all Israel were gathered about him.¹

The news of Absalom's revolt came on David like a thunderclap out of a clear sky. It struck him unsuspecting and utterly unprepared. David's rule must have excited discontent not only in Judah but also in the rest of Israel. He appears, for the moment, to have been able to count on but little support west of the Jordan, beyond his six hundred trusted veterans. It seems to have been only the east, which before held so fast by the house of Saul, that now remained true to him likewise. He did not feel himself sufficiently safe from a sudden attack by Absalom, even in his capital, strong as it was, and so determined to abandon it.²

David's trust in God, and his courage and shrewdness, which had so often stood him in good stead, did not fail him even in this predicament, the most trying he had fallen into in his life, full as it was of adventure. Leaving his harem in the palace, and crossing the brook Kidron, he fled to the Jordan. He was accompanied by his bodyguard, his household, and such as adhered to him, including the priests Zadok and Abiathar, bearing the ark of Yahvé. David directed the latter to return to Jerusalem, as he had a firm hope that Yahvé would not abandon his city. Moreover the priests, if they returned, could send him secret tidings by their sons, Jonathan and Ahimaaz, of what transpired in the city. With the same object in view he sent back Hushai, one of his trusted followers, with the commission to feign himself a partisan of Absalom's, and thwart the counsel of the wily Ahithophel, who had deserted to Absalom.³

David was now to learn that Absalom's appeal to Israel had found a willing ear in the house and tribe of Saul also. He was met at the Mount of Olives by Ziba, the steward of Meriba'al, with the tidings that his master had joined Absalom in the hope that he might recover through him his grandfather's throne.⁴ A distinguished Benjamite, Shimei by name, met him soon afterwards

---

¹ 2 Sam. xv. 7-12.   ² 2 Sam. xv. 13-15.
³ 2 Sam. xv. 16-37.   ⁴ 2 Sam. xvi. 1-4.

at Baḥûrim.¹ He received David with fierce invectives, which revealed clearly enough how fresh a memory many irreconcilable spirits retained of Saul, and of his house and its cruel fate, innocent as David was in the matter.²

The empty capital was taken possession of by Absalom, who showed the nation that he claimed the succession, by appropriating David's harem. He must get David out of the way if he wished to secure his throne. Since he was already supported by a goodly force, this would be easy to accomplish now before David had been able to collect an army. Such was Ahithophel's counsel, the only counsel that met the requirements of the situation. Absalom's unlucky fate, however, would not allow him to follow this advice. It flattered the vanity of the prince to consult also one of David's former trusty counsellors, and Hushai's cunning succeeded in duping the blinded prince: his fate was sealed. Hushai succeeded in awakening Absalom's alarm at the thought of David's brave and daring band of warriors, and led him to wait till he should have gathered the army of all Israel about him. At the same time Hushai sent David word by the priests of what had been decided on.³

Henceforth David was master of the situation. His decision was quickly made. He crossed the Jordan, proceeded to Mahanaim, the former royal residence of Eshba'al, and employed the time left him in gathering an army about him. There were naturally still thousands in Israel who, when David's call to arms went forth, were not deaf to the voice of duty and the glorious name of the old hero king. Important men of Gilead like Barzillai and Machir ben Ammiel, and even Shobi ben Nahash, the vanquished Ammonite king, granted him ample support.⁴

Meanwhile, Absalom had likewise crossed the Jordan. It was

---

¹ On the site of this place v. Marti, ZDPV. iii. 8 ff., and Van Kasteren, ibid. xiii. 101 ff. The latter decides in favour of a group of ruins on the ridge of Bīr Zennākī. ² 2 Sam. xvi. 5-13.

³ 2 Sam. xvi. 14-xvii. 23. Notice the pragmatism of the narrative (quite in the style of Ju. ix.) here, where the threads of the plot begin to be unravelled. Cf. espec. 2 Sam. xvii. 14b, 23, with Ju. ix. 20, 24, 56 f.

⁴ 2 Sam. xvii. 24-29. On the text see the translation in Kautzsch.

here, on the eastern side, that the contest was to be decided. David's army set out in three divisions, led by Joab, Abîshai, and Ittai the Gittite. Absalom had for general a nephew of David's named 'Amāsa, a son of David's sister Abigail by an Ishmaelite named Ithra. Yielding to the urgent entreaties of his followers, David remained behind in Mahanaim. The conflict took place in the forest of Ephraim—a name that must have been borne by some forest district east of the Jordan.[1] Absalom's forces were unable to stand before David's men, though far superior to them in point of numbers, representing indeed, in the eyes of the narrator, all 'Israel.' In the haste of his flight, Absalom was caught by his long flowing hair in the branches of a terebinth. His mule escaped, and he was found thus by a common soldier, hanging between heaven and earth. The soldier reported what he had seen to Joab. That fierce warrior knew no pity. He paid no heed even to the special command of David which the soldier had feared, but reproached the latter for his soft-heartedness, and thrust three arrows through Absalom's heart. Then he announced at once by trumpet-blast that the pursuit was at an end. The body of Absalom was cast into a pit and covered over with stones.[2]

David awaited the issue at Mahanaim, sitting in the gate. The porter saw a man running from the field of battle, and soon another. The first he recognised as Ahimaaz, the son of Zadok, who had already done good service as messenger in Jerusalem. Outstripping the courier sent by Joab, he brought word of the victory of David. The paternal heart of the king, however, was thinking only of Absalom. On being asked about him, Ahimaaz evaded the question. Meanwhile the other runner had arrived, and related plainly what had taken place. The king was quite broken down. Moved to the depths of his heart, he went up into the upper chamber of the gate-house, breaking out into loud laments over his son. He spent a long time here, heedless in his

---

[1] LXX. Luc. reads Mahanaim; *v.* Klost. *SaKö*, on 2 Sam. xviii. 6.
[2] 2 Sam. xviii. 1-18; *v.* 18 is in part a gloss; *v.* my translation.

grief even of the victorious army, which had in the meantime drawn near. Joab's anger over this neglect of his brave and trusty defenders, is not unreasonable. It was only his strong words that availed to rouse the king to master his grief.[1]

The conscience of the people awoke, as was to be expected, now that the sword had spoken. The tribes of Israel that had revolted returned in penitence to their king, remembering how much Israel owed to him, perhaps also under the influence of their old antipathy against Judah. Judah alone still held sullenly aloof. It was quite apparent that David's own tribe had been the seat of the conspiracy. David felt that the first thing to be done was to win it. He accordingly entered into negotiations with the elders of the tribe, and went so far as to offer 'Amāsa Joab's place in the army. Perhaps an old ground of discontent on the part of Judah was thus removed.

The men of Judah then brought David in state across the Jordan. They were joined by the Shimei already mentioned, at the head of a thousand Benjamites: David magnanimously pardoned him. Ziba also was zealous in his attendance on David, and soon even the lame Meriba'al appeared to clear himself from the charges made by his steward. David, not quite trusting his innocence, commanded the two to divide the property. The rest of the army of Israel joined David's procession at Gilgal.

It is not to be wondered at, however, that the precedence conceded by David to the headstrong Judæans produced discord. The quarrel between North and South threatened to break out anew.[2] Indeed, at least a part of the tribe of Benjamin was still unable to restrain its enmity against David. Sheba' ben Bichri sounded once more the call to arms against David. It would appear that on this occasion also, a considerable part of Israel responded to the summons to revolt. Judah, however, remained steadfast this time, and brought David back to Jerusalem. In accordance with David's promise, 'Amāsa was intrusted with the command of the army of Judah against the rebels. Joab, how-

---

[1] 2 Sam. xviii. 19–xix. 9.   [2] 2 Sam. xix. 10–44.

ever, was not the man to bear with patience this slight, which he had hardly fully deserved. As ʻAmāsa loitered, Joab was able to make himself again indispensable to the king.[1] David sent him also with the bodyguard to fight against Sheba. They came upon ʻAmāsa at Gibeon, where the latter fell, as Abner had done, by the treacherous sword of Joab.

The insurgents proceeded towards the north. Joab pursued them and drove them to the farthest limits of the territory of Israel. Sheba succeeded in establishing himself in Abel-beth-Maʻacah, close by Dan and the sources of the Jordan. Joab prepared to storm the city. Then in response to his demand, the head of the insurgent was flung to him over the wall, whereupon Joab withdrew and spared the faithful city.[2]

David's history is here at an end. In what followed he is hardly a voluntary agent. He may still have held the reins of government in Israel for some time[3] in peace, quiet and undisturbed. We next come upon him as an old man, hardly any longer capable of making up his own mind, quite in the hands of his court and harem—a society not over nice as to its aims and means. David has left the stage of history.[4] .

David's character stands forth more clearly in the light of history than that of Saul. Israel's greatness and Yahvè's honour were for David the first commandment. He has his reward, not only in Israel's gratitude, but in the undying love and respect of posterity. The giant-shadows of his career were powerless to destroy this feeling. David stands head and shoulders above the average of human rulers. Not only his predecessor Saul, but the kings of Israel that followed him, are far inferior to him in

---

[1] In the MT. of 2 Sam. xx. 6, Abishai has been wrongly substituted for Joab; v. Pesh. and Klost. *SaKö, ad loc.*   [2] 2 Sam. xx. 1-22.

[3] Absalom's insurrection took place in or near the last decade of David's reign. This is to be inferred from 2 Sam. iii. 3, in connection with xiii. 38; xiv. 28; xv. 7; if we suppose that when Absalom murdered Amnon he was already grown up. In this way, if we allow x years before Absalom's birth, we get for the period from the accession of David in Hebron to Absalom's insurrection: $x +$ about $20 + 3 + 2 + 4$, that is to say ± 31 years.

[4] [*Cf.* also Farrar, *The First Book of Kings*, p. 61 ff.]

nobility, in vigour and skill—both as a warrior and as a ruler—in magnanimity, sagacity, and tenacity of purpose. Even in unrestrained feeling and tyrannous passion, he is equalled by few.

David's weaknesses are patent; but even in these his greatness of soul always reappears in its native beauty. In his despotic caprice he seduced Bathsheba and basely murdered Uriah, but he bowed in genuine contrition and unfeigned penitence under the sentence of the nation, and the scathing judgment of Yahvé's prophet. His parental weakness was responsible for Amnon's offence, and for Absalom's insurrection and bloodshed; but his paternal heart did not cease to go out towards his son, low as he had fallen. David's weakness, as it meets us in noble fatherly grief, comes home to our human nature, and is transformed before us into an affecting picture of magnanimity and paternal fidelity. Although his magnanimity may have wavered in the case of Joab (our insight into the real relations of the events is too defective to warrant our passing final judgment), it is unquestioned as regards Saul and his house, and also Shimei and 'Amāsa. Poetic gifts and religious zeal were such marked characteristics of David's, that we can hardly deny the possibility of his having had an active share in the beginnings of religious lyric poetry in Israel.[1]

[1] [*Cf.* the character-sketches of David in W. R. Smith's article 'David,' *Enc. Britannica*, and Cheyne, *Aids to the Study of Criticism*, Part 1.]

CHAPTER IV.

SOLOMON.

§ 47. *Solomon's Accession.*

THE last days of the great king were disturbed by quarrels about the succession. As our information is so incomplete, the real circumstances of Solomon's accession will always be involved in a certain obscurity. We shall first of all reproduce the account given in the document that has reached us.

David had become so aged as to need nursing. The court could not avoid the question of the succession. Now that Absalom was dead, the nearest to the throne by order of birth was Adonijah, David's fourth son. Indeed, Adonijah regarded himself as his father's successor, and even allowed himself to go so far as to openly assert the rights of that position, as Absalom had done.[1] Accordingly, at court and among influential circles of the people, Adonijah seems to have been quite regarded as the future king.[2] David himself, who loved him fondly, and regarded him as taking the place of Absalom, whom he still mourned, did not venture to restrain him.[3]

But Adonijah's hopes did not meet with approval everywhere at court. He succeeded, indeed, in securing Joab and the priest Abiathar. But on the other side was Bathsheba, who was exerting herself to secure the succession for her son Solomon. She was supported by Zadok the priest, Nathan the prophet, and

---

[1] 1 Kings i. 5 f.   [2] 1 Kings i. 9.
[3] 1 Kings i. 6 (read עצי).

Benaiah, the captain of the guard. There were thus in David's last days two court parties violently opposed to each other.

One day Adonijah had a sacrificial feast at the 'Stone of the Serpent' [Zoheleth], a stone in the neighbourhood of Jerusalem at which sacrifices were offered.[1] Nathan, the moving spirit of the other party, appears to have been afraid that the banquet might end, like Absalom's at Hebron, in proclaiming Adonijah king. Were that to happen, Solomon's cause would be lost. It was, therefore, necessary to take immediate action. It was arranged that Bathsheba should at once convey word to the king of what was taking place at the Stone of the Serpent, remind him of a promise he had once made, which pointed to the succession of Solomon, and bring about its immediate confirmation.

Bathsheba did as she was instructed. After a short interval, Nathan himself followed her into the presence of the king, to give weight to her words. He asserted that he had even heard the shout of the conspirators: 'Long live King Adonijah!' By their united efforts they succeeded in awakening the suspicion of the king. He was convinced that he was to be deprived of his throne in his old age, and to fall a victim to a conspiracy of one of his sons. He forthwith formally adjudged the succession to Solomon. The latter was by his order conducted on the king's own mule to Gihon, a sacred spring near Jerusalem,[2] anointed by Zadok and Nathan, proclaimed king, and formally installed on the throne. The joyful acclamations of the people, and the blast of the trumpets, reached the ears of the feasters not far off. There was barely time to ask what the cause was, when word was brought by Jonathan, the son of Abiathar, of what had happened—Solomon was king. The only chance for Adonijah was to take refuge at the altar, holding to the horns of which he implored his more fortunate

---

[1] The site of this place is determined by the spring Rogel (now Job's Well), 1 Kings i. 9. See Bäd.² 113 (³ 103) [Eng. Transl.² p. 101], and Riehm in *HWB*.

[2] On the site of Gihon, *cf.* Furrer in *BL*. ii. 463; Bäd.² 111 ff. (³ 101 f.) [Eng. Transl.² 99 ff.]. It is the spring of Mary in the valley of the Kidron. It is only about 800 metres [slightly under half a mile] distant from Job's Well.

brother for his bare life. He professed his allegiance to his brother and was allowed to live.

Solomon had thus been proclaimed king. Before David expired he had a charge to give his successor that weighed on his mind. He reminded his son of Joab's still unexpiated murder of Abner and 'Amāsa, of Barzillai's kindness to him, and of the curses uttered by Shime'i against his house. Barzillai was to be royally rewarded; the other two were not to be suffered to go down to Sheol in peace.[1]

David's eyes were hardly closed in death when Adonijah, who had been pardoned by Solomon, was again seized with a longing after the throne. He wished to have Abishag, David's nurse, for his wife, and hoped to obtain Solomon's consent through the mediation of Bathsheba. We know from Absalom's conduct with regard to David's harem what this request implied according to the ideas of the age. Solomon saw through Adonijah's daring plans, and the latter paid the penalty with his life. At the same time Adonijah's most distinguished adherents were condemned. Abiathar was dismissed from his office as priest, but his life was spared in memory of the services he had rendered to David through good fortune and ill. He was banished to Anathoth, and his place was taken by his colleague Zadok. Joab, suspecting the worst, fled to the altar of Yahvé, but there was no mercy for him. Adducing in his condemnation his old bloody deeds, Solomon commanded him to be slain. Lastly, Shime'i, who had had no share in Adonijah's attempts, was provisionally confined to Jerusalem, and when, contrary to the king's orders, he shortly afterwards left the city, he was put to death.

So runs the narrative in 1 Kings i. and ii. Recently it has been supposed by many to contain in its first part a palace intrigue against the succession of Adonijah, set in motion in the interest of Solomon by Nathan and Bathsheba; while, in the second part of

---

[1] According to the text, it was not simply a 'warning' that was given to Solomon, or a command to interfere if certain contingencies occurred (Köhler, ii. 1, 372 f.).

the account, has been recognised a thinly veiled attempt to shift from the shoulders of Solomon the responsibility for the bloody deed with which he felt himself compelled to prop up his newly won throne.[1]

It seems to be decidedly in favour of this view that, up to this time, there has been no hint of such a thing as the succession's going to Solomon. If Adonijah fell an innocent victim to a court intrigue, we must suppose that Bathsheba and Nathan inveigled the imbecile old king into sanctioning a promise which he had never really made, but which, in his anxiety for peace in his last days, he weakly appropriated.[2] This view seems to be also favoured by the fact that the narrator, obviously with a touch of intentional irony, tells nothing in his own person of Adonijah's criminal objects in connection with the sacrificial banquet, although indeed he makes Nathan know all about them in his interview with the king. Finally, with reference to the second part of the narrative, there appear in the piece relating to David's last disposition clear traces of a later hand. These suggest the suspicion that the whole piece is of a later origin,[3] and support the view that in the original account, and hence in actual fact, Joab at least was put to death by Solomon on the ground not of his remote but of his immediate past, and not by desire of David, but as a partisan of Adonijah.

But the literary basis of this last supposition is not sufficiently ensured. The very parts of David's last words that relate to Joab and Shime'i are certainly old,[4] and the whole piece is derived

[1] So Duncker, Ed. Meyer, Wellhausen, and Stade. Otherwise, Dillmann in *Bib. Lex.* Art. 'Solomon'; Köhler, and others.

[2] So especially Wellh. *Bl.*[4] 226, note.

[3] See Wellh. *Bl.*[4] 226. He regards 1 Kings ii. 1-12 as a Deuteronomistic addition. So does Stade.

[4] See Kuen. § xxv. 1. He appeals above all to ver. 7; so also Budde, *RiSa*, 263. Vers. 5-9 cannot, in point of fact, be simply inferred from what follows them. It is easier to understand the failure to make special mention of the carrying out of David's wish with regard to Barzillai (ver. 7), than to suppose the wish itself an invention, when no corresponding fact is related. It is likewise in favour of the originality and historical character of vers. 5-9 that, as a matter of fact, Solomon's subsequent conduct is *not* determined exclusively by a reference to Adonijah (against Wellhausen and Stade). Abiathar was spared, while Joab was not. Shime'i had nothing whatever to do with Adonijah.

from our best document. In fact, a wish of this kind on the part of David does not raise such serious difficulties on the score of its contents as might appear. We must guard against trying to measure the distant past by our moral feelings. We must remember what David did to the house of Saul, in compliance with the terrible belief of his age, in order to wash away a taint of blood-guiltiness that still adhered to it. If we only do so, it will not seem strange, after all, that in the case before us David was haunted by an anxious dread lest the crime and the curse of a time long past might burst upon his house after his own death, as it had burst on the house of Saul.[1]

It seems to me as if the arguments in favour of David's having actually given the instructions in question are thus stronger than those against it. But light is thus also shed on the other parts of the narrative, whose parts are closely connected. If David really gave Solomon this commission, he was at least still so far in command of his mind and will that the promise regarding Solomon's succession attributed to him cannot have been pure invention.[2] Bathsheba and Nathan must have been able to refer to certain facts. We may probably draw conclusions regarding the succession to David's throne from the way in which Saul, and David himself, had become king. To all appearance, the succession was not yet so fixed that the eldest son would of necessity be the heir. Natural as it would be, there had not yet been established any law of this kind. Even if there had for long been no doubt that one of David's sons would be his successor, he had yet liberty to determine which of them it should be. David had probably taken no definite steps at all with regard to the succession. He regarded Adonijah's doings and aspirations as presumptuous, although he did not go so far as to forestall them. But it would be only human if, at the same time, urged to it perhaps by Adonijah's pretensions, on the one side, and Bathsheba's urgency on the other, he had at some time or other incidentally given some

---

[1] *Cf.* especially ii. 33, 44 f., where this thought clearly appears; and Budde, *RiSa*, 264.   [2] So especially Wellh. *Bl.*[4] 226, note.

promise on which Solomon's friends could build hopes for their man.

It was a clever game, although exceeding lawful bounds, that Nathan and Bathsheba played. Adonijah may indeed have held his meeting at the Stone of the Serpent not simply for the purpose of offering a harmless sacrifice; but the only fact that is really *known* is that he wished to be alone with his supporters, and that Solomon and his party were not invited.[1] This was sufficient to warrant apprehensions for the king—the case of Absalom made this only too natural—but to report treasonable *deeds*[2] was nothing else than a clever piece of palace intrigue. This at least is the result we must arrive at, if the relater of the incident tells all that he knew, and judges the events impartially. But it is quite possible that he knew more than he actually says, and had reasons for concealing his true opinion. On the other hand, it is possible that he had been a partisan of Adonijah—he makes 'all the men of Israel' belong to that party[3]—and therefore regarded events in a light too unfavourable to Solomon, although he had not the courage to express plainly his unfavourable judgment.[4]

Abiathar's removal from the priesthood was an event of the greatest importance in the history of the religious cultus in Israel. A new priesthood took the place of the house of Eli, which had been so seriously threatened under Saul, but had finally obtained favour again under David. The importance of the change appears from its having been prophetically referred to in the history of Eli. The latter traced his own and his family's priesthood to Egypt, and probably to Aaron as priestly ancestor. We do not know what the claims of Zadok were. He can hardly have begun an absolutely new line in the sense that he was not a Levite at all.[5] Solomon would have avoided appointing in Abiathar's place

---

[1] 1 Kings i. 10, 19, 26. [2] 1 Kings i. 25. [3] 1 Kings i. 9, *cf.* especially ii. 15.

[4] [On further consideration I am more inclined than formerly to regard Adonijah's guilt as proven. In this case there is still less ground for suspecting Nathan and Bathsheba of intrigue than is represented in the text above. There is thus, however, all the more reason for supposing that the narrator is not quite free from tendency.]

[5] *Cf. ThStW.* iii. 299 ff. ; Baudissin, *Gesch. des Priestert.* 194, 197 ff.

one who had no claim whatever to priestly descent. From this time forth the priesthood at Jerusalem belonged to the *benê Ṣadoq* (Zadok). After the erection of the temple they succeeded in raising their office, and consequently their house, to greater prosperity and power.

§ 48. *Solomon, King.*

Solomon's task as king was obvious. As David's successor he entered on a rich inheritance. All he had to do was to preserve what David had established, and to strengthen it. His foreign policy must be to maintain the extraordinary predominance that Israel had won: at home he had to render permanent the unification of the tribes that David had accomplished, and bind Israel to the house of the great king.

This last Solomon was not able to accomplish. He himself, however, so far as we can see, seems to have had strength and ability enough to maintain the position that Israel had reached. David's kingdom remained in his hands, if not uncontested yet substantially unimpaired, and although he was not able, or else was not concerned, to keep the tribes of Israel contented under his sceptre, there was no outbreak so long as he himself lived. The only attempt at an uprising of which we hear—that of Jeroboam—was vigorously suppressed. However great the desire of the northern tribes to withdraw from the house of David may have been, they did not attempt to emancipate themselves from the powerful sceptre of Solomon.

This shows, to begin with the internal relations, that Solomon was not the weak, inactive king that many have represented him as being. But in external affairs as well, he seems to have been equal to his task, at least in all important affairs.

There was no lack of difficulties. The death of the mighty David was doubtless an event long looked forward to by many of Israel's adversaries. When there was added to this the disappearance from the scene of his bravest soldier, Joab, the opportunity for attacking Israel became still more inviting. Hadad, a scion of the ancient royal house of Edom which David had overthrown,[1] had escaped to Egypt. Like Solomon himself, he had succeeded in obtaining for his wife a princess of the house of Pharaoh, the sister of the queen Taḥpeneûs.[2] Immediately on the death of David he returned home, and appears to have wrested from Solomon at least a part of Edom.[3] However, either his dominion was insignificant and harmless in the view of Solomon, or the latter succeeded in recovering possession of Edom, for the approach to the Red Sea at Eziongeber remained in the hands of Solomon.[4]

A second adversary is said to have sprung up for Solomon in the north, at Damascus. Rezôn ben Eliada‘, a general of that Hadad‘ezer of Aram Zoba whom David had conquered,[5] severed himself from his master. After living for some time a life of adventure, he founded a dominion of his own, and elevated the ancient city of Damascus to be its capital. He drove out the governor whom David is represented as having once placed there, and Solomon did not succeed in recovering the city. Here, therefore, if the narrative is historical,[6] Solomon must have suffered a real, and apparently a permanent, loss. Yet it is hard to say whether at the time it was much felt; for probably neither

---

[1] 2 Sam. viii. 13 f. On this see above, p. 163 f.
[2] The conjecture of Klost. *ad loc.* is uncalled for.
[3] 1 Kings xi. 14 ff. On the conclusion of the narrative, *cf.* LXX., and above, pp. 53, 57 f. The narrative belongs to So, and is probably historical. Yet it is remarkable that the names of both the Pharaoh and his sister-in-law are lacking. The same is true indeed in the case of Solomon's own marriage, but there we have to deal only with scanty notices, while here we have a detailed narrative. The conjecture of Stade (*Gesch. Isr.* i. 302), that Solomon's marriage with a daughter of Pharaoh was really brought about by this incident, is inviting.
[4] There is no reason to question this fact (Stade). The question suggests itself, how long the contempt for Israel (ver. 25*b*) lasted.
[5] 2 Sam. viii. 3 ff. *Cf.* above, p. 162.
[6] It is to be found in 1 Kings xi. 23 f., 25*a* of the MT., whereas in the LXX. it is lacking. See above, p. 53, where it is shown that the absence of the passage from the LXX. is most probably not accidental. Moreover, *v.* 24 offers special difficulties, so that the whole incident is brought into suspicion. See also Meyer, *Gesch. d. Alt.* 371. Nevertheless, the kingdom of Damascus must have come into existence not long after Solomon. To this extent some historical reminiscence or other may very well underlie the story.

David nor Solomon was ever really in possession of Damascus and Aram Damascus.¹ Here again, just as in the internal affairs of Solomon's kingdom, the prospect for the future seems to have been the most serious thing, for certainly in course of time the kingdom of Damascus was to become one of Israel's most dangerous adversaries.

If Solomon had thus in the south, perhaps also in the north, received a certain check, it was not a very important one, and elsewhere he appears to have accomplished not a little towards maintaining and strengthening the external position of Israel. It is possible that he laid the greatest stress not so much on the conquests of David that lay more on the outskirts of his kingdom, as on maintaining the territory of Israel proper. It is, at all events, a fact that he defended the latter against hostile attacks by the erection of strong fortresses, an undertaking the meritoriousness of which cannot be questioned. In the north, he fortified Ḥazor and Megiddo; in the neighbourhood of Jerusalem, Beth-ḥoron and the Canaanitish royal city of Gezer;² towards the south, as a protection for the frontier and the caravan route from Hebron to Elath, the city of Tamar.³ Gezer was conquered for Solomon by the Pharaoh of Egypt whose daughter he married. Mention is also made of a city called Ba'alath, of uncertain site, perhaps near Gezer, as being one of Solomon's fortified places.⁴ Moreover, he devoted a great deal of care to increasing and keeping in good condition the materials of war, and the cavalry that he had, stationed in a line of garrison cities. If the numbers given are open to suspicion, the fact itself cannot be doubted.⁵ All this shows that we can hardly speak of a decline of Israel's power under Solomon, even if he had to give up certain advance posts. Still, after all,

---

¹ See above, p. 163, note 2.
² On the site of this city see Klost. *SaKö.* 328*b* [and above, p. 151; also especially *ZDPV*. 1894, p. 36 ff. It is Tell Jezer; in Josephus, Γάζηρα, also Γάδαρα].
³ Tadmor (= Palmyra), which Klost. still retains, is certainly incorrect.
⁴ 1 Kings ix. 15*b*, 16-18. The notices are old and genuine (A), even if the present text is quite in disorder. See above, p. 52 f.
⁵ See below, p. 188 f., and especially p. 188, note 5.

Solomon did not attain the greatness of his father. Brought up as a king's son, without the opportunity or the necessity of steeling his will in the hard school of danger and self-denial, he was also destitute of his father's energy and originality. He was more interested in the privileges of the throne and its comforts, than in its lofty duties and mission. The despotic tendencies which, in the case of the father, appeared only occasionally, and were always restrained or suppressed, became, in the case of the son, a fundamental trait of character. His chief interest was in costly buildings, foreign wives, and gorgeous display.

At the same time he laid stress on the regular administration of justice, and his strongest point was the organisation of the government of the land. The final subjugation and absorption of the Canaanites went on simultaneously with this.[1] Both probably served the same end. Solomon needed plenty of money and workmen for his expensive buildings. This had to be supplied by his subjects. He recognised no distinction among the population; there was none that could escape the burdens that fell on the community.[2] He treated all Israel as a unity, and divided it, without any regard to diversity of tribes or the distinction of Israelite and Canaanite, into twelve districts. Each was superintended by an overseer, although the names have in part been lost.[3] The taxes were fixed on the basis of this division. It was doubtless on the same principle that the forced labour was regulated, which Solomon needed for the vast structures that he reared for

---

[1] 1 Kings ix. 20 f. MT. (in the LXX. following x. 22). The notice is certainly late (D²), but still pre-exilic ('unto this day,' v. 21), and, notwithstanding v. 22, not incredible. Yet see Stade, Gesch. p. 303.

[2] 1 Kings ix. 22 conflicts with iv. 7 ff.

[3] 1 Kings iv. 7-19 (A). Stade, Gesch. i. p. 305, speaks of thirteen districts. But the number twelve is guaranteed by the twelve months (iv. 7; v. 7), whereas iv. 19c is corrupt. The usual expedient (supplying *Judah* in v. 19) is probably a mistake. Moreover, taxation and forced labour are by no means the same thing (against Stade); cf. the distinction between persons and things recognised in the use of נציב and מס in iv. 5, 6; xi. 28 (house of Joseph). On iv. 7-19 MT., cf. the LXX. The MT. has only seven of the twelve names. Ed. Rom. has one name more (Βεεν [Βαιωρ] from בן or בן־חור?); Luc. has some more, specially corrupt (e.g. in v. 13).

purposes of war and peace. In Lebanon alone he is said to have had ten thousand labourers constantly at work under Adoniram.[1] The distinction between Israelite and Canaanite continued to be observed only to this extent, that the districts that had formerly been Canaanite were considerably smaller than the others. Hence if the contribution was rendered by each district in succession, it would fall on the Canaanites heavier. They were indeed become 'tributary' through this forcible incorporation into Israel.

The simple court kept by Saul and David had known nothing of such burdens. They would therefore now be felt all the more severe. There was just as little regard for the freedom as for the property of subjects. No wonder then that, in course of time, the discontent which had probably long been cherished in secret, burst forth in angry revolt. It was no accident that this originated with the house of Joseph, and so with Ephraim, and still less that it originated with one of Solomon's overseers. The old enmity of the northern tribes against the house of Jesse, and the discontent with the present severe *régime*, were two springs whose waters flowed into the same channel.

Jeroboam ben Nebāt, an Ephraimite of Zerēda, placed himself at the head of the movement. He seems to have been a young man of low station, the son of a poor widow. It was towards the end of his reign, as he was building Millo[2] and so 'closing up the breach of the city of David,' that the king made Jeroboam's acquaintance among his workmen, and learned to appreciate his value. Soon he had assigned to him the oversight of the forced labour of the house of Joseph—the very best opportunity for becoming acquainted with the complaints of the people and turning them to advantage. After a shorter or longer time, Jeroboam resolved to raise the flag of revolt. He achieved nothing, however: either the conspiracy was prematurely discovered, or the rising was suppressed. Jeroboam himself escaped

[1] 1 Kings v. 27 f. (So). The question arises how the following statement in v. 29 f. agrees with this. It is usually regarded as an addition by the hand of D².

[2] [See *ZDPV*. 1894, p. 6.]

to Egypt, where he met with a good reception from the Pharaoh Shishak, the Shishonq who founded the twenty-second dynasty of Manetho. It is worthy of note that Jeroboam was supported in his enterprise by a prophet, Ahijah of Shiloh.[1] The discontent with the *régime* of Solomon had affected all classes of the community.

The traditional view of Solomon represents him as a king equally rich in wisdom and justice, and in gold and treasures. His wisdom and justice are proved by his measures for securing his frontier and for regulating the administration of the kingdom, and by his celebrated, and certainly historical, judicial judgment,[2] which indeed leaves posterity to wonder to which of the great king's endowments the palm should be awarded, his wisdom or his justice. There was therefore good warrant for attributing to him many sayings of practical wisdom. It is also quite credible that, on the occasion of his accession, he had a vision pointing out to him his way and the will of Yahvé.[3] It can cause no surprise that vast treasure passed through his hands, when we reflect with what severity his taxes were collected, and remember that he also undertook many profitable enterprises.

It is beyond doubt that Solomon was the first to introduce the horse into Israel on a large scale, especially for military purposes.[4] It is remarkable that all allusions to this are to be found in connection with later statements concerning Solomon's magnificence and splendour.[5] Still, this cannot prevent us from regarding them as historically reliable, at least as far as regards the fact in question. If Egypt was, as it appears to have been, the land from which Syria got its supply of horses, and if

---

[1] The narrative is to be found in 1 Kings xi. 26-40. *Vv.* 26-28, 40 are certainly old. The intervening narrative concerning the insurrection proper has fallen out; but this does not show that *vv.* 29-39 have *taken its place*. The passage 29-39 has evidently been revised, but its kernel seems to be old. (See above, p. 58.) Note especially שֵׁבֶט אֶחָד, *v.* 32, 35. Stade (306 f.) takes a different view.

[2] 1 Kings iii. 16 ff. (So, or even A?).

[3] 1 Kings iii. 4 ff. See above, p. 57 f., esp. p. 57, note 5.

[4] See Rhiem in *HWB.* p. 865 [²885], and such passages as 1 Kings xvi. 9.

[5] 1 Kings v. 6, x. 26; *cf.* ix. 19. It is certainly very suspicious that two of these passages are wanting in the LXX.

Solomon was the son-in-law of the Pharaoh reigning there, there is probably also no serious objection to be made to the statement that Solomon was able to make a lucrative business of his importation of Egyptian horses.[1] The visit of the queen of the old Sabæan kingdom to Solomon's court was probably also, in the first instance, connected with commercial affairs. I am not inclined to relegate it either, once for all, to the region of legend.[2] For though later legend may have considerably exaggerated Solomon's splendour, all those legends could not have originated without some foundation in the facts themselves. Solomon's expeditions, on the other hand, to the Arabian gold land of Ophir,[3] seem to me to be specially well attested by the sources.[4] It was a case of a single ship, which Ḥiram of Tyre[5] manned with his skilled seamen, to bring natural products and articles of trade from Arabia Felix.

All this is not at all inconsistent[6] with Solomon's treasury often being empty, finally so empty that he was obliged to pledge twenty cities in Galilee to Ḥiram.[7] His marriage with a daughter of Pharaoh made his court expensive, and his castles and fortifications must have consumed enormous sums of money.

§ 49. *Solomon's Temple and Palace.*

We cannot deny Solomon also a deep interest in religion and cultus. His building the temple testifies to this. It was, indeed,

[1] 1 Kings x. 28 f. The text is almost hopelessly corrupt.
[2] We must assign the narrative (x. 1 ff.) to So. See above, p. 58. On the kingdom of Saba, see now esp. Glaser, *Skizze der Gesch. und Geogr. Arabiens* (1890), p. 357 ff., and thereon Sprenger in *ZDMG.* 1890, 501 ff.
[3] On its site see Glaser, *ibid.*; but esp. Sprenger, *ibid.* 514 ff.
[4] 1 Kings ix. 26 ff.; x. 11 (A and So). The two passages are in perfect agreement with each other, although they come from different hands. In x. 11 the ship is actually called Ḥiram's ship, which is fully accounted for by the facts set forth in ix. 26 ff. I would assign x. 22 to a third not very late source. Here there are two ships (of Tarshish). The passage is further interesting on account of the information it gives of the nature and cargo of these Tartessus ships. [On Tarshish compare now also Le Page Renouf, in *Proc. Soc. Bibl. Arch.* 1894, p. 104 ff., and 138 ff.]   [5] On Hiram see above, p. 157, note 2.
[6] On this and the preceding see Stade, *Gesch.* i. 303 f.
[7] 1 Kings ix. 10 f.

only as a constituent part of his magnificent royal city that he built it. But we can hardly suppose that he did not at the same time contemplate providing the nation with a sanctuary of special importance and attractive power. Nevertheless, it was certainly not a part of his design, at least for the present, to constitute the temple the one valid and legitimate sanctuary, as Deuteronomy afterwards did, although in time this result would follow of itself. But there is hardly any good reason for denying that the king was animated by the aim of constituting his sanctuary more and more the centre of the religious life of the nation, in the same way as Jerusalem had become, by David's influence and his own, and the presence of his magnificent court, more and more the centre of public and civil life. In fact, although the temple was only a constituent part of the palace buildings, it was at the same time so grandly and independently planned, as to betray a higher destination already present in the mind of Solomon. A mere palace sanctuary, were it ever so splendid, would be smaller and simpler in its plan.

A number of scholars have recently done meritorious work in the careful investigation of the subject of Solomon's buildings. In the first place, Stade advanced our knowledge of the subject by a thorough-going investigation of the text of our account in 1 Kings v.-vii.[1] Then, on the basis of his penetrating critical investigations, he accomplished the reconstruction of the temple and the other buildings of Solomon in a manner that is highly attractive, and, in many points, very satisfactory.[2] His results have been accepted in important points by a number of those who have taken up the subject more recently. In particular, his critical results have been acknowledged by Chipiez and Perrot in their great and splendid work.[3] Where they deviate from Stade in their restorations of the buildings themselves, they not infrequently wander from the basis of exact demonstration. Friedrich,[4] also, who notwithstanding

---

[1] *ZAW.* iii. 129 ff.   [2] *Gesch. Isr.* i. 311 ff.

[3] *Le temple de Jérusalem et la maison du bois-Liban.* Paris, 1889.

[4] *Tempel und Palast Salomos,* Innsbr. 1887, where special attention is devoted to the meaning of the word צלע. See still more recently, *Die vorderas. Holztektonik,* 1891. [Also the handbooks on Archæology.]

agreement with Stade on many matters, gives a different explanation of several important points, and thus reaches a considerably different general result, does not seem to me to be always happy in the points where he pursues an independent course. Although he is able to refer in several cases to the Septuagint and Targum, it must not be forgotten that these late translators themselves had no idea of the meaning of the disputed terms.[1] After all, it must be admitted that we have only a basis of hypothesis to go upon, and have often, in the absence of certainty, to seek the greatest probability.

The site of the temple of Solomon is, in all probability, to be sought in the neighbourhood of that spot on the hill of Zion which is still regarded as sacred by the Arabs of to-day, and is known as the Dome of the Rock. As is well known, there is to be found within the latter a sacred rock, of which there still lies exposed a portion of some fifty-seven feet in length, forty-three feet in breadth, and six and a half feet in height.[2]

We may assume that the altar erected by David at the threshing-floor of Araunah, and therefore, also, the altar of burnt-offering of Solomon, stood on this rock. There is still evidence, in the signs of an escape-channel connected with an aqueduct, that the rock once served as an altar.[3] From this rock as a starting-point, the position of the temple itself may be accurately determined, for the altar of burnt-offering was placed east of the temple, in front of its chief entrance in the outer court. The temple itself, therefore, extended lengthwise westward from the altar. As the hill slopes somewhat toward the west, there was need here of somewhat extensive artificial foundations.[4]

---

[1] *Cf.* also Wolff, *ZDPV.* xi. 60 ff., and his *Tempel v. Jerus.*, 1887.

[2] *Cf.* Adler, *Der Felsendom und die hl. Grabeskirche zu Jerus.* (1873), p. 17 ff.; Schick, *Beit el Makdas oder der alte Tempelplatz zu Jerus.* (1887), p. 7 ff., and the illustration on p. 14 (fig. 2); Bäd.³ 47 [Eng. Transl.² p. 45]; Ebers and Guthe, *Paläst.* 67.

[3] On this see Bäd.³ 47 [Eng. Transl.² p. 45]; and on its significance, esp. Guthe, *ZDPV.* xiii. 123 ff.

[4] The topographical investigations of recent times, founded on the results of excavations, have provided more detailed information on this subject. See esp.

It is only the inner dimensions of the temple that have been supplied us, so that we can form no exact idea either of the height or structure of the roof, or of the thickness of the outer wall. The details of Ezekiel can to some extent be applied here and there with great probability, since Ezekiel knew the temple of Solomon, and made it the basis of his description of the future temple.

The temple strictly so called, consisted of two principal compartments—the Debîr, or so-called Holy of Holies, at the back, perfectly dark and built in the shape of a cube; and before it an oblong front room. The latter was forty cubits in length, twenty in breadth, and thirty in height. There stood in it an altar made of cedar-wood, the so-called table of shew-bread. The sacrificial loaves of Yahvé were brought at regular intervals, as had been the case before at Nob, and probably at the ark. They were deposited on this altar-table before the face of Yahvé. The outer room probably also contained, even in the temple of Solomon, although this has latterly been contested, the altar of incense. This room also must have been comparatively dark, as the windows of moderate size through which it received its light, were at a height of not less than twenty cubits above the ground.

The back room which constituted the *adytum* proper, called in Hebrew *Debîr*, formed a cube, twenty cubits in length and breadth and height. It was enclosed above by a roof of its own, while the temple building itself was continued to a height of thirty cubits. There was thus over the Holy of Holies[1] an upper story ten cubits high. The Holy of Holies was the dwelling-place proper of Yahvé. It contained, in the case of the temple of Solomon, so far as we know, the ark and nothing else. Over this, representing the presence of God, and acting as guardians, so to speak, of the sacred place,[2] stood two cherubim carved in olive-wood, each ten cubits in height.

Zimmermann, *Karten und Plane zur Topogr. d. alt. Jerus. nebst Begleitschrift.* Also Warren, *Underground Jerusalem*; Wilson and Warren, *Recovery of Jerusalem* (1871); *Survey of Western Palestine* (1884). Also Ebers and Guthe, *Paläst. in Bild und Wort*; and Guthe in *ZDPV.* v. 7 ff., 271 ff.

[1] The name itself is younger. [2] *Cf.* the cherubim of Paradise.

In front of the building was an entrance-hall twenty cubits broad and ten cubits long, at the entrance to which stood two pillars cast in bronze, called Jachin and Boaz. The temple was surrounded on its three remaining sides—those facing north, west, and south—by a structure fifteen cubits high, attached directly to the outer wall. It enclosed the three sides of the temple to half their height, and consisted of three stories, each five cubits high, and each containing a number of apartments. These appear to have served for the accommodation of temple paraphernalia and votive offerings. The whole building was surrounded by the outer court, the size of which we do not know. This latter was the real place of worship for the people, where they presented their sacrifices and celebrated their feasts. The temple itself was entered by the priests alone.

The other buildings erected by Solomon on Zion immediately adjoined the temple enclosure proper, which constituted a considerable part of the whole. They lay in all probability farther south, where on the one hand there is more space, and on the other Zion slopes down in such a way that one would naturally speak of going up to the temple from the palace.[1] We are not told in what relation they stood to the old citadel of David. It is most natural to suppose that the latter was pulled down when Solomon's own palace and that of his Egyptian wife had been built. It may perhaps have stood on a site afterwards occupied by one of Solomon's halls. The buildings constituting Solomon's palace consisted of three parts. The first was the so-called House of the Forest of Lebanon. It was a hundred cubits long, and half as broad, and rested on forty-five cedar pillars; looking therefore, from a distance, like a cedar forest. The purpose of this stately building may be inferred from its hall-like plan. It may have served for gatherings of the nobility, the elders of Israel, while its upper apartments might very well form the armoury of the royal castle.[2]

---

[1] See Guthe, *ZDPV*. v. 314.
[2] *Cf.* Isa. xxxix. 2; xxii. 8; 1 Kings x. 16 f.

The second part, lying between the House of Lebanon and the palace proper, consisted of two halls. The first of them—that lying nearer the city—was a pillared hall, fifty cubits long and thirty cubits broad, provided with a stately vestibule. In immediate connection with it stood another hall which served as a hall of judgment. Here Solomon dispensed justice, while the first-mentioned hall, in front of it, probably formed only the entrance to it—a place where people seeking justice assembled to await their summons to appear before the throne.

The third part of the whole group of buildings forming Solomon's citadel, consisted of the royal palace itself, and that of the queen. It was enclosed between the temple with its outer court towards the north, and the above-mentioned halls used for state buildings toward the south, as if protected on both sides. We are not informed of the structure of these buildings forming the palace proper. The priestly narrator, accurately informed as he is about the temple and the outer buildings, seems not to have set foot in these. We know only that the palace consisted of two main buildings, the palace of Solomon and his family, and that of the daughter of Pharaoh, which immediately adjoined it.

So stately a building as Solomon's temple or his palace was for that age, could not indeed be carried through in Israel with native labour or native materials. The finer qualities of wood grew, in Israel itself, only in small quantities; cedars, hardly anywhere. The art of working in stone and building with squared stone seems to have been still unknown in Israel. Still less had casting in bronze, and in general the more artistic kinds of work in metal, been naturalised in Israel. Hence it was necessary to look for foreign help.

David had already employed Phœnician masons and carpenters, and Phœnician cedar, for his palace on Zion, which was at all events a much more unassuming structure, and the treaty with Ḥiram of Tyre was still in existence. It was thus a matter of course that Solomon would follow his father's example.[1] The wood was hewn on Lebanon by the forced labour of Israelites in the service of Solomon, transported by Ḥiram's men to the sea, and conveyed to a suitable harbour near Jerusalem (Joppa). For these services Solomon handed over to Ḥiram great quantities of wheat and oil from the produce of his land.

The time spent in building the temple was almost seven years. The bronze work was cast by a Tyrian artificer named Ḥuram-abî,[2] who erected his workshop at Succoth in the valley of the Jordan. On the completion of the temple, Solomon celebrated a splendid festival of dedication, and brought the ark with ceremonial pomp to the sacred inner apartment of the temple.[3] On this occasion Solomon pronounced a highly poetical dedication oracle, which is somewhat mutilated in the present text, but can be recovered from the LXX.[4] The later editor substituted for it a detailed dedicatory prayer of Solomon. The saying runs thus :—

> 'The sun hath Yahvé set in the canopy of heaven.
> Himself hath said, he will dwelt in darkness.
> I have built thee a house to dwell in,
> A place to dwell in for eternal ages.'

The importance of Solomon's temple[5] has been explained in what was said of the significance of David's choice of Jerusalem as capital of the land, and centre of the religious life of Israel. Solomon was in this respect only the executor of his father's designs. But what was thus accomplished—David preparing the way and Solomon carrying the work through—can hardly be estimated at too high a value. In particular, it was only through

---

[1] Doubtless the Phœnicians themselves worked for the most part according to foreign patterns (*cf.* Pietschmann, 140 ff., 265 ff.). Hence we may assume that Solomon's temple and its various fittings bore resemblance in many points not only to Phœnician, but also to other, and especially to Assyrian, temples of that age.

[2] [On this name see Giesebrecht, in *ZAW*. i. 239 ff.]

[3] 1 Kings viii. 1 ff. The piece has been repeatedly revised, as the numerous additions in the LXX. are enough to show. The kernel is old. See Wellh. *Bl.*[4] 234 ff., and above, p. 52.

[4] [Wellhausen, *Bl.*[4] 236 ; *cf.* Cheyne, *Origin of the Psalter*, pp. 193, 212.]

[5] See also Smend, in *StKr.* 1884, 689 ff.

the temple of Jerusalem that Judah and the dynasty of David, which were soon to be severed from the rest of Israel and lead for centuries a separate existence, were at all able, and especially for so long a time able, to maintain themselves. The religious side of David's work had attained through the temple a character of permanence. The ark had found its place, and God himself a home in Israel, for all time. If Judah was only partly able to administer this legacy of its two greatest kings, it would soon perceive what a treasure it had thus secured in its midst. From the point of view of religion, it was the place of the imageless worship of Yahvé, a worship that must more and more win general approbation; from the political point of view, it was the most splendid sanctuary in Israel, which surpassed all others, and soon became the ideal support of the house of David in time of trouble. In both these respects the temple became the corner-stone on which Israel's enemies shattered themselves, and the foundation-stone on which Israel's hope built up for itself a new future.

§ 50. *Civilisation and Religion of the First Period of the Monarchy.*[1]

1. *Mode of life. Political organisation. Literature.*—The transition from nomadic to agricultural life had been accomplished in the preceding period. It was simply the consequence of this change of life, and of what Israel saw of the life of the former possessors of the land, that people became more and more accustomed to dwell in cities and to adopt the forms of city life. Gibeah, Saul's royal seat, seems to have been nothing more than an unassuming peasant village, and his citadel there not much more than a dwelling-house, arranged after the primitive fashion of the age. In David's time things changed, and still more in Solomon's. The value of walled and fortified cities, and the

---

[1] [See also now the related sections in the Archæological Handbooks of Nowack and Benzinger, and in Smend's *A Tl. Religionsgeschichte.*]

charm and importance of royal castles and skilfully constructed stone buildings, came to be felt. We see at all points the wider prospect and changed mode of life.

It is easy to see that it was impossible to do justice to the higher claims of this age of progress without help from without. The original affinity of the Canaanites and the Phœnicians was not only no hindrance, but perhaps actually an incentive, to closer relations between Israel and Tyre and Sidon, the headquarters of the Phœnician city republics. Israel had, on the whole, come to terms in a peaceable manner with the former masters of the land. Occasional provocations and individual cases of oppression of Canaanite cities by Saul and Solomon, in no way altered the relation. The Phœnicians were hardly any longer conscious of the old connection.

The alliance with Ḥiram was fruitful of many results for Israel. Without it David's and Solomon's buildings would hardly be conceivable. The stimulus that Israel itself derived from them must, in any case, be estimated at a high value. Moreover Israel, which up to this time appears to have devoted itself exclusively to its own land, became now acquainted with the commerce of the world on a larger scale. It was at first a timid and very unassuming attempt that Israel made, in a sphere that was afterwards to become almost a second nature to it. Yet in view of this later development of the people of Israel, Solomon's expeditions to Ophir have a special interest.

An advance in political organisation and its institutions was just as much a matter of course, on the rise of the monarchy, as the development of intellectual and moral life.

The old associations of clan and tribe, the classical testimony to which is to be found in the Blessing of Jacob in Gen. xlix., still retained their vitality. Saul relied on his tribe of Benjamin,[1] David on Judah. The movements led by Shimei and Jeroboam also had their support in tribal feeling. Alongside of this, moreover, there existed at this time, especially in the cities, an

[1] *Cf.* 1 Sam. xxii. 7.

oligarchic communal polity after the Phœnician pattern.[1] But both of these lost in importance through the establishment of the monarchic system. They were supplanted either in part or altogether, by independent organisations. Solomon's partition of the land into districts for taxation, broke through the old tribal system. The requirements of the military organisation of David and Solomon would hardly be met by such a muster as the heads of tribes and elders of districts had had at their disposal. The object served by David's census of the nation was certainly similar to that of Solomon's division of the land into districts. With this was connected the appearance of definite offices, which can now be clearly discerned, and which became in time indispensable to the monarchy. A whole staff of officials was brought into existence, the highest representatives of which are named for us in the case of David and Solomon.[2] It was inevitable that there should soon spring up, in addition to the occupants of the highest position, a number of other holders of royal office.

Two of the highest court officials bore the names of *Mazkîr* and *Sôphēr*. These were the Chancellor, and the Secretary or Secretaries of State.[3] They indicate that we have reached a distinct turning-point in the intellectual life of the age. The art of writing, hitherto only exceptionally found, had become the rule.[4] Israel had thus attained the rank of a nation manifesting literary activity. If posterity has more than a vague knowledge of the past of Israel, it owes it to the circumstance just mentioned. It may be left undecided how far we still have records dating from the days of David—*e.g.* from the hand of his Mazkîr and Sôphēr. At all events, the documents Je and Da may be traced indirectly back to this officer. David's elegy on Saul and Jonathan may belong directly to him. With still greater probability was it argued above, that considerable fragments of the

[1] *Cf. e.g.* 1 Sam. xi. 3; xvi. 4; 2 Sam. iii. 17; v. 3; xvii. 4, 15; xix. 12; 1 Kings viii. 1, 3.

[2] 2 Sam. viii. 16-18; xx. 23-25; 1 Kings iv. 2-6; *cf. v.* 7 ff. Solomon took over several of these officers from his father. On the list of his officers, see above p. 186, note 3.   [3] In the time of Solomon there were two.

[4] At least, the name *Sôphēr* shows this. *Cf.* 2 Sam. xi. 14.

work of this officer of Solomon's have reached us.[1] In any case these were not the only products of the literary activity of the age of Solomon. Those songs, belonging in part to a much older age, which formed the contents of the *Book of the Wars of Yahvé*, —*i.e.* the wars of Israel during its heroic age—and of the *Book of the Excellent*,[2] were now also collected. Song-books and annals thus formed the continuation of a literature, the beginnings of which belonged to the preceding period, and the most magnificent fruits of which were to be matured in the period immediately following.

2. *Morals.*—Saul and David were men of the sword. The iron age did not belie itself in their conduct and that of their contemporaries. The usages of war had scarcely been at all mitigated as compared with the preceding age. The cruel custom of the *ḥerem*—the ban [3]—still continued in force. Nay, Samuel is represented as having enforced it with special severity.[4] Even where the *ḥerem* is not specially mentioned, the enemy seems to have been treated with the old severity. On being conquered they were massacred,[5] and in many predatory excursions not even women and children were spared.[6] Even where political or humane considerations might demand partial or complete clemency, the lot of the conquered was hard enough.[7]

The character of the age naturally brought with it other savage customs. It was a hundred foreskins of slaughtered Philistines that Saul demanded as a dowry at the hand of his prospective son-in-law.[8] Saul's posterity were sacrificed by David to a terrible superstition, and were exposed unburied, under the open sky, as food for the birds and beasts.[9] Under the

---

[1] See above, p. 56 f.
[2] On these see above, vol. i. p. 81 ff. [Eng. Transl., i. 90 ff.].
[3] See above, p. 64 f., and Driver, *Notes*, p. 100 f.
[4] 1 Sam. xv. 10 ff.   [5] 1 Kings xi. 14 f. (MT, 24); 2 Kings viii. 4 (?).
[6] 1 Sam. xxvii. 9 ff.
[7] 2 Sam. viii. 1 ff.; xii. 31. On this passage see above, p. 162, note 5.
[8] 1 Sam. xviii. 25 ff.
[9] 2 Sam. xxi. *Cf.* the hanging up of the bodies of Saul and Jonathan by the Philistines. 1 Sam. xxxi. 10, 12; 2 Sam. xxi. 12.

curse of the same dark delusion, Saul himself was ready to cut off his own heroic son on the very day of his victory.¹

But gross and savage customs were counterbalanced by gentler traits and kindlier usages. They show more and more how noble energies were gradually evolving themselves, which were destined, in alliance with the religion of Israel, to break through the old Semitic modes of thought and life. The friendship of David and Jonathan is for all ages the type of the purest and noblest human friendship. David's dirge over Saul and his noble son is a unique expression of noble sentiment. His conduct towards Nathan is a triumph of noble, truly royal feeling. Rizpah bath Aiah, Saul's concubine, is the Antigone of Hebrew antiquity. The noble, honest pride of Barzillai the Gileadite, and the grateful fidelity of the people of Jabesh towards Saul, find their parallel but seldom in any age.² Abel and Dan were a retreat for good old customs, which were clung to with piety.³ Above all, however, the monarchy itself was a guarantee of law.⁴ It abolished blood-revenge at least in principle,⁵ and procured rest for the citizen from aggressor and oppressor.

3. *Religion and Belief.*—Yahvé is undisputedly the God of Israel. Saul and David cannot for a moment be suspected of idolatry. It is only of Solomon that anything of that kind is related. He built his foreign wives altars for their gods. The author of our Book of Kings regards this toleration as a serious offence, and relates at the same time that Solomon gave his heart to foreign gods. However, this last charge is not placed beyond doubt;⁶ and if it is made good, Solomon's foreign worship forms an exception to all we know of the whole period.

---

¹ 1 Sam. xiv. 44. *Cf.* also 2 Sam. xxiv. 1 ff.
² 2 Sam. i. 19 ff. ; xxi. 10 ; xix. 32 ff. ; 1 Sam. xxxi. 11 f.
³ 2 Sam. xx. 18 f. ; *cf.* my translation.
⁴ 1 Kings iii. 5 ff., 16 ff. ; 2 Sam. xv. 1 ff. ; xiv. 4 ff.
⁵ 2 Sam. xiv. 6 ff. ; iii. 28 ; 1 Kings ii. 5.
⁶ 1 Kings xi. 4 ff. The whole chapter as far as *v.* 13 has, at all events, been very freely revised by D². See especially *v.* 11 ff. Only *v.* 7 is certainly old (A?). With *v.* 6 *cf.* Deut. i. 36 (מלא אחרי); עם שלם in *v.* 4 resembles the language of Chronicles.

On the other hand, in this age the worship of Yahvé was, in many respects, not regulated in the way that a later age supposed. Samuel himself sacrificed not at *one* place but at a whole series of high places. In the absence of an altar, Saul made use of an ordinary stone on occasion; and as soon as the stone had received the blood of the victim Yahvé was satisfied.¹ Solomon also did not confine himself to Jerusalem, but offered sacrifice on the high place of Gibeon.² Samuel, the priest of the ark at Shiloh, was not of Levitical descent, but was an Ephraimite. There were in David's time also non-Levitical occupants of priestly offices, along with Zadok and Abiathar. David wore priestly garments, and he and Saul offered sacrifice when they saw fit.⁴

In the earlier part of this period the name Ba'al was still without scruple used for Yahvé,⁵ although from the time of David the practice seems to have fallen out of use, at least in proper names. The worship of Yahvé under an image was likewise still practised. The shrines at Dan and Ophrah doubtless still continued to exist. After the destruction of the sanctuary at Shiloh, there was an *ephod* at Nob in the charge of Ahimelech ben Ahitub of the house of Eli. Another was to be found with Saul, in the charge of Ahijah ben Ahitub of the house of Eli, probably the brother of Ahimelech.⁶ Perhaps the latter *ephod* was that of Gideon of Ophrah; at all events, we have no reason to regard it as different from that of Ophrah. Ahimelech's *ephod* was afterwards brought by Abiathar to David. There was in connection with it

---

¹ 1 Sam. xiv. 32 ff. *Cf.* above, p. 99 (the oldest kind of *Maṣṣēba*).

² 1 Kings iii. 3, 4 (D² and A): *v.* 2 is a later addition which limits the admission made in *v.* 3. On the *Bama* at Gibeon, *cf.* 2 Sam. xxi. 6, 9.

³ 2 Sam. viii. 18; xx. 26. See, however, Baudissin, *Priestert.* 191.

⁴ 2 Sam. v. 17 f.; vi. 14; 1 Sam. xiv. 34, 35. The whole scene was enacted without the co-operation of the priest who was present with the army; moreover, in xiii. 8 ff. (R), it is probable that Saul's offence did not, in the original form of the document, consist in his sacrificing without the co-operation of Samuel.

⁵ Eshba'al, Meriba'al, Be'eliada', 2 Sam. v. 16. Note especially 1 Sam. xiv. 49, according to emended text, Ishiô = Eshba'al—*i.e.* Ba'al = Yahvé. On the significance of this fact see above, p. 98.

⁶ The genealogy of these priests, however, involves us in difficulty, as Zadok is also called a son of Ahitub. *Cf.* 1 Sam. xiv. 3; xxii. 11, 20; 2 Sam. viii. 17 (see my transl. and Wellh. *TBS.* 176 f.).

an oracle by sacred lot, *Urim* and *Thummim*.[1] If Gideon's *ephod* was an image, those of Saul and David would probably be so also.[2] There was most probably, even before Jeroboam's time, an important sanctuary at Gilgal, at which Yahvé was worshipped under the image of an ox.[3]

The *teraphim* cult was practised in the house of Saul, at least by one of its members. David himself did not prohibit it or succeed in putting a stop to it.[4] But we cannot infer from this the existence of polytheism in the case of David or Saul or their circle. It was simply a relic of the ancient Semitic worship of ancestors. Still David did not get beyond Henotheism. He gives expression to his belief in the existence of other gods.[5] Solomon went so far as to erect other altars in addition to those for Yahvé, although these may, on the most favourable interpretation, not have been intended for his own use.[6]

Human sacrifices cannot be proved with certainty to have been in use. What have been taken for such,[7] admit of other explanations. Nevertheless, there are other respects in which the age suffered from the curse of superstitious fears and scruples, that call to mind the early supremacy of the belief in demons. Some points in the character and fate of Saul can be understood

---

[1] 1 Sam. xiv. 18-37 ff. (on the text see my transl.); xxiii. 9 ff.; xxx. 7 f.; *cf.* xxviii. 6.

[2] In addition to the passages in the Book of Judges (see above, pp. 82, 101 f.), the following are decidedly in favour of this view: (*a*) Isa. xxx. 22, where אֱסַדָּה occurs in connection with statues; (*b*) Hos. iii. 4, where *ephod* and *teraphim* are mentioned as analogous things. But *teraphim* were also to be found with Saul and David. Note in this connection the passages where bringing forward the *ephod* is equivalent to inquiring of God (xxviii. 6; xiv. 37 ff.; *cf.* xxx. 7 f.); 1 Sam. xiv. 3, 18 (corrected text); xxiii. 6, 9 ff.; xxx. 7 f. (S and Da), and xxi. 10 ('behind the *ephod*,' SS). It is otherwise in the case of the *ephod* (or *ephod bād*) in ii. 18, 28 ('before me') SS and D²; xxii. 18, SS; 2 Sam. vi. 14, Je. Here it is the linen garment used by the priests of the ark, and hence by the house of Eli at Nob. *Cf.* moreover, König, *Hauptprobleme*, 59 ff.

[3] Hos. ix. 15 (*cf.* iv. 15); and *cf.* Köhl, ii. 2, 15, on this.

[4] 1 Sam. xix. 13 ff.; also xv. 23, and above, p. 39. We can infer from xix. 13 ff. that the *teraphim* were of human form.

[5] 1 Sam. xxvi. 19.   [6] On this see above, p. 200.

[7] 1 Sam. xiv. 15 (Jonathan, *cf.* above, p. 116, note 1); xv. 33 (Agag); 2 Sam. xxi. 1 ff. On this subject see Bäthgen, *Beitr.* 221.

only on the supposition that he was possessed by an overpowering tendency to superstitious fear of strange supernatural powers.[1] David allowed himself to be driven by such fears to do violence to the house of Saul.[2] There was no hope to comfort people in the presence of death.[3] The belief was, that exactly as a man was when he died,[4] he would join the company of his fathers,[5] and lead with them a shadowy existence. Perhaps the family sacrifice[6] and the *penates* cult (*teraphîm*) were supposed to influence the shades, whom popular superstition summoned for special ends to foretell good or evil.[7]

The Yahvism of the earlier period of the monarchy, like that of the pre-monarchic age, thus bore, in many respects, a half-heathen character. Still it was never merged in heathenism. The worship of God at the sanctuary of Shiloh, and the faith of its foremost priest Samuel, rose decidedly above the level of the common popular ideas of the age. It is only thus that we can explain the references to the special religious position occupied by Samuel in relation to his age. This was certainly one of the grounds of his conflict with Saul.

Shiloh was in possession of the ark, but it had no image of God. It is remarkable that Samuel also is never mentioned in connection with an *ephod* in the sense of an image of God. Only the more markedly, however, did *ephod* and *teraphîm* come into the foreground when the ark had disappeared from the scene, and Saul had begun to be estranged from Samuel. This concurrence of circumstances can hardly be accidental. It is interesting to notice, on the other hand, that when interest in the ark was revived by David, these elements, foreign to the higher Yahvism, retreated again. The Levitical priesthood, previously specially

---

[1] 1 Sam. xiv. 43 ff; xxviii. 1 ff. Also above, pp. 134, 136.
[2] 2 Sam. xxi. 1 ff. ; *cf.* 1 Kings ii. 5 ff., and above, p. 181.
[3] 2 Sam. xii. 23 : 'I shall go to him, he shall not return to me.'
[4] Thus *e.g.* a murdered man, blood-stained, like Banquo's ghost ; 1 Kings ii. 9, 6. Only thus can we explain the conduct of Rizpah in 2 Sam. xxi., and that of the Philistines and the people of Jabesh towards Saul and Jonathan in 1 Sam. xxxi.   [5] 1 Kings i. 21 ; xi. 21 ; *cf.* ii. 10 ; xi. 43.
[6] 1 Sam. xx. 6.   [7] 1 Sam. xxviii. 3 ff.

favoured, became more and more the rule. The use of the name Ba'al in proper names cannot be proved after David's time. After David ascended the throne in Jerusalem, and had brought back the ark, we do not again meet with *ephod* or other image of Yahvé. The ark must have gathered about itself, to a remarkable degree, the traditions of the age of Moses.

It is thus, on the whole, we understand the religious character of the age that preceded David, and the turning-point in religious life represented by his bringing back the ark and restoring it to honour. The destruction of the sanctuary at Shiloh, and the disaster that befell the ark at that time, had wrought a deep effect. The house of Eli held aloof from the shrine that had incurred the disgrace of captivity. They appear to have betaken themselves to the worship of the *ephod*, partly at Nob, partly at other places, perhaps at Ophrah. Saul, whether led by them, or himself urging them on, devoted himself to the same cult. David attained to greatness while practising this form of divine worship, and adhered to it for a time. But on being raised to the position of king over all Israel, he found the opportunity to claim for the ancient shrine, and the manner of worshipping God that clung to it, its rightful place.

BOOK III.

THE DECLINE OF NATIONALITY AND THE ADVANCE OF RELIGION.

A. THE SOURCES FOR THIS PERIOD.

§ 51. *The First Book of Kings: Chapter xii. and onwards.*[1]

1. *The Text.*—Here, too, first of all, certain important instances in which the Hebrew and Greek recensions of our text differ, claim our attention. At the beginning of chap. xii. there is something wrong with the M.T., as a comparison of $v.$ 2^b with 2 Chr. x. 2, and of $vv.$ 2^b, 3^a with $v.$ 20 will show. According to this, Jeroboam must have returned immediately after Solomon's death; while his entrance into Shechem, on the other hand, can only have taken place after the negotiations, as is also assumed by the LXX. Alex. in xii. 2. The correctness of this assumption is thoroughly confirmed by the LXX. Vat. and Luc. if the close of chap. xi. in the LXX. is taken over into chap. xii. There $v.$ 2 M.T. follows xi. 43^a, while $v.$ 3^a is wanting. We thus get the correct order of events as follows. Solomon dies, Jeroboam comes back, Rehoboam is made king provisionally, Shechem, Jeroboam. It follows from this that the text has to be altered, and that xii. 2 has to be put before $v.$ 1, while $v.$ 3^a has to be struck out as a later addition.[2]

A still more important difference between the two texts is

---

[1] On the literature of the Book of Kings *cf.* above, p. 49, note 4, to which has now to be added Kamphausen's translation of the Book in Kautzsch.

[2] See also Wellh. *Bl.*[4] 243. In $v.$ 12, too, in the LXX. Jeroboam's name is not mentioned.

found in the course of chap. xii. and at the beginning of chap. xiv. After xii. 24 the LXX. inserts a long narrative relating to Jeroboam, which is wanting in the M.T. In it, first of all, the death of Solomon and the accession of Rehoboam[1] are once more recounted, and, following on this, Jeroboam's earlier history is repeated pretty much in connection with xi. 26 ff. Before his return from Egypt Jeroboam allies himself by marriage with Pharaoh Shishak. He returns and gathers the tribe of Ephraim around him. His son falls ill, and, on account of this, he sends his wife to consult the prophet Ahijah of Shiloh, who, however, gives him an unfavourable answer. It is now that he first goes to Shechem, collects the tribes of Israel together there, and induces them to revolt. The circumstances are once more related very much in the same shape as that in which they had been already given in xii. 3 ff. From here onwards the LXX. again joins the M.T. (xii. 25 ff.), except that in chap. xiv. it, of course, omits verses 1-20, which, so far as their main substance is concerned, had been already given.

Leopold von Ranke[2] has accepted this piece with great warmth. He thinks that, in his character as historian, he is justified in preferring it to the M.T. But he has overlooked some essential points which cast grave suspicions on the piece. The reason which weighs most strongly with me against accepting it is, that if it belonged to the genuine LXX., the latter would thereby come to be in the most flagrant contradiction with itself. It assumes, as we have seen, and as is also in accordance with the course of events in xii. 1-24, that Jeroboam had kept away from Shechem until the matter was decided. How can it then here represent Jeroboam as having been in Shechem from the very first? Further, the scene in Shiloh has meaning only in the place where the M.T. gives it (xiv. 1 ff.), but not before Jeroboam has committed the real offences of his life. Kuenen is, accordingly, decidedly right when he gives the preference to the M.T. over the LXX.[3] He

---

[1] The Vat. assigns him a life of sixteen years, and a reign of twelve; and Luc. forty-one and seventeen.
[2] *Weltgeschichte*, iii. 2, 4 ff.   [3] *Ond.*[2] § xxvi. 10.

is in error, however, when he assumes that we have here to do with a narrative of the course of events which favours Jeroboam. The opposite is the case. His mother is represented as a harlot, and the revolt is laid at his door.[1] It is here, too, that the point of the whole lies. The intention is perfectly evident, and has, moreover, had its effect in the M.T. of xii. 1 ff.

I content myself simply with mentioning alterations of place such as are found in chaps. xx. and xxi., and in xxii. 41-51 (in the LXX. after xvi. 28).

2. *The Framework.*—If we consider the narrative matter of 1 Kings xii. to 2 Kings xxv., first of all as a whole, we at once meet with a feature which reminds us directly of the Book of Judges. Here each king is introduced and dismissed with some perfectly definite words, all of the same tenor, just as the individual Judges are there. Only here in the Book of Kings the formula is much more strictly adhered to than in the other case. Each king of Judah is introduced by a notice regarding the time of his accession in relation to the accession of his royal contemporary in Israel, his age at the time of his entrance into office, and the duration of his reign, as well as the name and home of his mother. From Manasseh onwards the information regarding the first of these points is, of course, wanting. In the case of the kings of Israel there is no mention of their age, or of their mothers; we only get information regarding the contemporary king of Judah and the length of the reign. In the case of each king it is stated whether he did or did not what was right before Yahvé. So, too, the history of each king winds up with a stereotyped formula, in which it is said that further information about his history is to be found in the Chronicles of the Kings of Judah, or Israel, as the case may be, and also where the king was buried and who was his successor.[2]

It ought to be clear that here we have not to do with a narrator who was contemporary with the earlier kings, but with a

---

[1] The omission of xiv. 7-9, 14-16 M.T. naturally followed, after the scene in Shiloh was put *before* Jeroboam's accession to the throne.

[2] On the proof passages in 1 Kings xiv. 19 f., 21, 29 ff., etc., see Kuen. § xxiv. 2. On the several exceptions, and the reasons for them, see *Bl.*[4] 241 f. in the notes.

later editor, who is able to survey the whole history of the kings, and thus stands at the end of the development. If we accordingly recall what we know from the Books of Judges and Samuel as well as regards 1 Kings i.-xi., the supposition is forced on us that the revision originated in the circle of writers belonging to the later period who were influenced by Deuteronomy (D^2). This supposition is made a certainty by the fact that the verdict passed on the individual kings is based on the standard supplied by the Deuteronomic Law.[1] That the author of the formula, however, is not merely a writer who is working over existing narratives, but is also the actual author of our Book of Kings, is shown in the most unmistakable way by his constant reference to the sources which he uses, or has not used, as the case may be.

The first question accordingly is as to what we can conclude regarding the documentary material used by him from the information which he himself supplies.

3. *The Annals of the Kings.*[2]—'The rest of the acts of King NN. and all that he did are written in the book of the history of the Kings of Judah (or Israel).' Already in the case of David and Solomon, amongst the officers of the crown, the chancellor and the state-recorder (Mazkîr and Sôphēr) are mentioned. One of them, presumably the first, is the historiographer-royal. The office, doubtless, continued to exist under the later kings, and the royal archives in Jerusalem and Samaria became more and more a valuable collection of data regarding the acts of the kings. Had our author access to these archives, and did he draw directly upon them ? So far as the kings of Israel are concerned, this question is *à priori* to be answered in the negative rather than in the affirmative. Otherwise we should have to adopt the supposition that when Samaria was pillaged, the contents of the Samaritan royal archives found their way to Jerusalem, which is, on the face of it, not very probable. It is, however, well possible that he was able

---

[1] See especially the reference to the Bamôth, 1 Kings xv. 14 ; 2 Kings xii. 3, xiv. 4, xv. 4, xxii. 44 ; and *cf.* 1 Kings iii. 2 f., and further Wellh. *Bl.*[4] 259 f.

[2] See Ewald, *Gesch. Isr.* i.[3], 198 ff. (English ed. i. 136 ff.). Wellh. *Bl.*[4] 260 ff. ; Kuen. § xxiv. 8 ff.

to make use of the Judaic Annals of the Kings which were preserved in Jerusalem.

Still the possibility of his having done even this ought not to be held to be a certainty without further consideration. It is rightly regarded as a remarkable circumstance that our author does not mention the Annals of the Kings themselves, but speaks of a *book* of the Annals of the Kings. Our discussion of 1 Kings i.-xi. has already shown that the two are not one and the same. We can quite as readily think of the 'Book of the Annals of the Kings of Israel,' or of Judah, as a book in which the contents of those Annals were set down verbally, as one in which the Annals were reproduced in an independent form. The plural 'kings,' too, makes this latter supposition a more likely one, in the case of Judah, than the former. It is thus in the highest degree probable that those writings cited by our author had a close connection with the official Annals of the Kings themselves, and there is no room for doubting that they—even if we think in this connection of other than the official Annals—take us back to sources of information which are genuinely ancient and trustworthy. Still this by no means proves that our author was in a position to draw *directly* on those original documents.

All the same, these two Books of Annals to which the author of the Book of Kings had access must have been sources of priceless value. If he had only reproduced them for us we should have been in an enviable position. Unfortunately, this he has done in an extremely restricted degree only. The way in which he at times mentions the Book of Annals in question, unmistakably shows that he refers us to it just when it is his intention *not* to let it speak for itself. He wishes it to be regarded as the complement of his own book for any one who wishes to get further information. Possibly the Books of the Annals chiefly contained the political history of the kings, an account of their doings in war, of their buildings, and of measures they carried out. For information regarding these matters we are accordingly referred to them. The author of our book, on the other hand, in accordance with his entire plan, has no intention of giving an exhaustive account of matters belonging to secular life. This can be got in the Books of the Annals. What interests him, and what, as he believes, will be more useful for his readers to know, has reference to the life of Israel in its *religious* aspect and in connection with the *service of God*, and to the merits or transgressions of the kings in this particular sphere. What belongs to this subject, so far as we have to do with facts and not with reflections, has been taken by him out of the Book of the Annals; everything of a different kind he either leaves out, or merely touches on it in passing.

From this standpoint we shall be able to form an approximate idea of the relation in which our author stood to the Book of Annals, or to the Annals themselves mentioned by him. So long as he mentions this source we have a right, in every case where he does not give us his own reflections, and where he supplies information regarding things that would naturally be found in the Book of Annals, to search out any traces of this latter. The extracts and statements which he has transferred to his pages from this Book, or the Books of the Annals of the Kings, we shall briefly designate by K. Should the trace of the documents on which the Book of the Annals of the Kings—*i.e.* of the Annals of the Kings themselves—is based, anywhere show itself, then in analogy with our method of procedure in 1 Kings i.-xi., this would be called A. The period of K is, for Israel (Ki) subsequent to 722, and for Judah (Kj) after Jehoiakim,[1] from which it directly follows that the former book was also written in Judah.[2]

According to what has been said, we cannot reckon as belonging to K, firstly, whatever has not to do with the kings—as, for instance, the detailed histories of the prophets Elijah and Elisha; next, whatever in general does not suit with the character of the Book of Annals, such as narratives of a specially popular or prophetic tendency. To this latter class particularly belong the

---

[1] See 2 Kings xxiv. 5. On Hosea, see Kuenen, § xxiv. 8.
[2] For a somewhat more precise determination of the date of the Israelitish Book, see below, p. 219.

detailed narratives referring to events connected with the house of Omri, which we meet with in 1 Kings xvii. to 2 Kings x. 'They contain what is partly naïve and partly prophetic tradition, and are distinguished by fine description, and have absolutely nothing of the dry annalistic tone.'[1] We are consequently led to suppose that our author had at his disposal other sources besides those actually mentioned by him.

4. *The separate narrative-pieces as far as* 2 Kings xx.—The history of the revolt of Israel from Rehoboam (1 Kings xii. 1-20) is an excellent bit of narrative.[2] It is not, however, easy to apportionate it to a definite source. It is evident, to begin with, that it was written before 722. The whole tone, as well as what is mentioned in *v.* 19, leaves no room for doubt regarding this. The author is a man who sees in Rehoboam's fate something which was deserved by him and Solomon.[3] Whether because of this, and because he is acquainted with the prophetical utterance of Ahijah and the words in 2 Sam. xx. 1, it is necessary[4] to consider him as belonging to Judah, is a point I leave undecided. In this case A would naturally be excluded, and the narrative is much too old to belong to K, if we do not wish to assume that K itself made use of other sources besides A. To me the narrative appears to be thoroughly Israelitish, just because of the triumphant tone of the reference to the events in 2 Sam. xx. The conjecture that it constituted the beginning of the Israelitish Annals of the Kings is a bold one, but perhaps not without some foundation in fact.[5]

Of a decidedly different kind is the remainder of chap. xii. Verses 21-24, at least in their present form, and probably in any form, are a later addition, and originated at earliest with the Deuteronomic editor, as is also the case with *vv.* 32 and 33.[6] Verses

---

[1] Wellh. *Bl.*[4] 260 f.

[2] On *vv.* 1-3, see above, p. 205. Verse 17 is also wanting in the LXX.

[3] See especially *v.* 15. It recalls the style of argument in Judges ix., and is accordingly not to be referred to D² (against Kuen. § xxv. 4).

[4] So Wellh. *Bl.*[4] 243.

[5] There is nothing to support the view that it belongs to E (Corn. *Grundr.* 124), and indeed צרה, *v.* 20, is against it.

[6] See Stade, *Gesch.* 350.

25-31 have also, without doubt, been worked over by D². The piece, however, because of *vv.* 25 and 28, points to an older original source. I would suggest Ki, since express mention of the fact that Shechem was in Ephraim could only have been made after 722 when the city was destroyed. In any case it has to be observed that *v.* 28ᵇ is not dependent upon Ex. xxxii. 8. This sentence, as well as the notices in *v.* 25, must in the present case rest on genuine historical tradition, from which it has come into Ex. xxxii. For it is only in the case of Jeroboam, and not in the case of Aaron, that the plural 'gods' has any meaning.

As regards chap. xiii., I refer readers to Wellhausen and Stade.[1] The piece is a later addition, of a Midrasch kind, to the Book of Kings; it is only the conclusion (*vv.* 33ᵇ, 34) which rests on an older basis, and it constitutes the continuation of xii. 31. The section in chap. xiv., to begin with, dealing with the wife of Jeroboam (*vv.* 1-18) has, indeed, been worked over by D², as is the case with other similar prophecies relating to Israelitish kings, but there is no mistaking the presence in it of an older original.[2] It can hardly, however, go back so far as the Hexateuch E, as Cornill[3] would have us believe, but rather to Ki. In chap. xiv. 21-31, we have the history of Rehoboam introduced. If we take out what belongs to D², then in any case an old kernel is left in *vv.* 25-28, 30. This belongs to Kj, and probably also in part to A. Verse 23, too, and especially *v.* 24, may possibly go back to some ancient traditions.

In chap. xv. the whole history of Abijam (*vv.* 1-8) belongs to D², though, of course, as has always to be remembered, this does not mean that the matters of fact in the framework regarding the king's mother and his burial do not go back to K or A. Verse 6 is similar to xiv. 30. In the history of Asa (*vv.* 9-24) the section 16-22 stands out pre-eminently as an ancient element. It points to Kj, and probably is based on A. Compare *v.* 16 with xiv. 30. So too *v.* 13, even if written by D², goes back to ancient data, and

---

[1] *Bl.*⁴ 244; Stade, 350 f.; further, Kuen. § xxv. 4; Köhler, *Gesch.* ii. 2, 51.
[2] So Wellhausen, Stade, Kuenen.　　　　　　　　　　[3] *Grundriss*, 124.

perhaps *v.* 15 also. The next bit dealing with Nadab (*vv.* 25-32) is entirely the work of D². He uses such freedom with the material taken from Ki that it is impossible to get to know the form which the details had originally in K. Verse 32, as its place clearly shows, has been inserted here. It may have come out of Aj, but it may also be a free imitation of xiv. 30; xv. 6.

As regards chap. xvi. also, to which xv. 33 f. belongs, the state of the case is similar. D², the chief author of our Book of Kings, is the main speaker. The portions, *vv.* 9-11 (12ª ?), 15ᵇ, 18, 21 f., 24, 31ᵇ, 32 (34 ?), may be recognised as belonging to the sources, apart, of course, from the names and such-like which were naturally fixed. They have their origin as a whole in Ki. A few things, *v.* 21 f. specially for example, where the narrative makes a fresh start, may be ascribed to A. Perhaps *v.* 34 belongs to A also; the end of the verse may be by D².[1]

Chaps. xvii.–xix. present us with something which is perfectly new as compared with the narratives hitherto given. Here we have no longer to do with mere extracts, as is the case in the last sections, but with detailed and independent descriptions. In addition to this, the chief *rôle* is not played by the king, but by the prophet; and the latter does not merely appear on the scene, as in chaps. xi. and xiii., with a prophecy for the special occasion, in order again to disappear, but he dominates the situation. This shows that we are no longer dealing with elements belonging to the Book of the Annals of the Kings. We have to do with an independent *Prophetical history* (Pr) from which our author transfers large portions to his book.[2] In chap. xix. the history of Elijah breaks off abruptly, so that we look in vain for the carrying out of

---

[1] I do not consider that it is necessarily so, spite of Jos. vi. 26. If we compare the two passages, Jos. vi. is obviously the later of the two. It is, besides, later than J (*cf.* 'riseth up and buildeth,' 'this city Jericho'). There is no reason to suppose that the author of 1 Kings xvi. was acquainted with Jos. vi. (Kuen. § xiii. 15), all that was necessary was that he should know the circumstance. That both passages have the same source, and that this is J (Corn. *Grundr.* 125), is, in my opinion, doubly improbable. The absence of the verse in a part of the LXX. recension is noteworthy, and because of this Klostermann regards it as a gloss.

[2] See especially Wellh. *Bl.*⁴ 245 ff.; Kuenen, § xxv. 6 ff.

the command given in xix. 15-18; for 2 Kings viii. and ix., as will be shown, are by another hand. The origin of Pr is, by xix. 3, placed beyond doubt; only an Ephraimite can express himself thus. That the piece is very old is shown by the absence of any polemic against bull-worship. Kuenen, accordingly, rightly ascribes it to the eighth, or perhaps to the ninth, century.

Chap. xxi. is the continuation of Pr. The difficulties which Kuenen finds in the way of accepting this view disappear, in my opinion, as soon as we assume that *vv.* 21-26 have been worked over by D^2. It is doubtful, on the other hand, if it is possible to discover any further continuation of Pr. What is further related of Elijah either does not belong at all to what has preceded, or does not absolutely belong to it. The former holds good with regard to 2 Kings i. We may attribute *v.* 1 to K. Verses 2-17 are of very late origin, and are probably an imitation of 1 Sam. xix. 18 ff. 2 Kings ii., again, although the chapter stands in such close connection with the history of Elijah, nevertheless appears to have rather belonged to another group[1] of prophetical histories of which Elisha was the central point. It is one of the most valuable pieces in this group (Pr^2), and was probably the beginning of it.

We next get a continuation of this group (Pr^2) consisting of a series of shorter and longer narratives, of which Elisha is the subject, and which can hardly be said to be altogether homogeneous either as regards value or origin. Some of them, such as 2 Kings ii. 1 ff., are good old narrative pieces; others, again, have the character of a legendary elaboration of older material. To these belong, as a whole, the following sections: 2 Kings ii. 19-22, 23-25; iv. 1-7, 8-37, 38-41, 42-44; v.; vi. 1-7, 8-23; viii. 1-6, 7-15; xiii. 14-21. In all of them the prophet Elisha occupies a central position, though, indeed, the relation in which he stands to the events described is not always exactly the same.[2] For the rest, there is

---

[1] Elijah has his fixed residence in Gilgal in the circle of the pupils of the prophets, 2 Kings ii. 1 ff. See Wellh. 248.

[2] Wellh. *Bl.*[4] 253. He is sometimes in Gilgal, sometimes in Samaria.

no mistaking the fact that the Elisha stories, even though they may have formed parts of a history of the prophets of some length, are not all due to the same author.[1]

As regards their origin, we can hardly doubt but that these narratives are Samaritan. They obviously have sprung up in the district which constituted the scene of the activity of their hero. It is difficult, however, to give any conclusive opinion as to their age, owing to the fact that the narratives of which Elisha is the subject are so little uniform. It is easy to see that, as a whole, they belong to a considerably later date, and are further away from the events than the Elijah stories.[2] At the same time they contain portions whose age and historical value show that they are not very far behind the Elijah narratives.[3] We have to consider, besides, that it is not the original composer who is to blame for the frequent clumsy insertion, into the body of the narrative, of separate stories taken from Pr^2, but the author of our present Book of Kings.[4] If we further bear in mind how quickly legends, such as we have, to some extent, here in the more recent elements, grow up round a celebrated man, we shall not be mistaken if we assume that Pr^2 dates from not long after the year 700.

If we now return from these stories of the prophets, which are continued far into the Second Book of Kings, to the end of the First Book, we have still left chaps. xx. and xxii. containing the narration of Ahab's Syrian Wars and his heroic death.[5] That they do not belong to the history of the prophets is already evident from the place which Ahab occupies in them. The king is portrayed in a decidedly sympathetic fashion, which is wholly different from what we have in Pr. There is not a syllable about Elijah. And, in this connection, it has to be noted that 2 Kings iii.[6] must also belong to the same body of narratives. The points

---

[1] *Cf.* vi. 8 ff. with chap. v. (war, spite of Naaman's cure); vi. 1 ff. with v. 26 f. (Gehazi, although leprous, transacts business with the king). See Kuen. § xxv. 12.
[2] *Cf.* viii. 1 ff. ; iv. 8 ff.
[3] So ii. 1 ff. ; viii. 7 ff.
[4] See especially Kuen. § xxv. 13.
[5] Naturally we have here to do with chap. xxii. only so far as *v.* 38. The rest of it is to be traced to D^2 who, especially in *vv.* 47-50, founds on his known sources (K and A, *cf. v.* 50.)
[6] Verses 1-3 belong to the author.

of contact between 2 Kings iii. 7, 11, and 1 Kings xxii. 4, 5, 7, are sufficiently obvious.

In it the prophet Elisha plays a definite *rôle*, while in contrast to this in 1 Kings xx. and xxii., the place of Elijah is taken by Micah ben Jimla. The work of the later reviser is more or less strongly marked in all three chapters; the anonymous prophets, especially in 1 Kings xx., must be traced to him.[1] The narratives are in substance historically true, but have been taken throughout from popular tradition, as the numbers given specially show.[2] For this reason neither A nor K can be regarded as the source. What we have here must therefore be some portions of a popular Ephraimite narrative-book which have come down to us. The obvious partiality with which the author treats the King of Judah is perhaps indicative of the period to which the composition of the book is to be assigned.[3] It reminds us of Amos, and especially of Hosea.

It is extremely probable that chap. vii., to which vi. 24-33 belongs and which now forms part of the Elisha stories, belongs to this group of Ephraimite histories of wars and kings with their prophetic colouring. It treats of the siege and marvellous deliverance of Samaria. How it has come to be in its present connection is easily explained by the part here played by Elisha. There is a great deal to be said for Kuenen's conjecture that the King of Israel here mentioned is not Joram ben Ahab, but Jehoahaz ben Jehu.[4] But even if it is correct, as I believe it is, it does not necessarily follow that vi. 24 to vii. 20 belongs to Pr.[2] The objections raised by Kuenen against the view that the piece is closely related to the Ephraimite history of the wars, do not seem to me to be decisive.[5]

The piece dealing with Jehu's revolution (chaps. ix. and x.) is, so far as the art of narrative is concerned, one of the very best bits in the Old Testament. The narrator, who describes the

---

[1] Wellh. *Bl.*[4] 249 ff. On xx. 35 ff. see also Kuen. xxv. 10.
[2] See xx. 1, 15, 29, 30.   [3] iii. 13 f. See below, § 66.
[4] § xxv. 12 f., and in addition, 2 Kings vi. 32.
[5] *Cf.* especially chap. iii. and *Bl.*[4] 251; on the other side, xiii. 14 ff.

scenes, writes with a vividness and a dramatic force which might seem to imply that he must have been there himself. That this was actually the case is, nevertheless, not very probable.[1] His information, however, must have been got from some one who had been directly concerned in the events. It is further worthy of notice that the narrator makes absolutely no pretence of glossing over Jehu's revolting cruelty, still less does he pretend to approve of it. His account is of an objective character, and he allows the facts themselves to testify against Jehu. So far as his private opinion is concerned, he leans to the judgment given in vi. 32 and Hos. i. 4.[2] From this his close relationship with the author of 1 Kings xx., xxii.; 2 Kings iii., vi. 24 ff., is plainly ✓ evident.[3] Stade, however, has shown, with some probability,[4] that in chap. x. a second, and perhaps later, account is united with the first. It is to be found in *vv.* 12-16. Kuenen has expressed some doubts regarding *v.* 17 ff. also,[5] still the difficulty may lie entirely in the restatement of the events.

From chap. xi. onwards, with the exception of the short formal statements regarding the individual kings, we have almost nothing but somewhat more detailed narratives dealing with matters in *Judah*. Chaps. xi. and xii. (more accurately xii. 5-19) in the first place, form a section by themselves. The subject is the accession and the reign of Joash of Judah. Both narratives are Judaic, and taken from the best source. They seem to have been transferred from A to K. Probably in xii. 5-17 we have a free version given by K of what was taken out of A; while, on the other hand, in xii. 18 A's own words are given. Chap. xii. 5 ff. is also a most valuable historical document owing to the thoroughly independent attitude of the writer towards the priesthood. In xi. 13-18ª Stade[6] has pointed out traces of a second account which may be regarded as a later insertion relatively to the main account.

[1] *Cf.* x. 1 ff., 27. Verse 28 ff. is an addition by D².
[2] *Cf.* especially x. 9 : 'Ye be guiltless.'   [3] See on this, Wellh. *Bl.*⁴ 252.
[4] *ZAW.* v. 275 ff.   [5] *Und.*² § xxv. 14.
[6] *ZAW.* v. 280 ff. On the text of xi. 1 ff. see Wellh. *Bl.*⁴ 258.

Chaps. xiii.-xv. give an account of the kings of Israel from Jehoahaz to Pekah. At the end of xv. Jotham and Amaziah of Judah, along with Joash of Israel, are briefly mentioned. We have already dealt with xiii. 14-21 (Pr^2). In the rest it is only exceptionally that the source itself is quoted along with D^2. The most important instance in which this has happened is xiv. 8-14: the account of how Amaziah was disposed of by Joash of Israel. The depreciatory style in which the king of Judah is spoken of makes us at once suspect an Ephraimite source. The suspicion is turned into a certainty by the remark that Bethshemesh belongs to Judah, *v.* 11. This last remark, however, according to what was formerly stated, excludes K. We have thus again, probably, a bit out of Ai. Besides this piece the following portions in this section are from the original sources: xiii. (6^b?) 7, 22, 24 ff.; xiv. 19-22; xv. 5, 10, 14, 16, 19 f., 25 (29 f. ?), 35^b, (37 ?). Bits such as xv. 19 f., 29 f., have been worked over by K himself relying on his recollections, the rest has been taken out of the Annals.

Chap. xvi., again, in *vv.* 5-18, contains a narrative of some length. The second half, *vv.* 10-18, strikes us at once by the *naïveté* of its point of view, as compared with the later conception of the Temple. Neither the priest Urijah nor the narrator finds anything to blame in what Ahaz does. This suggests that K had some material ready to hand which was taken over from a previous account, namely A. The resemblance to xii. 5 ff. confirms this supposition. The first piece, *vv.* 5-9, is not quite uniform, as is shown by the double statement, *vv.* 5 and 6. Besides the entire character of *v.* 6 ff., the judgment given in *v.* 6, as well as the time indicated, do not allow us to think of A; here we have K, but in *v.* 5 again A: the 'then,' *v.* 5, confirms this.

Chap. xvii. relates the end of the kingdom of Israel and the latest fortunes of the country. We are naturally led to expect that Ki should finish here. Accordingly we may attribute *vv.* 3-6, first of all, to this source. With *v.* 7 another author apparently is introduced, and he writes under the influence of the Deuteronomic point of view. But when we read on from *v.* 7, and compare *v.* 20

with v. 23, it is at once clear that here too we have to do with more than a single hand. Verse 21, to begin with, knows only of the Israelites whom Yahvé has given into captivity 'unto this day.' It thus occupies the same standpoint as v. 18. Verses 19 and 20, on the other hand, look back on the rejection of Israel *and* Judah, as v. 13 had already done. The original author D² (R^d, Dt) wrote, while Judah still existed, the verses in xviii. 21-23 by way of explaining the fate of Israel. A later author, R, after Judah's fall, added on vv. 7-17, 19 f.[1]

The rest of the chapter, vv. 24-41, treats of the origin and doings of the so-called Samaritans. Here we are struck by the fact that v. 34 says the opposite of v. 41. According to the former they did not fear Yahvé; according to the latter they did fear Him, only they kept their images. In keeping with this is the satisfied tone in which v. 28 ends: after they had practised the original idolatrous worship they are taught how to fear the God of the country and adopt His service; while, on the other hand, v. 29 ff. makes mention of a relapse into idol-worship, though certainly combined with the worship of Yahvé (32, 33). In addition to this, v. 34ª and v. 41 form each an independent conclusion. We shall thus have to take vv. 24-28 and 41 together. In this piece we have the by no means unfavourable judgment of a pre-exilic author on the Samaritans. Even the Bethel cult is not condemned in the uncompromising style of D². According to v. 41, the date is somewhere about the year 660. This points to K, and indicates at the same time the date of the composition of Ki. Verses 29-34 form a later addition of a decidedly less favourable character;[2] vv. 34ᵇ-40, on the other hand, are quite in the wrong place. Here we have not to do with the Samaritans at all, but with Israel, quite in the style of vv. 19 and 20. The proper place of the piece must therefore have been in the neighbourhood of these verses. In vv. 29-34ª we must recognise D², and in vv. 34ᵇ-40, R.

Of the still remaining Judaic narratives, those relating to the reign

---

[1] *Cf.* Wellh. *Bl.*⁴ 202 f. ; Stade, *ZAW*. vi. 163 ff. ; also Kuen. § xxvi. 5.
[2] See Stade, *ZAW*. vi. 168 f.

of Hezekiah, chaps. xviii.-xx., interest us in a pre-eminent degree, because they embody the accounts of the rescue of Jerusalem from Sennacherib. In xviii. 1-8 documentary elements are in any case to be found only in *vv.* 4 and 8.[1] Later on, we shall have to consider to what degree this is the case with regard to *v.* 4. Everything in *vv.* 9-12, with the exception of *v.* 12, may have come from the sources. Verses 9-11 form the counterpart of xvii. 3-6. The brief mention of these facts, which are of such importance, too, for Judah, could scarcely have been wanting in Kj. The piece, as well as *v.* 4 so far as it is old, and *v.* 8, are thus to be traced to K. We, accordingly, have here and in xvii. 6 a guarantee that in K definite statements of numbers were already to be found.

To the following piece, xviii. 13 to xix. 37,[2] we have, as is well known, an almost verbal parallel in Isaiah, chaps. xxxvi. and xxxvii. The most important difference between the two recensions consists in this, that the small section, 2 Kings xviii. 14-16, is wanting in Isaiah. The question as to which of the two texts is the more original[3] would have an interest for us only if we could go on to attribute the composition of the piece before us to the prophet Isaiah. But that he was the author is impossible, from the very nature of the case. Apart altogether from what will be further shown in detail, the matter is already settled by the single fact that both in the account in the Book of Kings and in that in Isaiah mention is made of the death of Sennacherib, which took place in 681 at a time when Isaiah was quite certainly no longer living.

The fact that the piece is not a unity takes us a step further. Verses 14-16 stand out plainly from the rest of the context of chap. xviii. They supply a striking justification of our whole critical method of dealing with the sources in connection with the Old Testament historical narratives. Even if they were not wanting in Isaiah, too, the peculiar way of writing the name

---

[1] See below, in § 70, in connection with Hezekiah's reforms.

[2] See on this, Wellh. *Bl.*[4] 244 ff. ; Stade, *ZAW.* vi. 172 ff. ; Kuen. § xxv. 17 ff., § xlv. ; Dillm. *Jesaja*, 310 ff. ; [Cheyne, *Introd. to Bk. of Isaiah*, 212 ff.].

[3] See on this Dillm. *Jesaja*, 310, and especially Kuen. § xlv. 3; [Cheyne, 212 f.].

Hezekiah,[1] as well as the fact that the subjection of the king to Sennacherib in *vv.* 17 ff., is not referred to in any way again, make it in the highest degree probable that we have here to do with a fragment of an independent description of the course of events. The Book of Isaiah turns this supposition into an absolute certainty. Chap. xviii. 14-16 is clearly an ancient and thoroughly trustworthy account. Both form and contents go to show this, and the Inscriptions are in harmony with this view of it. If we assume that the piece was continued beyond *v.* 16, and contained a narrative parallel to *v.* 17 f., in which Sennacherib's unjust action was made plain, then the frank way in which Hezekiah's humiliation under Sennacherib is related, in *v.* 14^b, cannot surprise us even in A. We may thus regard *vv.* 14-16 as a fragment taken from A. If it is merely a fragment, then there is scarcely any room for doubting that it is in its right place where it now stands.[2]

But neither are we to take it for granted that what remains, xviii. 13, 17, to xix. 37, was written by one and the same author. Stade has acutely pointed out[3] that from xix. 10 onwards a version of the narrative different from that given in what goes before is introduced. In *v.* 8 Rabshakeh returns to Sennacherib because his attempt to get Jerusalem to surrender was in vain. Sennacherib hears that Tirhakah is advancing against him, and thereupon resolves to send a letter to Hezekiah. And now the scenes in xviii. 27 ff., xix. 1 ff., 5 ff., are repeated in a very slightly altered form. This shows that we have two accounts of the same event. In the one case, the ambassadors speak themselves; in the other, they bring a *letter*. Chap. xix. 9^b and 10^a are parentheses due to redaction. The second is even wanting in the LXX. The continuation of xix. 9^a, and also the conclusion of the main account, are best looked for in xix. 36. For *v.* 9^a presupposes the departure of Sennacherib.

The origin of the main account, xviii. 13, 17, to xix. 9^a, 36, 37,

---

[1] Ḥizqija, otherwise Ḥizqijahu, a point to which Kuenen was the first to call attention.

[2] This is questioned by Wellh. 255 f.; Kuen. § xxv. 17; Stade, *ZAW.* vi. 180 f.

[3] *ZAW.* vi. 173 ff. *Cf.* Dillm. *Jes.* 320 f.; [Duhm, *Jes.* 234 ff.; Cheyne, *Introd. Is.* 214 ff.].

is to be looked for most naturally in K or in one of its documents. We have certainly not so far come upon any narrative here of such a detailed character, and for this reason one might be disposed to attribute it to an independent narrator writing under prophetical influence. But the special importance of the occurrence, and, in addition to this, the circumstance that the author is always approaching nearer and nearer to the present, might have led him here to quote the actual words of K with greater detail than usual. Still it is also quite possible that D² took only xviii. 14-16 out of K, and struck out the rest of the account in favour of other sources of information which lay to hand. This would naturally not interfere with the attribution of xviii. 14-16 to A.

With this the *relative dates* of the two accounts would in a measure correspond. Chap. xviii. 13, 17 ff., is in any case based on good information, though it is certainly not the work of a contemporary. The death of Sennacherib is brought into immediate connection with his return to Nineveh, and this does not correspond with the facts.[1] Chap. xix. 10 ff. brings us a step lower because of the enormous numbers given in v. 35, and also because of v. 32 ff., a piece which is neither in harmony with the facts nor the composition of Isaiah.[2] Since, further, xix. 32 ff. is, relatively to xix. 21-31, manifestly a duplicate, and since, besides, xix. 23 does not tally with the letter in xix. 10 ff., but with xviii. 17 ff., we may reckon this good Isaianic piece,[3] too, as belonging to the documents used in K.

The *illness* of the king, and the *embassy* of Merodach-Baladan, constitute the close of the history of Hezekiah in chap. xx. A parallel to the first piece is found in Isaiah xxxviii., which is there enlarged by the addition of a song of Hezekiah's. The words in xx. 17 cannot possibly, in their present form, have come from Isaiah. Isaiah has always in his mind only deportation to Assyria, not to Babylon. So, too, xx. 6 forms a parallel with xix. 34. The chapter must thus be attributed to K at the earliest.

---

[1] xix. 36, 37. See Wellh. *Bl.*⁴ 255.   [2] See Dillm. *Jes.* 330.
[3] Kuen. § xxv. 17; Dillm. *Jes.* 329; [but *cf.* Cheyne, *Introd.* 221 ff.].

5. **2 *Kings* xxi.–xxv. *and its Redaction*.**—From here onwards we more and more lose trace of K. It is conceivable that the nearer the author D² comes to his own day, the more he emancipates himself from dependence on his source, and writes on his own account. At any rate, it is now only in exceptional cases that it is possible to separate the two in any measure. The last mention of K is found in connection with Jehoiakim, xxiv. 5. Whether we have any right to assume that this verse is an imitation[1] by a later writer of the formula of D² is doubtful. If this is not the case, then 597 is the earliest date we can assign to the history by Kj. He must, in any case, have written his history a few years after 597 at the outside, since D², the principal author of our Book of Kings, as is repeatedly evident,[2] did not write after 588. K and D² are contemporaries, and—the latter after the former—composed their books between 597 and 590.

But we have already come on traces of the fact that besides D², and later than he, one or several writers worked at the Book, and these we have simply called R (Kuenen, Rd² together with Rd¹; Kamphausen, Dt² and Z with Dt). This peculiarity was specially evident in chap. xvii. We have to take it into consideration here. The very fact that the book goes down beyond 586 reminds us of it.

If the fact mentioned stood alone, Graf's assumption that xxv. 22 ff. is a later addition to the Book of Kings would be correct.[3] But if it is closely connected with the other fact, then this explanation is clearly no longer satisfactory.[4] R in the body of the book, and R at the end of it, match each other; and it is evident that our Book, after it left the hands of D², was further worked over and extended. Its author, in accordance with xxv. 30 and other hints, is to be placed in the middle or at the end of the Babylonian Exile.

[1] So Kuen. § xxvi. 6. The assumption seems to me somewhat forced.
[2] See especially 2 Kings xvii. 18, 21-23; further, viii. 22, xvii. 7, xvi. 6. Even if these utterances were actually contained in the source, D² could not have appropriated them if Judah was no longer in existence.
[3] *Gesch. Büch.* 110.   [4] See Kuen. § xxvi. 2, 3.

It is no longer possible to say with certainty what individual bits in chaps. xxi.-xxv. belong to R and what to D^2. I shall content myself here with enumerating the undoubtedly certain additions by R. One of these is to be found, first of all, in chap. xxi., where in *vv.* 7-15, in plain contrast to the view of D^2 which we elsewhere meet with, the peculiar view of the writer regarding the fall of Jerusalem is clearly apparent. The same is the case as regards xxii. 15-20; xxiii. 26-27. His hand is seemingly to be traced also in xxiv. 2-4. Apparently K had given an account of the reign of Jehoiakim, while D^2 had narrated the events of the reign of Jehoiakin to its close, and R, who in the course of the book had here and there made additions, continued the narrative down to Jehoiakin's death.

§ 52. *Chronicles.*

In our Biblical Book of Chronicles (1 and 2 Chron.)[1] we possess a narrative work which runs parallel with the historical books just mentioned. It is written with the intention of relating the history of the Temple of Jerusalem, and accordingly supplies us with information regarding the Kings of Judah from David and Solomon onwards, and their relation to the worship of God. The kings of the northern kingdom, as well as the history of this kingdom, are passed over. We get instead a long series of family registers, which forms the lengthy introduction to the historical accounts given in the book. It is at once evident that we have to hail here a specially welcome supplement to the older historical books—that is, of course, if we should be able to prove that the contents of this book rest on ancient and trustworthy sources of information.

In order to come to a decision regarding this point, we have

---

[1] See, on the whole subject, De Wette, *Beiträge Z. Einl. ins. AT.* i. 1806; Graf, *Gesch. BB. des. AT.* 114 ff.; Bertheau, *Komm. im exeg. H.B².* 1873; Wellh. *Prol.²* 177 ff. (Eng. Trans., p. 171 ff.); Dillm. *PRE²* iii. 219 ff.; Kuen. § xxviii. ff.; Öttli, *Komment.* 1889; Corn. *Grundr.* 268 ff.; Driver, *Introd.*, 484 ff. [König, *Einl.* § 54; Wildeboer, *De Letterkunde*, § 25. On the text and the separation of the sources see my translation of the book which is shortly to appear in P. Haupt's *Sacred Books of O.T.*]

first to settle the general question of the age of the book, and then the questions as to the sources from which the information given in it is drawn, and as to the way in which these have been used in it.

We are able from the contents to determine without difficulty the *approximate date* of the composition of the Book of Chronicles. Cyrus is mentioned in 2 Chron. xxxvi. 22 ff. as King 'of Persia,' and the descendants of David are enumerated in 1 Chron. iii. 19 ff. to the sixth generation after Zerubbabel. This brings us down to the borders of the Greek period.

If to this it be added that in the last-mentioned place the text is uncertain, and that perhaps originally eleven generations after Zerubbabel were mentioned, and further, that in all probability the man who wrote the Books of Ezra and Nehemiah also composed the Book of Chronicles, we have cogent reasons for fixing upon a still later age. So far as we are here concerned, it is enough to know that the book can hardly have been written before the year 332, and perhaps not till towards the middle of the third century B.C.[1]

In Chronicles a large number of writings is mentioned as the *sources* from which the material has been drawn, namely: (1) a Book of the Kings of Israel and Judah; a Book of the Kings of Judah and Israel; a Book of the Kings of Israel; a Midrash to the Book of Kings;[2] (2) the Words of the Seer Samuel, of the Prophet Nathan, of the Seer Gad; the Words of the Prophet Nathan, the Prophecy of Ahijah of Shiloh, and the Vision of the Seer Iddo; the Words of the Prophet Shemaiah and of the Seer Iddo; a Midrash of the Prophet Iddo; the Words of the Prophet Jehu ben Hanani, which are recorded in the Book of the Kings of Israel; a History of Uzziah by Isaiah; the Vision of the Prophet Isaiah in the Book of the Kings of Judah and Israel; the Words of the Seers.[3]

---

[1] See Dillm. *PRE.*[2] iii. 221; Kuen. § xxix. 7 ff.; Öttli, 10.

[2] 1 Chron. ix. 1; 2 Chron. xxvii. 7, xxxv. 27, xxxvi. 8; 2 Chron. xvi. 11, xxv. 26, xxviii. 26, xxxii. 32; 2 Chron. xxxiii. 18, xx. 34; 2 Chron. xxiv. 27.

[3] 1 Chron. xxix. 29; 2 Chron. ix. 29; 2 Chron. xii. 15; 2 Chron. xiii. 22; 2 Chron. xx. 34; 2 Chron. xxvi. 22; 2 Chron. xxxii. 32; 2 Chron. xxxiii. 19 (according to the corrected reading in the last place).

The large number of sources here mentioned is, however, very considerably simplified when we look at them a little more closely. The whole of the first category, which we may briefly describe as the historical sources, refers most probably to *one and the same book*, or at the outside to two books which the author of Chronicles had before him. The Book of the Kings of 'Israel and Judah' can hardly be a different book from that of the Kings of 'Judah and Israel.' Then again, since Chronicles in general takes to do only with the Kings of Judah, the Book of the Kings of 'Israel' cannot be a separate book either. Consequently we have left only the Midrash, or commentary on the Book of Kings, along with this book itself. The relation in which it stands to this book will be seen when we get to know the nature of that Book of Kings itself.

The Book of the Kings of 'Israel and Judah' made use of by the chronicler is, in any case, not to be identified with the two books quoted in our Book of Kings—namely, the Book of the Annals of the Kings of Israel, and that of the Kings of Judah (Ki and Kj).[1] The title, on the contrary, rather points to a single book in which the matter contained in those two had been, directly or indirectly, worked up into a whole. The most probable supposition at first sight is that this was our present Book of Kings. As a matter of fact, the large number of parallel sections in which Chronicles repeats[2] more or less verbally the text of the Book of Kings or of the Book of Samuel, as the case may be, shows that the chronicler was acquainted with our canonical Book of Kings, or with a work which was in many instances verbally the same. Spite of this, it is not probable that the source cited by the chronicler as the Book of Kings was our canonical Book of Kings itself. For that source, spite of its close agreement with the canonical Book of Kings, contained elements which are not found in this latter.[3] That book was thus an independent revision of the historical

---

[1] So according to Keil, 19 f. ; *Bleek*,[4] 289.

[2] See the parallel arrangement of them in Kuen. § xxx.

[3] *Cf.* 1 Chron. ix. 1 ; 2 Chron. xx. 34 ; xxvii. 7 ; xxxvi. 8 ; xxxiii. 18. See Graf, *Gesch. B.B.* 189 ff. (as against Movers and de Wette) ; Kuen. § xxxii. 12.

matter, having many points of agreement with the Biblical Books of Samuel and Kings, but containing also very considerable additions. Since, therefore, in accordance with the prevailing usage of language, by a Midrash was simply meant an edifying explanation and reshaping of the actual Sacred Writings,[1] we have to regard the Book of Kings which the chronicler had before him as in point of fact a *Midrash* to our canonical Books of Samuel and Kings. The question raised above as to the relation of the Midrash mentioned in 2 Chron. xxiv. 27 to the historical main source used by the chronicler, is consequently settled without further discussion. Both must have been one and the same; if not, then they must have been very closely related to one another.

The second class of quotations has reference to *prophetical* sources. Here too, however, it is extremely impossible that we have to do with different and independent writings. Bertheau[2] especially has fully shown that all those references are to one and the same book, and that the different designations refer to the customary titles or headings of the separate sections in it. Thus, even in the New Testament, we have the expression, 'the Scripture saith in Elijah' (R.V. Margin)[3] in a case in which it is plainly the section of the Book of Kings dealing with Elijah that is meant. The want of any division of the text according to chapters and verses led to the custom of using the name of the leading person of a period, or of a section of history, as a catchword for that particular section. Prophets especially lent themselves to this,[4] and soon it came to be believed that each of these prophets had himself written the section referring to him. This is how we must explain the transference of the history of Sennacherib from the Book of Kings to the Book of Isaiah, and perhaps also the name 'prophetae priores' as applied to the older historical books.

This book which is thus quoted under the names of different

---

[1] Otherwise Ewald, *Gesch. d. V. Isr.*³ i. 265, note 1 [Eng. Trans. i. 183].
[2] *Chronik*, § xxxi. f.
[3] Rom. xi. 2. See Wellh. *Prol.*² 235 [Eng. Trans. 226, note].
[4] See Josephus, *C. Ap.* i. 8 : ἀκριβὴς τῶν προφητῶν διαδοχή.

prophets, is again, however, in reality no other than that Midrash to the Book of Kings upon which Chronicles is based. As to the words, or the history (*debārîm*) of Jehu ben Hanani and the Vision of Isaiah ben Amos, it is expressly said, as we saw, that they were component parts of the Book of Kings.[1] Owing to the similarity between these narratives and the others whose origin in that great Book of Kings is not directly attested, it is extremely probable that the others, too, belong to the same source; and the mode especially in which the chronicler is accustomed to cite his authorities, favours this view. In the two cases just referred to, he calls the history of the prophets a part of the Book of the Kings, and thus cites the two together; in all the other cases he cites either the one or the other, and yet in each individual case we do not come upon any such perceptible difference between the sections in question as would justify the expectation that we are dealing with sections having a different origin.[2]

It is evident that we can judge of the chronicler's *way of handling* his sources only in so far as it is possible for us to get acquainted with them. Now, as a matter of fact, we are acquainted only with the canonical Books of Samuel and Kings,[3] and we have already reached the conclusion that they were not—not directly at least—the main sources used by the author. But, on the other hand, we know from those portions of Chronicles which run parallel with certain sections of the canonical books referred to, that the document on which Chronicles is directly based stood in a very close relation to the Biblical Books of Samuel and Kings. The indirect connection, consequently, between Chronicles too and these canonical historical books is very marked. We should thus, more strictly speaking, have two questions to deal with: first, as to the relation of the main source of Chronicles (the enlarged Book of Kings referred to) to our canonical historical books; and next, the question as to relation

---

[1] 2 Chron. xx. 34; xxxii. 32.   [2] See Bertheau, § xxxi. ff.

[3] It is not necessary for us in the present connection to deal with the question as to what the chronicler, in his introduction, has taken out of earlier books such as Genesis. See on this the commentaries.

of Chronicles to its main source. If, however, the two questions are practically one so far as the main point is concerned, we have not to regret very much the impossibility of answering the second question. For even if we take the most favourable view of the matter, and grant that the chronicler was perfectly faithful to his source, and added practically nothing of importance to it, still, though he certainly in that case must have gone entirely 'by his sources,' we do not thereby escape the duty of discussing the sources of his source, and the relation of the latter to the information we get elsewhere. There could be no more naïve, and no more fatal error than to regard the source and historical information in Chronicles as equivalent.

The question as to how Chronicles—whether it be its author or the document on which he directly drew—deals with the older traditional material, can be answered in individual instances only by the comparison of the parallel texts. In more important instances we shall have to fall back, in the descriptive part, on this method. It may, however, be said in a general way here that Chronicles treats the older material with great freedom, reshapes it, freely makes additions to it, and leaves out parts of the older narrative. At the same time, there is no mistaking the fact that the alterations made on it serve pre-eminently to illustrate one and the same thought, in which we rightly recognise the leading thought of Chronicles—namely, that the temple in Jerusalem, the Levitical priesthood of this temple, and the pious Kings of Judah who were devoted to the temple service, should appear to posterity as great and glorious.

To what extent Chronicles is to be regarded as a *trustworthy historical document* will be easily shown if we gather up the threads of the previous discussions. The book is of very late origin; in all probability it possesses only *one* source from which it takes its material; so far as we are able to study the relation of the source to the older traditional material, everything points to great freedom, and not seldom to actual arbitrariness, in the handling of tradition—a handling which has been prompted by a definite and frequently visible tendency. It necessarily follows from these facts that Chronicles as an historical source is to be used *only with the greatest caution*. We may say in advance that the information it gives is to be received with distrust rather than with trust, since the whole character of the book shows it to be anything but a purely documentary narrative-book. But caution and essential distrust should not lead us into the error of considering that we are relieved from the necessity of testing the actual state of matters in each individual case. Considering the defectiveness of the information given in our Biblical Book of Kings, we cannot avoid supposing it possible that Chronicles has occasionally supplied us with more detailed information based on trustworthy ancient sources. Even in the cases in which Chronicles 'has looked at and represented things entirely through the medium of Levitical priestly ideas,'[1] it, or its authority, may quite well have drawn its facts from older narratives which are given in the Biblical Book of Kings only in the form of abstracts or epitomes. The decision on this point must depend on each individual instance; still, no one can say it is unlikely that, in the time of Alexander the Great, somewhat more was known about the older Israelitish history than we are able to-day to gather from the Book of Kings.[2]

§ 53. *Information from Foreign Sources.*

1. *Palestinian-Phœnician.*—We do not possess for this period of the history either, a single document from *Israelitish* antiquity from which we could get any considerable addition to our knowledge. The only ancient Israelitish inscription which has, up to the present, been discovered—that, namely, found in 1880 in the so-called Siloah aqueduct—is historically without value.[3] It shows us, however, that we should not give up the hope of finding still

---

[1] Öttli, *Chronik.* 14.   [2] See also Kamphausen, *Chronol.* 21.

[3] See on it Kautzsch, in *ZDPV.* iv. (1881), 102 ff., 260 ff.; v. 205 ff.; and Guthe, *ZDPV.* iv. 250 ff., *ZDMG.* 1882, 725 ff.; Driver, *Notes*, xv. f. On the latest fortunes of the Stone, see *ZDPV.* xiii. (1891), 286 ff.

further and richer treasures in the way of inscriptions even on the soil of Israel. And so, too, the large number of *Phœnician* inscriptions which have been found—partly in the mother-country and partly in the colonies—yield very little for the ascertaining of the historical facts. They may, however, be consulted with profit for our knowledge of the religious life and thought of the Canaanites in this, and especially in the preceding period. They will be found arranged in a model fashion in the *Corpus Inscriptionum Semiticarum*.

On the other hand, we have succeeded in finding in the land of ancient Moab an historical inscription in the proper sense of that term—the pillar of victory of King Mêsha' of Moab. It is an historical monument of the first rank, and is all the more valuable for us that in the Old Testament also, in 2 Kings iii., we possess an account which has reference to the events mentioned in the inscription. It was discovered in the year 1868 by the German clergyman Klein on the site of ancient Daibon, and is now in the Louvre at Paris. There can no longer be any doubt as to its genuineness. Its significance for the historian is almost outweighed by the value which it possesses for the history of the Hebrew language and Hebrew writing.[1]

2. *Egyptian*.—Under Solomon and Rehoboam, Israel repeatedly stood in a close relationship with Egypt, as it did also from the time of the Assyrian wars. But with the exception of the inscription of Sheshonq, which will be mentioned later, there is no mention whatever of the Israel of the times of the Kings in Egyptian monuments. Besides, the defectiveness of the Egyptian chronology, and the gaps in Egyptian history, occur just in the very period in which Egypt is more frequently mentioned in the Old Testament. However important it may be that we should be able to bring in the history of the Empire of Pharaoh to help us in understanding the Israelitish history of the Kings, still the

---

[1] See on it, Schlottmann, *Die Siegessäule Mesas* (1870), and in *ZDMG*. 1870, 1871; Nöldeke, *Die Inschrift d. K. Mesa*, 1870; Driver, *Notes*, lxxxv. ff. The best edition: Smend and Socin: Freib. 1886.

yield which we can expect from this quarter is in the present condition of Egyptology not particularly great.

3. *Assyrio-Babylonian.*—Mesopotamia, on the other hand, yields us an incomparably richer supply. The history of Israel is bound up in the closest way with the steady advance of Assyria in Western Asia. The Northern Kingdom as well as the Southern Kingdom underwent one shock after another at the hands of the Assyrian kings, and so far as Judah was concerned, Babylon finally entered on the inheritance of Assyria. It can, accordingly, not astonish us that, by the deciphering of the Assyrio-Babylonian cuneiform inscriptions, a wholly unexpected light has been cast on the history of Israel in the time of the Kings. What the rulers of Assyria and Babylon relate regarding their expeditions to Palestine is all the more welcome to us the more defective and incomplete we find the native Hebrew accounts to be in reference to such political events.

The peculiar nature of the cuneiform accounts gives the information they supply a special value.[1] These accounts are to a large extent historical documents in the strictest sense of the term, and are based on contemporary and official reports. Of course, in spite of this, they cannot be used without criticism. Exaggeration of the deeds of the king, omission or extenuation of native defeats and misfortunes, giving prominence to, and making too much of, those of foreign nations, mistakes in writing, mistakes of memory, and errors of various kinds—all this plays its part in them as it does in other documents. But their real worth is not thereby put in question.[2] And, first of all, we have the splendid series of so-called *Royal Inscriptions.* These were placed in temples and palaces with a view to extol the deeds of the builders, or possessors, as the case might be. They are found on clay vessels (called cylinders), on prisms, and on the wall-lining of the palaces. The Royal Inscriptions are not all of the same kind. The most valuable certainly are the annalist inscrip-

---

[1] See Meyer, *Gesch. d. Alt.* i. 148 ff. ; Tiele, *Bab.-ass. Gesch.* 18 f.
[2] See Schrader, *Keilinschr. und Geschichtsforschung,* Giessen, 1878.

tions, since they give the deeds of their heroes in historical series and arranged according to the years of the reign; while the so-called show-inscriptions, on the other hand, arrange the material in an independent way, and naturally thereby make it difficult for us to get a view of the real course of events.

Besides these Royal Inscriptions the various cuneiform *Lists* have a special importance for the history of Israel. They serve as the necessary basis of the Biblical chronology. It is true, indeed, that neither the Babylonians nor the Assyrians had any special era; but, on the other hand, both peoples constructed lists of their dynasties and rulers, or of their highest officials, and in such lists the names and succession of these, together with the number of the years of each individual reign, are given. The so-called eponym-lists which were customary in Assyria are of special importance. In Assyria it was the practice to name each year after some high official of the Empire, the Archon-Eponymos of the year, and this custom prevailed from ancient times. The names of these officers, sometimes accompanied with short notes on the important events of the special year of their administration, are given in continuous registers, called in the latter case administration lists. An eclipse which took place in the year 763 B.C., and which is mentioned in the administration list, supplies the definite date from which to reckon. It shows at the same time that the dates supplied by the lists agree with those of the Ptolemaic Canon which contains the names of the later Egyptian, Persian, and Babylonian rulers, down to Nabonassar. We thus get the starting-point for the Hebrew chronology.

It is *Schrader* especially who has the merit of having turned to account the information supplied by the cuneiform inscriptions for the elucidation of Hebrew history.[1]

---

[1] *Die Keilinschriften u. d. Alte Test.*[2] 1883. *Keilinschriftliche Biblioth.* 1889 ff. To this add Winckler, *Keilinschr. Textbuch z. A T.* 1892.

§ 53a. *Supplement. The Chronology of the Hebrew Kings.*[1]

The Book of Kings supplies us with definite data regarding the time of the reign of the individual kings, so that it may appear as if all we have to do is to arrange the numbers, in order to get a perfectly accurate picture of the chronology of the period of the Israelitish kings. As a matter of fact this is not the case. The mere addition of the numbers used in connection with the two sets of kings—those of Israel and those of Judah—leads to different results, and shows that we have here quite a series of difficulties to get over.

When we look at the matter more closely, we find that the Book of Kings, in fact, puts two kinds of numbers alongside of each other which do not directly fit in. In the case of each king there is a notice of the duration of his reign, and also a synchronistic statement regarding his accession in relation to the accession of his contemporary in the other kingdom. According to the result of the examination of the Book of Kings given in § 51, the synchronisms as well as the statements regarding the duration of the reigns of the individual kings, belong to the framework of the Book of Kings. All the same, there is a difference between them. It has been already shown that the Book of Kings underwent more than *one* redaction. The first revision of the older material was the work of D^2, and belongs to the period before the destruction of Jerusalem; a second (R) belongs to a later period. Wellhausen has shown, by convincing reasons, that the synchronisms within the Book of Kings cannot possibly rest on ancient tradition, but are on the contrary simply the products of artificial reckoning,[2] and that in addition to this, in their literary aspect, they belong

---

[1] See especially Brandes, *Abhandl. z. Gesch. des Orients im Altert.* 1874; Wellhausen, in *JDTh.* xx. 607 ff.; Kamphausen, *Die Chronologie der hebr. Könige*, 1883; Riehm, in the *HWB. Art. Zeitrechnung*; Köhler, *Bibl. Gesch.* II., i. 460 ff.; Klost. *SaKö*, 493 ff.; Strack, in the *Handb. d. theol. Wissensch.* i.[3] 328 ff. [A most interesting essay by Rühl on this subject, containing many new points of view, has lately appeared in the *Deutsch. Zeitschr. für Geschichtswissensch.* 1894, 44 ff.]

[2] See Ewald, *Gesch. Isr.*[2] i. 242; iii. 464; further, Wellh. *JDTh.* xx. 612 ff.

to the second stratum within the framework of our Book of Kings.[1]

It may further be asked if the same can be said of the numbers which specify the duration of the separate reigns. Wellhausen and others have reached results regarding them similar to those reached in reference to the synchronisms.[2] But this assumption is not probable either from the literary or from the historical point of view. If we look at the question in its literary aspect, it becomes evident that certain chronological statements may even yet be traced back with the greatest probability to the older documentary works K and A, which lie at the basis of D^2.[3] A study of the matter from the historical point of view confirms this result, at least for the numbers referring to the later reigns. From Josiah onwards, we can check them by the data supplied by Jeremiah. We may consequently assume that the numbers of the other reigns were also known to D^2, and were not merely reckoned by him artificially—in other words, that at the end of the period of the kings of Judah, those then living were still in possession of information regarding the length of the reigns of the separate kings.

It does not of course follow that *we* still possess them. Various circumstances throw light on this point. The Israelitish numbers and the parallel numbers referring to Judah do not agree at the points at which we are able to compare them. Besides, the well-established Assyrian dates differ considerably from those deduced from the Old Testament. Both facts show either that the numbers, originally given accurately, of the Book of Kings, were in course of time altered by disturbing influences (errors of scribes, misapprehensions of the meaning, etc.), or else that we are no longer in a position to discover the original method of reckoning according to which the sums of the several items were bound to agree;

---

[1] Wellh. *op. cit.* 611; Kuen. § xxvi. 8.

[2] See *Bleek*,[4] 264 f.; Krey, *Z. f. wiss. Theol.* 1877, 404 ff.; Stade, *Gesch.* 95 f. Against this view especially Kamphausen, *Chronologie.*

[3] See for example, 1 Kings vi. 1*b*, 37, 38; vii. 1; xiv. 25; 2 Kings xi. 3, 4 (xii. 1, 2); xvii. 6; xviii. 10*a*, 13.

or, finally, that both causes have contributed to bring about the present state of things. The latter is most likely the case. We have to reckon with two important sources of error. The first class of errors can, of course, be corrected in the majority of instances in no other way save by that of pure conjecture. We could remedy those of the second class if only we could in any way find out how the Hebrews summed up the years of their kings. It has been usual of late to suppose that the system of 'post-dating' was in vogue—that is to say, any year begun by a king was reckoned as a full year of his reign, while the length of the reign of his successor was reckoned only from the following calendar year. A certain amount of evidence may be adduced for this method of reckoning, especially as regards the later period.[1] But it is at the same time evident that everything would depend on knowing *when* this method of reckoning became usual.[2] For certainly before it was in use no one ever thought of indicating the time of a king's reign otherwise than by its absolute duration. If it was necessary to round off the time, this was not done in accordance with any system, but from considerations of convenience. A considerable fragment of a year might be reckoned as a whole year, a small fragment might not be counted at all. There was in any case no occasion for reducing it to a calendar year.

It follows from this that we are on really sure ground only when the basis of reckoning is supplied from other sources, and also that if we start from this basis we are not in a position, in most cases, to get beyond *probable reckonings*.

The following are the most important fixed dates got from Assyrian sources:—[3]

854.	The Battle of Qarqar.
842.	Jehu's tribute to Salmanassar II.
739-8.	Azariah-Uzziah of Judah still living.
738.	Menahem of Israel tributary to Assyria.
734.	The Syrio-Ephraimite War.
722.	Samaria's Fall.
702.	Sennacherib's Invasion.

---

[1] M. v. Niebuhr; Wellh. *JDTh.* xx. 620 ff.
[2] See Riehm, in *HWB.* 1804.　　　[3] See above, p. 232.

Starting from this it is possible, in the first instance, to determine in a measure the period from Jehu upwards. We have to assume that he paid the tribute soon after his accession. As a usurper he is forced to buttress up his throne. Then we have the fact which is chronologically helpful, that by Ahaziah's murder he is the means of raising a new ruler, Athaliah, to the throne of Judah also, at the same time as he himself becomes King of Samaria. Now the Book of Kings gives the following numbers in connection with the different reigns up to the time of Jehu :—

Jeroboam I., . 22 years		Rehoboam, . 17 years	
Nadab, . . 2 ,,		Abijam, . . 3 ,,	
Baasha, . . 24 ,,		Asa, . . . 41 ,,	
Elah, . . 2 ,,			
Zimri, ... 7 days			
Omri, . . 12 ,,			
Ahab, . . 22 ,,		Jehoshaphat, . 25 ,,	
Ahaziah, . . 2 ,,		Joram, . . 8 ,,	
Joram, . . 12 ,,		Ahaziah, . . 1 ,,	
98 years 7 days		95 years	

The totals do not agree. If the figures in the two columns were correctly given, and if we were at the same time able to sum them up as the author did, they would, as is self-evident, necessarily agree. We cannot say where the error is. Still it is probable that it is on the Israelitish rather than on the Judaic side, because the larger number of items given in the case of the former leaves greater room for error. It is possible that each of the double years in the case of Nadab, Elah, and Ahaziah would have to be reckoned only as a single year, according to our present mode of calculation. The error may, however, lurk somewhere else. Kamphausen assigns one year to Nadab and none to Elah. In any case we only get approximate numbers. Still they certainly impress us as being throughout figures which have been handed down by tradition. Taking them in this sense we get the following numbers of years :—

Jeroboam I.,	937-917	Rehoboam,	937-920
Nadab,	915-914	Abijam,	920-917
Baasha,	914-890	Asa,	917-876
Elah,	890-889		
Zimri,	889		
Omri,	889-877		
Ahab,	877-855	Jehoshaphat,	876-851
Ahaziah,	855-842	Joram,	851-843
Joram,	854-842	Ahaziah,	843-842

A second period extends to the fall of Samaria. The numbers supplied by the Book of Kings are:—

Jehu,	28 years	Athaliah,	6 years
Jehoahaz,	17 ,,	Joash,	40 ,,
Jehoash,	16 ,,	Amaziah,	20 ,,
Jeroboam II.,	41 ,,	Azariah-Uzziah,	52 ,,
Zachariah,	6 months		
Shallum,	1 ,,		
Menahem,	10 ,,	Jotham,	16 ,,
Pekahiah,	2 ,,		
Pekah,	20 ,,	Ahaz,	16 ,,
Hoshea,	9 ,,	Hezekiah,	6 ,,
	143 years 7 months		165 years

The difficulties accumulate here at the very first glance. Not only does the difference between Judah and Israel amount to over 21 years, but even the smaller of the two totals—that referring to Israel, $143\frac{1}{2}$—has a surplus of more than 22 years when compared with the number of years given in the Assyrian lists, namely, $842-722=121$. Then besides, we have a second palpable error in the Bible accounts. According to 2 Kings, chap. xviii. 13, Sennacherib's invasion in 701 coincided with the fourteenth year of Hezekiah's reign, while in verse 10 of the same chapter it is stated that the year 722 was the sixth year of Hezekiah's reign, so that Hezekiah must have begun to reign as early as 729, and 701 would thus represent the twenty-eighth year of his reign. One of the two statements must necessarily be false. We shall be more inclined to conclude that it is verse 10 which is wrong, than to give up the other verse, because the former is directly connected with the synchronism referred to (*cf. v.* 1). Hezekiah's accession is consequently to be assigned to the year 714, and we thus save the first six years of Hezekiah's reign, at least so far as the series belonging to Judah is concerned. If we go in for further reductions we are met, first of all, by the peculiar relation which exists between Azariah-Uzziah and his son Jotham. It is necessary, for other reasons,[1] to suppose that Jotham was regent along with his father, but the fact of a regency does excellent service here. Since the father was still living in 739-38, Jotham can have been sole ruler only a few years at most, for Ahaz was king in 734. We can thus, without much trouble, win from fourteen to fifteen years in the case of Jotham. On the other hand, the sixteen years of Ahaz suggest the opposite difficulty, namely, that they appear to represent too short a period. It is possible that we ought to assign twenty years to Ahaz.[2] In any case, however, since Ahaz began his reign in 734, 722 must be his thirteenth year. Here, too, we also gain three years. How are we to get rid of what still remains—the twenty to twenty-one years? We are almost entirely driven to guess-work. We can only say this much, that the six years of Athaliah and the forty of Joash appear to be well-established on internal grounds. Kamphausen wishes, for this reason, to take other ten years from Amaziah and Azariah. For safety's sake it is necessary to abandon the idea of coming to any definite decision. The Judah series will accordingly run thus:—

Athaliah,	842-836
Joash,	836-796
Amaziah,	796-78?
Azariah-Uzziah,	78?-737
Jotham,	737-735
Ahaz,	735-715
Hezekiah,	715-686

The Israelitish series takes a somewhat simpler form from Jehu to Hoshea. Here the ten years ascribed to Menahem ought, on internal grounds, to be shortened by from two to three years.[3] So, too, it is impossible to assign twenty and nine years respectively to Pekah and Hoshea before 722, if Menahem paid tribute in 738, and if after him Pekahiah has still to get two years. We shall be

---

[1] See below, in § 67.   [2] See Kamph. *Chron.* 37.
[3] See below, § 68, at the beginning.

justified in assigning to Pekah, or Hoshea, or both, a shorter period for their reign. Since, however, the ninth year of Hoshea must certainly be the year 722, Hoshea ought to get his full number. In addition to this, Pekah's death undoubtedly took place, 734-3. As regards Israel we accordingly reach the result represented by the following:—

Jehu,	842-814
Jehoahaz,	814-797
Jehoash,	797-781
Jeroboam II.,	781-740
Zachariah-Shallum,	740
Menahem,	740-737
Pekahiah,	737-735
Pekah,	735-734-3
Hoshea,[1]	733-725

The last third of the series of the kings of Judah presents the fewest difficulties. The nearer we get, in the matter of the length of the reigns, to the age of the author himself, the more trustworthy do the figures become. If Hezekiah is placed within the period from 714 to 686, then, since 586 is certainly the year of the destruction of Jerusalem, exactly a hundred years are left; while the sum-total of the numbers assigned to the reigns from Manasseh to Zedekiah is, on the other hand, one hundred and ten. If this period must be shortened somewhere or other by ten years, the reign of Manasseh seems the one that may most appropriately be cut down.[2] What we get then is this:—

Manasseh,	686-641
Amon,	641-639
Josiah,	639-608
Jehoahaz,	608
Jehoiakim,	608-597
Zedekiah,	597-586

By way of conclusion, I add the probable numbers for the first three kings:—

Solomon,	977-937
David,	1017-977
Saul,	1037-1017

---

[1] On his accession and Pekah's death, see below, § 68.
[2] See Kamph. *Chron.* 36.

B. THE HISTORY OF THE PERIOD.

CHAPTER I.

REHOBOAM AND JEROBOAM AND THEIR IMMEDIATE SUCCESSORS.

§ 54. *The Division of the Kingdom* (937).

THERE was in Solomon's government an unsound element which might easily lead to a rupture, but there was no actual necessity that this should occur just yet. However, if the man who was fitted to bring it about, and who was resolved that it should come about, did appear on the scene, everything was ready for the crisis. The general feeling throughout Israel had been sufficiently prepared beforehand for this.

The transition from an elective monarchy to a rigidly despotic rule had been accomplished too quickly. The tribes of Israel had, even in David's case, set the crown upon his head after a free choice, just as they had done formerly in the case of Saul. Israel had been a purely elective monarchy. David's sons, however, played in succession the *rôle* of hereditary successors to the throne. Neither Absalom, nor Adonijah, nor Solomon, thought it necessary that he should be first chosen by the tribes. According to their view of it, the succession to the throne of their father belonged to them as the sons of David. Israel had become a hereditary monarchy. This development was a perfectly natural one in the circumstances. It would have come about even in the case of the house of Saul, if Jonathan had lived, or if Ishbaal had been more capable and more fortunate. Still there was an increased danger just at this time in the way of any such change, since the exclusion of the house of Saul had brought home to the tribes, for the second time, a consciousness of the independence of the popular will.

The change, however, could have been successfully brought about only if it had been, meanwhile, made possible actually to attach the tribes of Israel to the house of David. David himself had certainly not completely solved this problem, a specially difficult one in the then existing circumstances. The northern tribes and Benjamin always showed a certain distrust of his rule. Still less was Solomon equal to this task. His despotic tendencies, and especially the oppressive taxation, were certainly not calculated to make the tribes forget that only a short time before this, not birth but the will of the people, was what entitled a man to sit on the royal throne.

How widespread the ferment was amongst the northern tribes already in the reign of Solomon, is plainly enough evident from the fact that a rising broke out even during his lifetime. It was only by force that it was suppressed, and that the revolt of the northern tribes from Solomon was postponed. Jeroboam, one of the royal overseers, was the originator of the rising.[1] He had to flee to Egypt, and, as would seem, was received there with open arms. But Solomon's government was strong enough to prevent him and his supporters from thinking of making any attempt to repeat the rising, so long as Solomon occupied the throne. It may astonish us that an Israelitish rebel should have found protection in Egypt of all places, seeing that a Pharaoh was the father of one of Solomon's wives. The explanation of this is that Shishak, the Egyptian Sheshonq, was the beginner of a new dynasty,[2] and consequently 'knew nothing' of Solomon.

After Solomon's death, which we may put in the year 937, the succession of his son Rehoboam appears at first as something which was taken for granted. We cannot tell what gave him the pre-

---

[1] See above, p. 187 f.   [2] *Cf.* Meyer, *Gesch. Ägypt.* 332.

ference over the other sons[1] of Solomon. As a matter of fact, he seems to have mounted the throne, and to have occupied it for some time. But the long-suppressed and smouldering discontent of the northern tribes with Solomon's rule plainly breaks out, if not actually at his accession, at any rate soon after it. There may, indeed, have been many negotiations and attempts to smooth things over before Rehoboam finally resolved to treat with the discontented in Shechem.[2] Meanwhile Jeroboam, too, had had time to return from Egypt and to take up the threads of the movement.[3]

The representatives of Israel point out to Rehoboam how heavily Solomon had burdened them, and demand a lightening of the burdens. For a time Rehoboam seems to have been inclined to yield to the wish of the tribes, and at the same time to the voice of reason. The older counsellors, who had most likely known the times of David and the better traditions of the earlier times of Solomon, advised him to this. Soon, however, Rehoboam, after consulting with those about him whom he had himself selected from amongst the 'present' generation, resolves to dismiss the demand. His advisers are the representatives of the younger generation in Judah,[4] who had grown up under the influence of the main principles acted upon by Solomon, and who revere them as the pattern of royal prudence and the basis of royal authority. Force and inflexible severity will, they believe, be sufficient, as was the case under Solomon, to quieten the rebels. They have no idea that they have a man behind them who has not the power and determination of Solomon to fall back upon.

[1] Spite of xi. 1, only Rehoboam is mentioned.

[2] The expression, להמליך, xii. 1, cannot possibly signify here the choice of a king in the ordinary sense. (See the notes which follow.) It can only refer to the formal recognition of Rehoboam's accession to the throne by the northern tribes.

[3] 1 Kings xii. 1-3. See on this above, p. 205. Verse 2 should precede *v.* 1, for it is Jeroboam's return which is referred to here (וַיֵּשֶׁב שָׁם), and which had already become an accomplished fact at the gathering in Shechem. Verse 3a is to be struck out.

[4] The designation, ילדים, xii. 8, 10, makes the age of forty-one assigned to Rehoboam in xiv. 21 appear somewhat doubtful. *Cf.* 2 Chron. xiii. 7, but especially 1 Kings xii. 24a in LXX. cod. B. (see Swete).

An arrogantly defiant answer to the earnest request of the tribes is the only act on the part of Rehoboam. And when they withdraw their allegiance from him, he has not the strength to make his threat good. An attempt made to appease them, which ends disastrously for Rehoboam's aged overseer Adoram,[1] miscarries. The people advance to open rebellion. The king's officer is stoned to death. Rehoboam is not sure of his own life. He prefers to mount his chariot, and in hasty flight to make for his capital Jerusalem. Jeroboam is quickly fetched, and chosen as king over Israel. Rehoboam is actually dethroned, and Jeroboam is his successor in the kingship. Only the capital and his own tribe, Judah,[2] are left to Rehoboam.[3] What David once was in Hebron before he became king of Israel, his grandson now again is. The national kingship has once more become a tribal kingship.

Truly a tragic destiny this which now overtakes Israel! David's creation had lasted barely two generations, in order now to fall a sacrifice to the folly of his grandson, joined to the faults of his son and the ancient wranglings of the tribes. All the fair beginnings and the promising prospects which the union and strengthening of the nation under David seemed to offer, and which had been barely recognised and enjoyed, are already lost again beyond hope of recovery. In their place there rise before our vision all the countless sufferings and sorrows which are yet to come upon Judah and Israel as the consequence, almost without exception, of the unhappy state of rupture.

What Israel could do when it was one, and was conscious of its power, had been plainly seen. It is not a matter of accident that even Egypt does not dare to oppose David's rule in Syria, and that its Pharaoh accepts the friendship of Solomon. Egypt

---

[1] He had held the same post under Solomon, and even under David, 2 Sam. xx. 24 (see Wellh. *TBS.*); 1 Kings iv. 6; v. 14.

[2] The mention of Benjamin, *vv.* 21 and 24 (in itself not very probable), rests on a later addition. Verse 20 at the end makes this perfectly plain.

[3] 1 Kings xii. 1-20. The account is, at all events, old and trustworthy (perhaps A). It must in any case belong to a time not long after the events. See above, p. 211. On a considerably different representation of the circumstances in the LXX., see above, p. 206.

by this time had long got past the zenith of its power; and even supposing a time did come again in which Egypt was stronger and more fortunate than it actually was at this period, if Israel had been united, and had kept the undisputed predominance in Syria which it had under David and Solomon, it would have been, even for this stronger Egypt, an opponent well worthy of respect. Besides this, the kingdom of Damascus was only now in the course of formation. The best part of its strength was drawn from the weakness and disunion of Israel. If Israel had been united and on its guard, Damascus could not have done it any harm. It may confidently be asserted that if Israel had pursued the course on which it was started by David and Solomon, its position in Syria would have been assured up till the time when it came into contact with Assyria.

We may, in fact, ask whether it would not have been better, if the house of David was to lose the throne at all, that it should have been entirely got out of the way, and that Jeroboam should have become king of all Israel? We can imagine that in this case the unity of the nation might at all events have been secured, and the nation itself preserved as a whole. Besides, it would have been saved from wearing itself out in a civil strife which lasted for centuries. But it was soon to become evident that the idea of unity, and the conception of a fixed and lasting order of things, had not taken that firm root amongst these northern tribes which alone would have enabled them permanently to assume the guidance of the nation. In fact, if the government of all Israel was to be committed to any one tribe at all, it looked almost as if Judah alone could be this tribe. And it was the fate of this tribe, after David and Solomon, not to possess any man who was fitted to assume the leadership and to guide the nation with power and skill.

One thing certainly was left to the tribe of Judah, and for this reason a throne was left to it, even if it were only that of a tribal kingdom. This was *Jerusalem*, with the Temple and the glorious memories of David and Solomon. As a matter of fact, it was the position held by Jerusalem as the capital, and as the city of the Temple, and at the same time as the city which reminded the Israelites of the glorious past, which alone made it possible for David's dynasty, spite of the smallness and weakness of the kingdom, to prolong its existence for centuries.[1]

§ 55. *Rehoboam. Abijah. Asa.*

If the spirit of his fathers had lived on in Rehoboam (937-920), he must necessarily have succeeded in gathering together the brave in Judah, and perhaps also many in Israel who still clung to the house of David, and in wresting the crown once more from the usurper, as David had done from Absalom and Sheba, and Solomon from Jeroboam. Instead of doing this, he never gets beyond the carrying on of a feeble feud with Jeroboam. The civil war drags on without any real earnestness or result on either side, so long as Rehoboam lives.[2] The statement in the Book of Kings that he once intended to strike a decisive blow at the usurper of his authority, but was hindered from engaging in what was a war between brethren by a prophetic oracle, sounds like a friendly excuse for his inaction and indifference.[3] For, as a matter of fact, the fraternal quarrel is continued.

The evil consequences of the internal weakening of the kingdom become soon enough evident in Israel's relation to foreign countries. Egypt, which was suffering from its own weakness, and had not up to this time dared to disturb Israel's powerful unity, suddenly appears in the character of an enemy. In the time of Solomon the Egyptians had contented themselves with offering a place of abode to the enemies of Israel and to refugees from that country, and they had done this in one case spite of the close alliance between Solomon and the house of Pharaoh.[4]

[1] See on this also above, p. 157 and p. 195.
[2] 1 Kings xiv. 30. Differently, Wellh. *History of Israel and Judah*, p. 58 f.
[3] 1 Kings xii. 21-24. See on this above, p. 211.
[4] How this circumstance is to be explained in both instances, see above, p. 242, and p. 184, note 3 ; also p. 187 f.

Scarcely, however, is the kingdom split up, when its power too appears to be shattered. Pharaoh Sheshonq (Hebrew, Shishaq) organises a marauding expedition against Judah and Israel. He plunders Jerusalem, and carries off the treasures of the Temple which Solomon had collected together there.[1] His inscription in the temple at Karnak shows that his expedition had not to do with Jerusalem only, and that it was not undertaken merely to protect his former *protégé*, Jeroboam.[2] It is an ordinary marauding expedition, which even this Pharaoh, who had a little more experience of war than his immediate successors, would hardly have ventured on if the disastrous breach in Israel had not continued. For we do not hear of any other warlike deeds on the part of Sheshonq.

Sheshonq's invasion took place in the fifth year of Rehoboam. He continued to reign other twelve years after this, apparently in the same inactive manner as at the beginning. In Chronicles we are told of some fortress building, and this information, so far as Judah is concerned, may probably rest on good enough authority.[3] Rehoboam is sharply blamed, by the redactor of the Book of Kings, in reference to his position in the matter of religion and worship. According to this writer, he favoured worship on high-places and religious prostitution.

It is, however, very questionable whether this remark refers to Rehoboam personally and not to the kingdom of Judah generally.[4] That high-places with Maççebas, and probably Ashéras[5] as well, still maintained their position beside the Temple, and perhaps, too, under the influence of the northern kingdom, to some extent became still more prevalent, is not improbable. Besides, Rehoboam's mother was a heathen.

---

[1] 1 Kings xiv. 25-28, 30.
[2] See Brugsch, *Geogr. Inschr.* ii. 58 ff.; Blau, *ZDMG.* 15, 233 ff.; Meyer, *Gesch. Ägypt*, 330 ff.; Stade, *Gesch.* i. 353 f. [See, further, Dedekind, in the *Proceedings of the Stock. Orient. Congress*, iv. 191 ff.; also Conder, in *Pal. Expl. Fund Qly. Stat.* 1893, 245 f.]   [3] 2 Chron. xi. 5 ff.
[4] 1 Kings xiv. 22-24. Verse 22 f. at all events seems to refer to the sins of Judah in general; while v. 24, on the other hand, looks like an anticipation of xv. 12.   [5] See on this in §§ 38 and 64.

His son Abijah (920-917) was his successor. He reigns three years, and continues the futile resistance to Jeroboam which his father had carried on. He too, like Rehoboam, is classed as a king who did evil.[1] His mother was Maachah, the daughter of Absalom. Since the name Absalom is not qualified in any way, it can only be the well-known bearer of this name—namely, the son of David, who is intended here. Abijah is thus, both on his father's and mother's side, a great-grandson of David.[2]

Abijah, after his early death, is succeeded by his son Asa. His mother, too, is called Maachah.[3] His reign is supposed to have lasted forty-one years (917-876). So far as religious worship is concerned, he seems to have been more inclined to the purer service of Yahvé than his father and grandfather. He permits only the worship of Yahvé even on the high-places outside of the Temple. He puts away the Ḳedeshas who were now known in Judah also (*i.e.* those who prostituted themselves in the service of Ashtoreth), and with them the worship of their goddess as well as other foreign cults. How far-reaching the influence of these foreign forms of worship which thus threatened the service of Yahvé already was at this time in Judah, and how thorough Asa's measures were, is evident from the statement that Asa deprived his own mother of the special honour which was due to her as the mother of the king, because she had taken a prominent part in idolatrous forms of worship. She is said to have set up the Ashēra, 'an abomination'[4] which was destroyed by Asa, and burned in the Kedron valley. On the other hand, he gave greater attention to the Temple and brought offerings into it.[5]

If Asa decidedly deserves credit for what he did in the matter

---

[1] 1 Kings xv. 1 ff.; 2 Chron. xv. is a later Midrash.

[2] But see 2 Sam. xiv. 27 (xviii. 18). The LXX. in xiv. 27 has undoubtedly a false correction; 2 Chron. xiii. 2 is a copyist's mistake. Rehoboam's age presents some difficulties too. Does *bat* = grandchild (*cf.* Gen. xxix. 5), or were Abijam and Asa brothers? So Wellh. *Prol.*[3] 216.

[3] By an obvious error she is also called a daughter of Absalom, xv. 10.

[4] In view of the well-known confusion of Ashēra and Ashtoreth it can only be an image of Ashtoreth, or an Ashēra sacred to Ashtoreth, which is referred to here under this phrase. Perhaps this Maachah, too, was a heathen, like Rehoboam's mother.

[5] 1 Kings xv. 9-15.

of the worship of Yahvé and the Temple, such renown as he gained in the political sphere was, on the contrary, of a doubtful kind. It is true that our informant is acquainted with certain brave deeds in war which Asa is said to have done, and what he did in the way of planning cities and fortresses seems to have brought him renown.[1] But the detailed information regarding all this is supplied only in the Book of Chronicles, and, in fact, in a form which, though it rests on older traditions, hardly deserves to be implicitly trusted.[2] It is specially mentioned that he gained a brilliant victory over an otherwise unknown Ethiopian king called Serah. This is perhaps based on some recollection of the fact that Asa had the good fortune to repel a dangerous raid. We shall, in any case, be well advised if we construct our authentic picture of Asa from the little which the Book of Kings itself, with more accuracy, hands down to us of his long reign. If, however we follow it, the judgment we have to pass upon him is, that all the rest of his—perhaps worthy enough—deeds are far more than counterbalanced by the unpatriotic short-sightedness with which he sought to keep off his rival in Israel.

The old feud between north and south, which was inherited from Rehoboam, still continues. They do not seem yet to have arrived at any right settlement of it. Baasha, who has meanwhile ascended the throne in Israel, takes up with fresh zeal the war which for a long time had not been carried on with any real earnestness. He fortifies Ramah on the southern boundaries of Benjamin, hardly ten miles north from Jerusalem, in order thus to keep Jerusalem in check and to cut it off from intercourse with the outer world. In this strait Asa has recourse to a policy of despair. He collects together all the treasures which happen to be in the Temple and in his palace, and by means of these seeks to induce Benhadad ben Tabrimmon,[3] King of Aram Damascus, to attack his opponent. Benhadad responds to the appeal, invades

---

[1] 1 Kings xv. 23.   [2] 2 Chron. xiv. 6 f., 8 ff.
[3] This is how a grandson of Hezion is styled; or, perhaps, we ought to read Hezron = Rezon. See Klost. here.

the kingdom of Israel from the north, and takes a number of towns from Baasha, amongst which were Dan and Abel-beth-maachah, and probably also the whole of Naphtali. Baasha is naturally forced to retire. Asa is free, and is now able in turn, with the material collected by Baasha, to fortify Geba and Mizpah,[1] by way of protecting himself against his opponent.[2]

Asa had attained his end, but in a way which could not possibly bring blessing to Judah itself. Nothing could have been more inglorious and humiliating for a great-grandson of Solomon —even although Damascus had never actually once been a vassal state under David—than to have been compelled to beg for assistance from one of the neighbouring Syrian kingdoms. There could not possibly have been a more ignominious way of escape from a momentary pressing danger than this of having recourse to a foreign country. This is the first time, but not the only time, that Judah called in the aid of foreign help against its northern oppressor allied to it by ties of race, instead of seeking to compose the fraternal strife in its own house. It is accordingly not to be wondered at that, as is related in Chronicles, a prophet should have sharply censured this action.[3] That with which, later on, Isaiah[4] threatened King Ahaz, held good already of Asa. In the former case it was Assyria which rendered a service to Judah, only to end by threatening the latter herself. For the present it is the Syrian interference in the affairs of Canaan, dangerous to the kingdom of Israel—and, at the same time, to Judah herself—which has thus been evoked by Asa's short-sighted policy. Judah will, by and by, have to repent this means of strengthening herself. And, in fact, it is to be Judah's opponent, thus worsted for the time being, who will yet join with Judah's present friend in threatening her.

But we now return to the revolted tribes.

§ 56. *Jeroboam, Nadab, Baasha, Elah, Omri.*

Whether it be that Jeroboam had from the first a hand in the rising against Rehoboam, which is certainly likely enough, or

---

[1] A part of Benjamin thus already belonged to Judah.
[2] 1 Kings xv. 16-22.   [3] 2 Chron. xvi. 7 ff.   [4] Isaiah vii. 1 ff.

whether it be that he hastened out of Egypt and looked on merely as a spectator, in any case he is welcomed by the revolted tribes as being an old and tried enemy of the house of David, and is by them elected king. Jeroboam and his successors are entirely within their rights in calling themselves kings of Israel. For the kingdom was taken from the house of David. The king of Israel is he whom the nation invites to fill David's place.

Regarding Jeroboam's reign of twenty-two years (937-915) we have little trustworthy information. How far he was able to maintain Solomon's authority we can only conjecture. He, too, at any rate had to submit to the raid of Shishak, king of Egypt. This proves that he did not possess any great amount of military skill or strong patriotic feeling. We do not even hear of any attempt at energetic resistance. Had he been bold enough to make any such attempt, it would not, in all probability, have been quietly passed over in the accounts we have of his reign. We can gather from his conduct in this case how he acted in other cases. Besides, we have special means of judging. Jeroboam had, during his whole life, to defend himself against Rehoboam and his successors.[1] There is no mention of his having had any real success in his contest with the former of these, and it is indeed not probable that he had, otherwise the war would not have been handed on by Rehoboam to his successors. On the contrary, at first, at any rate, perhaps Jeroboam's opponent gave him serious trouble. We have, in any case, to explain the fact that he suddenly leaves the residence he had built in Shechem and migrates to Penuel, in the country east of the Jordan.[2]

As regards home matters, on the other hand, there is one measure which is ever after referred back in the most emphatic way to Jeroboam. Solomon's Temple, the building of which can hardly have been undertaken wholly without the design of creating in time a central place of worship for Israel, had certainly

---

[1] 1 Kings xiv. 30; xv. 7b.
[2] 1 Kings xii. 25. Stade conjectures that the invasion of Shishak was the occasion of the change of residence.

under Solomon's long and stern rule already definitely begun to fulfil this aim. Jeroboam was obliged to counteract its influence. The centre of gravity of public life until the time of David and Solomon had always been in the northern tribes and in the house of Joseph. If it once more came back to the same place, nothing was more natural than that the centre of gravity of the religious life should also return thither. Israel possessed ancient sanctuaries within its bounds. It was only necessary that they should anew be brought into remembrance, under the protection and patronage of the kingship which had now been transferred to Ephraim, in order soon to replace the Temple of Jerusalem in the eyes of the nation.

Bethel and Dan—the former in the south, the latter in the north, lying almost at the extreme boundary of the kingdom—are selected for this purpose. Bethel is the ancient sanctuary of the house of Ephraim, and had moreover been held in reverence by the patriarchs. Its holy stone had doubtless been an object of veneration for the Canaanites. Since David and Solomon, the nearness of Jerusalem may have endangered its position. Until the disappearance of the sanctuary in Shiloh, and thus until the break-up of the Philistine rule by Saul, Dan contained a graven image, and then after this it seems to have been disused as a sacred place.[1] To both of these once venerated temples Jeroboam gives new sacred objects. These consist of golden bulls, which, doubtless in accordance with certain ancient Israelitish tastes, were supposed to represent Jehovah in symbolic form.[2] Jeroboam therewith takes these old sanctuaries under his special protection. He poses as the patron of the ancient places of worship which the fathers had formerly held in reverence.[3]

---

[1] *Cf.* Judges xviii. 31, and also Wellh. *TBS.* 176 f., and also above, p. 101. The sanctuary itself naturally continues to exist. In the most arbitrary way Klost. *SaKö* alters the text.

[2] See on bull-worship Baudissin, *Stud.* i. 137. Dillm. *Ex. Lev.* 337. König, *Hauptprobl.* 53 ff.; Kautzsch in *PRE.*² vi. 536 f. Köhler, ii. 1, 13 ff.

[3] Bethel and Dan are certainly not the only sanctuaries of this kind. They were specially preferred by Jeroboam merely on account of their geographical position. *Cf. e.g.* Hos. ix. 15; iv. 13 ff.; and Köhler, *Gesch.* ii. 2, 15, 46.

They sheltered 'the God who had brought Israel out of Egypt.'[1]

As is well known, the furnishing of these sanctuaries with images of Yahvé in the form of a bull came to be reckoned to Jeroboam as his special sin; and, as a matter of fact, it was that. What Jeroboam did may have been an act of political prudence, and may have meant a strengthening of the Northern Kingdom as against Judah, but the measures he adopted give no proof of any deeper understanding of the spirit which guided the religion of Israel. They were, as compared with the Temple at Jerusalem, a backward step. There had indeed been high-places for long all over the country; even in Judah we find them both before and after the building of the Temple. Nor did public opinion in Israel, if we except the few who were under the influence of the views of the prophets, take any great offence at Jeroboam's bull-worship. For the worship of Yahvé under the form of an image had long been carried on, not in Dan only, but in many places ever since the time of the Judges. Still it was always an abuse, and must have been regarded by the best in the nation as such. And the very fact that the Temple alone amongst all the sanctuaries throughout the entire land of Israel had no image, must have secured for it a special pre-eminence.

Jeroboam's crime was all the greater that he, as king of Israel, did not treat the Temple with respect. For political separatist interests he had in this way lightly sacrificed what was a vital interest for Israel as a whole. We may hold what opinion we choose regarding the Deuteronomic redactor of our Book of Kings in his character as historian, but nothing witnesses so strongly to his deep religious insight as the fact that he cannot sufficiently censure Jeroboam's abandonment of the Temple, and his falling away into the worship of Yahvé under the form of an image. Regarding the matter from this point of view, nothing is more probable than that those circles which had sympathised with

---

[1] 1 Kings xii. 25-31. On Klostermann's fantasies in connection with this section, cf. Köhler, ii. 2, 11 f., 16 f.

Solomon's temple-building and had been discontented with the tolerance shown to foreign cults, the circles headed by the prophets Nathan, Gad, and Ahijah of Shiloh, now broke away from Jeroboam with similar decidedness.[1] The Levites, too, who were specially sought after for priestly service, seem to have repeatedly transferred their services to the Temple, so that Jeroboam was under the necessity of getting the help of non-Levites, which can hardly have been quite such a serious fault in the eyes of his contemporaries as it was in the eyes of those in later days.[2]

The seed of rebellion which Jeroboam had sown, was destined soon enough to bear evil fruits in his own house. And once begun, rebellion and king-murder continue to be an almost permanent characteristic of the northern kingdom. It must have already seemed to contemporaries as if the curse of God rested on the kingdom which had, by its own will, separated itself from David and his house. Conspiracy and usurpation hardly ever cease at certain times. Dynasty follows dynasty; while the kingdom of David, in the midst of much weakness and many faults, could still give evidence of the protecting care of Yahvé in the uninterrupted succession of Davidic kings for centuries.

The dynasty already comes to an end with Jeroboam's successor, his son Nadab. After a reign of only two years (915-914), he is murdered by Baasha ben Ahijah of Issachar, during the siege of the Philistine town of Gibbethon. Baasha usurps the throne, and in order to secure himself he extirpates the whole race of Jeroboam.[3] Baasha was probably one of Nadab's generals. The latter doubtless fell a victim to a military revolution. We must look for the occasion of this in the fact that wars with the Philistines could recommence. For, apart from very considerable weakness on the part of Israel, Philistia was not, after what had happened under David, in a position to wage war with Israel.

---

[1] 1 Kings xiv. 1-18. The narrative rests on an historical basis. See above, p. 212

[2] 1 Kings xii. 31; xiii. 33. *Cf.* also Köhler, 20 f. Baudissin *Priestert*. 199 can hardly be right.   [3] 1 Kings xv. 25-31.

A reign of twenty-four years is allotted to Baasha himself (914-890).[1] The way in which he carries on operations against Asa, king of Judah, shows him to us as an energetic prince of military skill. That he had to beat a retreat without accomplishing his design was not his fault. So when our informant attributes to him other brave deeds, the statement is most likely founded on facts.[2] Unfortunately the details have been lost. It is possible that he may have been successful in keeping off the Syrians. Nadab, during his life, may possibly have continued to reside in Penuel. Baasha, however, transfers the royal residence back to the west again—to Tirzah, in fact.[3] In this, too, we may trace his more powerful hand. The prophet Jehu ben Hanani is mentioned as his contemporary.[4]

Baasha is one of the few kings of Israel who die a natural death. But an untoward fate overtakes his son Elah.[5] After a reign of only two years (890-889), he falls a victim to a conspiracy. The circumstances are quite similar to those in the case of Nadab. Gibbethon has once more to be besieged, and Elah, who has doubtless again lost the Philistine town, has even taken the field, but lies drunk at home at a feast which his palace steward Arza has arranged in his honour. One of his officers, Zimri, murders him here, and treats his house as Baasha had formerly treated the house of Jeroboam.

Zimri's act would have been a foolhardy venture if he had not previously obtained the co-operation of the army of Gibbethon and Omri its general. The latter, however, is not inclined to recognise a subordinate as king. He gets himself called to the throne by the army, and moves with it against Tirzah. Zimri is not able to hold out here, and seeks his death amid the flames of his palace. His royal authority had lasted only seven days.

---

[1] See on him, 1 Kings xv. 32-34; xvi. 1-7; and also above, p. 213.
[2] 1 Kings xvi. 5.
[3] 1 Kings xv. 33. On the situation of the place see Guérin, *Samarie*, i. 365 ff.; and Mühlau in the *HWB*. Perhaps Jeroboam had resided here before Baasha (during the later years of his reign?—see xiv. 17).
[4] 1 Kings xvi. 1 ff.   [5] 1 Kings xvi. 8-14.

Nevertheless, Omri has even yet to fight for his throne. A certain Tibni ben Ginath sets up as a pretender to the throne along with him, and seems to have gained a strong following in the nation. After what seems to have been a somewhat long civil war, Omri finally gains the upper hand.[1]

[1] 1 Kings xvi. 14-22.

CHAPTER II.

THE DYNASTY OF OMRI.

§ 57. *The Assyrians. Omri.*

OMRI is the first King of Israel who is mentioned in the Assyrian inscriptions. This points to a new period. *Assyria* now comes within the horizon of Israel. It becomes more and more a factor which has to be reckoned with. Soon enough it will become the factor which decisively determines the history of Israel.

Two hundred years before this period, about the turning-point of the twelfth century, the powerful Tiglathpileser I. had already carried his ensigns beyond the Euphrates. He had even penetrated as far as Lebanon.[1] If his successors had followed up his movements, the kingdom of David and Solomon would hardly have been possible. But it was a remarkably fortunate arrangement of things that the two great kingdoms between which Israel was wedged—namely, Egypt and Assyria—were not in a position to interfere with Israel just in those very days when it was her lot to produce a David, and a Solomon. After the powerful forward step which it had taken under Tiglathpileser I., the Assyrian Empire had to pass through a period of weakness and incapacity,[2] extending from the middle of the eleventh to the middle of the tenth century, which certainly did not allow it to think of any further extension of its authority in Syria.

---

[1] Meyer, *Gesch. d. Alt.* 331.
[2] *Cf.* the monolith-inscription of Salmanassar II. (Col. ii. 37 f.) in Schrader, *KBibl.* i. 165.

Nor at the time of the disruption of the kingdom does Assyria seem to have been sufficiently strong to be able to oppose the kingdom of Aram Damascus, which had meanwhile sprung up, and was becoming more and more powerful. It was, apparently, Asurnaṣirpal, the contemporary of Omri and the father of Salmanassar II., who was the first to venture once more to advance against Syria. He reigned 884-860, and calls himself conqueror of the region beyond the Tigris and as far as Lebanon and the Great Sea. By the latter is meant the Mediterranean; since he, as a matter of fact, was receiving tribute from the Phœnician cities of Tyre, Sidon, Byblos, and others about the year 870, and consequently during the reign of Ahab.[1]

The course was already sketched out on which Assyria was to advance further. This, however, meant for Israel the appearance on the scene of what must soon enough awaken a lively interest in all who had eyes to see it. For the present, and in the period immediately following, the significance of what was taking place was scarcely realised. The Assyrian hosts which crossed through the northern part of Israel, even though they laid Sidon and Tyre under tribute—cities connected with Israel by ties of race and friendship—were welcome guests who kept off the more immediate, and therefore apparently more threatening, danger which came from the side of Aram Damascus. But the pleasing delusion could necessarily continue only for a time. It must soon become apparent that the further Israel was drawn into the affairs of the big world, and the nearer the greedy colossus, after having swallowed Israel's neighbours, approached her herself, the greater was the danger for her too.

The real point of importance, however, in connection with the entrance of Assyria within the historical horizon of Israel, is that the latter at the same time stepped out of the narrow bounds of her isolated existence and her petty surroundings. Outwardly, at any rate, this was certainly not to her advantage. So far as her outward condition was concerned, Israel, by her involuntary entrance

---

[1] Meyer, *Gesch. d. Alt.* 409; Tiele, *Gesch.* 175 f.

into world-history, could not possibly escape being crushed by the powers with which she was involved in conflict. Her appearance in the great world-theatre sealed her destiny as a state. For which of these powers would her troops be likely to defy? At the same time, however, those marvellous forces which slumber in the depths of the national consciousness, and which have hitherto manifested themselves merely in a timid and transitory fashion, begin now to develop and unfold themselves step by step until they reach their full and perfect strength and height. It is in misfortune and in the break-up of her outward existence that Israel's inner life is first to become what it is destined to be, and is capable of being. Every new blow will be for her religion a source of new and more complete advance. The nearer the state and the nation approach the abyss which must inevitably swallow them up, the surer and more certain of victory does the religious idea become as it gathers up its strength, the more proudly does it float above the wretchedness of the present.

Whether Omri himself already paid tribute to the Assyrians, and whether perhaps he may not even have gained the throne by their help, are points on which we have no information. Still this supposition is not altogether excluded when we consider the extraordinary niggardliness of the Biblical account of him.[1] In any case, he and the Assyrians must have come into contact. This is evident from the fact that, even in the Assyrian inscriptions belonging to a considerably later date, Israel is still briefly styled the house of Omri.[2] This circumstance certainly proves, at the same time, how slender was the impression made by Israel on Assyria; and, as will be readily understood, the importance of the connection for the latter country cannot for a moment be compared with that which Israel, on its part, had every reason to attach to the course of events in Assyria. It follows from this that the Assyrian accounts, spite of all the value we may attach

---

[1] 1 Kings xvi. 23-28.
[2] See Schrader, *KAT.*² 190 [Eng. Trans. i. 179]. On the question as to whether Omri put himself under the protection of Assyria, see Kamph. *Chronol.* 80.

to them, can hardly be regarded as supplying an absolute standard by which to judge of matters in Israel.

The little which the Bible tells us regarding Omri (889-877) allows us to conjecture that he was a prudent and powerful ruler. That he had a right perception of what was needful for his kingdom is unmistakably evident from his choice of a new capital in place of Tirzah, which owed more to the pleasantness of its situation than to any natural strength of position. He transfers his residence to *Samaria* (Shomrôn). The place of his choice cannot have been inferior to Tirzah in natural attractiveness. Isaiah calls it, 'The proud crown of Ephraim on the head of a rich valley.'[1] That it possessed the additional advantage of special strength is evident, both from its situation and its history. Samaria lay on a conical hill rising more than one hundred metres above a broad, deep valley.[2] It was, accordingly, a place which could be easily strengthened and made into an almost impregnable fortress when we consider the conditions of warfare in ancient times. As a matter of fact, it successfully came through more than one siege conducted by hostile forces superior in numbers. And when, at a later date, the Assyrians conquered Samaria, the possession of the town cost these masters of the art of war and besieging the labour of a three years' siege.

How clamant was Israel's need of such a capital which would be able to defy a hostile attack, is best understood when we consider the state of things which Omri had inherited from Baasha. For, doubtless, his successor Elah was not able to alter the situation in any essential points. The Syrians, invited by Asa of Judah, still constantly harassed Israel. Even Omri does not seem to have succeeded in altogether shaking them off. The fact that we have so little exact information on this head makes us again lament the defectiveness of what has been handed down. If we knew more about Omri, the picture which we

---

[1] Isaiah xxviii. 1.
[2] See on its situation, Rob. *Pal.* iii. 365 ff.; Bädek.[3] 225 f. On the name, *cf.* *ZAW.* v. 165 ff.

would, in all probability, be able to form of him would be that of one who sought by heroic struggles to get rid of the burdensome legacy which, owing to Asa's fault, he had to take over from Baasha, but did not succeed in perfectly freeing himself of it. As a matter of fact, we only gather from an incidental reference[1] that in the war with the Syrians he lost several towns and was even compelled to grant to the Syrian merchants a quarter of their own in Samaria.

Omri appears in the same character of a brave and frequently victorious soldier, in the inscription of King Mêsha‘ of Moab.[2] According to it, it was he who again brought the Moabites into subjection to Israel after they had for a long time enjoyed independence. The region of Mêdeba is specially mentioned by Mêsha‘ as having been conquered by Omri and held for a considerable time; while, on the other hand, the land round ‘Aṭarôt was never lost by Israel at all.[3]

This leads us to suppose that the Moabites, after that David had thoroughly subdued them, and, in fact, almost extirpated them, had been able to take advantage of the period of disturbance and civil war in Israel from the time of Solomon's death. Driven back to the south-east of the Dead Sea, they had, though slowly, recovered themselves, and, under Mêsha‘'s father Kemoshmelek, had re-established their authority over the southern half of the eastern bank of the Dead Sea. Daibon was his capital. We may regard Kemoshmelek as the contemporary of Baasha and Omri. He reigns thirty years.[4] The region of ‘Aṭarôt remained in the hands of the tribe of Gad. Kemoshmelek, however, seems to have extended his authority as far as Mêdeba.[5] Omri checks his progress and confines him to his more southerly regions; in them, too, he is Omri's vassal. This foreign domination lasted forty years.[6]

---

[1] 1 Kings xx. 34.   [2] On it, see above, p. 231.
[3] *Cf.* the Mêsha‘ stone, line 4 f., 10. Perhaps this had already taken place under Baasha. Kampf. *Chronol.* 41.   [4] Mêsha‘, line 2.
[5] On the situation of the place, see the hand-map of Fischer and Guthe.
[6] Mêsha‘, line 8. On the tribute which was paid till Ahab's death, see 2 Kings iii. 4.

§ 58. *Ahab. Elijah, and Prophecy in his time.*[1]

Omri, after having reigned for twelve years, is followed by his son Ahab. Twenty-two years are allotted to him (877-855). We do not only possess detailed, and, in part, excellent, accounts of him in the Old Testament, but the Assyrian inscriptions and the Moabite Mêsha'-tablet also give us information regarding him. According to all these accounts, Ahab appears as a man who worthily followed in his father's footsteps in the endeavour to advance Israel's independence and greatness. In the south-east he kept down the Moabites in the same way in which Omri had done before him. For the time being they do not dare to move. It is, at earliest, in the second half of his reign, and perhaps not till towards the end of it, that Mêsha' becomes bold enough to revolt.[2] And, what was still more important, he settled an old quarrel on the one hand, and, on the other, confirmed anew an old friendship. It is possible that the two last things, as well as the first, were owing to Omri's initiative. The founder of the dynasty would, if this supposition be correct, be raised a stage higher so far as his historical importance is concerned. These measures were, at any rate, first practically carried out in the reign of Ahab, so far as we can judge from our sources of information. Accordingly we are justified in referring them to him.

Amongst the considerations which led Ahab to make friends of his neighbours, the increasing perception of the danger which threatened the kingdom from the side of Assyria was probably one of the most important. What befell the Phœnician cities under Asurnaṣirpal could leave no possible doubt as to what was to be expected in course of time from that quarter. This perception of the coming danger reveals Ahab's statesmanlike insight. Besides, Israel was still at feud with Damascus. This state of things had, without doubt, its influence with Ahab.

---

[1] *Cf.* Rosch in *StKr.* 1892, 551 ff ; [W. R. Smith, *Prophets of Israel*, 75 ff.].

[2] Mêsha', line 8, according to the reading of Smend and Socin. See also Driver, *Notes*, § lxxxviii. f. The 'middle of the days' can hardly be understood literally.

Accordingly the fraternal strife between Israel and Judah, which had gone on uninterruptedly, as it would seem, from the time of the revolt of Jeroboam, is at last brought to a peaceful settlement. Jehoshaphat of Judah, Asa's successor, is the first of the kings of Judah to bring himself to recognise as an established fact the state of things which had existed since Solomon's death. Not only is peace concluded, but the good understanding which was now beginning is sealed by a marriage alliance between the two neighbourly royal houses. Jehoshaphat's son Joram weds Ahab's daughter Athaliah.

The ancient alliance with the Phœnicians had probably been renewed before this time. It had been in abeyance since the days of Solomon. The two kingdoms in Israel had been too much occupied with their own inner feuds to be able to turn their attention to foreign countries. Besides, as they had been weakened by civil war, they were not valuable allies for anybody. Now, however, the common danger which threatened from the east, and the recollection of their racial kinship and common interests, force Israel and her western neighbour once more together. Even before the time of David, Tyre (Ṣôr) seems to have taken the place of the more ancient Sidon, and to have exercised, as it did at this period, a predominant authority amongst the Phœnician cities.[1] Ahab enters into a marriage alliance with the Syrian king, Ethbaal, and weds his daughter Jezebel.[2] This points to a friendly alliance of the same kind as that which existed between Israel and Judah.[3] Ethbaal had, perhaps, the same name as Saul's son and successor; the Greeks call him Ittobalos.[4]

This alliance was destined to be one fraught with dire consequences for Ahab. It is certainly not without good reason that our narrator mentions in connection with it the measures

---

[1] See Pietschmann, *Gesch. d. Phön.* 294.

[2] 1 Kings xvi. 31. After what has just been said, it ought not to surprise us that Eshbaal is here called king of the Sidonians.

[3] *Cf.* also Amos i. 9: 'Brotherly covenant.'

[4] See Menander of Ephesus in Josephus, *Ant.* viii. 3, 1·2, and *C. Ap.* i. 18. Possibly, according to this, the original form was Ittoba'al. *Cf.* on him, Pietschm. *Gesch.* 298.

taken by Ahab for the naturalisation of the Phœnician Baal-worship in Israel.[1] He builds a temple in Samaria to the chief Phœnician god. According to what we learn later, this temple must have been of very considerable extent.[2] In accordance with the nature of the Phœnician worship, it has a Maççēba and an Ashēra.[3] A splendid priesthood conducts the worship of the god, who naturally has in Ahab's Syrian wife his most zealous champion. The worshippers of Yahvé seem actually to have been seriously threatened and persecuted, although probably the persecutions did not attain the dimensions ascribed to them by our documents.[4] The account we have bears the mark of having been influenced by a strong feeling of the injustice practised by Jezebel and permitted by Ahab, and represents it as still worse than it appears in reality to have been.

The proof that such is the case is supplied by the fact that Ahab himself, although he tolerated and even patronised the worship of Baal *alongside of* Yahvéism, did not renounce the latter so far as he himself personally and his family were concerned, and consequently did not, in all probability, renounce it so far as his kingdom was concerned. He names his children, Ahaziah, Joram, and Athaliah, after Yahvé, not after Baal, and has prophets of Yahvé in considerable numbers about him.[5] We have thus here a kind of mixed religion. It was necessary that Baal, as being the god of the queen of the kingdom, and, above all, as being the chief god of the closely allied neighbour country, should also possess his temple and altar in Israel.

Nothing was more natural than that a feeling of profound discontent with these syncretic tendencies should be roused amongst the best in the nation. Granting that the Canaanitish-Phœnician nature-worship had long exercised its seductive charm on many in Israel; granting that others who up to this time had

---

[1] 1 Kings xvi. 32 f.   [2] 2 Kings x. 18 ff.
[3] 2 Kings iii. 2 ; 1 Kings xvi. 33. There is no authority for interpreting this as referring to an image of 'Ashtart, or, as the case may be, of Baal (Köhl. 72).
[4] 1 Kings xix. 18 ; but *cf.* viii. 4.
[5] *Cf.* especially 1 Kings xxii. 6 ff., 22 ff.

clung to Yahvé, now yield, willingly or unwillingly, to pressure from above; still, those who had regarded Jeroboam's lapse into bull-worship with distrust and anxiety, and whose influence at a somewhat later period had made itself felt from time to time, could not be silent regarding what was now happening. It was now seen more clearly than had ever been the case before, that the foundations of the Mosaic religion were being called in question. Its religion was for Israel what constituted its existence as a nation. Whatever else Ahab may have undertaken for the advancement of his kingdom, he was now about to surrender the national treasure. Even supposing that those who kicked against this were not aware of the far-reaching importance of what they did, still, regarded in the light of history, those who were thus zealous for Yahvé stand before us as the saviours of their fatherland. We cannot, in fact, be sure what might have become of Israel had the Phœnician Baal-worship maintained itself, and if, under the protection afforded by the alliance of the two states, it had found its way from Samaria into Jerusalem.

The representatives of that counter-tendency are the *prophets*,[1] called Nebî'îm. Since the days of the powerful national movement which led to the elevation of Saul to the throne, and, in fact, to the creation of a new form of life for the nation—namely, the royal constitution—they had not succeeded in any great measure in making their influence felt in public life. It is only now and again that one of them appears on the scene and shows that that peculiar phenomenon has not died away, and that the prophets are following with a watchful interest the course of things in Israel, and, above all, that of religious events. Now, however, as then, the nation as a whole is in danger. They accordingly reappear on the scene in order to prepare themselves for interfering, in a decisive way, in the affairs of their fatherland.

Many changes have in the meantime come over the Nebî'îm. Formerly they had gone through the land in troops under ecstatic

---

[1] [See W. R. Smith, *Prophets of Israel*²; Cornill, *Der israel. Profetismus*, 1895.]

influence, almost like madmen, preaching a holy war, and perhaps also the duty of honouring their God, and sweeping along with them in their frenzy whatever came in their way. They still continue to be conscious that they have been laid hold of by the Divinity. But, as time has gone on, the mode of their public appearance has altered too. The bands of wandering dervishes have become societies in which the art and gift of prophecy and of announcing the will of God are cultivated in a more regular way; but it is the fostering of religious thought which is specially attended to. Thus the Nebī'îm soon take a place alongside of the priests, and, at the same time, a place above them. The former are the soul, the latter the arm and hand, of religion.

The prophets are thus on the point of becoming an Order—they have, in fact, essentially become this already. As such, they call themselves sons of the prophets—*i.e.* disciples and companions of a prophet of rank. Single individuals among them tower high above the mass. Between them and men of the stamp of Amos and Isaiah, there is only a step.

One of these masters of the prophets—the most powerful perhaps of all Old Testament prophets, because the most original—now crosses Ahab's path, Elijah of Tishbe in Gilead. In him is embodied the protest of the national will which was raising itself in such powerful opposition against the insult which was about to be done to Yahvé. With a clear consciousness of the real point at issue, he takes the field for Yahvé against Baal, does battle *for the moral rights and freedom of the human spirit* as against the tendency to abandon them in the religion of Nature, which was demoralising and debasing to man; and in this he is the genuine counterpart of Moses, with whom the New Testament ranges him. Elijah introduced into prophecy that species of categorical imperative which distinguishes him as well as the later prophets; that brazen inflexibility, that diamond-like hardness of character which bids them hold fast by their moral demand, even should the nation be dashed to pieces against it. For him the demand means, to stand by Yahvé as against Baal. Their whole appearance in history, though it takes place within the limits of the national particularism of Israel, thus gets at the same time the character of something that is *supra-national*. Any one who retains so little understanding of the peculiar essence of prophecy in Israel and its moral power, as does Ernest Renan, in his *History of Israel*, will, indeed, see in their general attitude merely wild fanaticism and senseless barbarity.[1] And yet it is this attitude alone that history has to thank for the preservation of the people of Israel for posterity.

The history of Elijah is enveloped with miracle, and is at the same time drawn from good and ancient sources. To interpret it rationalistically, as Hitzig does,[2] is an offence both against good taste and against the spirit of the Hebrew religion. We must take it—so far as it is well attested—as it is, and be aware that Elijah is a prophet of Yahvé, of grand originality, all afire with zeal for his God, and conscious of the divine power which works in him. Even one with a scrupulous historical conscience will not for a moment allow himself to doubt that Elijah was, as a matter of fact, a marvellous man, who did many marvellous things; a strong, commanding character, before whom all willingly bent, and who had at his disposal certain extraordinary forces and secret powers. To this we have to add his strange appearance, the lightning-like suddenness of his emergence and disappearance, and, not least, his bold religious idealism. Nothing was easier than that, to the admiring eyes of the people, everything that Elijah did and all that happened to him, should in consequence appear extraordinary. What was more natural than that, in the popular accounts of his actions, legendary traits should be added on to what he actually did? It is impossible now perfectly to separate these two elements.

One day Elijah appears before the king with the announcement that, for three years, neither dew nor rain would fall from heaven. He had already before this apparently foretold to king

---

[1] *Cf.* Renan, *Histoire du peuple d'Israel*, ii., iii.
[2] Hitzig, *Geschichte des Volkes Israel*, i. 176.

and people the judgments of Yahvé as the punishment of their apostasy,[1] but without effect. He himself, after having delivered his message, retires again into solitude. At the brook Cherith, God sustains him in life in as wonderful a way as if the birds of the air had carried food to him. And when the brook dries up, he seeks safety outside of the land. In the Sidonian city of Zarephath he finds shelter in the house of a miserably poor widow. But Yahvé blesses her in the most wonderful way with abundance so long as he is her guest. And when the son of the widow becomes mortally ill and is lying lifeless on the bed, he succeeds in calling him back to life.

Thus almost three years pass away. Drought and famine press on the land, and Ahab himself sets off, with his palace overseer, to seek fodder for the royal horses. Then the prophet meets him and proposes that he should submit to a divine ordeal. He is to come to Mount Carmel to sacrifice with the four hundred and fifty prophets of Baal.[2] There the lighting of the altar-fire will decide who is God, Yahvé or Baal. The prayers and practices of the prophets of Baal avail nothing.[3] The divine decision pronounces in favour of Elijah and Yahvé. The four hundred and fifty prophets of Baal are conquered, and are consequently lost. Elijah orders them to be hewn to pieces at the Kishon.[4]

The queen, when she hears what has happened, broods vengeance. Elijah is once more banished from the country. He flees towards the south, and gets as far as Horeb. Here, at the ancient mount of God, he makes his complaint to the God of Moses. He gets a revelation, and Yahvé Himself comforts him by telling him that a terrible vengeance will one day be taken on Baal. Elijah himself is to appoint the instruments of the divine judgment—Elisha, Jehu, Hazael.[5]

[1] 1 Kings xviii. 10-17.
[2] The Ashēra prophets, xviii. 19, are a gloss. *Cf.* Wellh. *Bl.*[4] 245.
[3] See on this Pietschmann, *Phöniz.* 164-220; also Gutschmid, *Kleine Schriften,* ii. 39.
[4] 1 Kings xvii. and xviii. See on this above, p. 211 f.
[5] 1 Kings xix. Wellhausen was the first rightly to understand the grandiose passage, *v.* 9 ff. See *Bl.*[4] 226.

The last-mentioned statement is, however, not quite correct. It was only Elisha that Elijah himself appointed to the work. The two kings appear to have been anointed by his successor. The great famine, which is the starting-point of the entire tradition about Elijah, is an historical fact. Menander of Ephesus also knows about it.[1] If he makes it last one year, while the Old Testament puts it at three, the difference is not really a very essential one. It simply proves, like the circumstance just now touched upon, that the particulars mentioned in our Elijah-tradition have not an absolutely historical character.* When, on the other hand, Menander ascribes the ending of the distress to a religious procession of the Phœnicians, while the Old Testament tells us that it was brought about by the judgment of God on Carmel, there is no need for finding any contradiction here.[2] The one may have taken place as well as the other.

Elijah is further instructed to announce vengeance on Ahab and on his house. A tyrannical act on Ahab's part, in connection with a civic matter, affords the occasion for his doing this. It completely shattered the confidence of the nation in the house of Omri, which was already undermined by the religious position taken up by Ahab, and as a consequence smoothed the way for the demand of the prophetic party, which aimed directly at the setting aside of the dynasty.

We are here in a better position than we have hitherto been, in dealing with Elijah's relation to affairs, for ascertaining the real state of matters which lies at the basis of our sources of information. Along with the detailed account, in which, however, the facts are treated in a free manner, we have a shorter but more accurate statement of the course of events.[3] By means of it the former account can in several points be supplemented and corrected in a welcome fashion. According to it, Ahab unjustly appropriated the patrimonial estate of a citizen of Jezreel, *Naboth* by name.

---

[1] See Joseph. *Ant.* viii. 13. 2.   [2] So Stade, *Gesch.* i. 527.
[3] See besides 1 Kings xxi., 2 Kings ix. 25 f.; and on the character and age of the latter passage, above, p. 216 f.

Because Naboth refuses to surrender voluntarily the piece of land desired by the king, he is brought before the court on a trumped-up charge, and, in accordance with the harsh custom of the time, put to death with all his family. The field, as being a property without a possessor, goes to the king.

If the religious feeling of the true worshippers of Yahvé had already been deeply outraged by the position taken up by Ahab towards the worship of Baal, now the whole nation's sense of justice is in like manner outraged by this base murder in the name of the law. Again it is Elijah who gives clear and frank expression to what is exciting the mass of the people so profoundly. At the very instant when, on the day after the judicial murder, Ahab, accompanied by Jehu and Bidkar, is just on the point of taking possession of the field which has by law fallen to him, Elijah bursts in upon him with the words: 'Surely I have seen yesternight the blood of Naboth and of his children: to thee will I requite it on this field.'

The fate of the dynasty in the public judgment of the nation is thereby sealed, if Elijah possessed at all the authority which the accounts we have ascribe to him. So far as Ahab himself was concerned, these words were to find their fulfilment in his last battles with the Syrians, which end with the death of the king.

§ 59. *Ahab's Wars with Damascus and Assyria.*

It would appear that the information we have regarding Ahab's relations with foreign countries is very deficient, in spite of the fact, too, that our Biblical accounts are more detailed than usual. Salmanassar II. specially mentions Ahab of Israel amongst those whom he conquered in the year 754;[1] while, on the contrary, the Old Testament does not make the slightest mention of any hostile encounter between Ahab and Assyria. To this it has to be added that, according to Salmanassar's account, Ahab is represented as having gone to war, in alliance with Hadad'ezer (Daddaidri) of

---

[1] See Schrader, *KAT.*² 193 ff. [Eng. Trans. i. 189 ff., 195 ff.]; *KBibl.* i. 173; Tiele, *Gesch.* 200.

Syria, against Assyria, while in contrast to this, our Biblical accounts mention merely several hostile encounters of Ahab with the Syrian king called Benhadad (II.) The least of the difficulties is presented by the difference of the two last-mentioned Syrian names. They may, if we compare them with the variations on Hebrew names, very likely mean one and the same man.[1]

Still we may well ask how the fact of a co-operation, on Ahab's part, with his opponent against Assyria, can be reconciled with what we learn from the Old Testament of the fierce struggles with the Syrians. Following an hypothesis[2] which has been several times put forward of late, we have perhaps to seek for the key to this in the statement made in our Book of Kings: according to which, Ahab, after his second victory over Benhadad-Hadad'ezer, concluded a treaty with the latter.[3] In this way we get the following picture of Ahab's campaigns.

During Ahab's last years the old enmity between Israel and Aram Damascus is again renewed. We may probably place the revolt of Moab, too, in this period. Perhaps Ahab seeks to get rid of the degrading impost which Benhadad I. had laid upon his father.[4] After several battles which proved unfortunate for Ahab,[5] Hadad'ezer succeeds in advancing against Samaria. Ahab is prepared to give up his capital, which he considers as lost, on certain moderate conditions, as first proposed by Hadad'ezer. At the last moment Hadad'ezer changes his mind, and demands the unconditional surrender of the city. The presumptuous perfidy of the other raises Ahab's sunken courage. He risks a sally and drives the Syrians out of the land. They try their luck once more in the following year. A powerful Syrian host encamps at Aphek, in the Kishon valley; Israel takes up a position opposite, on the spurs of the mountains of Ephraim. After long deliberation Ahab ventures to make the attack and destroys the hostile army.

---

[1] See on this, Schrader *KAT.*[2] 200 f. [Eng. Trans. i. 189]; *KAT.* 539.
[2] So Schrader *op. cit.*; Meyer, *Gesch. d. Alt.* i. 393; Stade, *Gesch.* i. 528. Otherwise, Wellh. *JDTh.* xx. 626 ff.; Kamphausen, *Chronol.* 43, 80.
[3] 1 Kings xx. 34.   [4] See above, p. 260.
[5] This is not said, but it may be gathered from 1 Kings xx. 1 ff.

Benhadad-Hadad‘ezer himself becomes Ahab's prisoner. With what was apparently an excess of magnanimity, Ahab spares the life of this dangerous foe of Israel. He has to agree to certain terms of capitulation with the king of Israel, according to which the Syrian is to restore to Israel the conquests of his father, and Ahab's merchants are to get a quarter for themselves in the bazaars at Damascus.[1]

Ahab had good reasons for sparing his opponent for the present. He recognises the danger which threatens both of them from the side of Assyria, and resolves, in conjunction with Damascus, to oppose the dangerous intruder. A number of Syrian princes, as well as an Ammonite prince,[2] are said to have been concerned in the confederacy, and Ahab joins it with 10,000 foot soldiers and 2000 cavalry. A battle takes place at Qarqar in Syria.[3] Salmanassar is master of the field, but not to such a degree as to permit of his reaping at this time the fruits of his victory.

Both things together, the provisional check to the further advance of Salmanassar, as well as the fact that the allies had been weakened, must have again loosened the confederacy. Probably too, Benhadad-Hadad‘ezer, trusting to this, was slow in fulfilling his obligations in connection with the surrender of his conquests to Ahab. In any case, hostilities break out afresh three years after the foregoing war. The point in dispute is as to Ahab's claim to the possession of Ramah in Gilead. The approaches which Ahab had probably already before this made to Judah, lead now to the formation of a formal alliance. Perhaps the marriage alliance between the two royal houses dates from this period. Notwithstanding that *one* prophet at least, Micah ben Jimla—it is true, in opposition to the great mass of his companions—predicts misfortune, the two kings venture on war. An

---

[1] 1 Kings xx. 34. The whole account is contained in 1 Kings xx. and xxii. See on this above, p. 215.

[2] Also Muṣri=Egypt? See Meyer, *Gesch. d. Alt.* 413. Tiele, *Gesch.* 190. (Otherwise, Meyer, 450; and *Gesch. Ägypt.* 333.)

[3] See the description on Salmanassar's monolith-inscription, *Col.* ii. 87 ff.

THE DYNASTY OF OMRI

artifice by which Ahab seeks to make himself unrecognisable to the enemy, brings him little advantage. Spite of his disguise a hostile shot reaches him. Mortally wounded, he keeps standing in his chariot until night puts an end to the battle. Ahab himself has fallen as a hero. But he was not able to secure victory for his side. His heroic death doubtless made the people forget many of the wrong things he had done, and allowed much of the brighter side of his character to come out more clearly. The accounts of Ahab's wars show this.

If it cannot be denied that this account affords what is, on the whole, a satisfactory picture of the course of events, still it appears to me that a further possibility which presents itself ought by no means to be rejected. It is reasonable to think that Salmanassar—or, at any rate, the scribe who wrote the tablet—was not more accurately informed regarding the name of the king of Israel who opposed Syria at Qarqar, than regarding the relationship of Jehu and other Israelitish kings to Omri.[1] In this case the co-operation of Israel with Damascus would be, so far as Israel was concerned, the involuntary consequence of the unfortunate battle at Ramah, and the king of Israel who was conquered by Salmanassar would thus be, not Ahab, but Jehoram. Without wishing to pronounce any final decision, I give the preference to this supposition, for reasons which will be explained in connection with the history of Jehoram.

I adduce some further reasons against the ordinary assumption:—

(1) In the Book of Kings we possess information of a very detailed character regarding Ahab, and especially information which tells *against* him. It must be regarded as all the more inexplicable that such an important fact as a decisive defeat experienced by him at the hands of Assyria, should have been passed over in silence. In the case of Jehoram, on the contrary,

---

[1] See below, § 63 (Jehu 'son of Omri'; *cf.* also 2 Kings viii. 26, 'the daughter of Omri'). The number, too, of the enemy who fell in battle is not definitely fixed in Assyrian tradition. See Schrader, *KGF.* 47.

the silence of the Bible cannot astonish us, since we have hardly any information at all about him.

(2) Spite of 1 Kings xx. 24, a military alliance with Syria is hardly explicable in the case of Ahab, when we consider all that had gone before and all that followed. The attempts to make it intelligible remind one of the old harmony-process; it is quite natural in the case of Jehoram as the involuntary consequence of the death of Ahab.

(3) Jehoram's twelve years are thus kept intact.

§ 60. *Ahaziah ben Ahab. Jehoram ben Ahab.*

It was an evil inheritance that Ahab's son Ahaziah (855-854) got from his father. It is self-evident that, after the issue of the last battle, Ramah in Gilead remained in the possession of Aram. But without doubt the matter did not stop there. We can merely inquire what was the extent of the dependence into which Israel was brought relatively to Syria, and how far this condition of dependence was taken advantage of by the Syrians in the period immediately following. The answer to this will depend on the decision come to regarding the question as to whether it was Ahab or Jehoram who took part in the battle of Qarqar.

Naturally the altered state of things, which such a misfortune necessarily brought with it, makes itself felt soon enough on the other boundaries of the kingdom. The Moabites are at once prepared to make use of the fact that Ahab's troops have been beaten, and that his hand no longer holds the reins in Israel. After having already, during Ahab's lifetime, thrown off the heavy yoke which they had borne for practically forty years, and advanced northwards beyond the limits assigned to them by Omri, they seem immediately after Ahab's death to have organised a new attack on Israel.[1] Doubtless Ahaziah was not able to check them.

---

[1] This is possibly the sense in which we are to take 2 Kings iii. 5 (i. 1); *cf.* Mêsha‘, line 7, 'and to his house.'

In addition to all these disasters, a severe misfortune befell Ahaziah soon after his accession. He fell from the upper room of his royal palace through the window, and appears to have received such dangerous injuries that he never recovered. After a reign of only two years he succumbed to his sufferings. Elijah is said to have prophesied his end. However, it is a question if the prophet was still in life. The fact that in connection with the consultation before Ahab's expedition against Ramah, Micah ben Jimla takes the place of Elijah, is opposed to the idea that he was. Besides, the narrative bears many traces of being a late composition.[1]

Ahaziah's successor is his younger brother Jehoram. The Book of Kings assigns him twelve years (854-842). Whether or not it is correct in doing this, depends once more on how we decide the question as to the name of the king of Israel who fought against Salmanassar at Qarqar. If, in accordance with the Assyrian accounts, it was Ahab, then Jehoram can have reigned only about eight years.[2] But if those accounts, on the other hand, are incorrect, and if the king referred to was really Jehoram, then the Bible statement with regard to his twelve years' reign would be right. It is obvious that we have here an additional reason for our assumption.

The condition of things, besides, in Israel suits very well with this hypothesis. If the battle of Ramah brought Israel into a state of dependence on Damascus, the inevitable consequence of this would be that, on the occasion of the next encounter of the Syrians with Assyria, Ahaziah or Jehoram would be forced to join the army of their conquerors. Still we have no means of coming to any definite decision in this matter. It is sufficient to note that, when we consider everything which throws light on the relation in which Israel stood at this time to foreign countries, the weakness of the position of the Northern Kingdom since Ahab's unfortunate end comes out with perfect clearness.

---

[1] 1 Kings xxii. 52-54; 2 Kings i.; *cf* above, p. 214.
[2] See Stade, *Gesch.* 534, note 1.

The proof of this is afforded first of all by Jehoram's unsuccessful undertaking against Mêsha' of Moab. It will, of course, be understood that Jehoram could not quietly endure the revolt of Moab from Israel, which had become an accomplished fact after the death of Ahab. An attempt must accordingly be made to bring the Moabites once more into subjection. It is to this attempt that we owe the Mêsha'-stone, an altar stone which the Moabitish king Mêsha' dedicated to his god Chemosh in remembrance of his victorious wars with Israel.[1] In addition to this we possess in 2 Kings iii. an account of Jehoram's expedition against Mêsha'. It appears from the latter that Jehoshaphat of Judah, even at this period, still maintains the alliance entered into with Ahab. He gives Jehoram assistance, and also summons the Edomites who were subject to Judah.[2] The plan of invading the Moabitish territory from the south was certainly the right one, from what Mêsha' himself tells us of his defensive measures towards the north. Nor in the event of a retreat southwards was any danger to be apprehended from the side of the Syrians. On the march the army suffers severely from want of water. Elisha suggests a plan by which water is got. The Moabites attempt a sudden attack, relying on a false rumour of dissensions which were supposed to have broken out in the army of the allies. They are driven back and reduced to great extremities. Mêsha' escapes with his men to Kirharoseth. He is besieged, and, after an unsuccessful sally, in his sore straits he has recourse to a plan of despair. In full view of the besiegers, he sacrifices on the city wall his first-born to Chemosh. This final expedient inspires his troops with new courage and new faith in the help of their god. They break out and are free. Israel is compelled to retire.

Mêsha' had every reason for being proud of the result of his plan.

The siege of Samaria by the Syrians is also usually placed in

---

[1] See Mêsha', line 3. Jehoram's name is not mentioned. But, according to lines 7, 8, Ahab is evidently dead and his house is reigning.

[2] The expression 'king,' 2 Kings iii. 9, is, judged by 1 Kings xxii. 48 f., inaccurate. It can only be a vassal prince who is referred to.

Jehoram's reign. And it certainly is placed in immediate connection with his history in our Book of Kings. Still Kuenen has shown it to be very probable that that unnamed king of Israel is not Jehoram ben Ahab, but Jehoahaz ben Jehu.[1] Besides, for other reasons than those successfully urged by Kuenen, it suits better with Jehoahaz than with Jehoram. It is, indeed, not very probable that the Syrians had the time and the strength just then to engage with Israel, allied as it was with Judah, in such a protracted war as it is here taken for granted to have been. If, shortly after the battle of Qarqar, they had to endure three successive inroads of Salmanassar II. in the years 850, 849, and 846, they could hardly have had sufficient breathing time to be in a position to attack Israel in the period between 849 and 846, as they are generally supposed to have done.

It is, however, quite probable that Israel itself had meanwhile so far recovered from the blows inflicted at Ramah and Qarqar, as well as from the defeat by Mêsha', as to be able to profit by the critical state of Syria. Jehoram would gradually come to think of the possibility of reconquering the Gileadite towns, for the possession of which Ahab had vainly fought. Thus it happens that Ramah in Gilead is besieged anew, a siege which was destined to have grave consequences for affairs in Israel.

[1] See above, p. 216.

CHAPTER III.

JEHU AND HIS DYNASTY. THE KINGDOM OF JUDAH.

§ 61. *Jehu's Revolution.*

IN Israel the service of Baal is still carried on alongside of the worship of Yahvé. Neither Ahaziah nor Jehoram made any alteration of importance in the state of affairs in this respect. And yet the times in Israel were not, as a matter of fact, such as to allow people to forget the curses which Elijah had formerly hurled against Ahab and his house. So, too, the outrage committed against Naboth and his family was undoubtedly still fresh in every one's memory and called for vengeance. This was reason enough for the friends of Elijah, and those like-minded, to look for the time when the hour of retribution would at last strike for the wicked house.

At the head of the Nebî'îm and of the prophetic circles attached to them, now that Elijah has disappeared from the scene of his earthly activity, stands his old disciple and servant Elisha (Elisa). The great master had been snatched away in a thunderstorm; suddenly and violently had Yahvé caught him up to himself, in a way corresponding to his manner of moving about on this earth.[1] Elisha, too, like his powerful predecessor, seems to have been a man of special gifts and to have exercised an extraordinary influence on his nation. If he is perhaps wanting in the original force which marked his master, he has all his fire and all his unbounded zeal in the cause of Yahvé against Baal. The marvel-

---

[1] 2 Kings ii.

lous deeds which are ascribed in such large numbers to him, give eloquent testimony to the deep and lasting influence which this striking figure exercised upon his contemporaries. Without doubt, bold fiction and popular tradition are here mixed with what is true. It is, however, much more difficult than in the case of Elijah accurately to separate the two elements.[1] We find the figure of Elisha standing most clearly in the light of history in connection with the event which will immediately occupy our attention, the dethronement of the dynasty of Ahab. In this matter he plainly shows himself as the heir of Elijah and of his thoughts. He faithfully and resolutely carried out the policy of annihilating Baal and all belonging to him, which was Elijah's great legacy to the nation. Besides this, many of the other deeds ascribed to him may well stand the test. It is, at least, very possible, although not absolutely certain, that he followed in the train of Jehoram during the campaign against Mêsha' and gave his counsel for the good of Israel. It is not inconceivable either that Elisha's counsel and help were asked even by a heathen, namely the Syrian general Naaman. At any rate, the narrative[2] in which we are told about this is thoroughly in keeping with the state of things in the time of Elisha. On the other hand, it is difficult to say how far Elisha had a share in the displacement of Benhadad-Hadad'ezer of Syria by Hazael.[3] This is ascribed in another place to Elijah.[4] Besides, the relations between Israel and Aram, just at the time when this transference of the throne took place, were apparently not of such a kind as would lead us to expect that Elisha could have been in Damascus and have had the entry of the court. Moreover, the narrative is otherwise not altogether probable.

Towards the end of the reign of Jehoram ben Ahab in Israel, his fate at last overtakes Benhadad-Hadad'ezer, the man who for long years had been the opponent of Israel. He must have been a brave ruler and a man of note. If he had engaged in many a

---

[1] See the particulars about this (Pr²) above, p. 214 f.
[2] 2 Kings v.   [3] 2 Kings viii. 7 ff.   [4] 1 Kings xix. 15.

fray with Israel—though, indeed, with very varying fortune—and if he had to endure many an attack from Assyria which cost him blood, still he had always succeeded in keeping himself at the head of his people. At last old age seems to have laid him, too, on a sick-bed. There he ends his life by the hand of a murderer. One of his palace officials, Hazael, according to our Biblical tradition, was supposed to have smothered him.[1]

Jehoram apparently at once makes use of the change of throne in order to assert his old claims in Gilead. The alliance with Judah is still maintained; and this, spite of many ups and downs which it brought with it for Judah. If Israel had not itself been weak enough, one might have been inclined to regard Judah as a vassal. Ahaziah of Judah marches with the army of Israel to Ramah, as Jehoshaphat had done before. At the storming of the town Jehoram is wounded[2] so that he is forced to return home to Jezreel. Ahaziah is at this time on a visit to Jehoram in Jezreel. The command of the troops which remained behind in Ramah, is, in the king's absence, taken by Jehu ben Jehoshaphat ben Nimshi.[3]

Then Elisha suddenly sends one of the disciples of the prophets to Jehu armed with a commission to anoint him king in the name of Yahvé. The army acknowledges his authority, and Jehu is proclaimed king. At once Jehu takes the road to Jezreel. He leaves the army behind in Ramah. On hearing of Jehu's approach, the two kings go to meet him in their chariots. Not far from the field of Naboth, Jehu and Jehoram meet. To the king's question, whether he brings peace, Jehu replies: 'What peace? the apostasy of thy mother Jezebel and her many idolatries are still amongst us.' Jehoram perceives treachery, and turns to flee. Nevertheless, an arrow of Jehu's has already reached him. Remembering the words which he had formerly heard from the mouth of Elijah, Jehu has his body thrown by his

---

[1] 2 Kings viii. 7 ff.

[2] We have here to do with a wound to Jehoram personally, and not with a reverse; cf. 2 Kings viii. 28 with v. 29.

[3] See in connection with this and with what follows, 2 Kings viii. 28, 29; ix. 10; and on it above, p. 216 f.

shield-bearer, Bidkar, on to the field of Naboth. Nor does Ahaziah of Judah meet with any better fortune. Jehu pursues him in hot haste and inflicts on him a mortal wound, so that he soon after dies.

There is nothing now to hinder Jehu's entrance into Jezreel. Here Jehoram's mother, Jezebel, Ahab's widow, is still residing. In accordance with the character of the whole movement, she must first fall before the restoration of Yahvé to His old rights can begin. She sees that the hour of vengeance is coming. But she does not stoop to ask favour of the murderer of her son. Like the proud child of a king, and clothed in royal array, will she fall. She meets her death at the hand of a eunuch.

The capital however is now, as before, in Samaria. There is the king's palace, properly so called, in which the members of the royal family dwell. They too must be secured before Jehu can enjoy his throne, and in fact before one of the sons of Jehoram is actually chosen king. Jehu succeeds in getting the holders of power in the capital, and also the heads of the families and the tutors of the royal princes, to declare for him, and to promise that they will execute his commands. His demand is, the heads of the seventy royal princes. They fall, and, packed in baskets, are sent to Jezreel. Jehu, in face of the terrified mob, boasts that he has the word of Yahvé's promise.

But enough blood has not been shed even yet. All in Jezreel who held to the house of Omri are slain. Then he makes his entry into Samaria. There, too, blood and murder mark his steps amongst those who were loyal to Ahab. Already before his arrival, he is said to have slaughtered forty-two princes of the house of David whom he comes across on the way. This bit of information does not sound very probable, after Ahaziah's death had become known.[1] Still the statement made in conjunction with this, regarding the close connection which Jehonadab ben Rechab has with Jehu and the whole movement, appears to be trustworthy. Arrived in Samaria itself, Jehu prepares a horrible

---

[1] See on x. 12 ff. Stade, *ZAW*. v. 275 ff.

blood-bath for the worshippers of the Tyrian Baal. The separate details are not clear, but there is hardly any room for doubting the fact that they were surrounded and slaughtered in their own temple. Baal-worship is rooted out with fire and sword, never to return again. Still the streams of blood which had flowed, and the frightful cruelties practised, in the name of Yahvé, must have deeply shocked the nation. Traces of the excitement are still perceptible a whole century after.[1]

§ 62. *Jehoshaphat of Judah and his sons. Athaliah.*

It is time for us to direct our attention back to Jerusalem. The son and successor of that Asa who had called in the help of the Arameans of Damascus to save him from his opponents in Israel of his own kin, is Jehoshaphat (876-851). We are already acquainted with several important events of his reign. Spite of what had happened, he is prepared to enter into an alliance with Ahab of Israel. This is ratified by the marriage of his son Jehoram with Athaliah, the daughter of Ahab, and the consequence is that Jehoshaphat takes part in the expedition of Ahab against Ramah in Gilead, and soon after Ahab's death, in that of Jehoram of Israel against Moab. It has been shown above[2] what were the reasons which moved Ahab of Israel, whom we have to regard as the more powerful of the two parties, to enter into this alliance with Judah. Perhaps we have to add to these considerations the fact, that for the moment Judah, in consequence of Asa's policy, was, relatively to Israel, in a favourable position, and one which, as matters then stood, might easily prove dangerous to Ahab.

Certainly in these undertakings Jehoshaphat did not, any more than his allies, succeed in effecting anything of importance. And he has no better success in connection with another affair mentioned in the meagre account of his reign given in the Book of Kings.[3] Jehoshaphat, as Solomon had done before him, takes advantage of Edom's continued subjection to Judah in order to

---

[1] Hosea i. 4.   [2] See above, p. 262.   [3] 1 Kings xxii. 41-51.

make use of the entrance to the Red Sea, which was in his hands, for the purpose of developing a profitable carrying trade.¹ He has a Tarshish clipper built²—that is, a vessel of the kind used by the Phœnicians for the Tartessus traffic—in order to fetch gold from Ophir.³ This vessel is, however, wrecked in Ezion-Geber, and therefore before it has started on its journey. Ahaziah ben Ahab of Israel encourages him to make a second attempt, but Jehoshaphat has no desire to try it again after the failure of the first venture.

If, in the Book of Kings, Jehoshaphat appears as a man who does not accomplish anything particular in any direction, neither in war nor in peace, the Book of Chronicles, on the other hand, has a great deal more to tell us about him, and a great deal more to his favour. According to Chronicles, not only did Jehoshaphat attain to quite unusual power and collect extraordinary wealth,⁴ but he is also credited with a magnificent victory over foreign foes of which the Book of Kings makes but the barest mention.⁵ The whole manner in which Chronicles relates the details shows that both accounts are traditional elements belonging to a very late date. Still it is possible and probable that Jehoshaphat, during the long period over which his reign extended, had to engage in many a battle with his southern and eastern neighbours besides what is mentioned in the Book of Kings.⁶ If in one of these wars he gained a victory of which the Book of Kings does not tell us, still we cannot now look for the original representation of the actual state of matters in the present form of the account in Chronicles.

We may much more readily implicitly trust the accuracy of what Chronicles tells us regarding a measure of Jehoshaphat for

---

¹ On the text of 1 Kings xxii. 48 f. see Stade, *ZAW.* v. 178.

² If the reading נִצָּב instead of נָצָב is correct, this was done by his governor.

³ Chronicles has made actual Tarshish-journeys out of this (starting from Ezion-Geber!)—an evident misunderstanding of what is here said. See on Ophir, above, p. 189.

⁴ 2 Chron. xvii. 1 ff., 10 ff.   ⁵ 2 Chron. xx. 1-30.

⁶ *Cf.* in 1 Kings xxii. 46, the reference to the rest of his mighty deeds and wars.

the extension of 'the Law' in Judah. According to this, Jehoshaphat sent certain of the heads of the people and some Levites round the country with the Book of the Law of Yahvé, in order to make the people acquainted with it.[1] This piece of information, too, has been for the most part called in question. But if it be granted that writings containing laws were in existence[2] as early as the time of Jehoshaphat, there is no reason against supposing that a king of Judah did actually issue a regulation of the kind referred to. And if we have no idea of the date of this statement found in Chronicles, still, when we take into consideration the extraordinary brevity of the account of the reign of Jehoshaphat in the Book of Kings, we cannot draw from its silence regarding this matter any argument against the historical accuracy of what is related. We are consequently driven to fall back entirely on inner reasons.[3]

A further difficulty is presented by the account in Chronicles of an organisation of the courts of justice carried through by Jehoshaphat. According to it, Jehoshaphat set up courts of law in all the fortified towns in Judah, and in Jerusalem a supreme court under the presidency of the high priest and the prince of Judah.[4] Wellhausen has made the brilliant conjecture that the author of Chronicles is here transferring the organisation of justice belonging to his own age back to the past, and thinks the reference is to the provincial tribunals and the Jerusalem Sanhedrin.[5] It can scarcely be doubted that Chronicles has actually taken from these the colours for the finishing off of the picture it gives. How far, on the other hand, we are to look for an historical kernel in the rest of the narrative, is a point which must be left undecided.

Jehoshaphat's successor in Judah is his son Joram. The Book of Kings assigns him eight years (851-843). As the husband of the Samaritan princess, Athaliah, he is Ahab's son-in-law. The

---

[1] 2 Chron. xvii. 7-9.
[2] See on this above, i. 94, 244.
[3] *Cf.* Reuss, *Gesch. d. AT.*[2] § 200.
[4] 2 Chron. xix. 5-11.
[5] Wellh. *Prol.*[2] 198 ff. [Eng. Trans. 191 ff.].

statement in the Book of Kings that he favoured in Judah also the foreign worship introduced by Ahab into Samaria, is thus a perfectly credible one. So far as regards his foreign politics, Joram ben Jehoshaphat seems to have met with little success. For the Edomites, who in the period immediately preceding were always spoken of as the vassals of Judah, follow the example of Moab after the death of Jehoshaphat, and attempt to regain their independence. Joram, it is true, undertakes a campaign against them, but he is surrounded, and, although he succeeds in breaking through [1] the enemy's hosts, his army cannot be got to stay any longer, and makes for home.[2] According to Chronicles, which we can quite well trust as regards this, he died of a tedious and severe illness.[3] This explains the shortness of his reign. His successor is Ahaziah, Joram's son, borne to him by Athaliah, 'bat Omri.' He can in any case have reigned only for a short time ; according to our sources, only one year (843-842). We have described above how he was involved in the fate of the dynasty of Omri, and lost his life at Jehu's hand. It appears almost as if his participation in the campaign of Jehoram ben Ahab against the Syrians was the only noteworthy act of the reign of Ahaziah ben Joram.[4]

The position of the mother of the ruler in an Oriental kingdom is well known. By the sudden death of her yet youthful son, Athaliah is suddenly deprived of her authority and influence as the queen-mother. A daughter of the proud Jezebel, she was not disposed to vacate her place with any readiness. The road to the maintenance of it undoubtedly lay over the bodies of her own grandchildren and relations. But the ambitious king's daughter does not allow herself to be frightened from taking even this step. Athaliah has all the princes of the house of David murdered, and then places herself on the throne thus left without an occupant. It is the only case in which a woman occupied the

---

[1] It cannot well be a question of a victory (Reuss, § 198).
[2] 2 Kings viii. 16-24.
[3] 2 Chron. xxi. 18 ff.
[4] 2 Kings viii. 25-29. The usual formula even is wanting : 'and what more there is to tell,' etc.

throne in Israel. Athaliah is able to maintain her authority in Jerusalem for six years[1] (842-836).

It is not accidental that her fall is brought about by the priesthood of the Temple.[2] If in the Northern Kingdom the house of Omri had been wiped out, and Baal-worship along with it, it was impossible that, at the seat of the greatest sanctuary of Yahvé, the warning note sounded from Samaria should in the long-run fail to have its due effect. And even if what we are told regarding the religious motives of those who took part in the movement against Athaliah is drawn from relatively late sources,[3] it can hardly, in the nature of things, be a pure fabrication.

The princess Jehosheba, a sister—a half-sister probably—of King Ahaziah, succeeds in getting his young son Joash put into a place of safety before the execution of the bloody command of the queen. For six years the boy is kept hidden in the Temple with the high priest Jehoiada. With every appearance of correctness, Chronicles calls the princess Jehosheba the wife of the priest Jehoiada.[4] At last, in the seventh year of Athaliah's reign, Jehoiada considers that the time for action has come. He lets the captains of the bodyguard into the secret. His plan is based on the fact that one part of the royal bodyguard guards the Temple and the other the palace, and that on the Sabbath the Temple guard is relieved by the palace guard. It is thus possible on the Sabbath to empty the palace of troops for a time, and to collect them all together in the Temple.[5] One Sabbath Jehoiada makes use of the favourable opportunity afforded by the presence of the whole bodyguard. He suddenly presents the youthful Joash to the troops as their real king, and gets them to do him homage. Then Joash is conducted to the palace and is placed on the royal throne. Athaliah, on the other hand, is surprised in the palace and cut

---

[1] 2 Kings xi. 1 ff. See on the text, Wellh. *Bl.*[4] 257 f.
[2] Otherwise, but incorrectly, Renan, *Hist.* ii. 323, 409.
[3] See on this Stade, *ZAW.* v. 279 ff.; and above, p. 217.
[4] 2 Chron. xxii. 11.
[5] Wellh. *Bl.*[4] 258, has thrown light on the circumstances in 2 Kings xi. 4 ff. *Cf.* too, Klost. on this passage, and Köhler, ii. 2, 211 ff.

down. After she is dead, Joash binds the people down to serve Yahvé, and has the temple of Baal destroyed, and his priest Mattan slain.

It is little enough that we can learn of the long reign of Joash,[1] a reign which, according to the Book of Kings, lasted forty years (836-796), still it is more than we have in the case of many another king. At first, as was indeed made necessary by his youth, he must have been under the guardianship of his priestly uncle. That at this period he was specially devoted to the worship of Yahvé, and strongly sided with the efforts of the priests, may be easily imagined.[2] But at a still later time, too, he appears to have given special attention to the Temple.

For reasons which are not mentioned in the Book of Kings, and which are merely indicated in Chronicles in a very unsatisfactory way,[3] the Temple was in need of repair. Joash arranges that all the money collected at the Temple-treasury is to be the property of the priests, who, on the other hand, are to be responsible for the necessary repairs on the Temple buildings, and are to pay for these out of their income. After the lapse of some time it appeared that the priesthood spent the money which came in on themselves, without complying with the aforesaid obligation. Joash now hits on an arrangement whereby the moneys bestowed by the people on the Temple are not to go to the priests. On the contrary, a chest is to be placed at the entrance to the Temple. The gifts of the people are to be placed in it. From time to time the chancellor is to empty the chest, and deliver its contents to the workmen who have charge of the direct upkeep of the Temple buildings.[4]

According to this account, Joash until the twenty-third year of his reign gives proof of his ardent zeal for the worship of Yahvé and for the Temple, and therefore it may well astonish us when we find that Chronicles tells us of a relapse which occurred

---

[1] [*Cf.* Farrar on Joash in *Expositor*, 1894, p. 81 ff.]
[2] *Cf.* 2 Kings xii. 3.　　　　　　　　　　[3] 2 Chron. xxiv. 7.
[4] 2 Kings xii. 5 ff. *Cf.* above, p. 217.

in his later days. After the death of Jehoiada, Joash is said to have given himself up to idolatry. He is even said to have had Jehoiada's son, the priest Zechariah, executed because he reproved him for this crime.[1] But the whole style in which Chronicles remodels [2] the previous history of this king, is decidedly a pretty strong argument against its trustworthiness in this particular case.

On the other hand, the statement that Joash suffered severely from an inroad of the Syrians seems to rest on good authority. This invasion is doubtless closely connected with the miseries of all kinds inflicted at this time by the Syrians on the Northern Kingdom. During one of his expeditions Hazael makes as though, starting from Gath,[3] he would penetrate as far as Jerusalem, and Joash is reduced to the necessity of purchasing his departure by means of a large tribute.[4] Joash meets his death in a conspiracy. It is very possible that Chronicles is right in connecting this with his shameful subjection to Hazael.

His successor appears to have been his son Amaziah (796-78 ?). He has the murderers of his father executed. And, indeed, he appears to have been the first who, in connection with a judicial proceeding of this kind, broke with the old principle of club-law, according to which the avenger of blood does not only punish the murderer himself, but extirpates his whole race. Deuteronomy has codified this new form of justice in opposition to the ancient usage.[5]

Amaziah succeeded in again reducing to subjection the Edomites who had been in a state of revolt since the death of Jehoshaphat. But it is certainly a question as to what extent this was done, since Amos, by the way in which he speaks of the Edomites, does not convey the impression that at this time the whole of Edom was tributary to Judah.[6] It would seem that

---

[1] 2 Chron. xxiv. 15-22.   [2] 2 Chron. xxiii. ; xxiv. 1-14.
[3] *Cf.* on the fate of Gath, Amos vi. 2.
[4] 2 Kings xii. 18 f.   *Cf.* 2 Chron. xxiv. 23 ff.
[5] 2 Kings xiv. 1 ff.   *Cf.* Deut. xxiv. 16 ; further, Jos. vii. 24 f. ; 2 Kings ix. 26 ; 2 Sam. xxi. 1 ff.   [6] See Stade, *Gesch.* i. 567 f.

Amaziah, by his victory, got hold mainly of the land west from Arabia, with the capital Sela (= Petra) and the port Elath.[1]

His end is the same as that of his father. A conspiracy is formed to get him out of the way. He flees towards Lachish; is however delivered up there, and then slain by the rebels. We can easily guess the occasion of the rising. Amaziah had had to expiate with ignominy a thoughtless challenge to war, which he sent to his Ephraimitish neighbour Joash.[2] The thread of the narrative itself leads us at this point back to the Northern Kingdom.

§ 63. *Jehu and his successors until Jeroboam II.*

The war which Joram ben Ahab of Israel engaged in against the Syrians, for Ramah in Gilead, was fraught with grave consequences both to himself and to the whole dynasty of Omri. But the fact that the war came to be undertaken at all, has supplied us with proof that Israel, under Joram's rule, had gradually come to feel itself sufficiently strong again to be able to offer some resistance at any rate to the Syrians. And indeed it was feasible only in connection with the severe attacks to which Damascus was constantly exposed at the hands of the Assyrians. Israel could not venture to oppose Assyria itself, especially after her late experiences. Accordingly, we find amongst the princes who, in the year 842, submit to the powerful Assyrian conqueror Salmanassar II. (860-824), the name of Jehu, 'the son of Omri.' Israelitish ambassadors are represented on Salmanassar's obelisk in the act of bringing Jehu's tribute to Assyria, consisting of bars of gold and silver, golden vessels, and such like.[3]

When we consider the position in which Israel had recently stood in relation to Damascus, it is only too easy to understand that Jehu (842-814) should make use of the occasion of an

---

[1] 2 Kings xiv. 7 ; *cf. v.* 22, and in addition below, § 67, at the beginning.

[2] See below, § 63.

[3] See on this Schrader, *KAT.*² 208 f. [Eng. Trans. i. 200]; *KBibl.* i. 151 (*cf.* 141, note 1); in addition, the illustration in Stade, 562 ff.

expedition of Salmanassar against his enemy, Hazael, in order to gain the friendship of Assyria. Considering the state of things in his own kingdom, he had without doubt double need of some strong support. For we can hardly be wrong in supposing that Salmanassar's expedition against Syria in the year 842 occurred at a time when the traces of the bloody deeds by which Jehu had purchased his throne were still visible everywhere in Israel. Jehu must have mounted the throne a short time before.

It must have been all the more unfortunate for Jehu that Salmanassar's campaign against Syria had by no means the result that was expected. The great king does not, as a matter of fact, succeed in taking Damascus. At this time, as well as three years later when Salmanassar made a new attack on Syria, Hazael succeeds in maintaining his ground. The Assyrian had to retire from Damascus without effecting his purpose. The natural consequence of their deliverance is that the Syrians throw themselves on Israel with redoubled fury. And now begins for Israel a period of severe affliction and humiliation at the hands of the Syrians. The unfortunately extremely meagre accounts in our Book of Kings suggest the idea that a story told of the prophet Elisha rests on a thoroughly good foundation. Elisha is in Damascus, and has held out to Hazael, who was later on to be Benhadad's successor, the prospect of the sick king's death. Thereupon the prophet bursts into bitter tears before Hazael's eyes. When asked the reason of his weeping, he answers Hazael thus: 'I foresee the suffering that thou wilt inflict on Israel. Its fortresses wilt thou set on fire, its young men wilt thou slay with the sword, its sucklings wilt thou dash in pieces, and rip up its women with child.'[1]

Our Book of Kings, which enters so much into detail regarding the vengeance taken by Jehu on the house of Omri, describes his relation to Damascus with astonishing brevity in these few words: 'In those days began Yahvé to cut off parts of Israel; and Hazael smote them in the whole region of Israel;'[2] and a later addition

---

[1] 2 Kings viii. 12. [2] 2 Kings x. 32.

tells us that the whole of the country east of the Jordan as far as the Arnon, fell into the hands of the Syrians.¹ In all probability the retreat of the Assyrians from Damascus was followed on the part of Hazael by a series of retaliatory campaigns against Jehu. The extent to which the Syrians ravaged Israel is not only shown by the words put into the mouth of Elisha quoted above, but, at a somewhat later time, Amos refers with similar distinctness to the cruel revenge taken by Aram on Israel: 'They have threshed Gilead with threshing instruments of iron.'² In addition to this, Israel's day of need was shamefully taken advantage of by its ever greedy and revengeful neighbours. The Philistines, the Tyrians, the Edomites, and the Ammonites, make plundering expeditions into Israel, especially in the east Jordan country, so hardly treated already by Aram, and carry off captives.³

The same state of things must have continued, though partly perhaps in an even worse form than under Jehu, throughout the reign of his son Jehoahaz (814-797). Amos, in the first chapter of his Book, has his time also in his mind. Even in the reign of Joash we still hear of plundering hordes from Moab which burst in upon Israel, and these forays are mentioned as things of quite common occurrence at that time.⁴

In the reign of Jehu's son, Jehoahaz, according to our Israelitish documents, a change of throne occurs in Damascus. Benhadad III. takes the place of his father Hazael. Jehoahaz suffers such a severe humiliation at the hands of one of these, that he has only fifty horsemen, ten war-chariots, and ten thousand foot-soldiers left.⁵ Owing to the laconic brevity with which the Book of Kings relates the facts, it is not at all clear which of the two Syrian kings it was who placed such a restraint on the independence of Jehoahaz. For it is obvious that by this humiliation he has become simply a vassal of the king of Damascus. It looks as if the narrator shrank from revealing Israel's disgrace any more

---

[1] 2 Kings x. 33. See besides Stade, in *ZAW.* v. 279.
[2] Amos i. 3.   [3] Amos i. 6-15.   [4] 2 Kings xiii. 20 f.
[5] 2 Kings xiii. 3, 7. See also Stade, in *ZAW.* v. 295 ff. *Cf.* further, *vv.* 22, 24.

than was absolutely required to carry on the thread of the history. We may, however, reasonably suppose that here we have the conclusion of a long series of unfortunate wars which Jehoahaz waged, first with Hazael, and later on with his successor.

It is very probable that an episode in these wars, which was different from the others in having resulted favourably to Israel, has been preserved. Its issue supplied a sufficient reason for giving it in detail; while many other events regarding which we should have been glad to have known something, were, from the point of view of our narrator, only fit to be forgotten.

We know in fact that the prophet Elisha was contemporary with, and a witness of, these calamitous wars of Israel with Aram. He lives on for a time under Joash, the son of Jehoahaz. And both with king and people he holds the rank of a true counsellor and comforter. He receives no less a title than 'Israel's chariots and horsemen.' And it is not without reason that Kuenen[1] has proposed to transfer a narrative belonging to a period of the Syrian wars which the Book of Kings includes in the history of Joram ben Ahab—although it does not well accord with Jehu and his time[2]—to the time of Jehoahaz ben Jehu.

After Benhadad had beaten Israel in a battle he succeeded in penetrating with his army to the gates of Samaria. He lays siege to the city. Within the walls, however, a severe famine prevails and is gradually getting worse. The populace is on the verge of despair. Mothers slay their own children in order to prolong life. The king, in deep distress, wears on his naked body a dress of sackcloth, the sign of mourning. He vents all his wrath on Elisha, who hitherto had many a time given him advice and help, and who had in this time of distress, too, counselled him to trust to Yahvé. Nor even now does the prophet's hope in his God play him false. On the next day, he promises the distress will be at an end. Some lepers who are living outside the gates of the city summon up courage, before abandoning themselves to death by starvation, to slip into the enemy's camp that same evening.

---

[1] § xxv. 12, 13.   [2] 2 Kings vi. 24; vii. 20. See above, p. 277, and p. 216.

They find it empty, and bring into the city the news of what they have seen. The spies whom the king despatches confirm the tidings. Samaria is saved.

We cannot clearly determine what occasioned the sudden break-up of the siege by the Syrians. The narrator himself informs us that the enemy heard an unexpected noise in the air which in their dread they took to be the advance of Egyptian and Hittite troops. The presence of such a relieving army is hardly historically probable.[1] But when the narrator thus expresses himself in what is historically an inaccurate way, we can only conclude that he is treating his subject in a purely popular fashion, and is not well acquainted with the important events in the world outside. Still, it would be a mistake to conclude further that the whole episode of which he tells us was not based on any historical event. Whether or not we are justified simply in putting the Assyrians in place of those Egyptians and Hittites, is a point that may be left undecided.[2] Assyrian inroads into Syria certainly took place in the reign of Jehoahaz too.[3] Thus, about that period, Rammânnirâr III. brought the whole of the Syrian West, including Israel and Damascus under King Mari, into subjection.[4] Still, even apart from the difference in the Syrian kings' names, it is well to exercise caution in making such conjectures. There may have been other Assyrian inroads besides the expeditions of Assyrian kings with which we are acquainted. And leaving them out of account, when we consider the unsettled state of these times there were plenty of reasons which might induce an Aramæan army to beat a hasty retreat from a beleaguered town.

In any case, the renewal of the Assyrian campaigns against

---

[1] Though we have to consider that the Chatti are still mentioned as enemies of Assyria as late as the reign of Rammannirar III. (Meyer, *Gesch. d. Alt.* 415), and, besides, that Egyptian history just at this time is still completely wrapped in obscurity.

[2] So Stade, *Gesch.* i. 539. *Cf.* Wellh. *Abr.* 31.

[3] There is hardly room for doubt that he, and not Joram ben Ahab, is referred to under the designation 'son of a murderer' (2 Kings vi. 32).

[4] About 800. *Cf.* Meyer, 416; Schrader, *KAT*². 215 [Eng. Trans. i. 205]; *KBibl.* 191.

Syria by Rammânirâr III. relieved Israel once more. Thus we find the son and successor of Jehoahaz, Joash of Israel (797-781), immediately after engaging in a successful war with Syria. Elisha is still living under Joash, the grandson of Jehu, far advanced in years, and, after what had happened in the reign of Jehoahaz, revered, with double reason, as a father by the king. Before departing this life, he is said to have promised to the down-hearted king that he would yet be victorious over Aram.[1] As a matter of fact, Joash ben Jehoahaz, according to the account in our Book of Kings, succeeds in again taking from the Syrians under Benhadad the towns of which they had robbed his father Jehoahaz.[2]

This Joash ben Jehoahaz seems otherwise to have been a man who had a firm grip of his sword, and whose heart was in the right place. At anyrate this is the aspect under which he appears in the solitary circumstance recorded of him. Amaziah of Judah, who was his contemporary (from 796 onwards), may well have looked with a jealous eye on the freedom from the Syrian yoke which the Northern Kingdom was at last once more enjoying. In addition to this, some fortunate undertakings had increased his self-confidence. He accordingly breaks with the traditions of peaceful relationship between the two neighbouring kingdoms which had held good for more than a century. The account of the way in which he and Joash respectively conducted themselves may have an Ephraimite colouring. Still, the fact may be correctly enough stated that Amaziah wished for war and brought it on. Joash advances into Judah. At Bethshemesh Amaziah is disgracefully beaten and taken prisoner. Jerusalem itself is forced to open its gates and to submit to being plundered. Hostages are given to Joash, and in addition to this he is allowed to tear down a considerable portion of the city wall.[3]

---

[1] 2 Kings xiii. 10 ff., 14-21.

[2] 2 Kings xiii. 24 f. It is not clear in what relation the Benhadad III. of the Bible stands to the Mari of the Assyrian accounts. Perhaps in the same relation in which Benhadad II. stands to Hadad'ezer; in this case they would be *one* person. Besides, we have to remember that the Old Testament authors are not quite clear themselves in what they say about our Benhadad. *Cf.* 2 Kings xxiii. 3, with *vv.* 22, 24. [3] 2 Kings xiv. 8-14 (A). See above, p. 218.

In a still greater degree than Joash, his son, Jeroboam II., was favoured with good fortune and success. His reign which, according to the Book of Kings, lasted forty-one years (781–740), seems to have brought to Ephraim a renown such as it had not enjoyed for many a day. What the Book of Kings tells us on this head is brief but significant. 'He restored the coasts of Israel from the neighbourhood of Hamath unto the Sea of the Plain (Dead Sea).'[1] That he found it possible to do this is not due to his own merits only, but is to a large extent the consequence of favourable circumstances. The decisive blow struck by Assyria at Damascus in the reign of Rammânnirâr III. must also have been of service to him. Further attacks followed on this one in the days of Salmanassar III. (782–772) and Assurdân III.[2] (772–754), which, as it would seem, so completely crippled Damascus for the time being that it could scarcely be any longer regarded as a serious opponent. Besides, if Jeroboam wished to call the southern half of the land east of the Jordan his own too, he would have to subdue the Moabites, who, from the time of Joram ben Ahab, had occupied it. He seems to have succeeded in doing this too.

As a matter of fact, if our Book of Kings gives a true account of things at all, the boundaries of the kingdom were once more extended almost as far as David had put them. In addition to this, Israel was powerful and was not attacked by any enemy, a condition of things which had not existed since the days of Solomon. Still we ought not to forget, at the same time, that Jeroboam's successes were possible only in so far as Assyria allowed him a free hand. This certainly appears to have been the case as early as the time of Assurdân III., and still more in the reign of the peaceful and inactive[3] Assurnirâr. In fact, it looks as if Jeroboam, in alliance with Azariah-Uzziah of Judah, could venture at this time to extend his authority in Syria, even at the direct cost of the Assyrians.[4] With merely the brief statement in

---

[1] 2 Kings xiv. 25. *Cf.* also Amos vi. 14. *V.* 28 appears to be hopelessly corrupt.
[2] See Meyer, *Gesch. d. Alt.* 416.
[3] See on him, Meyer, *Gesch. d. Alt.* 419.
[4] See on this below, in § 67.

the Book of Kings to go upon, we should indeed scarcely venture to draw the picture of Jeroboam and his time in any clearly defined way if, besides the Book of Kings, we had not at our disposal a source of information which gives us perfect confidence in attempting this, and which, besides, fills in the bare sketch of the Book of Kings with strong, deep colours—the Books of the prophets Amos and Hosea.

We shall have to deal with these farther on.

§ 64. *Culture and Religion in the period after Solomon.*[1]

1. *Mode of life and customs.*—The occupation of the people in times of peace continues to be *agriculture*. Handicrafts and art have developed very little. Anything beyond what was required for ordinary domestic use was got from abroad. There was doubtless, however, often opportunity for making use of the services of foreigners since the *commercial* connections formed by Solomon had brought money into the land. Even the unfortunate times which followed his reign did not ever quite dry up the springs of wealth opened by him. And single mishaps, such as that under Jehoshaphat, merely prove how much the people were set on making use of the favourable position of Canaan for commerce. The Syrian merchants have their own quarter in Samaria, the Israelitish merchants had theirs in Damascus from the time of Ahab.[2] They had certainly established themselves in other countries and principal towns likewise, sometimes in greater, sometimes in smaller numbers. There must have been active commercial intercourse with Egypt since the days of Solomon, as is specially proved by the history of the patriarchs in E, where the narrator shows that he is familiar with things Egyptian.

The retention of the monarchical government, the constant

---

[1] [See now too the sections dealing with this in Nowack's and Benzinger's *Archäol.*, and also in Smend's *AT. Relig. gesch.*]

[2] 1 Kings xx. 34. *Cf.* also the description in Amos viii. 4 ff.

necessity for war, and the further development of commerce, all work together in an equal degree to promote *town* life. Besides the royal cities of Jerusalem, Tirzah, and Samaria, we meet, as time goes on, with a whole series of fortified towns, and new ones are added to the old, such as Shechem, Penuel, Ramah, and Lachish.[1] Jezreel becomes under Ahab a kind of second residence of the kings of Israel. Town life produces a well-to-do set of burghers and officials, and at the same time the old simple customs in a large measure disappear. Big fortunes make their appearance, and with them social contrasts begin to show themselves. Bribery and violence press hard on the lower classes; usury and the buying up of family holdings increase the possessions of the upper orders, and accentuate the contrast. The pursuit of pleasure and luxury, and, in addition to this, moral corruption, are the natural consequences of this state of things.[2] We can thus understand how the prophets often do not preach, merely as preachers of repentance, against the immorality of the people, but as social agitators against the whole present arrangement of society. The present is utterly corrupt; only an entirely new future can bring relief.

Naturally, the great mass of the people retained their simple ways and life, especially in the country and in small towns. The soil of Israel was indeed not rich enough for anything else. Alongside of the freestone houses, the cedar and ivory palaces of the great with their soft damask pillows for luxurious revels,[3] we find the simple style of house of the ordinary man who might also be a man of means; and alongside of the overdone love of dress which marked the gay, fashionable ladies of the capital,[4] we have the simple dress of the olden time. The history of Elisha gives us a good idea of the arrangement of a middle-class house. The one-story house of the poorer sort is enlarged by the addition of an upper story;[5] in the rooms we have table, chair, bed, and a

---

[1] 1 Kings xii. 25; xv. 21 f.; 2 Kings xiv. 19; xviii. 14. [Probably Akzib also, which is shown to have been a fortress by Micah i. 14.]

[2] See below, in § 65 and 66.

[3] 1 Kings xxii. 39; Amos iii. 12, 15; iv. 1; v. ii.; vi. 1 f, 4 ff.

[4] Isaiah iii. 16 ff. *Cf.* Amos iv. 1. [5] 2 Kings iv. 10; i. 2.

light;[1] the latter seems to have been kept constantly burning in every house.[2] In the better houses there was a special bed-chamber, probably in some retired part at the back.[3] Many are not satisfied merely with preserving the simple ways of the olden time. The enthusiast Elijah goes about in a hairy mantle, perhaps in what was merely the skin of the animal;[4] the Nazarites refrain from wine, and will not allow any razor to touch their heads;[5] the sect of the Rechabites do not only despise wine, the supreme product of culture, but living in built houses and the tilling of the earth are an offence in their eyes.[6] The retention of the nomad life is, in their view, the only guarantee for the preservation of the old customs of Israel which are pleasing to God. They supply the logical protest against all the mischiefs of culture, while the protest of the older prophets and the Nazarites is of the modest kind.

The great narrative books originating in this period supply us with certain information regarding the *family life* at this date and in the time previous to this. The histories of the patriarchs especially may be drawn upon here, since they are pre-eminently family histories. Naturally, we have to subtract what is said of the nomadic life and anything else that only suits with quite ancient times. With the exception of the king, part of whose brilliant court consists of a numerous harem, the ordinary Israelite seems, as a rule, to have only one wife. Still it is not considered in the least objectionable to marry a second wife, or to have a concubine in addition to the wife proper. And especially in the case where the couple are childless, the wife looks on it as her duty to bring one of her slaves to her husband. Examples of what is here alleged may easily be got from the history of Abraham, Jacob, and Samuel. The wife, so far as her position is concerned, although she is essentially the property of the man, is nevertheless held in high respect,

---

[1] 2 Kings iv. 10.   [2] Jer. xxv. 10. See Stade, 367.
[3] 2 Kings xi. 2. *Cf.* Amos vi. 10.   [4] 2 Kings i. 8.
[5] Judges xiii. and 1 Sam. i. may, in accordance with their date, be brought in here.   [6] 2 Kings x. 15; Jer. xxxv. 1 ff.

and is altogether more free than the majority of women in the East in the present day. The children are regarded as the property of their father. The paternal authority is evidenced, so far as the daughter is concerned, specially in the mode of betrothal, and both in the case of son and daughter it may go so far as to include the right of sacrificing the child, as may be proved from the action of Abraham and King Ahaz, not to speak of Jephthah.[1] The father may, without further ado, kill the rebellious son.[2] Man-servants and maid-servants are not treated as slaves in the modern sense of the word. If they, and especially the latter, are entirely the private property of their master, still they are protected by ancient established usage from being exploited and harshly treated. They belong to the family. Abraham's servant Eliezer is the type of a faithful and highly valued slave. We can see, both from the history of Abraham and from that of Elisha, how the rites of hospitality are practised, and how guests are held in honour.[3]

2. *Constitution and social organisation.*—The nature of these is essentially determined by the acquisition of the royal power which had been definitely introduced since the days of Saul. The old family and tribal bonds naturally lose more and more the importance they had at the beginning of the kingdom. They are not, indeed, even yet wholly discarded. The great main tribes of Judah and Ephraim have taken the place of the separate tribes of Deborah's song and Jacob's blessing, and have given their names to the two kingdoms. The old tribal constitution is certainly essentially replaced, or at any rate broken through, by the division of the land into provinces which have probably been the outcome of Solomon's taxation districts. On the other hand, the 'Elders'—that is, the heads of families and the representatives of the noble families—still continue to play a certain rôle in the individual communities, as, for instance, in Samaria

---

[1] Perhaps 1 Kings xvi. 34 is also connected with this.
[2] From the time of Deuteronomy after consultation with the elders of the town.
[3] Gen. xviii.; 2 Kings iv. 10; *cf.* Judges xix. 11 ff.

and Jezreel.[1] In fact, they still constitute as the popular assembly ('ēdā) the representative body of the whole nation, and in certain circumstances not only elect the king,[2] but hold an important place as advisers alongside of the king.[3] They share this influence, however, with the royal officials, who were naturally, as a rule, taken from the ranks of the nobility, though often enough they might owe their position to other considerations. The most powerful man after the king is the commander-in-chief,[4] and this was the case already in the time of David and Solomon. In the Northern Kingdom it was easy for a resolute man in this position to seize the crown for himself. Besides the chancellor, the scribe, the priest, the palace overseer, and master of works, who were doubtless introduced in the time of Solomon,[5] special mention is made of the king's confidential adjutant, 'the noble on whose arm he leans.'[6] Inside of the palace, as was the case everywhere in the East, the eunuchs play an important part.[7] At the head of the provinces there are governors whose armour-bearers formed a kind of select troop in war.[8] They had probably to supply definite contributions for the army out of the revenue of their provinces. A special dignity attaches to the mother of the king.[9]

The king himself, in accordance with the way in which the kingdom first originated, is, mainly in the Northern Kingdom, in the first place a soldier. His special care is the organisation of military matters in consequence of the continual wars. Fighting at a distance with bow and arrow against chariots and horsemen has taken the place of the old hand-to-hand combat with sword and spear. The history of Menahem supplies us

---

[1] 1 Kings xxi. 8; 2 Kings vi. 32; x. 1. On the significance of the family, see Wellh. *Isr. and Judah*,[3] 75.   [2] 1 Kings xii. 20.

[3] 1 Kings xx. 7 f. Isaiah iii. 2; ix. 14; *cf.* Exod. iii. 18; iv. 29, and elsewhere frequently.

[4] 2 Kings iv. 13; ix. 1 ff.   [5] *Cf. e.g.* 2 Kings xxiii.; 1 Kings xviii. 3.

[6] 2 Kings vii. 2, 17; ix. 25; x. 15 (called 'friend of the king' in Solomon's time, 1 Kings iv. 5).

[7] 2 Kings viii. 6; ix. 32.   [8] 1 Kings xx. 25.

[9] See mainly 1 Kings xv. 13; 2 Kings x. 13.

with some information regarding the organisation of the army. According to it, the landed proprietors had to bear the burden of military service. Naturally there must have been certain permanent troops at the disposal of the king.[1] The kernel of this standing army was the bodyguard, which could on occasion play an important part.[2]

In peace the most important duty of the king is the *giving of judgment*. As was the case in the time of David and Solomon, so even at this time, the common people come to the king to get justice.[3] But the king is probably only appealed to in specially important and difficult cases. For ordinary cases the primary court is constituted by the 'elders' of families and the royal officials—by the possessors of power, in short.[4] Any one who had sufficient power did not, in ordinary matters of law, require any judge: he got justice for himself, took the law into his own hands.[5] However frequent the perversion of justice may be amongst judges and magnates, a strict feeling of justice is not wanting in Israel. Even the king is not independent of it. It was largely owing to his disregard for it that Ahab brought about the fall of his house. How regular legal judicial procedure was conducted is illustrated by the proceedings against Naboth, and it shows at once how little the king was lord of the possessions and lives of his subjects in the usual fashion of Oriental despots.[6] Far into the time of the kings there was always a feeling that in Israel, too, things had once been different in this respect.[7] We can see in the case of Jehu and Joash[8] what happened when there was a change of throne, and especially when it was brought about by force. In the case of any

---

[1] 1 Kings xv. 20. See below, § 67, in connection with the history of Menahem.

[2] 2 Kings x. 25; xi. 4 (Kari=Kreti?). [The second after the king, 1 Sam. xxiii. 17, 2 Chron. xxviii. 7, is perhaps a special office in the kingdom (*cf.* Joseph).]

[3] 2 Kings vi. 26 ff.; viii. 5 f. *Cf.* 2 Sam. xiv. 1 ff.; xv. 1 ff. 1 Kings iii. 16 ff.

[4] 1 Kings xxi. 8, 11; Isaiah i. 10, 17, etc.; Exod. xviii, (E); *cf.* 2 Sam. xiv. 7, and especially Deuteronomy.

[5] 2 Kings iv. 1; Amos ii. 6.

[6] *Cf.* besides 1 Kings xxi. 1 ff. also xvi. 24.

[7] *Cf.* 1 Sam. viii. 10 ff.; Deut. xvii. 14 ff.

[8] 2 Kings ix. 1 ff., 13; xi. 12. *Cf.* 1 Kings i. 38 ff.

one intentionally inflicting a mortal blow in time of peace, recourse is still had to blood-revenge,[1] and at first the punishment takes the rude form of the extirpation of the whole house of the guilty person.[2] From the time of King Amaziah onwards it is restricted to the actual doer of the deed.[3]

3. *Literature.*—The general character of the period after Solomon leads us to expect that literature, too, will play an important part. Nor are we deceived in this expectation. As a matter of fact, we here enter on the *Golden Age* of Hebrew authorship. David and Solomon had made history: they had made Israel feel for the first time that it was a nation. The less posterity was able to preserve their great creation in actual reality, the more it strives to hold it firm in memory and thankfully to rejoice over the fair past. And when once the interest in Israel's past is awakened, the thoughts of the nation are carried farther and farther back, first to the predecessors of the great kings, to Saul and the men of the heroic age of Israel—Jerubbaal-Gideon, Jephthah, Barak—and afterwards to the great liberator of Israel who led them out of Egypt, and the patriarchs Abraham, Isaac, and Jacob.

We accordingly possess three or four narrative-books belonging to the beginning of this period which are of first-rate importance for our knowledge of the Israel of the older royal period. These are the writings already designated by the abbreviations Je, S, Da, So.[4] The three first, in all probability, originated in the very first years after the disruption of the kingdom. They are *histories of the first two kings*, written for the most part in an easy and diffuse style and entering into details, but they have also partly the character of brief and matter-of-fact annals. The authors treat the main figures in their history as the heroes of

---

[1] In the case of involuntary manslaughter, and for manslaughter in war, it had already been abrogated at an earlier period. Exod. xxi. 13; 2 Sam. iii. 28.

[2] *Cf.* 2 Kings ix. 26; Jos. vii. 24; also 1 Kings xv. 29.

[3] 2 Kings xiv. 6; *cf.* Deut. xxiv. 16.

[4] See on these writings above, pp. 33 f., 45-48, and the explanations at the end of Kautzsch's Old Testament.

a great national drama, which has been played before the eyes of their fathers and grandfathers. What they write is, with a few exceptions, anything but what we look for in annals, though at the same time it is not history with a purpose. It is *heroic history*, an epic in prose. S and Da are perhaps one and the same writing, which treats of the rise of the monarchy up to the time of Solomon's accession.

Of another kind, and probably of somewhat later date—written perhaps in the days of Jehoshaphat—is the work on Solomon (So), to which, next to the annals of that king, we owe most of the information we possess regarding Solomon. It supplies us with the first example of an historical work, in the higher sense, which we possess in the Old Testament.[1] The epic narrative has become a pragmatic working up of the material. We are able to estimate the spiritual elevation of the author by the freedom with which he treats his material.

The composition of a further historical work on the oldest period of the kings is to be assigned to the time between this and the days of Jeroboam II., though parts of it may have been written as late as the time of Hezekiah. It tells the story of Saul's *good fortune and of his end*, in the form of didactic narrative which was calculated to make posterity reflect. The monarchy, introduced in opposition to God's will and against the advice of the prophet, cannot bring blessing to Israel in so far as it does not take Yahvé and His word as its supreme standard. The kernel of this Samuel-Saul history (SS) was written in the time and in the spirit of Hosea.[2]

In addition to all these works by patriotic narrators dealing with the past, we have the *official* records of the royal annals of the two kingdoms running on from the time of David and Solomon.[3] Even if, as will be easily understood, they were not accessible to every one, still what was in them could hardly have reasonably been kept hidden. And when once the historical sense was

---

[1] See above, pp. 54, 57 f.   [2] See above, pp. 34, 45.
[3] See further, pp. 208, 209.

awakened and active, it could not but be that many a narrator should set himself to put together and hand down to posterity what he had got out of them. It is from this same impulse to supply more definite information regarding Israel's past, that the histories of the heroes sprung which constitute the chief basis of our present Book of Judges.[1] They do not form a unity, and some of them originated in the earliest part of the royal period, while others belong to the more recent portion of it.

The two great books on the *primitive history* of Israel which have already been described in detail in a previous section under the names of E and J, and which are in a very special degree ornaments of Hebrew literature, first saw the light in this period.[2] Without going back here again on the much debated question of their relative date, I simply remark that the development of Israelitish literature up to this time in the form in which we have just become acquainted with it, is most in harmony with the result previously gained, according to which the two books of the primitive history originated in the time of Kings Ahab and Jehu—the one in Israel, the other in Judah. To come any farther down seems to me still to be hazardous in the case of E, on account of the great *naïveté* with which the old holy places of Israel are treated. This implies a certain distance from Amos and Hosea.

4. *Religious Life.*—The split in the kingdom divided the religious Israel, as it did the political, into two camps. In the Northern Kingdom Jeroboam could appeal to the fact that the divine worship which he gave to his kingdom was, both as regards locality and the form in which it was celebrated, in harmony with the past traditions of a considerable part of Israel. Bethel and Dan were, as sanctuaries of Yahvé, far older than Jerusalem; and though He had not necessarily been worshipped hitherto under the symbol of bulls, still the worship of images had not been anything particularly rare.[3] Thus the cry, 'These are thy gods which have brought thee out of Egypt,' was intended

---

[1] See my essay in *StKr.*, 1892, 44 ff.

[2] See vol. i. pp. 81-90. (The time of Amos and Hosea is inaccurately specified at pp. 81 f.) [3] See above, § 50, 3; *cf.* also p. 99.

to remind Israel that what Jeroboam offered them, did not pretend to be anything new, but was a return to something widely practised long ago in Israel.

We can therefore scarcely go wrong in supposing that the worship of the Kingdom of Ephraim occupied the same level as *the worship on the high-places and the 'serving' of images* in the age before the kings, and in the early years of the period of the kings. The brief and very general terms in which our Book of Kings refers to religious matters in the Northern Kingdom makes it difficult for us to form a definite picture of them. Still it is possible to fix some of its features. Bethel and Dan are merely the principal, but not the only sanctuaries of the Northern Kingdom;[1] the former possesses a splendid temple which is under the special patronage of the king.[2] The same was probably the case with Samaria.[3] Besides these, the sanctuaries of Gilgal, Beersheba, Mizpah, and those on Mount Tabor and Mount Carmel[4] are held in special veneration, and, very probably, too, places such as Shechem, Penuel, and Succoth.[5] So far as its priesthood was concerned, Levitical descent is not considered an absolutely necessary qualification for office.[6] There is no want of sacrifices and crowded festivals. Sabbaths and new moons[8] are strictly celebrated, the tithe is dutifully rendered to Yahvé.[9]

Side by side with the worship of the bull, the worship of Yahvé by means of the *Ephod* and the adoration of the *Teraphim*, which had been previously practised, still go on. Hosea mentions them as parts of the ordinary divine service[10] in the Northern

---

[1] 1 Kings xiii. 32; 2 Kings xxiii. 19.
[2] 1 Kings xii. 31; Amos vii. 13; *cf.* ix. 1.   [3] *Cf.* 2 Kings x. 18 ff.
[4] Amos iv. 4; v. 5; Hos. ix. 15; iv. 15; xii. 12; Amos v. 5; viii. 14; Hos. v. 1; 1 Kings xviii. 30 (Micah vii. 14?).
[5] Gen. xii. 6 f., etc.; xxxii. 25 ff.; xxxiii. 17 [Lachish also, according to Micah i. 13, is apparently to be classed amongst these].
[6] 1 Kings xii. 31; xiii. 33; *cf.* Elias xviii. 30 ff.
[7] 1 Kings xii. 32 ff.; xviii. 26 ff.; 2 Kings iii. 20; Amos iv. 4 f.; v. 22. Hos. vi. 6; viii. 13; Amos v. 23; viii. 10.
[8] Amos v. 23; viii. 10; Isa. i. 13; 2 Kings iv. 23.   [9] Amos iv. 4.
[10] Hos. iii. 4. This does not mean that he approves of them. The kingly office is also referred to in this passage spite of Hosea's plainly expressed opinion regarding it in xiii. 10.

Kingdom in his day, and the narrative piece, Judges xvii. f., which belongs to the beginning of our period, mentions them without a trace of disapproval.[1] The older accounts, too, of Saul and David have very little to find fault with in them. Beside the altar of Yahvé, if not invariably, at any rate generally, stands the sacred pillar which had come down from Canaanitish times, called *Maççēba*.[2] Hosea mentions the Maççēba in the same way as the Ephod and the Teraphim, and in the two books of stories which deal with the primitive history of the nation, it is mentioned with the same enthusiasm as marks their references to the altars which Abraham and Jacob long ago set up.[3] Of all the sacred symbols of the Canaanites it appears to have been the most innocent, and the one which could most readily be tolerated together with Yahvéism. As a simple symbol of the presence of the Godhead, it had a very close resemblance to the Ark, and, like it, could be employed also in connection with a form of worship in which images were not used. That to have the Maççēba alongside of the altar could in any way be displeasing to Yahvé, is an idea that never occurs to J and E, any more than the thought that there is anything wrong in having several sanctuaries at the same time. It is all the more worthy of notice that the adoration of Yahvé by means of an image, or the erection of an image of Yahvé, is never ascribed to the patriarchs.

The *Ashēra*, too, the sacred post, which was for the Canaanites a symbol of fruitfulness, their chief female divinity, is entirely absent from the list of the means of worship ascribed by J and E to the patriarchs. Spite of this, the Ashēra was evidently in use in the Northern Kingdom. It is true that the Book of Kings mentions it here almost exclusively in connection with Baal-worship,[4]

---

[1] See above, p. 20, and § 50, 3.

[2] So Stade, ZAW. i. 345. Both in the references to the patriarchs as well as in the Book of Kings (Jeroboam, Elijah), and also in Judges and Samuel, the Maççēba is often enough absent where the altar is mentioned.

[3] Hos. iii. 4; x. 1 f.; Micah v. 12; Gen. xxviii. 18 f.; xxxi. 13; Ex. xxiv. 4, etc., and above, vol. i. p. 88. Deut. xvi. 22; xii. 3. In 2 Kings iii. 2; x. 27 (the text is doubtful here) the reference is to Baal-worship. Isa. xix. 19 is hardly in point here. [4] 1 Kings xvi. 33; 2 Kings x. 26; perhaps also xxiii. 15.

but the fact that we find it again under[1] a king belonging to the dynasty of Jehu, who had suppressed Baal-worship, shows that the sacred pillar of the Phœnicians had been also transferred to Yahvé. Still stronger evidence is afforded of this by the analogy of the Kingdom of Judah, and by the energetic protest of the prophetic and Deuteronomic writers against the Ashēras.[2] How near the worship of Northern Israel had been brought to Canaanitish heathendom by all these things is shown in the plainest way in what is said about them by Amos and Hosea, whose utterances for this very reason very frequently leave us in the dark as to whether they are thinking of actual heathenism, or of a Yahvéism which resembles heathenism.[3] From this, in fact, to the introduction of actual heathenism into Israel, there was only a step. Ahab, under the influence of his Phœnician wife, actually admits it. In Samaria, and probably in Jezreel also, there is a splendid temple of Baal[4] in which naturally Ashēras and the Maççēba are found.[5] Personally, Ahab seems to have held fast to Yahvé.[6]

Spite of all this, we cannot believe that the times of David and Solomon had gone past without leaving any trace in Northern Israel, or that the remembrance of them had been wholly blotted out. Our document, hardly without good reason, recalls the fact that Jeroboam dreaded the influence of the Temple of Jerusalem on his countrymen. Amongst the prophets trained in the school of Samuel and Nathan the worship of Yahvé without images, as it was practised in connection with the Ark, was held in high esteem. As Elijah and Elisha raised their voices in protest against Ahab's innovations, it is possible that the prophets of the time of Jeroboam may not have kept silence in face of his new departure. It is all the more striking that such a man as Elijah should not have uttered a single word by way of blame against

---

[1] 2 Kings xiii. 6. Incorrectly, Köhl. ii. 2, 44. In this case xxiii. 15 may also refer to a Yahvé-ashēra.

[2] Micah v. 13 ; Judges iii. 7 ; vi. 25 ff. ; Deut. vii. 5 ; xii. 3, etc. ; Isa. xvii. 8 is uncertain.

[3] See below, §§ 65 and 66.

[4] 1 Kings xvi. 32 ; 2 Kings x. 18 ff., 27 ; cf. v. 11.

[5] 1 Kings xvi. 33 ; 2 Kings iii. 2 ; x. 26 (27 ?) ; xiii. 6.   [6] See above, p. 264.

bull-worship. In view of this fact no one can contest the possibility of the view that Elijah and the prophets of his day may have regarded bull-worship as inoffensive. But there is a more likely supposition, namely, that Elijah and Elisha, in combating the actual idolatrous worship, may have kept in the background their opinions regarding the adoration of Yahvé under the symbol of a bull. If it was a question as to whether Yahvé or Baal was to be the God of Israel, the worship of Yahvé by the help of an image would seem to them by far the lesser evil of the two. The position taken up by J and E in Exodus xxxii. in reference to bull-worship, adds force to this supposition.

We are little better informed regarding the Kingdom of Judah at this period than we are regarding that of Israel. It was its good fortune to have the Temple and its worship of Yahvé without any image, which it continued to preserve although perhaps not without some curtailment, after the separation from Ephraim. Its priesthood is in the hands of the family of Zadok, who retained it until the time of the Exile. As Solomon did himself, his successors claimed the right to offer sacrifices without the intervention of the priesthood.[1] At a later period great offence was taken at this, but it is very questionable if their contemporaries too objected to it. Besides Jerusalem, there are here and there in the country local sanctuaries, called Bamôth, where Yahvé is worshipped without protest.

The head of the numerous priesthood of the Temple, as was already the case under David and Solomon, is classed amongst the highest dignitaries of the kingdom. The prominent position occupied by a high priest of this kind is clearly illustrated by the case of Jehoiada, who brings about the revolution against Athaliah and raises the young prince Joash to the throne. At the end of the period of the kings a 'second priest' is mentioned alongside of the high priest; the Temple guards, too, are priests of higher rank.[2] This points to the existence of a large number of individuals con-

---

[1] 2 Kings xvi. 12 f.; cf. 2 Chron. xxvi. 16 ff.
[2] 2 Kings xxiii. 4 (see Baudissin, *Priestert.* 216); xxv. 18; Jer. lii. 24.

nected with the Temple service and arranged in hierarchical gradation.[1] Corresponding to these there were also various subordinate officials engaged in the service of the sanctuary.[2] All these priests are essentially royal servants. The way in which Joash and Ahaz act, shows how freely the king can act as regards his priest.[3] We do not hear anything of any regular order of sacrifices, although this must have existed. Both in Israel and Judah the people themselves take part in the sacrificial service with the liveliest zeal.[4] We find mention of regular morning and evening sacrifice in addition to the special sacrifices of the king and those of private persons in the time of Ahaz; and in the time of Joash we hear of dedicatory and expiatory offerings given to the Temple, as well as of money payments, by which other duties were commuted in the shape of a tax.[5] Isaiah is acquainted with yearly festivals, especially with the Passover-night, and with joyous festival songs. Prayer too is for him a part of divine service.[6]

But spite of this, Judah did not escape heathen or half-heathen influences any more than Israel. The remembrance of the time before the carrying back of the Ark by David must inevitably have had an effect on people's minds, if not in Jerusalem, the seat of the Ark, at least in the various sanctuaries in the land. Besides, Solomon himself, although his religious position in other respects cannot be very clearly ascertained,[7] gave an example in this respect which was not greatly to the advantage of the Temple. Finally, we must not underrate the importance of the influences which came from the Northern Kingdom. Even if they proceeded from a kingdom which was frequently at feud with Judah, on the other hand they were in harmony with certain ancient tendencies of Israel which had not yet quite died out even in Judah.

We need not, accordingly, be astonished when we find the author of the Book of Kings mentioning that already in the time

---

[1] *Cf.* the name 'elders of the priests.'   [2] Kings xix. 2; Isa. xxxvii. 2.
[2] Jos. ix. 23.   [3] 2 Kings xii. 5 ff.; xvi. 11 ff.
[4] Isa. i. 11 ff; *cf.* Micah vi. 6.   [5] 2 Kings xii. 5, 17; xvi. 15.
[6] Isa. xxix. 1; xxx. 29; xxxiii. 20; i. 13 f.
[7] See above, p. 200, note 6.

of Rehoboam there were large numbers of *high-places* in Judah
which were provided with Maççēbas and Ashēras, and at which
religious prostitution was practised in the service of Astarte.[1] In
Asa's reign even Abijam's widow Maachah has to be deprived of her
rank as queen-mother, because the heathenism which had already
a strong hold on the country, and especially the lascivious Astarte-
worship, could appeal to her authority.[2] Even if Asa checked for
a time the practice of heathen customs which had already
begun to get a footing in Judah, still here too favourable circumstances were all that were wanted to allow of heathenism at once
springing into life again. The high-places still continue, and
images, Maççēbas, and Ashēras, which had been done away
with, are soon enough to return again. The brazen serpent, a relic
of ancient animal-worship, continues to be adored without protest
till the days of Hezekiah. It can hardly have been the only thing
of its kind. We have no proof that before the time of Ahaz
Ashēras were used in Judah, in the service of Yahvé in the Temple
at any rate, and no certain proof[3] of the employment of Maççēbas,
although in the history of the patriarchs the presence of the latter
would not seem to be anything out of place. The marriage
alliance between the House of David and the family of Ahab gave
the favourable opportunity referred to; and we hear directly of a
temple of Baal in Jerusalem with all its belongings, its own priest,
representations of Baal, and altars.[4]

Spite of this the Temple-service even under Athaliah seems to
have gone on unhindered. On the contrary, the Temple of Jerusalem and the worship of God practised in it constantly gain
ground not only in Judah itself, but beyond its boundaries too.
The way in which Amos speaks to Israel, and that in which Hosea,

---

[1] *Cf.* however in connection with this and with what follows what is given above at pp. 247, 248.

[2] 1 Kings xiv. 23, 24; xv. 12, 13.

[3] We should have evidence of this in Isaiah xix. 19 if it could be proved that a Maççēba for use in divine worship is referred to, and also in 2 Kings xii. 10, if with Stade (*ZAW.* v. 289 f.) we could read אֵל הַמַּצֵּבָה. Only, the Heb. צ is always rendered by σ and not by ζ in the LXX. (See also Köhler, ii. 2, 219).

[4] 2 Kings xi. 18. See on this above, p. 287.

although a citizen of the Northern Kingdom, expresses himself regarding Judah and the House of David,[1] is the best proof of this. And even if Isaiah has many complaints to utter regarding the numerous images [2] which are drawing away Judah from the pure worship of God—and these did not certainly represent idols only—still it was to be his special duty more than that of any other, to point out that Yahvé highly esteems his holy dwelling in Zion and is ready to protect it both against friend and foe.

[1] See below, § 66.
[2] Isa. ii. 8, 18, 20; xxx. 22; xxxi. f. [*cf.* further i. 29; x. 4 (Baltis and Osiris?); xvii. 4 (Adonis?); see *Isaiah* in a forthcoming part of Paul Haupt's Old Testament (Hebrew text revised, and English translation).]

CHAPTER IV.

THE INTERVENTION OF PROPHECY.

§ 65. *Prophecy from the Eighth Century.*[1]

THE further the history proceeds the more meagre the information becomes in the Book of Kings. It is only in exceptional instances that we get a more detailed account. If we had only the narrative in that Book to go to for information regarding the period of Jehu and Athaliah downwards, we should be badly equipped. It is of inestimable value for our knowledge of Israel's past that just when the information in the Book of Kings begins to fail, a source of fresh information is opened up in the writings of the prophets. The dry skeleton of the narrative in Kings is quickened into life by the fresh air of natural feeling which breathes from their utterances. It gets flesh and blood and all the freshness of natural colour. The prophets are moved to the very depths of their nature by what goes on in their nation; its troubles send a throb through their heart; its cares eat into their soul; its sins burn in their conscience. And what thus inwardly moves them and lays hold of them, finds natural expression in spontaneous and unadorned words.

We thus get a picture of the condition of things in Israel and Judah as this presents itself to Amos and his successors from the reign of Jeroboam II. onwards. It is the holy wrath of genuine patriots that wields the brush here; the colours are now of a lurid

---

[1] See in general Duhm, *Theol. d. Prof.*; Wellh. *Abriss.* 49 ff.; Stade, *Gesch.* 1, 550 ff.; Kuenen, *Hibbert Lectures for* 1882, 91 ff., 111 ff.; *Ond.*[2] § 39 (for bibliography). [Also Schultz's *OT. Theology* (E. T. 1894), and especially Dillmann's *Alttest. Theologie,* ed. Kittel (1895); besides W. R. Smith, art. *Prophecy* in *Encycl. Brit.*; *Prophets of Israel*[2] (1895); Cornill, *Profetismus,* 1895.]

glow, now darkly sombre, such as we see when an abyss is lit up by the play of the lightning flash.

The moral sense is blunted, the moral conditions are corrupted. The many wars have done their work. And even the better days which the reigns of Jeroboam and Uzziah brought with them for the kingdom cannot blind us to the damage which has been done. They have at most increased the evil. Insolent pride and wanton immorality have followed barbarity and violence. Amos[1] complains that father and son go together to visit harlots; and Isaiah reproaches Samaria as well as Jerusalem thus: 'They reel from wine and stagger from strong drink ... all tables are full of filthy vomit, so that there is no more room.'[2] The injustice in trade and business cries aloud to heaven; the right of the stronger has taken the place of the divine law. There seems to be no longer any administration of justice, and the social question is solved by the exploiting of the weak. 'They sell the righteous for money, the poor for a pair of shoes. They pant after the dust of the earth on the head of the poor, and twist justice in their dealings with the wretched.'[3] 'Woe to those,' continues Isaiah,[4] 'who join house to house, who lay field to field, till there is no single bit of room left; and woe to those who are strong to drink wine and heroes in the mingling of strong drink, who acquit the transgressor for a bribe, and withhold from the righteous their right.'

The religious life is in no better condition. Here, too, the earnestness of the prophetic call to repentance tears up without regard to consequences all deceptive and dazzling outward show. On the one side we see zeal for Yahvé based on the naïve delusion that quantity is everything, and that outward performance can cover inner defects which had indeed only too often plainly come to the surface already. On the other side there is open apostasy to foreign gods, or, at any rate, a worship of the God of Israel which is very like heathenism.

---

[1] Amos ii. 7.   [2] Isa. xxviii. 7 ff.; cf. i. ff.
[3] Amos ii. 6 f. (earth on the head signifies mourning); cf. viii. 4 ff.
[4] Isa. v. 8, 22 f.

Not that all this has come into existence for the first time in the days of Jeroboam and Uzziah. The mischief may have grown with the time, but in essence it has been there for long. The new thing that our time brings with it, does not lie in the circumstances themselves, but in the light which suddenly falls upon them. People in Israel spent their days in a careless fashion, thinking only of the immediate present. The Syrian wars and many other troubles of the time had indeed brought anxieties with them. But then there was always some kind of help or other at hand. Yahvé had never quite forsaken His people. But now a lurid flash suddenly lightens up the sky and shows to the startled glance of Israel that she is walking close to a yawning abyss. The lightning flash came from the east, from *Assyria*.

We have already several times come across Assyria since the days of Omri. The kings of Israel have also more than once made terms with her. But from the time of Jeroboam things have taken a decisive turn. The consequences of this become at once evident in the reigns of the next kings in Israel and Judah. The Syrian kingdom of Damascus, even if its existence is prolonged for a time, has now after a long struggle received its death-blow. Assyria is Israel's neighbour. Israel might have been long enough worried by Damascus; in Assyria, which chastised Aramean neighbours, she might often enough have beheld a welcome deliverer, but any one who saw into the heart of things could not be blinded by all this to the real facts. With Assyria as Israel's neighbour, with this mighty conquering kingdom ever gaining ground by the sword and brute force, regardless of consequences, placed close to the puny Israel, the issue of things could not possibly be doubtful. What had happened to Damascus and Hamath must with unfailing certainty come upon Israel some time or other.[1] Her independence was at an end, monarchy and people were irretrievably doomed to destruction, if God did not work a miracle.

The fact that many in Israel did not see this, did not make the situation any better. A calamity is always the greater the less

---

[1] Isa. x. 9.

it is expected. It was Israel's good fortune and her salvation—so far as salvation was here possible—that she had at least some men who did not allow themselves to be carried away by the general infatuation. These were the *Prophets*. They alone looked facts in the face. And, as servants of their God, they found courage to utter the terrifying things which they saw before king and people in the most direct way. Thus they penetrated the very centre of the national life. They became the intellectual leaders of their nation, it might be in harmony with the ruling powers, or it might be in opposition to them. At any rate, Israel could not put aside this guidance so long as it had any political existence. And even long after its political annihilation, the people which grew out of the old Israel stood, and one may say still stands, under the influence of this the most unique and powerful manifestation to which a national life ever gave birth. In Israel's prophets the genius of the Israelitish spirit is represented in its purest and grandest form. Incomparable in themselves, and as unique in their performances, these religious heroes saw into the innermost recesses of the soul of this people. Prophecy may not have been of Israelitish origin, but the prophets soon attained the truest feeling of what Israel in its inmost being was and could be.

If we wish to understand prophecy in its new form, our glance involuntarily turns backwards. We do not now hear for the first time the name prophets: *Nebî'îm*. Samuel and Nathan, and, after them, Elijah and Elisha, bore the title. What is the new element in the prophecy of the present? We must guard against laying too much stress on anything outward, even if much has been altered, and if gradually many new developments have shown themselves in the outward appearance and mode of action of the Nebî'îm. The fact that what the prophets have to say to the people is now partly written down and presented to the public in the form of books or fly-sheets, certainly presents them outwardly in a different aspect. Still, in reality, this is nothing but the natural consequence of the changed times. Israel has entered upon the period of literature. Was it likely that the guiding spirits of the nation would deny themselves the use of the most obviously effective means of bringing their thoughts under the notice of men, as soon as the employment of this medium had become the regular practice?

True, the bands of ecstatic enthusiasts whom we see parading the country in the times of Samuel belong to a long vanished past. Already, in the days of Elijah, their place had been taken by the societies of the prophets, the calm, clarified product of those loosely formed associations. These, too, have now lost much of their significance. It has, however, been left as a permanent reminiscence of them that the prophets form a kind of close order, a corporate body.[1] Whoever in the guild is distinguished by the possession of special prophetic endowment, naturally comes to the front. He takes the place of the Master, in this resembling the later Rabbi, who gathers round him his intimate pupils, and forms them into a narrower circle of disciples.[2] But any one, who through the inner impulse of the Spirit of God feels within himself the call to be a prophet, can put himself forward as a man of God without being a member of the prophetic order, or the son of a prophet. It is not membership of the order or society which makes the prophet, at least not the prophet of standing. The individual acts on his own responsibility, and comes forward on his own account in the name of Yahvé; what gives him authority is the might of the Spirit which breathes from him. It may, indeed, be that personality comes more to the front now than formerly; still we cannot assert that at an earlier period it was merged in the society, and so, in this respect too, it is evident that the advance of time does not mean any absolute change.

The same holds good of the psychological form of the expression of the prophetic spirit. The being directly laid hold of by God—an experience which is often independent of the will of man, and which not seldom takes the form of an ecstatic and visionary seizure—forms the main feature here as it did before. If, on the

---

[1] See Kuen. §§ 39, 12. On the older prophecy, see above, p. 265 and p. 109 f.
[2] Isa. viii. 16; Amos vii. 14.

one hand, the original connection with the 'mantikos' is more and more discarded, and if, on the other, the visionary element retires more into the background as time goes on, still, the consciousness the prophet has that he did not call himself, but that God compelled him and imposed His word upon him, always remains.

It is only one thing that is entirely new, namely, the direct interference of Assyria in the fortunes of Israel, and the mode in which this is reflected in the soul of the prophets. To their vision is revealed the yawning abyss at the edge of which Israel is standing; they see the horrible picture of a national body whose existence is shaken to the very core, and already catch the sound of the death-rattle, the sign that the life is approaching its end. But the life of a nation such as Israel *shall* not and *must* not come to an end, even suppose a world-empire were its enemy. The thought irresistibly forces prophecy out of its national limits, and leads it to regard Israel's goal and destiny in the light of what is *supra-national*, in the light of universal history. In the light of universal history Israel has left behind it Assyria and all the world-empires which did violence to it. The prophets perceived that. And what they perceived they effected.

Two questions weigh upon the souls of the men of God—a question of knowledge and a question of action. The one makes them teachers without a rival, restorers of their country's faith; the other makes them patriots without a rival, and reformers of conduct.

How, so runs the one question, how was what was being accomplished before their eyes *at all possible*? Was not Yahvé Israel's God from of old, who must protect it against all danger? How then could God thus deliver His people into the hands of the Assyrians? If, nevertheless, He did this, then either He was no longer Israel's God, or Israel was no longer His people. He did it. And since Yahvé's faithfulness and power could not waver, then the logical conclusion of the prophetic preaching was inevitable. Israel is no longer what it was, it is a rebellious nation, the people are degenerate sons who have broken faith with their Lord. It is Israel's *guilt*, it is its sin which is being avenged on it, which its God is avenging by the hand of the enemy. Thus the condition of Israel hitherto, its religious as well as its moral and social condition with its manifold evils, suddenly appears in a new light. It is because of these evils that the all-powerful enemy is allowed to knock at Israel's gates. Ay, and Yahvé himself thus suddenly appears in a new light; it is He Himself who, in His moral holiness, has decreed Israel's ruin, who has made its enemies its scourge.

The moral holiness of Yahvé is not new. Moses had long ago recognised the moral character of Yahvé.[1] Nathan had clearly and inexorably given expression to it in what he said to David, and Elijah in what he said to Ahab. It is, however, something new indeed that Yahvé's moral holiness does not only punish Israel, but may even let it go to ruin. The fiery spirit of a Moses and an Elijah comes to life again in Amos and Isaiah, but in a new form, no longer confined within the narrow circle of the nation. If Yahvé, through Elijah and Elisha, had threatened to destroy with fire and sword what stood in His way that he might continue to be Israel's God, in Amos, Hosea, and Isaiah, the God of the world has decreed the breaking in pieces of His own people that He may maintain justice in the world by means of His *moral world-order*. But even if the prophets of this period were not the first to discover the moral character of Yahvé, theirs must ever be the merit of having, with an energy and consistency before unheard of, made the moral element in the character of God the central point of all thought about Him. They thus give completion to the thoughts which constitute the Mosaic religious creation, and elevate that into *ethical monotheism*. The theological question was thereby solved.

And thus the second question, the question of action, pressed all the more strongly on the teachers of the period. It was impossible to stop short at Israel's ruin, which was demanded and announced beforehand by the moral order of the world. The

---

[1] See on this above, vol. i. pp. 242 f., 247 f.

prophets could not have been patriots, and they could not have been men of God and the religious guides of their nation, had they not sought after harmony in the discord, after a harmonious ending to the great tragedy. What then was to be done? There was only one way; the present state of things must pass away, now or at some future time. The religious, moral, and social evils in the nation are the cause of the divine wrath; if once they disappear, the divine wrath will cease too. With a radicalism which recalls some of the most uncompromising manifestations of socio-political and religious agitation in history, they loudly proclaim this fundamental principle: whatever exists in Israel is fit only to be destroyed! Only a thorough renovation of all the conditions of life on a perfectly new basis can avail. Often hopes were entertained of reaching this new state of things even yet by conversion and true repentance. But this hope is soon seen to be deceptive. The state, the whole present order of society, the present perverted practice of religion itself, must first pass away. Yahvé Himself, as sure as He is Israel's God, will effect the needed renewal through the King of the future, the *Messiah*. Under him Israel will be a kingdom of God, a holy nation, well-pleasing to God. Justice and morality will be in accordance with the demands of God, the practice of religion will be in accordance with His will.

Did the prophets attain what they here desire? In the eyes of their own nation and age they often enough occupied the position of betrayers of the Fatherland to the enemy; in the light of history they appear as the patriots to whom Israel owes it that she came forth from the storms which swept over the land—weakened indeed and humiliated, but not broken. Into the hand of their nation, which was too weak to fight with the sword against the world-powers, they pressed the banner of faith and hope. With it Israel has gained the victory. It has not only outlasted the world-powers, it has inwardly, spiritually, laid them at its feet. And as regards action, both moral and religious, what they say does indeed, in the first instance, meet with no response. But, nevertheless, under the weight of the divine judgments, Israel more and more inclined its ear to them. Israel has received a certain bent towards the doing of the divine will, which it never again let go, and which very soon gave the national life a new direction.

§ 66. *Amos. Hosea.*

We cannot in the case of all the prophets of this kind succeed in getting any certain information in regard to the time of their appearance. The first of them to whom we can with certainty assign a date is Amos.[1] A Judæan by birth, born in the little town of Tekoa near Bethlehem, he makes his appearance in the kingdom of Israel in the reign of Jeroboam II. preaching coming disaster. What leads him thus to preach is not that he is of the prophetic order and calling, nor is it long and diligent preparation within the circle of the 'sons of the prophets': his station is that of a herdsman and planter of sycomores. No; the call of Yahvé which, like an all-powerful natural force, irresistibly lays hold of men, has opened his mouth:

> 'Shall two walk together except they have agreed?
> Will a lion roar in the forest when he hath no prey?
> Will a young lion cry out of his den if he hath taken nothing?
> The lion hath roared—who will not fear?
> The Lord God hath spoken—who can but prophesy?'[2]

What he has to say in the name of Yahvé is nothing less than this, that it is all over with the state, the people, the royal house of Israel. Yahvé, who has made heaven and earth and guides the stars, is a just God, but the measure of Israel's sins has long been full, the judgment day of Yahvé is dawning, the ripe fruit is dropping.[3] One hears the voice of the herdsman from Bethlehem's pastures and Judah's desert, when he exclaims:

> 'As the shepherd rescueth out of the mouth of the lion
> Two legs, or a piece of an ear,
> So shall the children of Israel be rescued
> That sit in Samaria
> In the corner of a couch, and on the silken cushions of a bed'[4] ('damask pillow,' so Kittel).

---

[1] *Cf.* also Oort in *Th. Tijdschr.* 1891, 121 ff.
[2] Amos iii. 3, 4, 9 (R.V.).
[3] *Cf.* Amos viii. 1, 2.
[4] Amos iii. 12 (R.V.).

> Woe unto you that desire the day of the Lord!
> Wherefore would ye have the day of the Lord?
> It is darkness, and not light.
> As if a man did flee from a lion,
> And a bear met him;
> Or went into the house and leaned his hand on the wall,
> And a serpent bit him.'[1]

Not as though the great harvest day which Yahvé intends were the first judgment on His people. Guilt and sin were there long ago, and so too was God's punishment. But little blows, such as failure of crops and dearth, drought, canker, and the plague of locusts, even pestilence and earthquake, such as were experienced in recent times, no longer produce any effect.[2] All that can be done now is that Yahvé should let Israel itself perish, in order to reach His end. Already Amos sees the funeral procession and hears the lamentation for the dead, already he begins himself to sing the death-song over his nation:

> 'The virgin of Israel is fallen:
> She shall no more rise:
> She is cast down upon her land:
> There is none to raise her up.'[3]

> 'Wailing shall be in all the broad ways; and they shall say in all the street, Alas! alas!
> And they shall call the husbandman to mourning, and such as are skilful of lamentation to wailing.
> And in all vineyards shall be wailing: for I will pass through the midst of thee, saith the Lord.'[4]

The cause of all this calamity is evident. Unrighteousness and dishonesty; heartless oppression of the poor, shameless corruption of the judges, open exploiting of the weak, and at the same time luxury, debauch, and a life of ease and pleasure lived by the help of these ill-gotten gains, are to be met with everywhere. Debtors who cannot pay go into slavery for the sake

---

[1] Amos v. 18, 19 (R.V.).
[2] Amos iv. 6 ff. The earthquake, according to i. 1 (cf. Zech. xiv. 7), is to be placed two years after the first public appearance of Amos. It accordingly occurred in the period between this and the writing down and editing of his book.
[3] Amos v. 1 (R.V.).   [4] Amos v. 16 ff. (R.V.); cf. vi. 9 f., 14.

of a wretched pair of shoes; in their greed of unjust gain some can hardly wait till the holy days of rest, the Sabbath and the new moon, are past, in order that they may practise usury and cheat with false weights and measures.[1] Men and women have an equal share in all this wrong-doing, in fact the women incite the men to a base pursuit of gain—'Make money that we may carouse.'[2] They understand how to make use of the money thus unjustly acquired in other ways besides in carousals. Splendid freestone buildings with costly ivory panelling, town-dwellings for the winter, and country-seats for the summer, gardens and vineyards, luxurious pillows for their riotous banquets, balm, the music of stringed instruments and song, all help to sweeten life in Samaria and lead men to forget the affliction of Joseph.[3]

But still worse than these things is the open apostasy from Yahvé. There is no want of zeal in honouring God outwardly. But will Yahvé, like Israel's judges, be bribed by presents? Is He to be gained over by feasts and sacrifices, by songs and the music of the harp?[4] It is true, if only this were at least done in a right way, it would be something. But what Israel practises is really nothing but idolatry. Its holy places, Bethel, Gilgal, Beersheba, are the places of idols, its altars have become places of sin, which must fall. It is sacrilege to swear by the God of Dan and by the pilgrimage to Beersheba.[5] Not as if they practised a real foreign worship, the worship of Baal perhaps. The dynasty of Jehu owed its throne to the fight against Baal, and in the time of Amos, as was indeed always the case in the Northern Kingdom, Bethel is the royal sanctuary. The religious views of Jeroboam II. are not likely to have been different from those of his namesake or of Jehu. But prophecy has meanwhile taught a different view of these things. The image-worship of Bethel and Dan, which Elijah had tolerated, whose seats are still held in honour and glorified by E and J, has now become a worship of idols, while

---

[1] Amos ii. 6 ff.; v. 10; viii. 4 ff. [2] Amos iv. 1.
[3] Amos iii. 12-15; iv. 1*b*; v. 11; vi. 1 ff., 4 ff. [4] Amos v. 21 ff.
[5] Amos iii. 14; iv. 4 f.; v. 4 f.; vii. 9; viii. 14.

its holy places have become the same as the high-places of Baal.

But if Yahvé has sworn that Israel will for the present be destroyed, this does not mean that it will disappear from the earth. The grace of God is greater than the guilt of man. The House of Israel shall indeed be shaken out amongst all the nations as one shakes corn in a sieve. But in the far future Yahvé is again to set up the dwellings of David which have been cast down, so that they will be glorious as in former days. Then a time of blessing will come upon Israel. 'The mountains shall drop sweet wine and the hills shall melt. And I will plant them upon their land, and they shall no more be plucked up out of their land which I have given them, saith the Lord thy God.'[1]

It cannot astonish us when we find that the sharp words of Amos made him few friends in Samaria. When in Bethel he had prophesied the destruction of the sanctuaries of Israel together with that of the House of Jeroboam, he was arraigned before the king by the priest Amaziah on a charge of blasphemy, and expelled the country.[2] What became of him we do not know; it is sufficient that he has left us his book.

But the sowing of Amos was not in vain. A short time after him, and while Jeroboam II.[3] is still reigning, a man appears on the scene amongst the Ephraimites themselves, who takes up afresh the preaching of Amos against Ephraim: Hosea ben Be'ēri.

It is a personal experience [4] which turns him into a prophet. His wife, whom he tenderly loves, is unfaithful to him. How could Yahvé send this sorrow on him? His own trial and his wife's degeneracy blend in his thoughts with what he daily sees amongst his own people. The one becomes for him a picture of the other, and thus it becomes clear to him that what he has come through has happened that he may feel in his own experi-

---

[1] Amos ix. 9 ff. 15 (R.V.). *Cf.* on *v.* 11 Hoffmann in *ZAW.* iii. 125.
[2] Amos vii. 9 ff.   [3] On Hosea i. 1, see Kuen. § 66, 5-8.
[4] On the different attempts to explain this, see besides the Commentaries especially Kuen. § 66, 9 ff.; [and W. R. Smith, *Prophets of Israel*, 179 ff.].

ence, and teach others to declare how Israel is treating its God, and how God is treating Israel. The nation has committed adultery against its Lord. The recognition of this fact makes Hosea a prophet. It continues to be throughout the central point of his prophecy. But does not he himself, spite of all that has happened, still love the wife of his choice? And so Yahvé does indeed reject His unfaithful people, but He cannot withdraw His love from them. He must once more bring them back to Himself.

Israel is like the adulterous wife, Yahvé is like the faithful loving husband; and thus two conceptions are introduced into the Old Testament, which, from this time onwards, were never again absent from it. Hosea is the prophet of the Divine love; no Old Testament writer has spoken of it with more fervour and depth of feeling than he. In utterances which are harsh, compressed, and which often break off abruptly, but which are full of bold flights, and rich in grotesque images and turns, he pours forth his whole heart. Hosea does not shrink from being bizarre and almost repulsive. He is not afraid, in the interests of Yahvé and of His great cause in Israel, to lay open to the gaze of the whole world the depths of his inner life and the secrets of his house and heart.

It is his endeavour above all to set forth the sins of Israel in their true form, and in all their offensiveness. The main evil from which Hosea sees his nation to be suffering, is that Israel has forsaken the true God. It is all the same to him whether they run after Baal and other idols, or whether they worship Yahvé in a way which is not worthy of Him—it is idolatry. Israel is forsaking her own husband and running after strange men. He appeals to the sons of Israel thus:[1]

> 'Plead with your mother, plead;
> For she is not my wife, neither am I her husband:
> And let her put away her whoredoms from her face,
> And her adulteries from between her breasts; . . .

---

[1] Hosea ii. 2, 5, 8 (R.V.).

> For their mother hath played the harlot: she that conceived them
> hath done shamefully:
> For she said, I will go after my lovers,
> That give me my bread and my water, my wool and my flax, mine oil
> and my drink. . . .
> For she did not know that I gave her
> The corn, and the wine, and the oil,
> And multiplied unto her silver and gold,
> Which they used for Baal.'—('From which they made a Baal'—so
> Kittel.)

The great part of the prophecies of Hosea, and probably the composition of his book generally, belongs to the time after the death of Jeroboam II. With the fall of the dynasty of Jehu, the worship of strange gods had doubtless again penetrated anew into Israel. Before this, bull-worship and worship on high-places had roused the prophet to utter denunciations, because this material representation of God was a denial of the holy character of Yahvé, and because, besides this, the lascivious orgies of the Canaanitish nature-worship often went along with it. It must have all the more kindled his anger when he saw that this very nature-worship itself had again begun in an undisguised form to get a lodgment in Israel:

> 'Whoredom and wine and new wine take away the understanding.
> My people ask counsel at their stock, and their staff declareth unto
> them. . . .
> They sacrifice upon the tops of the mountains, and burn incense upon
> the hills,
> Under oaks and poplars and terebinths, because the shadow thereof
> is good:
> Therefore your daughters commit whoredom, and your daughters-in-law
> commit adultery.
> I will not punish your daughters when they commit whoredom,
> Nor your daughters-in-law when they commit adultery,
> For they themselves go apart with whores,
> And they sacrifice with the harlots.'[1]—('Consecrated harlots'=Kedeshas
> —so Kittel).

But, indeed, the calf and image-worship is itself wickedness enough. It is bringing about the fall of Israel once more, after

---

[1] Hosea iv. 11 ff. (R.V.).

the revolt from Baal and the return to Yahvé under Jehu had again exalted it:

> 'When Ephraim spake, there was trembling;
> He exalted himself in Israel:
> But when he became guilty in Baal, he died.
> And now they sin more and more, and have made them molten images of their silver,
> Even idols according to their own understanding,
> All of them the work of the craftsmen;
> They say of them:
> Let the men that sacrifice kiss the calves.'[1]

Israel's guilt is added to also by the open immorality in which high and low, and, above all, the accredited leaders of the nation, the priests and prophets, have a share.[2] Usurpation, tyranny, and anarchy, such as had been the order of the day since the death of Jeroboam, could not possibly improve matters.[3] Nor, in Hosea's judgment, can Menahem's attempt to gain over the Assyrians who, since the fall of Syria, have been standing close to the borders of Israel, avert destruction, any more than the efforts made probably about the same time to turn Egypt into Israel's friend.[4] They only confuse the judgment and turn men's eyes from Him who alone is able to help, if He willed to be gracious. But though for the present He has rejected His people, and given them up to misery, His love cannot allow Him to abandon them for ever. Israel must fall together with its monarchy, which from the first was contrary to Yahvé's will. But when that has happened, the judgment will have purified it, and God will then have pity on it:

> 'It is thy destruction, O Israel, that thou art against me, against thy help.
> Where now is thy king, that he may save thee in all thy cities?
> And thy judges, of whom thou saidst, Give me a king and princes?
> I have given thee a king in mine anger,
> And have taken him away in my wrath, . . .

---

[1] Hosea xiii. 1-2 (R.V.).
[2] Hosea iv. 1 ff., 5 ff.; v. 1; vi. 8 ff.; vii. 1 ff.; ix. 15; x. 9; xii. 9.
[3] *Cf.* Hosea vii. 7; viii. 3 f.; x. 3, 15; xiii. 10 f.
[4] *Cf.* Hosea v. 13; vii. 11; viii. 9; x. 6; xii. 2; xiv 4.

> O death, where are thy plagues?
> O Sheol, where is thy destruction? ("pestilences," so Kittel).
> Repentance shall be hid from mine eyes. . . .
> They shall fall by the sword,
> Their infants shall be dashed in pieces,
> And their women with child shall be ripped up.'[1]

But now the picture changes. God's merciful love opens up a path for itself:

> 'I will betroth thee unto me for ever;
> Yea, I will betroth thee unto me in righteousness, and in judgment, and in loving-kindness, and in mercies, . . .
> And it shall come to pass in that day, I will answer, saith the LORD,
> I will answer the heavens, and they shall answer the earth,
> And the earth shall answer the corn, and the wine, and the oil;
> And they shall answer Jezreel (= Israel). . . .[2]
> I will heal their backslidings, I will love them freely;
> For mine anger is turned away from him. . . .
> O Ephraim, what have I to do any more with idols?
> I have answered, and will regard him:
> I am like a green fir tree:
> From me is thy fruit found.'[3]

Still more than Amos, the man of Judah, did Hosea direct his glance hopefully to the 'fallen dwellings of David.' Judah is indeed far from being free from sin,[4] still it is at least better than Israel, and the future belongs to it and to its royal house. Sometime those belonging to the Northern Kingdom will return to Judah from which they have revolted, and again recognise David as their rightful king.[5] This can hardly astonish us. And there is accordingly no occasion for declaring such passages to be spurious additions.[6] If once Ephraim's worship of God, 'the calf of Bethel

---

[1] Hosea xiii. 9-11, 14^b; xiv. 1^b (R.V.).   [2] Hosea ii. 21, 23 f.
[3] Hosea xiv. 5, 9 (R.V.).   [4] *Cf.* Hosea v. 10, 13, 14; vi. 4; viii. 14.
[5] Hosea iii. 5; ii. 2; x. 11; *cf.* iv. 15.
[6] So Wellhausen, Stade, Cornill. See also against, Kuen. § 66, 8 ff. The passages are no more to be disputed than Amos ix. 11. If Hosea shows himself to be acquainted with the thoughts in 1 Sam. viii. (*cf.* xiii. 10; on the other hand, viii. 4 may very well refer to usurpers such as Shallum and Menahem, and ix. 9, on account of x. 9, may refer to Judges xix. ff.), no objection whatever can be drawn from his fundamental dislike of the monarchical constitution against the fact of his actual preference for the Davidic dynasty. *Cf.* further, Oort in *T. Tijd.* 1890, 345 ff.; [Cheyne, Introd. to new ed. of W. R. Smith's *Prophets*, p. xxviii. f.].

and Samaria,'[1] were recognised as 'vanity,' a prophet's love of his fatherland could not hinder him from casting his eye towards Jerusalem and its Temple. Judah and Jerusalem appeared to him clothed in fresh splendour, and their House of David in its security which defied the centuries, stood exalted high above the kingdom of Ephraim, which was slowly consuming itself.

It is only in the form of a supplement that I venture here to say a word on Joel. The age of this prophet is still a subject of keen controversy. If previously Joel was regarded as the oldest of the prophets who wrote down their prophecies, from year to year the number of those is increasing who assign him to the latest period of prophecy.[2] Still there are not wanting even in the present day defenders of the earlier date.[3] So far as my own opinion goes, the latter seems more and more doubtful, still I recognise the weight of the reasons which can be alleged in its support

If we could with reason maintain that Joel is older than Amos, then a good deal of what has been ascribed to Amos above would have to be referred to Joel. The history of prophecy would in this case be altered in more than one direction. The literary activity of the prophets would, according to this view, have begun at least a half a century earlier than we have hitherto supposed. The ideas of the unity, the spirituality, and the moral righteousness of Yahvé[4] would, in this case, have been expressed all this earlier, with the same clearness with which they are stated by Amos and Hosea. We have no right whatever to assert that in itself all this is impossible. Still, even granting this, we cannot but allow that the time of Jeroboam II. and of the prophets Amos and Hosea, with the prospect which it offered, was suited as no other was, for giving a central position to those thoughts in the religion of Israel.

---

[1] See *e.g.* Hosea viii. 5, 6 ; x. 5.

[2] Best worked out in Kuen. § 68, 1. In addition, see Holzinger, *ZAW.* ix. 89 ff. ; Cornill, *Grundr.* 174 ff. ; Driver, *Introd.* 287 ff.

[3] To these belongs also, Reuss, *Gesch. d. AT.*² 257 ff.

[4] *Cf.* Joel ii. 27 ; iii. 1 ff. ; chap. iv.

CHAPTER V.

THE END OF THE NORTHERN KINGDOM.

§ 67. *Azariah-Uzziah. Menahem.*

THE successor of that Amaziah of Judah, who in all probability had to pay by his death for his arrogant conduct towards Israel, was his son *Azariah*. In Isaiah and Chronicles[1] he is called *Uzziah*. This latter name has also to a certain extent got into the Book of Kings, but it is not original there.[2] The relation between the two names is not very clear. However, the Assyrian inscriptions seem to point to the fact that as king he bore the name of Azariah.[3] It is possible that he may have changed his name when he ascended the throne.[4]

The Book of Kings dwells very briefly on his long reign, put by it at fifty-two years (78- ?–737).[5] The only bit of information given regarding his deeds refers to the fortifying of Elath, which is ascribed to him. This is, in any case, closely connected with his father's successful campaigns against Edom. From the statement that he restored Elath to Judah, we may perhaps conclude that this town had already been taken by his father, and that it had been lost after his death, so that Azariah had to get possession of it again.[6] In any case, the possession of this important seaport on the Red Sea points to a revival of trade and to new pros-

---

[1] With the exception of 1 Chron. iii. 12.
[2] *Cf.* LXX. in 2 Kings xv. 13, 30, 32, 34.
[3] See Schrader, *KAT.*² 223 ff. [Eng. Trans. i. 215 ff.]. But see below, p. 336, note 1.
[4] Another possibility supported by Wellhausen; see in Stade, *Gesch.* i. 569, note 1.
[5] 2 Kings xv. 1-6; *cf.* xiv. 21 f.   [6] See above, § 62, at the end.

perity.¹ Besides this, the Book of Kings mentions only Azariah's illness and death. 'And Yahvé,' it is said, 'sent a plague upon the king, so that he was leprous unto the day of his death.'² As he was no longer able to carry on the affairs of government, his son Jotham appears to have exercised a kind of regency during the king's lifetime. The text of the Book of Kings points at any rate to this, when, although it mentions the formal accession of Jotham only after Azariah's death, it at the same time tells us that Jotham had already during the king's illness carried on the most important part of the work of government, namely, the giving of decisions. It is only by means of this assumption that the serious chronological difficulties presented by the relation in which the two kings Azariah-Uzziah and Jotham stand to one another can be in a measure got over. It is extremely probable that Jotham's regency, entirely or in great part, coincides with his reign. The year of Azariah's death must be very close to that of Jotham.³

Chronicles is able to give us more detailed information regarding Azariah, whom it calls Uzziah, than the Book of Kings. According to it Uzziah had no inconsiderable success in his undertakings against Judah's neighbours to the south, the west, and the east—a success which won for him a respected name. His later illness, on the other hand, is connected in the Book of Chronicles with a conflict which he had with the Temple priesthood. His successes in war, it is said, puffed up his heart, so that he presumed to enter the Temple with the burnt-offering. In vain did the priests seek to prevent him from committing this act of presumption; but for this he was smitten with leprosy as a punishment from Yahvé.⁴

I cannot, on internal grounds, entirely reject the first of these

---

¹ *Cf.* Isa. ii. 16.

² 2 Kings xv. 5. Regarding the place of his residence, *cf.* Stade, *ZAW.* vi. 156 ff. ; also Klost. *Sa. Kö.*, on this passage.

³ See, on this and generally on the chronology of the period of the Kings, above, § 53 *a*

⁴ 2 Chron. xxvi. 1-15, 16-23.

narratives. What Isaiah says presupposes, in the time before the outbreak of the Syro-Ephraimitish war, a certain measure of prosperity and military strength in Judah. After the mournful defeat at the hands of Israel, with which Amaziah ended his reign, the description given by Isaiah of the times of Uzziah and Jotham is not intelligible unless Azariah had meanwhile succeeded, in some way or other, in making good the damage again. Successes on the part of Judah against the Northern Kingdom are not probable so long as Jeroboam II. lived. On the contrary, the perfect silence of our accounts regarding any conflict between the two kingdoms during this period, points in all probability to the fact that Judah was to a certain extent in subjection to Israel. The more Israel, under Jeroboam II., was able to act independently with reference to the Syrians, the less would it be disposed to allow the success it had gained against Amaziah to remain unused. All this goes to prove that the account in Chronicles of certain successes of Azariah on the other borders of his kingdom is based on historical reminiscences. It was at the price of an involuntary alliance with the Northern Kingdom that Azariah was free to proceed unhindered against his neighbours. We have, in fact, good grounds for supposing that Azariah directly supplied a contingent to Jeroboam II. in connection with his Syrian conquests, and that, after Jeroboam's death, he advanced into Syria on his own account.[1] If he was in a condition to do this, he must have had strength enough to advance against his nearest neighbours.

Nor ought we to reject straight off the other account in Chronicles of an encounter between Azariah and the Temple priesthood which was fraught with serious consequences for him. When we consider what an influence the priest Jehoiada was able in the time of Athaliah to exercise on the destinies of the royal house, we shall see that here too the inner reasons are not wholly wanting which make it probable that Azariah's removal from the government had a close connection with a conflict in which he had been involved with the Temple priesthood.

---

[1] See on this below, p. 335 ff.

Under Azariah's son, Jotham[1] (737, rel. 751-753), according to the Book of Kings, the first attacks on Judah by the united Syrians and Ephraimites took place. These form the beginning of the so-called Syro-Ephraimite war, which will have to occupy our attention again. With the exception of certain services rendered in connection with the Temple fabric, our source is not able to supply any further information regarding Jotham.[2]

In the Northern Kingdom, with the death of Jeroboam II., the star of the dynasty of Jehu sinks, and at the same time that of the kingdom. Usurpers follow one another in quick succession. The sword of the one removes the other, until finally the last one, and with him the kingdom, becomes the prey of a mightier power. Of the few kings of the kingdom of Ephraim who died a natural death, Jeroboam II. is the last. He is followed by his son Zachariah,[3] who, after a reign of only six months (740), is murdered by Shallum[4] ben Jabesh, the head of a conspiracy formed against him.

The murderer himself holds possession of the throne only for a month. Menahem ben Gadi[5] (740-737) marches 'from Tirzah' against him, takes Samaria, and there deprives him of his life. This shows that Shallum had never been undisputed king. We are at the same time able to get a glimpse of the seething anarchy after the death of Jeroboam II. Tirzah had formerly been the capital of the Northern Kingdom. It is still a strong fortress, and is in fact in the possession of Menahem—in any case in the time of Shallum, and probably also in the reign of Zachariah. This means that after Jeroboam's death Menahem ben Gadi was able to get hold of the one half of the kingdom, and Shallum ben Jabesh of the other. Shallum may have been the more prompt of the two, and so he succeeds in getting Zachariah out of the way, and thus, for the moment, secures the throne for himself. But he

---

[1] 2 Kings xv. 32-37.
[2] Chronicles tells us further of a war against Ammon (2 Chron. xxvii.), which is to be judged of in the same way as the wars of Uzziah.
[3] 2 Kings xv. 8-12.   [4] 2 Kings xv. 13-16.
[5] 2 Kings xv. 17-22; cf. 14, 16.

has to reckon with his rival who is in possession of the strong Tirzah, and from this as his headquarters he fiercely attacks with fire and sword all who do not submit to him,[1] and, after a month, he gets Samaria itself into his power. But even this does not end the civil war. It is extremely probable that even as early as this the two neighbouring great powers, Egypt and Assyria, played a certain *rôle* in Israel. The one party appears to have favoured a junction with Egypt, the other, a junction with Assyria.

We can easily understand what an overwhelming impression must have been made on contemporaries by the state of things of which we here get a glimpse in the Book of Kings. However modest the circumstances of Judah might be, still it had the advantage of a fixed dynasty, which put it out of the reach of commotions of this kind which endangered the very existence of the kingdom. The extent to which the seed of rebellion, out of which the Northern Kingdom had grown, represented at the same time the curse of this whole kingdom, had never before been shown in such a vivid form. It came to be more and more clearly recognised that it was radically diseased and could not possibly be healed. Anarchy and usurpation were, and continued to be, its mark of Cain. 'They chose kings,' cries Hosea, 'without me rulers of whom I knew nothing. . . . They all glow like an oven and devour their judges; all their kings fall, not one among them calleth unto me.'[2] And Isaiah, with clear reference to these times of the civil war, says of Ephraim: 'Each eats the flesh of his own arm, Manasseh Ephraim and Ephraim Manasseh.'[3]

The consequences of this self-laceration are soon evident. 'In his day,' says the Book of Kings in reference to Menahem, 'the Assyrian king Pul came into the land, and Menahem gave Pul one thousand talents of silver, in order that he might stand by him and confirm his authority.'[4] *This is the first occasion on which Assyria sets foot on the native soil of Israel.*

---

[1] 2 Kings xv. 16. The text must be altered in accordance with the LXX. See in part Stade, *ZA W.* vi. 160, and also Kamph. in Kautzsch's translation.
[2] Hosea viii. 4; vii. 7. *Cf.* also above, pp. 326, 327, and note 6.   [3] Isa. ix. 19, 20.
[4] 2 Kings xv. 19. The beginning of the verse is to be restored as in the LXX.

An encounter between Israel and Assyria in Israel's own land was, of course, inevitable. After the opposition of Damascus had been actually broken down, it was only a question of time. But it is certainly no mere accident that it takes place just at this time. Tyranny and civil war have weakened the kingdom; no one party is able by its own strength to become master in the country. The one side seems, as Hosea tells us,[1] to have sought support in Egypt, the other in Assyria. Menahem too does not yet feel secure upon his throne. Civil strife still goes on. Even if Menahem had had uncontested possession of his throne, it would have been an easy matter for Assyria, after what had happened, to have undertaken an invasion of Israel. If we in the first instance allow the Old Testament to speak for itself, the supposition suggests itself that Pul, invited by Menahem and his party, was able to make good use of the disturbed state of things in Israel in order to organise an expedition for the conquest of Samaria. It will also be seen to be probable that Pul had other reasons for advancing against Israel. Menahem secures the withdrawal of the enemy and, at the same time, purchases the safety of his throne against the attacks of his opponents at home, by paying a shameful tribute.

The means employed by Menahem to raise the tribute claim our attention. The sum required is assessed on those bound to bear arms.[2] This is only intelligible if those bound to bear arms are at the same time the holders of property. It would thus seem that at this period the old custom was still in vogue in Israel, according to which those who had no property were exempt from military service. The possessors of landed property share the burdens of the state and also military service amongst themselves. If we reckon the talent at 3000 shekels,[3] the result we arrive at, on the basis of an assessment of 50 shekels for each individual proprietor, is, that in the time of Menahem there were in the Northern Kingdom 60,000 families who possessed heritable lands.

---

[1] See above, § 66, p. 326.
[2] 2 Kings xv. 20. See also Meyer, *Gesch. d. Alt.* 449.
[3] See Schrader in the *HWB.*, under Talent and Sekel.

We are now in the favourable position of being able to throw some further light on this expedition of the Assyrian king Pul against Menahem of Israel, by the aid of the Assyrian monuments. It was for a long time supposed, and it has now been proved with certainty,[1] that Pul was no other than Tiglathpileser III.,[2] one of the most powerful of the Assyrian conquerors (745-727). He informs us in his Annals that he exacted tribute from Menahem of Samaria, as he did from Hiram of Tyre and Rezin of Damascus.[3] We gather at the same time from the Assyrian accounts that this paying of homage by Menahem to the Assyrian king is to be placed in the eighth year of the reign of Tiglathpileser, and so in the year 738 B.C.[4]

In order, however, to reach the inferences which we are able to draw from our present standpoint in connection with Israelitish history, mention must be made here of another event in the history of Tiglathpileser to which our attention is called solely by what we find in the Assyrian accounts. In the annals of Tiglathpileser III. we find two important fragments,[5] which, spite of the defectiveness of the text, make this much at least perfectly clear, namely, that Azariah of Judah is here mentioned as the opponent of Tiglathpileser, and in fact as being at the head of a coalition of Syrian towns formed against Assyria, which 'in their wickedness and sin had attached themselves to the party of Azariah.'[6] These events too must be referred to the year 738, or to a time a little previous to this.[7]

It is preferable to examine these last-mentioned accounts first. Azariah of Judah cannot possibly be any other than the king long known to us as Azariah-Uzziah. All attempts to

---

[1] See especially Schrader, *KGF*. 422 ff. ; *KAT*.² 227 ff. [Eng. Trans. i. 219 ff.] ; Tiele, *Gesch*. 227.

[2] He is the third, and not, as was supposed until recently, the second of this name. See Schrader, *KBibl*. ii. 2, note 1.

[3] See Schrader *KAT*.² 223 [Eng. Trans. i. 215]; *KBibl*. ii. 31.

[4] See Schrader, *KAT*.² 222 f. [Eng. Trans. i. 214 ff.]; Tiele, *Gesch*. 231.

[5] See Schrader, *KAT*.² 218 ff. [Eng. Trans. i. 209]; *KBibl*. ii. 25 ff.

[6] See especially iii. R. 9, Nr. 2, Z. 3, 4 (8 ?), 10, and iii. R. 9, Nr. 3, Z. 23, 31.

[7] Schrader, *KAT*.² 223 [Eng. Trans. i. 215]; Tiele, *Gesch*. 229 f.

combat this identification,[1] partly on the ground that according to our established chronology, Azariah must at this time have been long since dead, partly on the ground that the Bible accounts do not lead us to suppose that Azariah mixed himself up with affairs in Northern Syria, are of no avail. However unlikely it may seem from the standpoint of the Bible account, still, as a matter of fact, Azariah must have been involved in some way or other in the battles in the region of Hamath, and our task simply is to bring the sudden appearance of this king in Syria into connection with what we otherwise know regarding him.

If we recollect that Jeroboam II. is supposed to have extended the borders of Israel as far as Hamath,[2] further, that Azariah-Uzziah in all probability stood in some kind of relation of dependence to Jeroboam,[3] we may find in this the key to the understanding of these further accounts of Azariah. Azariah supplied Jeroboam with a contingent in the wars of the latter against the Syrians of Damascus already weakened by Assyria. At the time of the decline of the Assyrian Empire under Assurnirâr, they succeeded in extending their own authority in Northern Syria at the cost of the Assyrians. After Jeroboam's death (about 740) Azariah takes advantage of the disturbances in the kingdom of Ephraim in order to continue on his own account in Syria the policy hitherto pursued in common with Israel. The change of throne in Assyria seemed to supply a favourable opportunity. Hamath makes common cause with

---

[1] Gutschmid, *Neue Beitr. z. Gesch. d. alt. Orients*, 55 ff.; Wellh. *JDTh.* xx. 632; Klost. *Sa. Kö.* 496. [If I had to write on this subject now, the treatment of it would necessarily differ considerably from that given in the text, written three years ago. Since then an unexpectedly new light has been cast on this question by the discovery of the ancient Aramæan inscriptions of Sendschirli (*Mittheilungen aus den Orient. Sammlungen der Königl. Museen zu Berlin*, xi. 1893) in which likewise a land Jaudi plays a part. This renders it again doubtful if the king mentioned in the cuneiform writings is really our Azariah-Uzziah. If the view that they are one and the same becomes untenable, then of course the conclusions based on this identification go too. I hope very soon to be able to take up a definite position with regard to the whole question. Meanwhile compare Winckler, *Altor. Forsch.* i. 1 ff.; M'Curdy, *Hist. Proph. and the Monuments*, i. 413-415.]

[2] 2 Kings xiv. 25. See above, p. 295.   [3] See above, p. 331.

Azariah against Assyria, and perhaps Damascus also. But the powerful Tiglathpileser was not the man to look calmly on plottings of this kind: in 739 or 738 Hamath is reduced to subjection, after its army, together with that of Azariah, had been beaten.

The only difficulty still remaining has reference to the relationship between Azariah-Uzziah and his son Jotham. Judging from the Biblical accounts we would necessarily expect that at this time Jotham had for a long period been occupying the place of his sick father. If we do not wish to put Azariah's illness so far down, we can still fall back on the possibility that Azariah is mentioned only as the nominal king of Judah, while, as a matter of fact, Jotham was regent. The same view may be taken of the statements in Isaiah.[1]

As soon as Hamath is reduced to subjection, Tiglathpileser (738) turns against the rest of Syria. Israel, too, in which the Egyptian party represented at once the party of Jeroboam II., and the party opposed to Menahem, is to be punished for the encroachments of Jeroboam. Assyria's interference may have been welcomed by Menahem's party,[2] which was the Assyrian party, since it propped up Menahem's still shaking throne. But it was in truth merely a miserable momentary success. It appears, further, that Tiglathpileser advanced as far as Samaria.

§ 68. *The Syro-Ephraimitish War. Isaiah's first appearances.*

Menahem cannot have long survived his disgrace. For in 734 we already find his second successor on the throne. He must thus have died soon after 738. For this reason it is not probable that the ten years' reign assigned to him in the Book of Kings[3] corresponds to the actual facts. His successor is his son Pekahiah,[4] who, however, after a short reign—of two years

---

[1] Isaiah vi. 1. See also above, at the beginning of this paragraph.

[2] For Hosea's judgment on this see above, p. 326.

[3] 2 Kings xv. 17. See on his and Pekah's times above, § 53a.

[4] 2 Kings xv. 23-26. The text in *v.* 25 is corrupt. See Stade, *ZAW.* vi. 160.

(737-735), according to the Book of Kings—was slain by his charioteer Pekah ben Remaliah (735-734/3). He is said to have broken into the royal palace, at the head of a band of Gileadites.

Pekahiah's dethronement was undoubtedly the consequence of the disgraceful agreement which his father had made with the Assyrians. For if those in Syria were not entirely smitten with blindness, it must have been seen that the sole hope of resisting the renewed and reckless advance of Assyria lay in a close combination of all the Syrian states. If that succeeded, then there was, at any rate, some hope of Syria being able once more, as it had done one hundred and twenty years earlier, to meet the assault of the enemy. Naturally enough, the Egyptian party also renewed its activity. Pekah was probably its tool even. Only, as things were at that moment in Egypt, no help was to be looked for from that quarter. The national Egyptian rulers had used every endeavour to keep off the Ethiopians,[1] who were constantly making new assaults on them. However much they may have been interested in warding off the Assyrian danger, it was little that they could contribute in the way of help.

We can thus understand how in Syria use was made of the first opportunity which presented itself of abandoning the ancient feuds, in order with united strength to keep off the all-powerful foe. During the years 737-735 Tiglathpileser is occupied in the far East,[2] and he would certainly have had occasion for remaining longer there if he had not been called back to Syria by the pressing state of things in that region. Here in his absence two old enemies have come to an agreement. The common danger makes Pekah of Israel and Rezin of Damascus forget the quarrel between the two kingdoms, which was centuries old. The two principal Phœnician cities, Tyre and Sidon, join them, as does also an Arabian queen, Shamsî.

Only, on the other hand, a not inconsiderable portion of Syria will have nothing to do with the confederation. Its fate was thus sealed beforehand, if it did not succeed in compelling the waverers

---

[1] See Meyer, *Gesch. d. Alt.* 428.   [2] Tiele, *Gesch.* 231.

to join. To these belong, on the one side, the Northern Phœnicians, and especially the Hittites; and on the other, the countries of Southern Palestine: Judah, Ammon, Moab, Edom, and the Philistines.[1] To win them over is necessarily the grand aim of the allies.

In Judah King Jotham is reigning about this time (± 736) either by himself or as regent for his invalid father Azariah.[2] The Book of Kings informs us that at this time Yahvé stirred up the two kings, Rezin of Aram-Damascus and Pekah of Israel, against Judah.[3] If it is at all allowable to take the meagre statements in our Bible sources in connection with world-events, then we are justified in regarding the common attack of Rezin and Pekah on Judah as a consequence of the refusal of Jotham to join the confederacy against Assyria. The Book of Kings connects the account of Jotham's death[4] with the statement referred to, and does this in a fashion which suggests the thought that Jotham died soon after the beginning of the war. This is in harmony with the picture which we are otherwise able to form of the course of events. According to it, the war must have been continued into the reign of Ahaz of Judah.

The strife which thus broke out in Palestine itself is known in history as *the Syro-Ephraimitish War*. We have three different sources of information regarding the events in it—the Book of Kings, Tiglathpileser, and the prophet Isaiah. And we cannot speak of it without thinking of this last-mentioned powerful man, who for some years had been taking part in public life, and who impressed the stamp of his character on his whole age.

Isaiah ben Amoz[5] is a native of Judah, but his thoughts are not occupied with Judah alone. From the days of Uzziah to the the end of the reign of Hezekiah, and consequently for more than

---

[1] See on these points Tiele, *Gesch.* 233; and in addition, 3 R. 10, Nr. 2, 12 ff.; 2 R. 67, 57 ff. However, see now on the Phœnician cities, Winckler, *Gesch. Bab.* 333.   [2] See on this above, pp. 330, 331, 332.   [3] 2 Kings xv. 37.

[4] 2 Kings xv. 38. Verses 37 and 38 form together a supplement to the history of Jotham. *Cf. v.* 36.

[5] See Duhm, *Theol. d. Prof.*; Guthe, *Das Zukunftsbild des Prof. Jesaja*; Driver, *Isaiah: His Life and Times*; Dillmann, in the Exeg. Handb.; Kuen. § 41 ff.

a generation, he closely followed all the events of any consequence which happened in the nation, and dealt with them in his prophetic utterances. He lived through the Syro-Ephraimitish war, the fall of Samaria, the threatening of Jerusalem by Sennacherib, and in all these changes of fortune he represented the voice of Yahvé to his nation. His thoughts are not entirely new. He stands on the shoulders of his predecessors, Amos and Hosea. But he far surpasses them both in manysidedness, depth and force of thought, and in the energy and breadth of his religious views of things. His language is sustained and lofty, frequently full of colour and highly poetic; his imagination is rich in striking comparisons and appropriate images. Isaiah is a master of eloquence, and excels in producing an overpowering effect.

But, above all, Isaiah is the type *par excellence* of a prophet of God in Israel. What holds good of the prophets of Israel generally is true of him in a very special degree. He is eminently a *religious personality*,[1] wholly steeped in the great religious thoughts supplied by the religion of Yahvé, and by them he is borne onward to the highest flights of enthusiasm and hope. Like Moses and Elijah, he belongs to the religious heroes of his nation, in whom the really peculiar and deepest side of the national character of Israel, and its world-historical mission to the nations of the world, found their most complete expression. The figure of Isaiah stands out as a landmark, visible far and wide, in the history of his nation. He was, in fact, one of those lamps which spread their light far beyond the limits of this one people. His thoughts have become history. They breathed new breath into the expiring Israel, and new life into generations long after. He who recognises and reveres the traces of God in history, will not fail to see in a figure such as that of Isaiah, the man of God.[2]

Isaiah's first appearance in public life was in the last year of Uzziah. Perhaps at the time of his first utterances Uzziah had

---

[1] See on this above, § 65.

[2] [See my little work: *Aus dem Leben des Prof. Jesaja* (Akademische Kanzelreden) 1894.]

Chap. V.]   THE END OF THE NORTHERN KINGDOM   341

not yet been humiliated by Tiglathpileser; at any rate, Jotham does not seem to be as yet threatened by the two allies. The power of Judah is still unbroken: 'their land also is full of silver and gold, neither is there any end of their treasures; their land also is full of horses, neither is there any end of their chariots.'[1] But behind the dazzling outside, Isaiah sees the corruption within; injustice and oppression of the poor, the frivolous pursuit of pleasure, along with superstition and shameless apostasy:

> 'Woe unto them that join house to house,
> That lay field to field, till there be no room,
> And ye be made to dwell alone in the midst of the land! . . .
> Of a truth many houses shall be desolate,
> Even great and fair, without inhabitant! . . .
> Woe unto them that rise up early in the morning, that they may follow strong drink;
> That tarry late into the night, till wine inflame them!
> And the harp, and the lute, the tabret and the pipe, and wine, are in their feasts:
> But they regard not the work of the Lord, neither have they considered the operation of his hands.
> Therefore my people are gone into captivity, for lack of knowledge:
> And their honourable men are famished, and their multitude ["revellers," so Kittel] are parched with thirst.'[2]

A terrible judgment must accordingly come upon Judah. The Holy One of Israel does not suffer himself to be mocked. A 'day of Yahvé of Hosts' is about to come on all the still existing glory of Judah:

> 'Upon all the cedars of Lebanon, that are high and lifted up, and upon all the oaks of Bashan; . . .
> Upon all the ships of Tarshish, and upon all pleasant imagery ["costly curiosities," so Kittel]. . . .
> And the idols shall utterly pass away.
> And men shall go into the caves of the rocks, and into the holes of the earth,
> From before the terror of the Lord, and from the glory of his majesty,
> When he ariseth to shake mightily the earth.'[3]

As soon, however, as the threatening clouds show themselves

---

[1] Isaiah ii. 7 (R.V.).   [2] Isaiah v. 8, 9, 11-13 (R.V.).
[3] Isaiah ii. 13 f., 16, 18 f. (R.V.).

on the horizon of Judah, and it becomes evident that the alliance between Ephraim and Aram threatens Judah first of all, Isaiah straightway takes up a new position. The judgment of Judah will not fail to arrive; but what threatens here is not the scourge of God, but the work of man: a torch which is already burned out has only smoke, not fire. Ephraim's policy, and all its doings, have for years been marked by blind infatuation; its destiny is a chain of divine judgments which has not yet reached it end. They said:

> 'The bricks are fallen, but we will build with hewn stone:
> The sycomores are cut down, but we will change them into cedars.
> Therefore the Lord hath set up on high against him the adversaries of Rezin ["oppressors," so Kittel] and hath stirred up his enemies:
> The Syrians on the east, and the Philistines on the west, and they have devoured Israel with open mouth. . . .
> Yet the people hath not turned unto him that smote them. . . .
> Therefore the Lord hath cut off from Israel head and tail, palm-branch and rush, in one day. . . .
> For all this his anger is not turned away, but his hand is stretched out still.'[1]

And Ephraim's ally, Damascus, will fare no better than Ephraim itself. If Ephraim's fortresses must become like the long desolate and ruined dwelling-places of the Hivites and Amorites who once fled before Israel, the same lot is in store for Damascus and its inland towns. 'They shall be for flocks, which shall lie down, and none shall make them afraid. The fortress also shall cease from Ephraim and the kingdom from Damascus; and the remnant of Syria shall be as the glory of the children of Israel, saith the Lord of Hosts.'[2]

This, perhaps, was how Isaiah judged of things at the beginning of the war, while Jotham still lived and the traditions of Azariah's successes had still an influence on people's minds. But Jotham dies, and then what Isaiah had already anticipated takes place. 'I will give children to be their princes, and babes shall

---

[1] Isaiah ix. 10 ff. (R.V.). See on the only correct interpretation of the passage, Dillmann in his Commentary.

[2] Isaiah xvii. 2, 3 (R.V.). *Cf.* v. 9, and for the text the Commentaries.

rule over them. O my people! children are their oppressors, and women rule over them.'[1] Jotham's place is taken by his still youthful son, Ahaz.[2] Judah, which at this time so urgently needed a strong and resolute man to guide it, falls into the hands of a youth of twenty, who possessed neither experience of life nor the moral force and stability which come from a firm faith in God. The whole burden of looking after the good of the land rests, as it so often did, on the shoulders of prophecy—the best proof of the peculiar significance and importance of this unique phenomenon in Israel.

It is highly probable that it was the death of Jotham, and the accession of the youthful Ahaz who succeeded him, which spurred on the allies to make a fresh attempt to win over Judah to their side. In any case, their main action in the matter occurs in the reign of Ahaz. Rezin undertakes an expedition in a southern direction which costs Judah the possession of Elath, the source of the wealth of the kingdom of Judah under Azariah and Jotham. It goes back to its old possessors, the Edomites. But the allies next prepare to make a direct attack on Ahaz. With their united forces they move towards Judah in order to capture Jerusalem, and, if possible, to dethrone the obstinate Ahaz.[3]

When matters took this turn, Judah did not know what to do. The Assyrian party in Jerusalem and at the court of Ahaz could point to the example of Menahem, for whom, in his sore straits, Tiglathpileser had, a few years before, proved himself a deliverer. In that instance, as in the present one, those against whom Judah had appealed to Assyria were the enemies of the latter. On receipt of the bare news of the advance of the enemies against Judah, Ahaz and all Jerusalem, in their dismay, lost their heads,[4] and the king seems to have formed his resolution before the

---

[1] Isaiah iii. 4, 12 (R.V.).   [2] 2 Kings xvi.
[3] 2 Kings xvi. 5, 6; Isaiah vii. 2, 5 f. The events of 2 Kings xvi. 6 may precede those of v. 5, since a fresh beginning is made in each verse.
[4] Isaiah vii. 2. Perhaps Ahaz on this occasion offered up his son. *Cf.* 2 Kings xvi. 3. Stade, p. 596, places the event slightly later; but the text of Isaiah viii. 6 is much too uncertain.

prudent among his counsellors could check him by their advice. He sends ambassadors to Tiglathpileser, and, in humble language, submits himself to the great king. His humble prayer for help against his enemy is backed up by the despatch of the whole store of silver and gold which was laid up in the Temple treasury and the royal exchequer.[1]

In following this short-sighted policy, Ahaz had the public opinion of Jerusalem on his side. Modern historians, too, have taken him under their protection. Ahaz, it seems, did what any other in the circumstances would have done.[2] Isaiah's judgment is different, and he knows that it is in harmony with the counsel and will of Yahvé. While Ahaz is at the aqueduct leading from the upper pool,[3] superintending the preparations which it was most needful to make in the event of the capital being besieged, Isaiah seeks him out with the words: 'Take heed, and be quiet; fear not, neither let thine heart be faint, because of these two tails of smoking firebrands, for the fierce anger of Rezin and Syria, and of the son of Remaliah. ... It shall not stand, neither shall it come to pass. For the head of Syria is Damascus, and the head of Damascus is Rezin; and the head of Ephraim is Samaria, and the head of Samaria is Remaliah's son. *If ye will not believe, surely ye shall not be established.*'[4]

What the prophet in these words preached to the king is faith, trust in God. Isaiah was hardly fool enough to imagine that a hostile attack could be met with folded arms and eyes directed to heaven. But as things now stood, his conviction undoubtedly is that nothing can help Judah save God alone. If He does not help, then Judah is lost—wherever it may turn to among men for help. And there is only *one* means of getting this help, to be quiet and trust in God. The issue proved that Isaiah was right. In the present distress his advice was undoubtedly

---

[1] 2 Kings xvi. 7-9. [2] Stade, *Gesch. Isr.* i. 595.
[3] On this locality see Dillm. *Isaiah*, p. 65 f.
[4] Isaiah vii. 3 f., 8 f. (R.V.). 8*b* is a gloss. [The assonance of the original Hebrew is so far preserved in the German —' *Glaubet ihr nicht so bleibet ihr nicht.*' We might perhaps say, 'If ye will not confide, ye shall not abide.'—Tr.]

the right one. Jerusalem could hold out against a siege for a time. Meanwhile Tiglathpileser, if he had the interests of his empire at heart, had on his own account to march against the allies, whose cause was lost from the first, seeing that all Syria did not unite. In this case the Assyrian had no occasion for troubling himself about Judah at all, and Ahaz preserved for the present, at any rate, that measure of independence which his father had handed down to him.

Isaiah accordingly, so long as there is still time, works with all his might to convince the king how disastrous for Judah the interference of Assyria must necessarily be. He sees in spirit the Assyrian troops on the one side and the Egyptian on the other, spreading themselves over the fields of Judah,[1] and he sees how Judah is already playing the *rôle* of the unfortunate apple of contention between the two world-powers, if Ahaz means voluntarily to tear down the last bulwark that still separates Assyria and Egypt. Isaiah, certain of what he says, and full of belief in his God, has recourse to a last expedient. He offers even to work a miracle for the king, in order to prove that he is speaking the truth. But even this does not move the feeble Ahaz; he will not tempt God.

And so the die is cast; the ambassadors are not brought back; Isaiah's words and trouble are all in vain. Isaiah sees what must be the inevitable result, and he lets it be known. Judah's terrible fate and its mournful ruin are clear to him. But now as a proof that faith is no empty delusion, he rises in the very midst of these so depressing circumstances to the loftiest heights of hope and trust. If for the present only misery and wretchedness are the lot of Judah, and if the house of David itself has sunk down to the ground, the 'if ye will believe ye shall be established' must nevertheless retain its truth. A new generation, which will spring from the tearful sowing of the present, will know this in its own experience. It will, with a strong arm, drive the enemy out of the land, and will see a new king of the stock of David at its

[1] Isaiah vii. 18 f.

head—but it will no longer be a kingdom of war and of this world, but a kingdom of God, a kingdom of peace and of righteousness.

The hour in which Isaiah parted from Ahaz gave to the world the thought of the Messiah.

'Hear ye now, O house of David: Is it a small thing for you to weary men, that ye will weary my God also? Therefore the Lord himself shall give you a sign: Behold, a maiden shall conceive, and bear a son, and shall call him "God-with-us" ('Immanu'ēl). Curds and honey shall he eat when ["until," so Kittel] he knoweth to refuse the evil and to choose the good. For before the child shall know to refuse the evil and choose the good, the land whose two kings thou abhorrest shall be forsaken. The Lord shall bring upon thee, and upon thy people, and thy father's house, days that have not come, from the day that Ephraim departed from Judah.'[1] Assyria will afflict the land and make it desolate, so that it soon will be the haunt of cattle and sheep, and its inhabitants, instead of bread and wine, shall live on milk and wild honey. But the time of distress will pass away; the child with the name so full of promise is growing up, and founds in Zion a new kingdom of David:

'For unto us a child is born, unto us a son is given;
And the government shall be upon his shoulder;
And his name shall be called Wonderful, Counsellor, Mighty God, Everlasting Father, Prince of Peace.'[2]

When and where the ambassadors of Ahaz fell in with Tiglath-pileser, we do not know. It is not impossible that he was already on the way to Syria, which he meant once more to reduce to subjection without the co-operation of Ahaz. At any rate, we find the great king actually present in Syria in the year 734, with the intention of chastising the rebels. As Isaiah had foreseen, the work was not one of particular difficulty, owing to the disunion amongst the smaller states. Damascus alone seems to have offered an energetic resistance.

[1] Isaiah vii. 13-17 (R.V.).   [2] Isaiah ix. 6 (R.V.).

The Book of Kings relates that Tiglathpileser took away from Pekah, Ijon, Abel-beth-Maachah, Janoah, Kedesh, and Hazor, also Gilead, Galilee, and all the land of Naphtali, and carried their inhabitants away to Assyria.[1] With this agrees both what we learn from Isaiah,[2] and what the great king himself tells us.[3] Samaria itself was saved for this time from capture and destruction, owing to the fact that the party opposed to Pekah promptly murdered him, and presented his murderer, Hoshea, to the great king as his successor (734/3).[4] After Israel is thus chastised and Jerusalem delivered, Tiglathpileser (733) turns his attention to Damascus. The Bible briefly relates that he conquered Damascus, carried off its inhabitants, and slew Rezin.[5] From the information supplied by the great king himself, on the other hand, we gather that the siege and capture of the strong Syrian capital occupied him for two years.[6]

Ahaz has attained his immediate end; his two opponents have been slain by the sword, and their lands wholly or in part have fallen to the enemy. But amongst other things, a narrative in the Old Testament which proves that the matter was not ended by the paying of tribute once, shows us at what a price Ahaz bought the advantage of being a *protégé* of the great king. The great king expected further acts of homage, and it was taken for granted that Ahaz, as his loyal vassal, would henceforth take Assyrian customs and usages as the pattern to copy, both in the affairs of daily life and in matters of worship. Accordingly Ahaz, after the capture of Damascus, waits on Tiglathpileser in that city. There he happens to see an altar, a model of which he sends straight to his priest Uriah in Jerusalem, and has one made the same for the Temple.

---

[1] 2 Kings xv. 29. But see also Stade, *ZAW*. vi. 160.

[2] Isaiah viii. 23.

[3] See on this Schrader, *KAT*.[2] 258 ff. [Eng. Trans. i. 251 ff.]; *KBibl*. 30 ff.; Tiele, *Gesch*. 234 f. There also on the chronology. It will not do to identify the names, 3 R. 10, 2, 17, with Gilead and Abel-Maachah.

[4] 2 Kings xv. 30 = 3 R. 10, 2, 28 f. The Assyrian date determines the end of the reign of Pekah.   [5] 2 Kings xvi. 9.

[6] See the Eponym lists with the notices attached under 733 and 732, and on Lay. 72 f., see *KBibl*. ii. 31 f., note.

The new altar takes the place of what, up to this time, had been the altar of burnt-offering.[1] This does not mean in the least that the worship of Yahvé was displaced. It can hardly have been an altar of Rezin's that is referred to.[2] As soon as Damascus came into the possession of the Assyrians, they would introduce their own form of worship. Ahaz sees the Assyrian chief altar in Damascus, and thinks he will gain the favour of the great king by imitating it. Ahaz otherwise does not show any very particular regard for the Solomonic Temple.[3] Most of the measures drawn up by him in this connection are to be attributed to the necessity he was under of getting money, while we undoubtedly have incidental references which suggest the view that Ahaz introduced the star- and sun-worship of Assyria into Jerusalem, and had even sacred horses of the sun at the Temple of Jerusalem.[4]

§ 69. *Samaria's End.*

Both kingdoms—Israel and Judah—could have enjoyed for the immediate future undisturbed peace under the protection of Assyria, if they had kept quiet and rested content with the actual condition of things. Ahaz took this way, and succeeded in keeping his throne for many years. In Israel, on the other hand, things do not calm down. Since 732 Tiglathpileser has been occupied in the east, and in 727 he quits the scene. Salmanassar IV. takes his place (727-722). The absence of the great king, and, still more, the change of throne in Assyria, inspire the independent party in Samaria with new hope.

Egypt does its best to nourish these hopes. For the further Assyria had in recent years penetrated into Syria, the more the kingdom of Pharaoh must have felt that the position it had hitherto held was being seriously threatened. It was simply aiming

---

[1] 2 Kings xvi. 10-16.   [2] So Stade, *Gesch.* 598.
[3] 2 Kings xvi. 17, 18; text and translation are, however, doubtful.
[4] 2 Kings xxiii. 11-12. Ahaz, in any case, is to be included amongst the 'Kings of Judah' who are there mentioned; whether or not still earlier kings are referred to is a point which may be left undecided.

a blow at itself if it did not do all that was in its power to check Assyria and incite the Syrian states to resist the great king. It was high time that Egypt was abandoning its old policy of inactivity which it had been compelled to adopt owing to the state of affairs at home. The victory of the Ethiopian Sabako by which, after long struggles inside the country, Egypt was at last delivered into the hands of the Ethiopian ruler, brought with it for a time at least an orderly state of things for Egypt, and consequently made it possible to pay some attention to affairs in Syria.[1] We accordingly find Sabako in alliance with the Syrian states; and from this time till the days of Assarhaddon, Egypt continues to be the constant disturber of the peace who labours to stir up the Syrian states against their oppressor. Hanno of Gaza, who had remained for a while as a fugitive in Egypt, returns home either immediately after the death of Tiglathpileser, or some years later, in order, under the influence of Egypt, to urge the Syrian states to revolt; and the Old Testament informs us that Hoshea of Israel, in consequence of an understanding with King Seve of Egypt,[2] had given up paying the tribute.[3] One is inclined to identify Seve with Sabako; but if they were not one and the same, then Seve must have been an under-king of Sabako's.[4]

Salmanassar could not look calmly on at the revolt of Samaria, because the Assyrian supremacy over all Syria was at stake. He must have set out soon after his accession, possibly in the second year of his reign. For if the statement that Hoshea reigned nine years is correct, then Salmanassar must have come against him as early as 725. He seems to have surrendered at discretion to the great king on the latter's advance. Hoshea is taken captive, and very likely

[1] See Meyer, *Gesch. Ägypt.* 343 ff.
[2] The MT. gives it, though in all probability erroneously, Sô; *cf.* Ass. Sab'i.
[3] *Cf.* 2 Kings xvii. 3-6. The whole section, although possibly originating with K, or going back to it, gives us nevertheless a very inexact account. (See Stade 600, note 1.) We can for this reason hardly infer from *v.* 3 that there was an earlier expedition of Salmanassar against Hoshea. The verse merely says that Hoshea did homage to Salmanassar, first of all, on his accession.
[4] So Winckler, *Unters. z. altorient. Gesch.* 91 ff. *Cf.* Schrader, *KAT.*² 269 f. [Eng. Trans. i. 261 ff.].

shared the fate of the other prisoners. His capital, Samaria, on the other hand, is not disposed to yield on such cheap terms to Assyria. Salmanassar has to set about a regular siege; and, owing to its strong position, Samaria succeeds in holding out for three full years. Salmanassar himself is not fated to live to see the capture of the city.[1] According to the well-authenticated Assyrian accounts, Samaria fell into the hands of his successor Sargon (722).

During the time of Salmanassar's advance and the siege of Samaria, Judah, as will be readily understood, has been earnestly directing her gaze towards her northern neighbour. It was doubtless owing to Isaiah's influence that Ahaz kept quiet, and resisted all the attempts which were undoubtedly made to allure him to revolt.[2] Had he acted otherwise, it would probably have been all over with Judah at this time. But Isaiah is convinced that Samaria, too, will gain little this time by her foolhardy attempt. Her measure is full. But Judah may learn a lesson from what it sees being accomplished here. 'Woe to the crown of pride of the drunkards of Ephraim,' he cries, in reference to Samaria, 'and to the fading flower of his glorious beauty, which is on the head of the fat valley of them that are overcome with wine! Behold, the Lord hath a mighty and strong one; like a tempest of hail, a destroying storm, as a tempest of mighty waters overflowing, shall he with violence cast it down to the earth. The crown of pride of the drunkards of Ephraim shall be trodden under foot.'[3]

About the same time, besides Isaiah, there rises up in Judah a like-minded prophet—perhaps a pupil of Isaiah's—Micah ben Moresheth. He too is certain about Samaria's downfall and destruction:

> 'Behold, the Lord cometh forth out of his place,
> And will come down, and tread upon the high places of the earth.
> And the mountains shall be molten under him,

---

[1] Incorrectly 2 Kings xviii. 10.

[2] Perhaps the statement about Judah's subjection by Sargon in the inscription from Nimrûd refers to this. See Tiele, *Gesch.* 238; [but *cf.* Cheyne, *Introd. Is.* p. 4].

[3] Isaiah xxviii. 1 ff. (R.V.).

> And the valleys shall be cleft
> As wax before the fire,
> As waters that are poured down a steep place.
> For the transgression of Jacob is all this,
> And for the sins of the house of Israel.
> What is the transgression of Jacob? is it not Samaria?
> What are the high places of Judah? are they not Jerusalem?
> Therefore I will make Samaria as an heap of the field,
> And as the plantings of a vineyard :
> And I will pour down the stones thereof into the valley,
> And I will discover the foundations thereof.'[1]

Micah has no fear that for the present Jerusalem will be destroyed.[2] For as it did not oppose Assyria, there was no ground for any quarrel. But it was easy to see that the waves which swept Samaria away would not leave Judah wholly unharmed. Moreover, Judah's sins were like those of Ephraim; if Yahvé were again to swing His scourge, the end would have come for Judah too.[3] The blows which strike Ephraim are not deadly for Samaria only: 'They come even unto Judah, and reach unto the gate of my people, unto Jerusalem.'

It is only to a limited extent that we can say with certainty what became of the inhabitants of the conquered country. Part of them, in accordance with the custom of the Syrian and Babylonian kings which we hear of first in connection with Tiglathpileser, were carried away from their homes. According to Sargon's inscriptions,[4] he carried into captivity 27,290 of the inhabitants of

---

[1] Micah i. 3 ff. (R.V.). The prophecy must clearly be put before 722, and with this the indication of the date of the Book of Micah in i. 1 agrees. For this reason, only ch. iii. (see v. 12) can be claimed for the reign of Hezekiah, to which Kuenen, on account of Jer. xxvi. 18 f., would refer it. There is no unanimity of opinion regarding the original extent of the Book of Micah. See Stade, ZAW. i. 165 ff.; iii. 1 ff.; iv. 291 ff.; Nowack, ZAW. iv. 277 ff.; Ryssel, Unterss. über Textgestalt und Echtheit d. B. Micha, 1887; Kuen. § 73 f. An essential part of the question is as to the position of the prophecy on the Maççēbas and Ashēras (cf. v. 12), regarding which it is difficult to come to any satisfactory conclusion, owing to the small number of instances in which they are certainly mentioned. But cf. above, § 64, and below, p. 357.

[2] Micah iii. 12 (against Kuen. § 74, 3) (R.V.).   [3] Micah i. 8 ff.

[4] See Winckler, Die Keilschrifttexte Sargons (1889), (not accessible to me). Further, Schrader, KAT.² 266 ff. [Eng. Trans. i. 260 ff.]; KBibl. ii. 35 ff., especially 55.

Samaria, while he left the remainder in the country under an Assyrian governor. Those carried away doubtless represented the leading element in the state: officials and proprietors, army and priesthood. According to our Bible Book of Kings, they were transplanted to Assyria; amongst other places, the Habor, a tributary of the Euphrates, and the 'towns of the Medes,' are mentioned as their new place of abode.[1]

Those who remain behind, and who naturally form the great mass of the people, are Assyrian subjects; while the country from being a tributary vassal-state has become a regular Assyrian province. But it does not reconcile itself to this fate without once more attempting to find deliverance in revolt. The Old Testament tells us nothing about it, but it is mentioned in Sargon's inscriptions.[2] According to them, it appears that immediately after Sargon's departure from Syria the opposition to Assyria was organised anew. Ilubi'di of Hamath headed the party of resistance. Almost all Syria to the north of Samaria joined in the rising. Samaria itself, willingly or not, was drawn into the movement. In the south, Hanno of Gaza and the Egyptian Seve (Sab'i) support the confederates. Judah belongs to the few exceptions who prefer to remain on the side of Assyria. In the year 720 Sargon is accordingly once more back in Syria. He does not allow his opponents to unite. Ilubi'di is promptly beaten at Qarqar. Thereupon the great king proceeds towards the south, and defeats the united Philistines and Egyptians at Rapihi, doubtless the place which was afterwards the Raphia of the Greeks, not far from Gaza on the Egyptian frontier. Samaria's resistance is thus finally broken; at all events, the Assyrian accounts tell us nothing further of any attempt to shake off the foreign yoke.

Probably in consequence of these disturbances Sargon, at this time and on other occasions later on, settled foreign colonists in

---

[1] 2 Kings xvii. 6; xviii. 2. See on each of the places Schrader, *KAT.*[2] 275 f. [Eng. Trans. i. 267 ff.]; and Siegfr. and Stade in their *Lex.* It is, however, worthy of notice that the LXX. gives what is partly a different text. [*Cf.* also Ainsworth, *Proc. Soc. Bibl. Arch.* 1892, p. 70 ff. (The two Captivities)].

[2] Tiele, *Gesch.* 259 f., and *KBibl.* ii. 55, 57.

Samaria. Thus Sargon himself mentions 'prisoners from different lands,' whom he had transported to Syria,[1] and he mentions in particular some Arabian desert-tribes, who had refused to pay tribute to him, and who were accordingly transplanted from their home.[2] Along with them the Old Testament mentions some Babylonian towns, the inhabitants of which Sargon transferred to Samaria.[3] These may be the same as those who, according to Sargon's own account, were transferred to the land of the Hittites in consequence of the disturbances in Babylon.[4] Some decades later, in the reign of Assarhaddon, a new addition of foreign elements was made to that already existing.[5]

The Northern Kingdom has now reached its end. Even if the great majority of the inhabitants remain, still the vital pith of the nation is gone, and the last shadow of freedom has disappeared for ever. A foreign nationality and a foreign religion mingle with those of Israel. Assyrian governors and officials bear rule in the land; Assyrian, Babylonian, and Arabian blood destroys the purity of the old native families, and foreign gods are worshipped at the sanctuaries. At first the Israelites struggle against them as well as they can. Bethel for some time longer preserves its ancient character as a sanctuary of Yahvé, indeed it even seeks to exercise an influence on the heathen colonists.[6] To a certain extent it must have succeeded too, for the altar of Bethel[7] is still standing in the time of Josiah, and the pre-exilic narrator in the Book of Kings passes a not exactly unfavourable judgment on the religious worship practised there.[8] Indeed, when the inhabitants of Judah return, they find here a people who had

---

[1] In his Annals, l. 16, *cf.* Winckler, *Keilinschr. Textb.* 27. On the time, see Tiele, *Bab.-ass. Gesch.* 258.

[2] Schrader, *KBibl.* ii. 43 (cylinder inscription, l. 20).

[3] 2 Kings xvii. 24.

[4] Schrader, *KAT.*² 276 [Eng. Trans. i. 276].

[5] *Cf.* Ezr. iv. 2 (*KAT.*² 373 f.). In Ezra iv. 10 the reference is clearly to the same event.

[6] 2 Kings xvii. 26 ff. *Cf.* Jer. xli. 4 ff.

[7] 2 Kings xxiii. 15; *cf.* 19 ff.

[8] 2 Kings xvii. 24-28, 41. See on this, and generally on chap. xvii. above, p. 219.

clung to the worship of Yahvé. But those who returned no longer recognise them to be flesh of their flesh, nor do they recognise their God to be the old Yahvé of the prophets. They separate themselves from the *Samaritans*. Foreign rule and foreign influences have made them into something different from what they were. And if they themselves wished to be sons of ancient Israel also, still it was hardly pure pride on the part of the returned exiles that they could barely discover in them the features of ancient Israel.[1]

---

[1] See further on the Samaritans in Kautzsch, *PRE.*³ xiii. 340 ff.

CHAPTER VI.

THE ASSYRIANS IN JUDAH. JUDAH'S END.

§ 70. *Hezekiah* (715-686).

IN the fierce storms which burst over Samaria and had swept it away, Ahaz of Judah had succeeded in escaping untouched. He had made a prudent calculation of all circumstances, and had firmly supported the Assyrian rule, and he consequently kept his throne until the end of his life, and at his death handed it over to his son Hezekiah. The change of throne took place probably in the year 715.[1] Hezekiah began to rule while still undoubtedly very young, perhaps while barely a youth.[2] It was his good fortune to have men like Isaiah and Micah at his side.

It is to their influence that we have to trace certain measures taken by Hezekiah for the improvement of the worship of Yahvé, which our narrator tells us about—and probably rightly[3]—in connection with his accession. Hezekiah did not only, according to this account, break in pieces a brazen image of a serpent, called Nehushtan—a relic of ancient serpent-worship[4]—which had had divine honours paid to it in Jerusalem since ancient times, but the suppression of the high-places as well as of the Maççēbas and Ashēras is also ascribed to him.[5]

---

[1] See above, p. 238; and on Mic. iii. 12 above, p. 351, note 1.

[2] See Kamphausen, *Chronol.* 37.

[3] Differently Rob. Smith, *Prophets of Isr.* 363; Stade, *Gesch.* 608, 623; Renan, *Hist.* ii. 518; [Cheyne, *Introd. to Isaiah*, 365]. Isaiah xxx. 22 has not reference to public sanctuaries, but to household images which had been still preserved.

[4] *Cf.* the snake-stone in Jerusalem, above, p. 178. Perhaps, too, Nehushtan was connected with it.   [5] 2 Kings xviii. 4; *cf.* 22.

This account in our Book of Kings, so far as it deals with high-places, Maççēbas and Ashēras, has of late been described in certain quarters as unhistorical. Grammatical as well as historical arguments have been advanced against its genuineness.[1] As a matter of fact, the mode of expression in this verse cannot possibly be made to harmonise with the laws of the older Hebrew language.[2] There can accordingly hardly be any doubt but that the sentence in its present form was not written by a pre-exilic narrator. Nor is the circumstance that the abolition of high-places is presupposed in *v.* 22 necessarily conclusive for the historicity of this fact. For it is evident that if this bit was written by a later author, things may very probably be put into Rabshakeh's mouth that he never actually said. It is further urged that neither Isaiah nor any other prophet of the eighth century declaimed against the high-places, Maççēbas and Ashēras, which it is here presumed were suppressed by Hezekiah. We are, it is argued, precluded from supposing that Hezekiah went further than prophecy itself.

Spite of this I do not think that the information regarding Hezekiah's reform should be rejected. The account, of which *v.* 22 forms part, leaving out of view the incorrect supposition in reference to Sennacherib's death, seems based on sound information, and nowhere shows traces of post-exilic, or in fact of any specially late origin.[3] We are justified in doubting the correctness of its statements only if they are contradicted by really weighty facts. These, however, I am not able to find. That Isaiah does not directly declaim against high-places is correct enough; but his contemporary Micah certainly did it. If the former did not show any interest in their suppression, the latter

---

[1] See Wellh. *Bl.*[4] 255; *Prol.*[2] 26 [Eng. Trans. 23]; Stade, *ZAW*. iii. 8 ff.; vi. 170 ff.; *Gesch.* 607 f.

[2] See an attempt in Köhler, ii. 2, 263. But the example in 2 Sam. vii. 8-10 offers no analogy to our text. There we have perfect tenses which reach down to the present; here we have not, since the Maççēbas and Ashēras return again. So, too, the instances adduced by Driver, *Notes* on 1 Sam. i. 12 (*cf.* also 2 Sam. xvi. 5) are all of a different kind. *Cf.* further Gesen.-Kautzsch, *Gramm.*[25] 325 f.

[3] See above, p. 221 f.

undoubtedly did.[1] But Isaiah would in this case be guilty of a want of thoroughness which, though certainly intelligible enough in J and E, which are not acquainted with the peculiar importance of Zion, would hardly be intelligible in his case. He declaims against images and stands up for Zion; but what are the altars in the land without their images as compared with Zion? If they fall, the altars must fall too. Apart from Yahvé's unity, His spirituality has no meaning. If thus 2 Kings xxii. 4 in its present form is also late, this by no means proves that it is unhistorical. The reviser appears to have enlarged the verse because of *v.* 22.

If, then, Hezekiah abolished the sanctuaries of Yahvé outside Jerusalem, he must at the same time have felt it necessary to remove the old Canaanitish sacred symbols—the Maççēbas and Ashēras[2]—which were attached to them. We may indeed assume that it was because of these appendages that the altars were put down. And supposing that even in recent years they made their way into the Temple of Jerusalem,[3] Hezekiah was bound, when he once began to put away the heathen and half-heathen rubbish, to remove them twice over. This lay in the nature of the case. Probably, therefore, we have no occasion to deny that the Micah from whom we have complaints respecting the high-places also spoke against Maççēbas and Ashēras.[4] And if we find no such denunciation in Isaiah, there may be accidental reasons for this; but even supposing it proved that Isaiah allowed[5] the Maççēbas, though not the Ashēras, it would be more reasonable to suppose that Micah, followed by the king, went a step further

---

[1] Mic. i. 5. The explanation given of this passage in vol. i. p. 108, note 4, is now purposeless. I have meanwhile come to the conviction that the reading of the MT. is correct as opposed to the LXX. The LXX. gives merely a simplification.

[2] The text in *v.* 4 mentions only *one* Ashēra, while the translations, on the contrary, have the plural. If the singular is correct, the reference must be to an Ashēra which had found its way into the Temple in the time of Ahaz.

[3] See the foregoing note, and above in § 64, 4.

[4] Mic. v. 12 f. See on this Stade, *ZAW.* iii. 8 ff.; iv. 291 ff.; Nowack, *ZAW.* iv. 277 ff.; Ryssel, *Micha*, on this passage; Kuen. § 74, 6; and above, p. 351.

[5] Isa. xix. 19. But the interpretation is uncertain.

than Isaiah, than to claim the right of correcting him in accordance with Isaiah.

There can be no doubt as to the intention of Hezekiah and those who supported him in thus limiting the worship of Yahvé to Jerusalem. Samaria's fall so loudly proclaimed Yahvé's destroying wrath, that they felt compelled to try and turn it away. Priests and prophets were at one in maintaining that Israel's apostasy from the Yahvé in Zion, who had no image, had been its destruction. The same fate awaited Judah and Jerusalem if they did not thoroughly repent.[1] The youthful king listened to them more readily than his father had done. If Judah wished to escape Israel's fate, it was necessary that her worship of God should be kept free of those elements which had brought about Israel's fall. But this end could be perfectly attained only if all the other sanctuaries outside of Zion were put down. For even if in favourable cases it was Yahvé who was worshipped, still there was always a great danger that the Yahvé of Hebron or Beersheba should be regarded as different from the Yahvé of Zion,[2] and in this case polytheism and heathenism would be once more secured in all their rights. But it is just the very greatness and far-reaching significance of this thought which supplies the explanation of the defective way in which it was carried out in the reign of Hezekiah. The revolution which was now aimed at was too great to allow of its being carried through all at once. The axe was laid at the root of the tree, the decisive blows which brought it down followed later on. But it does not follow that because the first blows did not at once lay it flat with the ground that they were not given.

Hezekiah resembled his father Ahaz in few points. One might rather say that in many points he fell back on the fundamental principles of his great-grandfather Uzziah. He, like Uzziah, takes certain measures, the object of which is to secure the military

---

[1] *Cf.* Mic. iii. 12. Some of the threatenings of Isaiah may belong to this period.

[2] Wellh. *Prol.*² 27 [Eng. Trans. p. 24].

safety of his country, and especially of his capital: as, in Uzziah's time, Judah's treasuries and arsenals are now also well filled; like Uzziah, he ventures to take up a hostile attitude towards Assyria. We have unfortunately very little information regarding the chronology of the events of his long reign. We neither know when he was victorious over the Philistines,[1] nor at what period of his reign the aqueduct ascribed to him was constructed. Perhaps the war with the Philistines was a legacy left him by his father Ahaz as a consequence of Judah's refusal to join the rising under Hanno of Gaza. And since we know that Hezekiah's revolt from Assyria had been prepared long beforehand, we may reasonably suppose that the construction of his aqueduct[2] is to be referred to the earlier years of his reign.

His object in making the *aqueduct* was doubtless to add to the defence of Jerusalem in the case of a siege.[3] Jerusalem does not possess any flowing water inside the city walls. The only important spring in the immediate neighbourhood of the city is the Gihon on the eastern declivity of the ridge on which the ancient fortress of David had been built, and on which the royal palace now stood. The project readily suggested itself of conducting the water of the Gihon inside the city wall in order to be perfectly protected against the possibility of a want of water in any circumstances that might arise. If at first an attempt was perhaps made to have the aqueduct above ground, reasons were soon forthcoming for making the connection underground. It was thus that aqueducts originated of the same sort as the conduit from the Gihon, the Maria-spring of the present day, which leads to the Pool of Siloah, regarding the construction of which the old Hebrew inscription[4] found in it in 1880 gives us some information. Unfortunately the inscription tells us nothing of the time when the cutting through the Temple hill was made. But since the Book of Kings tells us that Hezekiah 'made the pool

---

[1] 2 Kings xviii. 6; *cf.* also below, p. 371.

[2] 2 Kings xx. 20; *cf.* 2 Chron. xxxii. 30.

[3] *Cf.* the statement in 2 Chron. xxxii. 5, which certainly rests on a correct reminiscence.   [4] See on it also above, p. 230.

and the conduit, and brought water into the city,' and Chronicles expressly connects this statement with the Siloah conduit, there is scarcely any room for doubting that Hezekiah is the constructor of that very Siloah conduit and of one of the Siloah pools.[1]

If the youthful Hezekiah was thus intent from the beginning of his reign on strengthening his defences and making sure of his military equipment, we may gather from this that, as in religious matters, so also in political life, a new spirit had entered Judah with the change in the throne. The party which was under the influence of Egypt and hostile to Assyria, the party of the 'Patriots' who were strong for a revolt from Assyria, must very soon have gained the ear of the young king. The fact that the breach did not take place a great deal sooner than it actually did is apparently to be ascribed wholly to the influence of Isaiah.

§ 71. *Sennacherib in Palestine.*

As soon as Sargon had withdrawn from Palestine after the battle at Raphia, the opposition to Assyria was again reorganised. Ashdod now formed the centre of the movement, taking the place of Gaza, which had been suppressed. Its king Azuri, relying on help from Egypt, seems to have succeeded in getting the South-Palestine nationalities, and amongst them Judah, to band together to resist Assyria. This is, at all events, Sargon's[2] account; while, on the contrary, the Old Testament is silent as regards Hezekiah's share in the undertaking of Ashdod. Probably when Sargon sent his army to Palestine the allies abandoned Azuri in time to save themselves, so that the Assyrian general, called

---

[1] *Cf.* the plan of Jerusalem as it is to-day in Ebers and Gunthe, *Pal.* i.; further Riehm, *HWB.* Art. *Jerus.*, Nʳ. 10 and Siloah; *Bädeker,*[3] 102. Differently Stade, *Gesch.* 593 f. He considers the Siloah conduit to be older, chiefly on account of Isaiah viii. 6. But there may quite well have been a 'water of Siloah' before this, as the name, 'Ain Silwan, still attached to the place, seems to indicate. See also Dillm. on Isaiah viii. 6.

[2] See the fragment in Winckler, *Keilinschr. Textbuch*, 31. [Cheyne, *Introd. Is.* 20.]

Tartan, had practically only Ashdod to deal with. The siege of Ashdod ended, as was to have been expected, in the capture of the town. Its inhabitants were carried away into captivity, 711.[1]

In this case, too, Egypt's blandishments had had a very decided influence. We are not left in any doubt as to Isaiah's opinion about them, which is expressed in one of the few utterances of his to which we can with certainty assign a date. In chap. xx., on the occasion of the siege of Ashdod, he prophesies the speedy downfall of the Egyptians and Ethiopians at the hands of Assyria, an event which is to happen within three years. And to Judah, which relies upon the untrustworthy friend, Egypt's downfall will bring shame and confusion. 'When this has been the fate of those in whom we hoped, to whom we fled for help and deliverance from the king of Assyria, how can *we* possibly escape?' That will be in brief the cry of Judah and of the rest of Palestine.[2]

From the first Isaiah was thus determinedly opposed to any junction with Assyria, but he was now quite as much against any thought of a revolt. If Assyrian protection inevitably involved many humiliations for Judah, the least of which was perhaps after all the yearly tribute, still, the friendship of Egypt appeared to him to be as little disinterested, and, as regards what it could actually offer in the way of help, to be far more unsafe.

After the fall of Ashdod, so long as Sargon lived, no Assyrian army again entered Palestine. Sargon was uninterruptedly occupied in the north and east until the end of his life. After a reign of seventeen years, which was rich in memorable deeds, and was crowned with unparalleled successes, Sargon died in 705, apparently by the hand of an assassin. He was succeeded by his son Sennacherib, more correctly Sanherib (705-681). If, as will readily be understood, the long absence of the Assyrian armies from the west had inspired the Syro-Palestine peoples anew with the thought of regaining their independence, the murder of Sargon, and the confusion in Assyria and Babylon which resulted from it,

---

[1] *Cf.* the Khorsabad inscription, line 90 ff., in Schrader, *KBibl.* ii. 65 ff. [*RP.* ix. 11.]   [2] Isa. xx. 1-6.

probably supplied the occasion desired for the formal renewal of the old offensive and defensive alliance against Assyria.

The circumstances just at this time appeared specially favourable for the carrying out of such a project. In Egypt, where the defeat of Sabako at Raphia and the fall of Ashdod were naturally followed by unfortunate results so far as the internal state of the country was concerned, the usurper Tirhaqa secured the throne just about the time of Sargon's death. He energetically resumed the policy of combating Assyrian influence in Syria, doubtless in the hope of thereby strengthening his throne. On the other hand, there appeared once more in Babylon one who was a dangerous opponent for the Assyrians, the Chaldean Merodach-Baladan.[1] Sargon had already had many a brush with Merodach-Baladan. On Sargon's accession he got himself elected king in Babylon, and he had succeeded in maintaining his position alongside of Sargon for twelve whole years. It was not till towards the end of his reign (710 or 709) that Sargon succeeded in becoming Merodach-Baladan's master. He fled to Elam. But scarcely had Sargon closed his eyes, when the indefatigable Merodach-Baladan again appears on the scene. In 702 he succeeds in regaining his kingship in Babylon by force.

Merodach-Baladan seems to have spent his long life in constant conflict with Assyria. The fact that he is found seeking alliance in the far West with Assyrian opponents proves what a serious view this tenacious and enterprising warrior took of his life's task. The Bible Book of Kings has preserved the recollection of this in the statement that Merodach-Baladan sent an embassy to Hezekiah to congratulate him on his recovery from a severe illness, and that Hezekiah showed his well-stocked treasures and arsenals to the ambassadors. There can be no doubt but that the main end of the embassy, regarding which, indeed, the Bible narrator is silent,[2]

---

[1] See on him Winckler, *Unters. z. altorient. Gesch.* 47 ff.

[2] The narrative will be found in 2 Kings xx. 12 ff.; it is preceded by that of the king's illness and recovery. It is clear from the position of chap. xx. after xviii. 13-19, 37, that the Bible narrator (see above, p. 222) no longer understands the proper purpose and connection of these events. Still, both narratives rest on historical recollection. [*Cf.* Cheyne, *Introd. to Isaiah*, 287 ff.]

was to urge Hezekiah to enter into the confederacy against Assyria. We thus get the date both of the embassy and of Hezekiah's illness and recovery. Both occurred shortly before Hezekiah's breach with Assyria.

When Egypt in the south and Babylon in the east were urging active measures and promised their help, it was certainly not easy for the Palestinian States to remain quiet. Who could tell whether they, too, might not succeed in doing what Merodach-Baladan had now for the second time been successful in doing in Babylon. They had only to remain unanimous and seize the right moment. In the north, Sidon specially seems to have been the centre of the movement; in the south, now that the power of Gaza and Ashdod had been broken, the Philistine cities of Ashkelon and Ekron seem to have occupied a similar position. It would appear that great importance was attached to the co-operation of Hezekiah in the movement, as is proved both by the embassy and by the leading place which he seems later on to have taken within the confederacy.

We are not able to say how far Hezekiah was from the first disposed to listen to those who were urging on a breach with Assyria. As we saw, the attitude he had so far taken up makes it probable that he needed very little persuasion. Besides, the war-party was without doubt strongly represented in Jerusalem and at the court. It had an easy task with the unthinking mob, as the party of the extreme patriots always has. On the other side, however, stood the party of the moderates and cautious-minded. It was, of course, as is always the case, in the minority, and at its head stood Isaiah. In the breach with Assyria he sees simply the seed of fresh disaster which will come upon Judah, and his recognition of this is not connected with friendly feelings towards Assyria—this he had shown under Ahaz—but springs from a clear insight into the actual condition of things.

Thus, soon after Sargon's murder, Isaiah, reflecting upon the fate of Gaza and Ashdod, had declared to the Philistines that Philistia should not too readily congratulate itself that the stick which had beaten them was broken; from the serpent an adder will spring, and its fruit shall be a dragon.[1] And now, while the plan of the rising is getting ripe for being carried into execution, he shows Jerusalem the fate which threatens it. Perhaps he will even yet succeed in preventing them from taking the decisive step. Apparently a whole cycle of Isaiah's utterances, chaps. xxix.-xxxii.,[2] belongs to this period of deliberation and planning. He employs all the force of his eloquence to keep king and people to the path of reason and prudence.

> ' Woe to the hearth of God, hearth of God, the city where David encamped!
> Add ye year to year, and let the feasts come round,
> Then will I distress the hearth of God, and there shall be mourning and lamentation,
> And she shall be unto me as a hearth of God!
> And I will camp against thee round about,
> And will lay siege against thee with a fort, and I will raise siege works against thee.'[3] . . .

The alliance with Egypt is a subject of special anxiety for Isaiah. He speaks of the kingdom of the Pharaohs with the utmost contempt. He hopes for no blessing for Judah from it, and only dreads further complications.

> ' Woe to the rebellious children, saith the Lord,
> That take counsel, but not of me,
> And make a league, but not of my spirit. . . .
> That walk to go down to Egypt. . . .
> To strengthen themselves in the strength of Pharaoh ("To shelter yourselves in the shelter of Pharaoh"—so Kittel)
> And to trust in the shadow of Egypt. . . .
> Through the land of trouble and anguish,
> From whence come the lioness and lion, the viper and fiery flying serpent ("flying dragon"—so Kittel),
> They carry their riches upon the shoulders of young asses,
> And their treasures upon the bunches of the camels
> To a people that shall not profit them!
> For Egypt helpeth in vain and to no purpose,
> Therefore have I called her, Rahab, that sitteth still'[4]—('Monster, that sitteth still'—so Kittel).

---

[1] Isa. xiv. 29-32. Perhaps v. 32 refers to the envoys of Merodach-Baladan, who had come to Philistia too. [Cf. Cheyne, Intr. Is. p. 82.]

[2] See e.g., Driver, Isaiah, 55 ff., and now also Guthe in Kautzsch. Somewhat differently, Dillmann in his Comm.   [3] Isa. xxix. 1-3 (R.V.)

[4] Isa. xxx. 1, 2, 6, 7 (R.V.); cf. Isa. xxxi. 1 ff.

The last-mentioned utterances of Isaiah against Egypt show that the prophet's efforts were in vain. Hezekiah's ambassadors are already on the way to Egypt, naturally laden with rich presents. Isaiah can at most only hope that they will be recalled, and that the alliance will be broken off. But neither does this take place. The anti-Assyrian party in Jerusalem, the party friendly with Egypt, seems more and more to have gained the upper hand. Hezekiah has made up his mind not to let the favourable moment slip past, in order to re-establish Judah's independence, and perhaps even the throne of David. He unreservedly joins the general rising, and, in fact, he appears to have taken a prominent position amongst the confederates; King Padi of Ekron, who remains true to Assyria, is vanquished by Hezekiah and taken prisoner.[1]

For the second time Isaiah appears here in all his religious greatness. Even at this stage, although he sees his nation taking the wrong road, he does not give up hope. Spite even of its folly Judah cannot yet perish. Yahvé will not forsake the House of David, nor abandon His holy place. But certainly deliverance will not come from the quarter in which Judah's leaders are seeking for it, and least of all from Egypt. Yahvé alone will be Judah's help. Those great thoughts which Isaiah had formerly cherished regarding Judah's future he still firmly clings to, even in this the time of supreme distress. The glorious future appears to his vision to be almost nearer than before. But it is no longer to issue from Judah's destruction. The misery of the siege of Jerusalem by Assyria appears to him in the light of the purifying judgment from which Judah, gloriously delivered, will come forth as a purified and new race, well pleasing to God. It will be only the sinners whom the judgment will sweep away; the city and temple of Yahvé will stand in the judgment. Zion is a sure corner-stone, against which every hostile power shall be dashed to pieces.[2]

---

[1] *Cf.* Sennacherib's prism-inscription, col. ii. 70-72 (Schrader, *KBibl.* ii. 93).

[2] [Differently, Cheyne, *Intr. Is.* pp. 83, 109.]

Sennacherib himself certainly acted with prudence in taking no notice at first of the Palestinian rising, although it was backed up by Egypt. He makes it his aim to deal with the evil at its root, and that lay in Babylon. The old rebel Merodach-Baladan must first be overcome. Sennacherib succeeds in crushing him in 702, and now he is free to turn his attention to the West in 701. According to Sennacherib's own detailed accounts,[1] his campaign in Syria divided itself into several sections. He is first of all occupied in reducing to submission the Phœnician cities from Sidon to Akko. In Sidon Sennacherib places a certain Eshbaal on the throne, and hands over to him by way of counterpoise to Tyre a certain number of Phœnician towns. He does not seem to have succeeded in capturing Tyre. From here he turns southward to attack the Philistine cities of Ashkelon and Ekron. King Ṣedeq (Ṣidqa) is conquered and is sent a prisoner to Assyria. Simultaneously with the advance of the Assyrians against Ekron a body of Egyptian and Ethiopian troops comes to the relief of Ekron. A battle takes place at Altaqu (Eltekeh). Sennacherib boasts of having gained a great victory here. In any case, the Assyrians hold the field, and the road to Ekron is now open for Sennacherib. The town falls into Sennacherib's hands, who executes a cruel judgment on the rebels, and later on compels them to accept the banished Padi once more as king.

Meanwhile most of the other rebels had preferred to yield to Sennacherib, and this was what Ammon, Moab, and Edom did. Judah alone persists in her attitude of resistance. The last stage of the whole campaign is occupied with the measures taken against Hezekiah. The Bible accounts come in here. It is astonishing that Sennacherib did not follow up his victory at Eltekeh, and that he thus gave the Egyptians an opportunity for rallying again. This leads us to suppose that the victory did such serious damage to Sennacherib himself that Hezekiah could venture to persist in his resistance. The Bible accounts, if we understand them

---

[1] See Schrader, *KAT.*[2] 285 ff. [Eng. Trans. i. 278 ff.]; *KBibl.* ii. 91 ff., and in addition Tiele, *Gesch.* 289 ff., 314 ff.

correctly, are in harmony with this view.¹ They tell us that Sennacherib advanced against all the fortified towns of Judah and took them. There would have been no occasion for this unless we suppose that Hezekiah had not yet consented to abandon his attitude of resistance. It is only now that Hezekiah resolves to submit to Sennacherib. Hezekiah's ambassadors announce his resolve in Lachish in the Shephela, the Assyrian headquarters. Sennacherib demands a tribute of 300 talents of silver and 30 talents of gold. After making the utmost exertions, Hezekiah is able to deliver it to him. The Temple and the treasuries of the king have to yield up their best in order that the sum may be got together. It was on this occasion that Hezekiah handed over Padi of Ekron, whom he had kept a prisoner, to Sennacherib, who restored him to his throne. But Sennacherib is not satisfied with the tribute. After he has it in his hands, he demands the cession of the capital. He sends a part of his army to Jerusalem under Rabshakeh, doubtless a general,² to compel Hezekiah to yield the city up. Negotiations entered into between Rabshakeh and Hezekiah's chief officials, the palace governor, Eliakim ben Hilkiah, the State-recorder Shebna, and the chancellor Joah ben Asaph, came to nothing. Rabshakeh prepares to besiege the city.³

In Jerusalem the unfavourable result of the negotiations produces a feeling of dismay. Hezekiah rends his clothes and appeals to Isaiah to plead for him unto Yahvé. But even at this juncture Isaiah is certain of the issue. 'Behold,' he is reported to have said to Hezekiah in a divine oracle pronounced regarding Sennacherib, 'I will put a spirit in him, and he shall hear a

---

¹ The two accounts, 2 Kings xviii. 14-16 and 2 Kings xviii. 13, 17-19, 9a, may, in accordance with the explanation given above, p. 220, be used as complementary parallel narratives.

² See on him Tiele, *Gesch.* 497. In a gloss the Book of Kings further mentions Tartan (the commander-in-chief) and Rabsaris (see on him Winckler, *Unters. z. altor. Gesch.* 138).

³ This is not actually said, but is the evident meaning of 2 Kings xviii. 26-37. He certainly advances with an army. This disposes of Stade's assumption (p. 621) that there never was an actual attack.

rumour, and shall return unto his own land, and I will cause him to fall by the sword in his own land' (R.V.). On hearing of Sennacherib's departure from Lachish, Rabshakeh seems for the moment to have raised the siege of Jerusalem, doubtless with the intention of returning again later on. But the breaking up of the headquarters at Lachish must itself have been connected with the news of Tirhakah's advance against Sennacherib. According to one account in the Bible Book of Kings, the same news not only leads Sennacherib to resolve not to resume the siege of Jerusalem, but to beat a retreat from Palestine altogether. He may have been haunted by the doubtful result of the battle of Eltekeh.[1] At the same time the disturbing news, too, which reached him from the East, without doubt led Sennacherib to decide on retiring. One can easily understand how the Old Testament had not more definite knowledge regarding these rumours. There is a second account in our Book of Kings, the one which Herodotus[2] also adopted, according to which a great pestilence breaks out in the Assyrian camp, with the help of which the angel of Yahvé destroys in one night 185,000 Assyrians. It is very possible that it too is historical,[3] and that all these circumstances contributed to the result.

There is hardly any room to doubt that the account here given corresponds in all essential points with the actual facts. For those very portions of it which we might expect to find again in the Assyrian accounts, agree in a remarkable way with it. These are the references to Sennacherib's attack on Judah, the submission of Hezekiah, and the siege of Jerusalem. Sennacherib[4] informs us that he took from Hezekiah of Judah, who would not submit to him, forty-six strong towns, and countless fortresses and small places, and captured 200,150 prisoners of every age and station. 'Him

---

[1] See Tiele, *Gesch.* 296.

[2] See Herod. ii. 141. Field mice are supposed to have taken up their quarters in Sennacherib's camp overnight. The mouse is the emblem of pestilence. *Cf.* 1 Sam. vi. [For a different view see Cheyne, *Introd. to Isaiah*, p. 233.]

[3] [On the other side, see Cheyne, *Introd. Is.*, *l.c.*]

[4] See Prism-inscription, Col. iii. 10 ff.

himself I shut up like a bird in his royal city Jerusalem. . . .' He laid on him a new tribute in addition to the former, since Hezekiah, he says, had been overpowered by the splendour of his sovereignty—namely, thirty talents of gold and eight hundred talents of silver, as well as utensils of ivory and fine woods, besides forcing him to deliver up his daughters and wives, his male singers and female singers.

If we make allowance for the obvious exaggeration of which the great king is guilty as regards the number of the prisoners captured, and also in the statement about the tribute,[1] and if we remember, on the other hand, that Sennacherib *is not speaking of the capture of Jerusalem* but only of a sending of tribute, we can still plainly see reflected in these Assyrian accounts the consciousness of the fact that Sennacherib had to retire before he had succeeded in making himself master of Jerusalem.

Isaiah had triumphantly shown himself to be in the right, and so too had his God Yahvé. Never had a prediction been more splendidly verified than this which Isaiah had here held out to his king and nation. When Sennacherib was still far distant—indeed, before the final breach with Assyria at all—he had reached a sure conviction that Yahvé would not abandon His city.[2] He is still more sure of this after Sennacherib has set out and is advancing against Judah. The greater the anxiety in Jerusalem becomes, the more joyous is Isaiah's certainty of victory. And as one after another the reports reach Jerusalem, bringing the bad news of Sennacherib's victories in Phœnicia and Philistia, and the politicians of Judah are becoming dejected, Isaiah sees in all this his previous threatenings gloriously justified. He can even venture to utter harsh threatenings against the king's chief advisers.[3]

---

[1] We may with Brandis, *Münz-, Mass- und Gewichtswesen in Vorderas.*, p. 98, perhaps explain the difference in respect of the sum mentioned by Hezekiah (300 and 800 talents), by supposing that the method of reckoning was different in the two cases. Still this is uncertain.

[2] *Cf.* Isaiah xxix. 5 ff. ; xxx. 27 ff. ; [and Dillm. *Comm.* ; Cheyne, *Intr. Is.*, pp. 183, 199 ff.].

[3] *Cf.* Isaiah xxii. 15 ff. ; and Dillm. in his *Comm.*

When Sennacherib's army left Phœnicia and turned towards the south, it was greeted by Isaiah in a prophetic utterance which, for grandeur of conception and for force and beauty of description, is amongst the most powerful of any of his which we possess. Assyria is the rod of God's anger, 'howbeit he meaneth not so, neither doth his heart think so, but it is in his heart to destroy and cut off nations without number,' and therefore his pride is bringing him to his ruin.[1] And when, finally, Sennacherib has received Hezekiah's tribute, and, spite of this, inflicts a siege on Jerusalem, he sees in this a base piece of treachery which Yahvé will not allow to go unpunished :[2]

> 'Woe to thee that spoilest, and thou wast not spoiled,
> And dealest treacherously, and they dealt not treacherously with thee!
> When thou hast ceased to spoil, thou shalt be spoiled.
> . . . The high ways lie waste, the wayfaring man ceaseth:
> He hath broken the covenant,
> He hath despised the cities ("done violence to," so Kittel),
> He regardeth not man.'

Jerusalem, on the other hand, will finally triumph:

> 'Thine heart shall muse on the terror:
> Where is he that counted, where is he that weighed [the tribute]?
> Where is he that counted the towers?
> Thou shalt not see the fierce ("foreign," so Kittel) people.
> A people of a deep speech that thou canst not perceive;
> Of a strange tongue that thou canst not understand.'
> ('The people of the dark, unintelligible language,' so Kittel).[3]

§ 72. *Manasseh. Amon.*

Of Hezekiah's further proceedings we can learn nothing. Isaiah, too, vanishes in 701, and we see no more of him. The position of Judah after Sennacherib's retreat was not an enviable

---

[1] Isaiah x. 5 ff. *V.* 11 determines the time.
[2] For other ideas of the date and significance of Isa. xxxiii. see König, *Einleitung*, p. 321 ; Duhm's *Commentary* ; and Cheyne, *Introd. to Isaiah*, pp. 163-172.]
[3] Isaiah xxxii. 1 ff., 18 f. (R.V.) ; Isaiah xiv. 24-27, xvii. 12-14, and besides, 2 Kings xix. 21-24 (note the 'messengers'), also probably belong to the period of the siege.

one. Hezekiah is, and continues to be, Assyria's vassal; and his country, after what it had suffered during the war and the siege, must have certainly been in a pitiable condition.[1] But all the distress of the present is nevertheless far more than outweighed by the proud and exalted feeling which Judah alone, amongst all the states of Southern Palestine, had a right to indulge in. The giant amongst the rulers of the earth, before whom all the kingdoms of the earth bowed down, was shattered on the rock of Zion. This joyous consciousness of victory would, of course, help Judah soon to recover again from its wounds. The account of Hezekiah's successful battles with the Philistines is perhaps also to be referred to this period.[2] In any case, the reputation of Yahvé and of Zion would necessarily gain infinitely by the marvellous issue of the struggle. Isaiah had been right when he said that the Hill of Zion was higher than all hills, and that Yahvé would protect His dwelling-place. It is extremely probable that he now enjoyed the triumph of seeing the disappearance of the idols which still remained everywhere in the hands of the common people, and that Hezekiah, by way of honouring Yahvé of Jerusalem, proceeded with greater earnestness than before with the work of suppressing the high-places.[3]

But after Hezekiah's death things soon assumed a totally different aspect. The Book of Kings[4] informs us that his son Manasseh (686-641) restored and introduced again into Judah all kinds of heathen customs. He allowed the high-places which had been suppressed by Hezekiah to be used again; built altars to Baal, and put back again into the Temple the Ashēra which had been

---

[1] Perhaps Isaiah i. 5-9 has a reference to this.

[2] 2 Kings xviii. 8. *Cf.* Stade, 624.

[3] By most recent writers the whole of Hezekiah's reforms have been referred to this period. But it is difficult to understand how, in this case, the author of the Book of Kings passes a favourable judgment on the whole reign of Hezekiah, if the latter did not begin his reforms till near the end of it. Seeing he wrote only a short time after Hezekiah's day, he may quite well have had a correct recollection of what took place. No objection can be drawn from the case of Josiah; he begins his reign at an earlier age, and he began his reforms before 621.

[4] 2 Kings xxi. The chapter is probably not quite uniform (see Stade, *ZAW*. vi. 186 ff.), but its statements as regards matters of fact can hardly be objected to.

removed from it. He restored to a place of honour again the Canaanitish practice of sacrificing children, and also the various black arts which have for long been forbidden in Israel, at least by law, and which were carried on only in secrecy. And even the Assyrian star-worship finds in him a zealous patron.

How are we to account for this phenomenon? Wellhausen's explanation is certainly right: 'The popular half-heathen Yahvé must at all costs be restored to His place of honour in opposition to the stern and holy God of the prophets.'[1] Sennacherib's retreat from Jerusalem, and the brilliant fulfilment of Isaiah's preaching, necessarily resulted in the victory of the prophetic party. The prophets would be able to maintain their place so long as the king lived who owed everything to Isaiah. As soon as Hezekiah's eyes are closed, the old popular religion which had been combated by the prophets, raises its head again and fights—for the last time, and therefore all the more desperately —for its existence. What we see being accomplished under Manasseh is nothing but the strong violent *reaction* of the old syncretism which had got firmly implanted in the hearts of the masses, against the endeavours of prophecy to give the strict ethical Monotheism the place of authority in life. Those who clung to the popular religion did not wish its fresh, joyous worship of Nature, with its altars on high places and images, and its indulgent and voluptuous accompaniments, to be starved out of existence in favour of that strict and sober conception of God and of His Will which the prophets represented. If Hezekiah had leant an ear to the prophets, why should his successor not reverse the process and side with the other party?

Political considerations may also have had an effect, at least so far as the introduction of Assyrian forms of worship was concerned. Hezekiah owed his deliverance to Yahvé, and in what he did he expressed his thankfulness that Yahvé had proved Himself more powerful than all the gods of the heathen.

[1] Wellh. *Abriss*, 67.

If Isaiah's prophecy was to be believed, the time of salvation and blessing for Judah was now at length truly to dawn. Assyria must perish, and Jerusalem and Judah might raise their heads more proudly than ever. There were certainly few enough signs of this. As a matter of fact it was just at this very time that Assyria reached the pinnacle of its power, and although Judah had offered a glorious resistance to the giant, it could not hope to get any further than it had been before. It was, and continued to be, Assyria's vassal.[1]

Thoughts such as these were calculated to damp enthusiasm for Yahvé. One might, in fact, ask: Who, after all, gained the victory—Sennacherib or Hezekiah, Yahvé or the gods of Assyria? Judah after 701 enjoyed a long, and, as it seemed, an undisturbed time of peace; but what was this repose under the sceptre of Assyria as compared with the prospect held out by Isaiah? If Judah, as a matter of fact, thus lived merely by the grace of Assyria, it seemed illogical to withhold from the gods of Assyria the worship which was their due as well as Yahvé's.

Thus the Canaanitish and Assyrian deities, and foreign modes of worshipping God, gradually found their way into Jerusalem and into the Temple. The high-places and the altars are restored; the Ashēras and Maççēbas become once more parts of Israelitish worship; and even Ḳedeshas—*i.e.* those dedicated to prostitution in the service of Astarte, or in connection with her worship—settle in the immediate neighbourhood of the Temple.[2] In addition to all this that strange dark feature, which is often enough peculiar to the religion of Nature together with lascivious festivals and wild orgies, gets special prominence here, and the inhuman custom of sacrificing children appears to have flourished with exceptional vigour in the reign of Manasseh. In the valley of Hinnom, a gorge on the southern or western side of the Temple hill, are the places for sacrifice where children, slaughtered in honour of Melek

[1] See Schrader, *KAT.*[2] 354 ff. [Eng. Trans. ii. 40 ff.]; Tiele, *Gesch.* 328 ff., 346.
[2] 2 Kings xxiii. 7.

(Moloch), are burnt.[1] Besides this, we have the Assyrian star-worship in its various forms. Manasseh, in fact, more than any other, is to be certainly classed amongst those kings of Judah before the time of Josiah, who kept sun-chariots and sun-horses close to the Temple:[2] he carries on, at the same time, the worship of 'the host of heaven'; the sun-god is surrounded by a whole court of heavenly beings—the stars, who, as being his under-gods, claim their own peculiar worship.[3] Even if Ahaz was the first to begin the worship of these Assyrian deities, it was under Manasseh, according to all the indications we have, that the worship was first carried on on an extended scale. The period from now to the reformation under Josiah is dominated by this mode of worship. That very reformation, and Deuteronomy, which was spiritually so closely related to it, show what a hold it had got in Judah. Even after this reform it was not quite rooted out. We still find Jeremiah and Ezekiel complaining of it.[4]

There can scarcely be any doubt but that this close alliance with Assyrian modes of worship, which made such a deep impression on the life of Judah, is merely a symptom of something of a more general kind. If Assyrian religion was imitated to such an extent as was the case here, Judah, in Manasseh's time, must in general have drawn closer to Assyria in political matters, as in all the other departments of life. People got reconciled to the fact of the Assyrian vassalage, and began to admire and imitate the whilom enemy. Assyrian life and thought, the customs and culture of Assyria, along with its religion, certainly became more familiar to Israel at this time than had ever been the case before.

Unfortunately, the information we possess regarding these eighty important years of Israelitish history—from 701 to 621—is so very scanty, that we cannot venture to pronounce upon

---

[1] 2 Kings xxi. 6; xxiii. 10. On the pronunciation of Molek, see in Kautzsch, critical notes on 1 Kings xi. 7. The same holds good of Ashtoreth and Astarte.

[2] 2 Kings xxiii. 11, 12. [3] 2 Kings xxi. 5.

[4] Jer. xliv. 4.; Ezek. viii. 6 ff.; cf. Zeph. i. 5.

the influences exercised by Assyria in any other sphere save in that of worship, nor do anything beyond mentioning the general fact of its existence. Any conjectures regarding anything beyond this cannot be proved. Stade,[1] for instance, thinks he can show that the Assyrio-Babylonian mythology found its way, to a very large extent, into Judah at this very period of syncretism and blended with the ancient Israelite stories regarding the primitive history of the world and of man. But to whatever extent Israelitish primitive history may have been influenced by Assyria, the adoption of Assyrian elements may belong to a considerably earlier time. Ahaz, for instance, did not only worship sun-horses, but set up an Assyrian sun-dial in Jerusalem.[2] It will be seen from this that the influence of Assyria on the life and thought of Israel, though it may have been specially strong in the reign of Manasseh, goes back to a considerably earlier period.

Naturally, such a thorough change as took place under Manasseh, and which so entirely altered things from what they were in Hezekiah's days, could not be carried through without the application of force. Those who remained faithful to Yahvé, and especially those who had gathered round Isaiah, could not be silent about Manasseh's ongoings. Manasseh, however, seems to have punished with death any resistance to his measures. It is only by supposing this to have been the case that we can understand why, in the very closest connection with the king's apostasy from Yahvé, the Book of Kings reproaches him with having caused streams of innocent blood to flow, so that Jerusalem, like an over-full dish, was filled with blood to the very rim.[3] Tradition has numbered Isaiah amongst the martyrs in Yahvé's cause whose blood flowed under Manasseh. If he himself was not actually amongst them, many of his pupils doubtless were. Jeremiah is apparently thinking of the horrors under Manasseh when he speaks of the sword as having devoured Judah's prophets like a destroying lion.[4]

---

[1] Stade, *Gesch*. 631 f.
[2] See 2 Kings xx. 11; cf. Herod. ii. 109.
[3] 2 Kings xxi. 16.
[4] Jer. ii. 30.

But though brute force might indeed silence the prophets of Yahvé, it could not compel them to apostatise. In their seclusion the prophets, and the faithful worshippers of Yahvé belonging to the ranks of the priesthood and the people, may have set themselves all the more earnestly to work for Yahvé and His honour. The evil of the time was apostasy from Yahvé. That could be checked only if what Hezekiah had without much success striven after, could be permanently accomplished. The high-places, with their altars, their images of the gods, and the secret worship of various kinds which was bound up with them, were the real seats of idolatrous worship. If they were once suppressed it would be easy to restore Yahvé once more to honour, and once more to make of Israel a people holy to Yahvé. It was in thoughts such as these that there originated, within the prophetic circle in the time of Manasseh, a book which was not to play an important part till the days of Josiah, namely, *Deuteronomy*. The ancient Mosaic law of the Book of the Covenant was to be freshly presented to Judah in a new form corresponding to the special needs of the time. The unfavourable circumstances of the time, especially the heavy weight of persecution which, in Manasseh's days, lay upon Yahvé's brave confessors, did not allow of the book being made public as yet. It is accordingly laid up in the Temple, and remains concealed there till it is brought to light in the eighteenth year of Josiah's reign.[1]

As regards literature generally, the time of Hezekiah and Manasseh seems otherwise to have been a period of active production. As was shown before, the later elements in the group of narratives in the Book of Samuel, designated SS, belong in all probability to the reign of Hezekiah.[2] The writers worked on the basis of the older traditions, and partly by freely developing the old material, sought to revive anew, for the benefit of the younger generation, the traditions which had been handed down regarding

---

[1] See the detailed examination of the composition and of the date of the writing of the book above, in the first volume, § 7, 1, 2.

[2] See above, pp. 34 f., 45.

the heroes of the past—Samuel, Saul, and David. To these were doubtless joined narratives dealing with the period of the later kings which, unfortunately owing to the peculiar plan of our Book of Kings, have been to a large extent lost. Some bits may be preserved in the books we have called K. And, in particular, we previously arrived at the conclusion that the Israelitish Book of Kings (Ki) must belong to the time of Manasseh.[1]

If the detailed proof of this, previously given, be correct, then the most suitable time to which to assign the composition of essential parts of the great Hexateuch Law and History-book will also be in this period—the book, namely, with which we are acquainted under the name of the Elohistic *Priestly-writing* (P). Ever since the Temple service had been regularly going on, and had more and more increased in importance, a ritual must have become a necessity. In course of time it came to be prescribed in writing. Many other regulations were added on to this, especially those having to do with cultus and the worship of God. When Hezekiah undertook his scheme of reform, he was able, like Josiah at a later date, to count on the support not only of the prophets, but quite as much on that of the Jerusalem priesthood. The shape this support took was the redaction of the older laws from the point of view of the centralisation of divine worship in Jerusalem. Thus important parts of that priestly writing (P^2) were composed as early as the time of Hezekiah. From this point onwards the work of the priestly lawgivers is continued beyond the time of Manasseh, and, in fact, some portions seem not to have been included in the book till the time of the Exile. For the proof of these statements, so far as I am able to give it, I refer readers to the investigation in an earlier section of this book.[2] A fresh examination of this very difficult and very big question cannot be looked for here. This would require a fresh and detailed estimate of the reasons for and against, and consequently a fresh critical examination of the sources. For general statements are

---

[1] See above, pp. 210, 218.
[2] *Cf.* the examination of this point in vol. i., §§ 9 and 10.

of no value here. If my view is the correct one, it does not require any new arguments in its support; if when examined it cannot stand the test, its rejection is simply a matter of time.

A later narrative, preserved in the Book of Chronicles, tells us that Manasseh was taken prisoner by the Assyrians. He was carried away in chains to Babylon, but was, in answer to his prayer, afterwards set free and restored to his throne.[1] The Book of Kings knows nothing of this. Even if it were not altogether probable that the narrative originated in the necessity felt of bringing Manasseh's long and peaceful reign into harmony with the theocratic standpoint of the Book, still, taking into account the well-known character of Chronicles, very few serious reasons can be advanced in favour of its historicity. Besides, it cannot be denied that the narrative possesses a striking analogy in the history of Pharaoh Necho I. who was carried away in chains to Nineveh, and was afterwards set at liberty.[2]

Manasseh's son and successor, Amon (641-639), appears to have gone entirely in his father's footsteps. After a reign of two years, he loses his life in a palace revolution.[3] It would be of the highest importance in enabling us to form an opinion regarding the general condition of that period, if we knew whether religious reasons had anything to do with his dethronement, as in the case of Joram of Israel. If they had, then the fact that Amon was specially popular with the common people would appear in a new light. A bloody revenge was taken by the populace for his murder on those who had instigated the conspiracy against Amon's life. Are we to suppose that these occurrences were closely connected with reforms similar to those carried through by Josiah, and for the accomplishment of which, on the death of Manasseh, the change of throne seemed to supply the fitting opportunity? We may suppose that Amon resisted the reforming tendencies of the court, trusting to the favour in which the system, which had become the

---

[1] 2 Chron. xxxiii. 10 ff. See on this Graf, in *StKr.* 1859, 467 ff., and Wellh. *Prol.*² 215 [Eng. Trans. 207]; on the other side, Köhler, *Gesch.* ii. 2, 279 ff.

[2] See Schrader, *KAT.*² 371 [Eng. Trans. ii. 58]; Tiele, *Gesch.* 356.

[3] 2 Kings xxi. 19-26.

dominant one in the country under Manasseh, was held. He would pay for his resistance by his death, but the party of the country people who supported him, together with the country priests, would, we may imagine, take a bloody revenge for this attack on their interests. This party would thus succeed in delaying the carrying out of those plans of reform for almost twenty years. Owing to the scanty nature of our information, it is perfectly impossible to answer questions of this kind. Still the state of the case is such, that it is permissible at least to mention conjectures of this sort.

§ 73. *Josiah.*

In place of the murdered Amon, his son Josiah, a boy of only eight years (639-608), is set on the throne. With his accession Israel is once more seen taking an active part in connection with events which were happening in the big world. The mighty empire of Assyria, which had risen to the supreme point of its power under the great and noble-minded Assurhaddon, now began under Assurbanipal (669-625), the Sardanapal of the Greeks, gradually to fulfil its destiny. In the first years of his reign Assyria was still in full possession of its power and greatness. But now those mighty movements of the nations which in the second half of the seventh century shook all Western Asia, began more and more to make their appearance, and under their influence Judah's despot, the empire of Assyria, broke up. As early as the middle of his reign (about 645) Psammetich of Egypt had thrown off the Assyrian rule, which since the time of Assurhaddon had weighed upon his kingdom. Others followed suit, and the final result was that the dominion of the world was taken from the Semites, who had carried it on for a thousand years, and transferred to the Aryans.[1] The first deadly blow struck at the Assyrian Empire was dealt by the *Medes*. They revolt from Assyria about the middle of the seventh century, and under Dejokes, and especially Phraortes,

[1] On what follows, see especially Meyer, *Gesch. d. Alt.* 543 ff.

begin to found a kingdom of their own. Phraortes meets his death (about 625) while fighting with the Assyrians. The decisive battle is delayed for a time by the appearance of the *Scythians*. About this time (± 630) hordes of an Eastern equestrian people come swarming over all Western Asia, robbing and plundering as they go, an event which may be compared with the later inroad of the Huns and Mongols into the West. They, too, shook the Assyrian Empire to its foundations. According to Herodotus, they even penetrated into Syria and knocked at the gates of Egypt. But the Scythian shock is scarcely past when the Medes unite with Babylon to strike a decisive blow at Nineveh (608).

Judah was drawn, directly or indirectly, into all these movements. Since the revolt of Egypt and Media from Assyria, it was felt that the all-powerful colossus, before which the world had for centuries trembled, had begun to totter. A fresh breath of new life and hope must have gone through the vassal-states. In Judah too, people began to think that Isaiah was, after all, right when he had prophesied the end of the proud braggart. Assyria's deities sank in value. The spirit of Isaiah, though it had almost died out amongst the masses, revived again. Prophecy began again to gain ground and could venture into the light of day. And when now, finally, the Scythians inundated Western Asia and touched even the borders of Judah, it was all perfectly clear: Yahvé is rising up once more to execute judgment on the nations. The gravity of the situation, and the threatening danger (for Judah herself as well as for others) supplied the soil on which a new phase of prophecy sprang up.

Of the representatives of this new prophetic development Zephaniah[1] is the first whom we come across. Whether it is that the revolt of Egypt or the inroad of the Scythians appears to him to be a special sign of the divine punitive wrath, his conviction is that the day of Yahvé will come with all its terrors. It will

---

[1] See Kuen. § 78; Schwally, *ZAW*. 1890, 165 ff.; Reuss, *Gesch. d. AT.*[2] 364 ff.

destroy the heathen round about; it is, however, over Assyria especially that the divine judgment hangs.[1] But the day of God will certainly come upon Judah itself, and will come upon it first if an end is not put to its idolatry.[2] The 'remnant of Baal,' as well as violence and all foreign practices, must first be abolished before Judah can be safe in the day of the wrath of Yahvé. At a short interval apparently, and previous to Josiah's reforms, Zephaniah is followed by Nahum. Assyria must fall; Nineveh will be destroyed, for out of it went 'he who thought evil against Yahvé, and counselled wickedness.' 'I will break his yoke and burst his bonds ... of thy name let there be no more any sprout, out of the house of thy god will I cut off graven images and molten images; I will make thy grave—for thou art vile.'[3] Sure of victory, and filled with an unutterable contempt for Assyria, Judah rejoices over the fall of her powerful foe. Nahum pictures the latter in such clear and brilliant colours that one might think he is painting what he has actually seen. But this may be so only in appearance; it is sufficient that Nahum foresees Assyria's destruction as a certain fact. This points to the time when Assyria was being hard pressed, in the days of Kyaxares the Mede, by the Medes and the Scythians together. For Judah must still have been nominally subject to Assyria.[4]

The spirit of prophecy once wakened from its slumber must continue to exert its influence. And when, a few years after the time in which Nahum probably prophesied Deuteronomy was brought to light, it must have fallen on fruitful soil. Even in Manasseh's reign the worshippers of Yahvé had not been idle: the production of Deuteronomy shows this, according to my view of how we ought to explain its origin. Later on, at Manasseh's death, and under the influence of what was happening in the outside world, the hopes of the patriots revived; but all in vain. Amon fell. Josiah was still a docile boy when he mounted the throne. The more he approaches maturity, and the more the course

---

[1] Zeph. ii. 4-5. [2] Zeph. i. 4-ii. 3. [3] Nah. i. 11, 13, 14.
[4] See Kuen. § lxxv., especially Nr. 8 and 10.

of events itself proves favourable to him, the more he seems to have lent an ear to the prophetic party. And on this occasion, moreover, it was the party of the patriots which spoke against Assyria.

Since the death of Assurbanipal, Josiah, who had meanwhile from a child become a man, had been loosening the ties which made him the vassal of Assyria. Later on, at all events, he considers himself the lord and master of Palestine. He introduces reforms into Samaria, and attacks Necho on his march through Canaan as if he had always had the right to exercise authority everywhere in the country.[1] At the same time the Assyrian deities, and perhaps the foreign deities generally, lose credit. The Yahvé of the prophets is again restored to honour, and along with Him the Temple of Zion. The proclamation of *Deuteronomy* is only a link in the chain of events. Before the book made its appearance, Josiah had set himself to work to get the Temple put in order. Then he gets to know of this ' Book of Doctrine,' and it supplies a new basis for his efforts.[2]

This happened in the king's eighteenth year (621). The book was plainly the outcome of the prophetic spirit. What the prophets had always demanded, namely, that Yahvé's precepts should be observed and His will fulfilled, was now expressed in easily understood and definite statements which showed how Israel must live in order to be holy and worthy of the 'Holy One of Israel.' Prophecy had thus become statute, law; it had entered into the priestly sphere. The holiness of Yahvé, and His unique nature as the only God, form the fundamental thought of

---

[1] *Cf.* Kuen. § lxxv. 10.

[2] 2 Kings xxii. and xxiii. See also remarks in vol. i. pp. 58, 59. The account is certainly not all of a piece, but, on the contrary, has been richly supplied with additions (Stade, *ZAW.* v. 292 f., and now especially in Kautzsch). But this does not essentially detract from its trustworthiness. The new French school, however, holds very different views about it. *Cf.* Vernes, *Une Nouvelle Hypoth. sur* . . . *du Deutéron.* 1887 (*Essais Bibliques*, i. ff.), and *Précis d'Hist. Juive*, 1889, 470; Horst, *Étude sur le Deut.* in *Rev. de l'Hist. des Relig.* 1888, 11 ff. Against, especially Kuenen in *T. Tijd.* 1888, 35 ff. [See now also Piepenbring, in *Revue de l'Hist. des Religions*, 1894, 123 f.]

the book. But the necessary preparation for the carrying out of its principles is, to a large extent, a renewed purifying of worship. Deuteronomy does indeed also contain a considerable number of ethical and especially social rules, the aim of which is to realise the prophetic ideal of righteousness in the nation. But in many respects they remained ideal demands, such as the nation had to a certain extent been long familiar with in the older prophets. What could be directly accomplished, and what at the same time was in complete harmony with the trend of the age, and promised to effect the most thoroughgoing changes in the actual state of religious matters, was the energetic enforcement of the thought of the centralisation of worship. This, however, was an affair of the priests quite as much as of the prophets.

Thus both parties, prophets and priests, had a share in bringing about the public recognition of the book and in carrying out its demands. It is the priest Hilkiah who makes the book public,[1] and the prophetess Huldah guides the king in his resolutions by her prophetic utterance. The heathen symbols and altars which had sprung up since Manasseh's time are again put away, and a thorough purification of the Temple is undertaken. It was to be done in a more effectual fashion than under Hezekiah. To this end, the priests belonging to the country towns are transferred to Jerusalem, and their sanctuaries in the high places are profaned. And, owing to the weakness of the Assyrian government just at this time, Josiah is able even to go beyond the borders of what was properly his own land. The worshippers of Yahvé in what was formerly Israelitish territory, but has been for exactly a hundred years Assyrian, are included in his reforms, and the altar of Bethel is destroyed. It is, moreover, sufficiently significant for the character of the movement that the priests of the sanctuaries of the high places which were suppressed were not treated either in accordance with the letter of the new law or with the original

---

[1] Why did Hilkiah not make P public, if the book was actually in existence (Horst, *Th. Hitt. Z.* 1888, Nr. 22)? Because he found D, and did not only pretend to have found it.

intention of the king. The law had desired that they should remain where they were, and simply give up priestly service. They might come occasionally to Jerusalem and take part as guests in the Temple sacrifices. Josiah had evidently intended to indemnify the priests who had been deprived of their living by incorporating them in the Temple priesthood. The Jerusalem priests, on the other hand, seem to have struggled against this undesirable increase in their numbers, and would not admit their country brethren to the altar.[1] *De facto*, the Temple priests from this time onwards are the possessors of a monopoly, while those who had hitherto been the country Levites are degraded from their office; *de jure*, this state of things is approved by Ezekiel.

The reform which was demanded and introduced by prophecy has in this way become a priestly ordinance. It supplied the very strongest support to the position of the priesthood. This is the one effect of the new law. The other is, however, of a much more far-reaching character. By means of a national assembly at which king and people respectively bind themselves to obey Yahvé, the law is made the law of the community of Israel. Up to this time the law had consisted partly of the oral utterances of the priests, and partly of written common law preserved and safe-guarded by custom. Now there exists a recognised legal codex—a 'canonical' book. We thus come on the first trace of a sacred book, in the strict sense of a *holy scripture*. What the Christian Church, the Church of the Reformation above all, owes to Holy Scripture, has its roots in this conception which we here meet with for the first time. But, on the other hand, we have here finally the source, too, of all the evils which, like the shadow alongside of the light, have come into Judaism and Christianity as the result of outward reliance on the written Word, and of an unspiritual adherence to the authority of the letter.

[1] *Cf.* Deut. xviii. 1 ff., with 2 Kings xxiii. 8, and the discussions in vol. i. p. 122 f.

§ 74. *Jeremiah. The End.*

When we consider the course which Josiah's reforms, carried out on the basis of that law, had actually taken, we can understand how the very man who above all might have been expected to take an interest in it, was more and more at a loss to know what to make of the spirit which these reforms had called forth in Judah—the prophet Jeremiah.[1]

The prophetic figure of Jeremiah is the bright evening sun which, with its golden beams, sheds a glory over Judah as it sinks into the night. No single one of all the Old Testament prophets comes so near to us in a human way as he. He has all the powerful utterance of a Hosea, and can deal blows as heavy as Isaiah's; but at the same time his heart is overflowing with a human feeling for the misery of his people, and he weeps hot tears over the piteous fate of his fatherland. He is consumed by a warm love for his unhappy nation. And yet duty to his God calls him and compels him to blame, when he would willingly console. With a bleeding heart he enters on the terrible struggle with himself, and, although the noblest patriot who ever lived, bears the stigma of a traitor to his country for the sake of Yahvé and truth. More surely than any other he foresees the end. To seek to arrest it would be arrogant, to bewail it would be vain. Like the older prophets, he too has only hope left. But his hope speaks a different language from theirs. It is not the thought of outward restoration which lies nearest to his heart, though he is acquainted with that too, nor is it the restoration of a remnant. God's law in the heart, and along with this a *new covenant*—that will be the mark of the Israel of the future. And thus he stands at the point where the ancient Israel terminates, as the pioneer who anticipates a new time.

Jeremiah's first appearance in the character of prophet belongs

---

[1] *Cf.* Köstlin, *Jes. u. Jerem.*; Cheyne, *Jeremiah: His Life and Times*, 1888; Marti, *Der Prophet Jeremia*, 1889. The best characterisation in a short form is in Wellh. *Abr.* 75 ff.; *Israel and Judah*,[3] 117 ff. [*Cf.* Giesebrecht, *Jeremia*, 1894, Introd.]

to the thirteenth year of Josiah's reign, and thus to the period of idolatry previous to the king's reforms. It is at the same time the period of the Scythian invasion which threatens Judah too. Probably both things, in fact, Judah's apostasy and the danger which threatened from the side of the Scythians, are brought into close connection in the words uttered by Jeremiah at that time:

> 'Assemble yourselves, and let us go into the fenced cities.
> Set up a standard toward Zion!
> Flee for safety, stay not!
> For I will bring evil from the north,
> And a great destruction.
> A lion is gone up from his thicket, and a destroyer of nations;
> He is on his way, he is gone forth from his place;
> To make thy land desolate,
> That thy cities be laid waste, without inhabitant. . . .
> A people cometh from the north country,
> And a great nation shall be stirred up from the uttermost parts of the earth.
> They lay hold on bow and spear;
> They are cruel, and have no mercy.'[1]

Josiah's reform took place soon after this. We do not know whether or in what way Jeremiah took an active part in it. He must in any case have taken the liveliest interest in it. But when we consider the direction which things took soon after Josiah's action based on Deuteronomy, we can only too easily understand how Jeremiah has still the old complaints to make against Judah.[2] He will have nothing to do with outward precepts and man's commandments which have been learned; he demands circumcision of the heart. But he cannot find this now any more than before.

We know nothing definite regarding Josiah's reign after the reform. But it was apparently peaceful and successful. All was quiet at home, and since the downfall of Assyria there had been nothing to fear from abroad in the way of the oppression of foreign

---

[1] Jer. iv. 5-7; vi. 22, 23 (R.V.). *Cf.* especially vi. 27-30.
[2] See Marti in *Zeitschr. f. Theol. und Kirche*, ii. 52 ff.

rule. It is not till thirteen years after his reforms that we again learn something about Josiah. Owing to the alliance of the Medes with Babylon, the attacks on the Assyrian World-Empire had entered on a new stage. In the year 608 we find the Mede Kyaxares in company with Nabopolassar of Babylon occupied with the struggle against Assyria. Assyria is approaching its end. Egypt feels it should not let slip this opportunity of making good its old claim to Syria. The son of Psammetich, who had just mounted the throne as Pharaoh-Necho (II.), approaches with the intention, as the Book of Kings informs us, of marching towards the Euphrates against the king of Assyria. He means to dispute the sovereignty of Syria with the Assyrians. The other States apparently join him; but Josiah, on the contrary, is not disposed to give up to a new despot the independence which he has barely tasted. He opposes Necho's advance. An engagement takes place at Megiddo in the Kishon Plain. Josiah falls; his people carry his body back to Jerusalem.[1]

Here everything is in the most terrible confusion in consequence of Josiah's defeat. Nobody had reckoned on a result of this kind. Apparently Josiah's reform and Assyria's downfall had awakened in the nation a confident feeling that Judah now possessed Yahvé's approval, and consequently could count on the help of His arm. Any one who took a sensible view of things could only pronounce Josiah's conduct to be foolhardy and rash. And this appears to have been Jeremiah's opinion. When after Josiah's defeat the people in their alarm came thronging to the Temple to keep a fast day, under the idea that they had simply not been zealous enough in worship, but that God could not possibly abandon His city, he pronounces their hope to be superstition. 'Will ye steal, murder, and commit adultery, and swear falsely, and burn incense unto strange gods? Then ye come and stand before me in this house, which is called by my name, and say: Here we are safe! that ye may do all these abominations.' On the contrary, as the Temple of Shiloh became a prey to the enemy, so too can the

[1] 2 Kings xxiii. 29, 30. *Cf.* Herod. ii. 159, and Meyer, *Gesch. d. Alt.* 578.

Temple of Jerusalem.[1] In saying this, Jeremiah of course came into the sharpest conflict with public opinion in Jerusalem, as represented by the holders of power, and as reflected in the current patriotism of the masses. His outspokenness involves him in a prosecution. But he is able to appeal to the example of Micah before him.[2]

The fear that Necho would immediately appear before Jerusalem proved to be unfounded. Pharaoh hastens towards the Euphrates. Meanwhile the army had made Josiah's younger son, Jehoahaz, king in Jerusalem. Apparently the elder son, Eliakim, was inclined to submit to Necho, and was for that reason passed over. But Jehoahaz only reigns for three months. Pharaoh does not appear to have been satisfied with the choice; he sends from Ribla, in Cœlesyria, where he was, and imposes a fine on the inhabitants of Judah, and forces them to dethrone their king. Eliakim is put by Necho in Jehoahaz's place, and mounts the throne of his fathers under the name of Jehoiakim (608-597). Jehoahaz is carried away to Egypt, and later on he died there. A heavy tribute is imposed on Jehoiakim, which he assesses on the holders of property, and collects by the aid of the army.[3]

Jehoiakim seems to have returned completely to the paths of Manasseh. A different moral theory became prevalent. People said, 'The fathers have eaten sour grapes, and the sons' teeth have been set on edge,' as they reflected on the fate which had overtaken Josiah spite of his piety. And in the same spirit is the complaint: 'When we burned incense to the Queen of Heaven[4] in Judah and Jerusalem, we had plenty of bread. Things went well with us, and we saw no evil. But since we left off burning incense we have wanted all things, and have been consumed by the sword and by hunger.' Besides this, Jehoiakim seems to have been

---

[1] Jer. vii. 9 ff. See Wellh. *Abr.* 73.   [2] Jer. xxvi. *Cf.* Marti, *Jerem.* xxiii.
[3] 2 Kings xxiii. 31-35. עַם הָאָרֶץ = Militia? [But see Klostermann.]
[4] See on this Stade, *ZAW.* vi. 123 ff., 289 ff.; Schrader, *Berl. Akad. d. Wiss.* 1886, 477 ff. [Cheyne, *Jeremiah*, 1888, p. 198 f.]
[5] Jer. xxxi. 29; xliv. 17, 18.

fond of display and a ruler of despotic tendencies;[1] while just then, when the times were so critical, Judah required a man who was backed up by the confidence of the people.

Pharaoh was still in Syria, which seems to have submitted to him without much trouble on his part. But when Nineveh fell it was necessary that there should be some clear definite understanding between Egypt and the new lord of the East as to which was to be master. In place of Nabopolassar, who had already fallen ill, his son, Nebuchadrezzar, advanced against Pharaoh-Necho. The latter was completely defeated in 604 at Carchemish on the Euphrates.

Syria has fallen into the hands of the Chaldeans. Jehoiakim, like the other Syrian rulers, submits to the victor after having for some years indulged the vain hope of complete freedom (about 601). He has paid his tribute for three years, and then he feels a desire to revolt again from Nebuchadrezzar. Jeremiah was now in evil case. As early as the time of Necho's defeat he had clearly foreseen the fate of Egypt:—

> 'Go up into Gilead and take balm,
> Oh virgin daughter of Egypt!
> In vain dost thou use many medicines,
> There is no healing for thee.
> The nations have heard of thy shame,
> And the earth is full of thy cry :
> For the mighty man hath stumbled against the mighty.
> They are fallen, both of them together.'[2]

Jeremiah had even at that time feared that Jerusalem would be destroyed by Nebuchadrezzar. In Jerusalem itself, too, similar fears seem to have been entertained. And so a fast is arranged in order to ward off the threatened evil. Jeremiah cannot now keep silence any more than on a former and similar occasion. He must point his people to the right path of help. He is forbidden to appear in public, and so he arranges to have his words read

---

[1] See Jer. xxii. 13 ff.
[2] Jer. xlvi. 11, 12 (R.V.). [Some critics doubt the prophet's authorship. See Giesebrecht.]

aloud by his scribe Baruch. In the book which was read there must have been threatenings such as we meet with in Jeremiah here and there. Nations from the north, the king of Babylon himself, will burst in on Jerusalem and Judah, destroy them, and take away from them 'the voice of the bridegroom and of the bride, the sound of the mill and the light of the lamp.'[1] Informed of this by his ministers, Jehoiakim cuts Jeremiah's book in pieces and throws it into a brazier. Jeremiah had fallen into disfavour; and his unpopularity necessarily increased the more determinedly he, as Isaiah had done before him, sought to thwart the party composed of the rabid patriots, and the more he endeavoured to prevent Jehoiakim from revolting from Nebuchadrezzar.

When the revolt, nevertheless, actually took place, Nebuchadrezzar, first of all, incited the neighbours to make attacks on Judah in conjunction with Babylonian guerilla bands. Soon after this, however (597), he enters Palestine himself with an army.[2] Jehoiakim's sudden death saves him from a bitter humiliation. His son Jehoiachin, a youth of eighteen, also known as Jeconiah, enters on his very unattractive inheritance. Nebuchadrezzar proceeds to besiege Jerusalem. In order to escape extremities, Jeconiah yields before the city is actually stormed. He has to repair to the enemy's headquarters as Nebuchadrezzar's prisoner, accompanied by his mother and his whole court and staff. Nebuchadrezzar demands, besides, the surrender of seven thousand men, capable of bearing arms—that is, possessors of land—as well as one thousand workers in iron. Along with Jeconiah and his court and harem they are carried away to Babylon—naturally with their families.[3] A part of the sacred utensils is also carried off.[4] Seeing that Jerusalem had, for the second time, resisted him, Nebuchadrezzar was now determined to break its

---

[1] *Cf.* Jer. xxv. 8 ff., and in addition chap. xxxvi.

[2] 2 Kings xxiv. 1 ff. Verse 2 ff. is a later addition, but cannot be objected to so far as the substance is concerned.

[3] For some exceptions, see Ezek. xxiv. 21.

[4] 2 Kings xxiv. 8 ff. Verses 13 and 14 are an addition, see below. But see Jer. xxvii. 8 ff.; xxviii. 3.

pride and to make further resistance impossible. He had underestimated the tenacious love of freedom and the fierce fanaticism which marked the Jewish spirit. The prophet Ezekiel is amongst those who were carried away. From him we learn that the captives were settled near the river Chebar. The youthful Jeconiah himself languished for thirty-seven years in Babylonian dungeons. Jeremiah calls after him: 'O land, land, land! hear the word of Yahvé. Thus saith Yahvé, Write ye this man childless, a man that shall not prosper in his days: for no man of his seed shall prosper, sitting upon the throne of David, and ruling any more in Judah.'[1]

During this period the *literary impulse* has not yet died out in Judah any more than prophecy. It is as if men with the spirit of the prophets had, in anticipation of the end, sought to arrange the literary 'remains' of the nation. In the days of Jehoiakim or Jeconiah, the history of the kings was put together in a form which differs very little from our present Book of Kings. It was anything indeed but a perfect work; still, in the absence of anything better, it is a monument of priceless value. The real author of the Book of Kings, who is clearly a child of the spirit which first manifested itself in Deuteronomy, has comrades in aim and endeavour in the men who put together and revised the stories of the Judges and the earliest narratives of the Kings. They, too, belong to this last period of the history of Judah. And, in fact, the Deuteronomic School had probably by this time extended its labours even to the Law.[2]

In *Habakkuk*, prophecy, in the strict sense of the term, makes its appearance once more at this time side by side with Jeremiah. He speaks of the Chaldeans as an enemy who has already done grievous violence to Judah. How can the Holy One of Israel suffer this? It must be the punishing hand of Yahvé: 'But the plunderer will one day be plundered because of men's blood and

---

[1] Jer. xxii. 29, 30 (R.V.).
[2] See on K and D² above, p. 223; on *Ri.* pp. 5, 13, 25 ff.

of the violence done to lands, and cities, and to all their inhabitants.'¹

On David's throne is placed yet another son of Josiah, called Mattaniah, who is twenty-one years old. As king he bears the name Zedekiah (597 to 586).² Although willing enough, in a way, to act up to Jeremiah's advice and to accept the inevitable, he did not possess either the skill or the force to make himself master of the difficult situation in which he was placed. The deportation of the propertied and influential element was a source of many complications for the new constitution. Now that all offices and possessions were free, the door was open for the incapable, the ambitious, and the self-seeking. The new possessors of property and power, with the usual zeal of upstarts, were still less inclined than their predecessors had been to renounce the right of Judah to play an independent rôle. Judah's sole task for the present, namely, to regain internal order and new strength under the overlordship of Babylon, appears to them, in their blind zeal, far too insignificant a part. They begin once more to listen to Egypt's blandishments, which had always proved disastrous, and, especially after the predictions uttered by Habakkuk, hope for the speedy downfall of Babylon. Thus factions of all kinds are formed; there seem even to have been instances of violence and bloodshed. In a word, those who had been carried away to Babylon, with Ezekiel at their head, regard with contempt the state of matters in Jerusalem, as if those who remained behind were the real authors of all the misfortune, and see in it a proof of their lawlessness and corruption.³

But it was not in Judah only that men began to look forward to the speedy destruction of Babylon, and to think of how it might be made use of to enable them to cast off the foreign yoke. As had happened in the days of Hezekiah, foreign embassies arrive and importune Judah. Edom, Ammon, Moab, Tyre, and

---

¹ Probably only i.-ii. 8, belonged to the book in its original form. See especially Kuen. §§ 76, 77. [Differently Budde, *StKr.*, 1893, 383 ff.; *cf.* also Rothstein, *StKr.*, 1894, 51 ff.]

² 2 Kings xxiv. 18-25, 21; also Jer. lii.

³ *Cf.* Ezek. xi. 15; xxii. 25 ff.; chaps. viii., xvii.

Sidon take part in the confederacy. Jeremiah, as Isaiah had done on a former occasion, uses every endeavour to keep his king to the path of reason, but in vain. The hope of the speedy break-up of Babylon, a hope which is even now nourished by fanatical prophets, as well as the prospect of support from Egypt, carry away the masses, and they are stronger than the king's will. Even the exiles themselves are drawn into the general commotion.[1] The report goes that they are already preparing to return. Jeremiah is the only one, as Isaiah had been before him, who perceives the mad foolhardiness of such a hazardous enterprise, not because he has less trust in Yahvé than the rest, but because he has no confidence in the moral condition of his people. And his voice is not listened to.

The confederacy of his vassals does not seem to have troubled Nebuchadrezzar much. In the winter of the year 587 he however appears with his army before Jerusalem. He proceeds at once to invest the city. In the city itself terror and despair begin to manifest themselves. Still the inhabitants are determined to resist to the uttermost. And, as a matter of fact, the walls of Jerusalem prove strong enough, and its garrison brave enough, to offer resistance to the Great King. And when the long-looked-for help from Egypt at last came with the appearance of Pharaoh Hofra, whose army marched into Palestine, Nebuchadrezzar is forced to raise the siege. The rejoicing is universal—Jeremiah alone does not rejoice. The enemy will return in a short time; even if Zedekiah's army were to inflict a total defeat on the Babylonians, Yahvé would in the end deliver Jerusalem into the hands of Nebuchadrezzar.[2]

Jeremiah has to pay for his outspokenness by imprisonment.[3] But while he is bearing the disgrace of being considered an enemy and a traitor to his own city, his words are being actually fulfilled. The besiegers have returned. Famine rages in the city. After besieging it for a year and a half, Nebuchadrezzar's troops

---

[1] Jer. xxvii., xxix. [2] Jer. xxxvii. 11; xxxiv. 8 ff.
[3] Jer. xxxviii. [*Cf.* Cheyne, *Jeremiah*, p. 172 ff.]

succeed in making a breach in the walls. Zedekiah is seized with the courage of despair. He attempts a sortie. On the south side he succeeds in breaking through the ranks of the besiegers. He has already gained the open, and tries to flee to the country east of the Jordan. He is overtaken at Jericho and made prisoner, and his troops are dispersed. He is blinded by Nebuchadrezzar and carried off in chains to Babylon. His sons were executed before his very eyes. The city is given up for a month to the plundering troops of the enemy, and then set fire to, together with the Temple and the king's fortress. The walls fall; what still remained of the Temple utensils is carried off. A frightful doom overtakes those who are found alive within the city. The populace is subjected to a second deportation. Unfortunately, we cannot now determine the number of those carried away.[1]

A final attempt to raise once more a Judaic commonwealth on the ruins of the ancient state miscarries after a few months.[2] Nebuchadrezzar makes a friend and partisan of Jeremiah, the noble Gedaliah ben Ahikam ben Shaphan, governor of Judah, and fixes his headquarters at Mizpah. He endeavours to collect together the scattered remnant and to reintroduce order and prosperity into Judah under Babylonian authority. But the jealousy of the neighbouring Ammonites prevents the unhappy country from settling down peacefully. The Ammonite king incites a certain Ishmael, a member of the House of David, to murder Gedaliah. Three months after the fall of Jerusalem Ishmael and his party make a fierce and cruel attack on all in Mizpah who acknowledge themselves as Babylonian subjects. Ishmael flees towards Ammon. Those still left in the country are afraid of Nebuchadrezzar's vengeance. They resolve to emigrate to Egypt. Along with the emigrants, though against his will, goes Jeremiah. He was still a prisoner when Jerusalem was captured. The conquerors set him free, and he is carried away along with the exiles as far as Ramah, and then set at liberty.

[1] *Cf.* 2 Kings xxv. 20; xxiv. 13, 14; Jer. lii. 28-30; and thereon, Stade, *ZAW*. iv. 271 ff.   [2] 2 Kings xxv. 22 ff., and especially Jer. xli. ff.

The Hebrew nation has thus reached its end. It has not become extinct, but it has been uprooted. Its shoots are planted in two foreign regions, in Babylonia and Egypt, where they grow luxuriantly and take on new forms. What springs from them, even when it is once more replanted in the old soil, is no longer the old tree. Hebraism has become Judaism.

INDEX

A = Annals of the Kings, ii. 208 ff.
Aahmes, i. 190 f.
Aaron, i. 119 ff., 194 ff., 199, 205 *n.*, 207 f., 216 ff., 219.
Abarim, i. 221 f.
Abdon, ii. 76.
Abel-beth-Ma'acah, ii. 175, 200, 250, 347, 347 *n.*
Abiathar, ii. 126, 171, 177 ff., 182.
Abibaal, ii. 157 *n.*
Abiezer, ii. 80.
Abigail, sister of David, ii. 173.
—— wife of David, ii. 128.
Abijah, King, ii. 238 f., 248.
Abimelech, of Gerar, i. 138, 153.
—— of Shechem, ii. 13 *n.*, 18 *n.*, 82 *n.*, 85 ff.
Abinadab, ii. 135.
Abiram, i. 212, 219.
Abishag, ii. 179.
Abishai, ii. 144, 162, 173.
Abner, ii. 124, 138 ff., 143 ff., 146 f.
Aborigines of Canaan, i. 18 ff.
Abraham, i. 136 ff., 149 ff., 162 f., 171 ff.
Absalom, ii. 163, 169 ff., 248.
Accad, i. 148, 178, 258.
Accho, i. 269 ; ii. 366.
Achish, ii. 129 f., 141.
Achsah, i. 268, 299.
Achzib, i. 269.
Adma, i. 137.
Adon, i. 179.
Adonijah, ii. 177 ff.
Adonibezek, i. 266, 276, 299, 306.
Adoram (Adoniram), ii. 187, 244.
Adonizedek, i. 306 ff.
Adriel, ii. 167.
Adullam, ii. 125 f., 151.
Agag, ii. 117 f.
Agriculture, ii. 93, 296.

Ahab, ii. 215, 237 f., 262 ff.
Ahaz, ii. 239 f., 343 ff.
Ahaziah, King of Judah, ii. 237 f., 281, 285.
—— King of Israel, ii. 237 f., 274 f.
Ahijah, priest, ii. 201 f.
—— prophet, ii. 188, 254.
Ahimaaz, ii. 171 ff.
Ahiman, i. 201, 267.
Ahimelech, ii. 125 f., 201.
Ahithophel, ii. 171 f.
Ahlab, i. 269.
Ai, i. 285 ff., 299 ; ii. 64.
Aijalon, i. 270, 301 ; ii. 63, 76.
Alisphragmutosis, i. 257.
Altaqu, ii. 366 ff.
Amalek, i. 95, 197, 201, 207, 233 f., 268, 276 ; ii. 78 f., 117 f., 133, 140, 163.
Amarna Tablets, ii. 60, 96 *n.*
'Amāsa, ii. 173 ff.
Amaziah, King, ii. 218, 238 f., 288 f., 294 f.
—— priest, ii. 323.
Amenhotep, i. 261.
Amenmeses, i. 261.
Amenophis, i. 258 ff.
Ammonites, i. 24, 152, 202, 224, 231 *n.* ; ii. 29 *n.*, 78, 90, 113, 139, 161 ff., 172, 291, 332 *n.*, 339, 366, 392, 394.
Amnon, ii. 169 f.
Amon, King, ii. 240, 378, 381.
Amorites, i. 21, 211, 213, 224, 230, 270.
Amos, father of Isaiah, ii. 339.
—— prophet, i. 81, 129 ; ii. 291, 320 ff.
Amu, i. 185.
Anakim, i. 23.
Anat, goddess, ii. 98.
—— person, ii. 76 *n.*
Anathoth, ii. 179.
Ancestor-worship, ii. 203.

Apepi, i. 189.
Aphek, i. 269; ii. 104, 132, 158, 271.
Apuriu, i. 184.
Arabah, i. 24; ii. 295.
Arabia, ii. 131, 189, 338, 353.
Arad, i. 202, 268.
Aram. *See* Syria and Damascus.
Ararat, i. 182.
Araunah, ii. 191.
Arioch, i. 177.
Ark of Yahvé, i. 209, 224, 238 f., 275, 279; ii. 46, 105, 107 f., 136, 158, 171, 192, 195, 203 f., 306.
Armenia, i. 182.
Army, ii. 164, 198, 300, 334.
Arnon, i. 11, 212 f., 224.
Arpachsad, i. 162, 184.
Arsa, ii. 255.
Art, ii. 94 f., 194.
Asa, ii. 237, 248 f., 255.
Asahel, ii. 144 f., 148.
Asenath, i. 145.
Ashdod, i. 25; ii. 360, 363.
Asher, i. 155, 269; ii. 63, 74, 80, 98 *n.*
Ashēra, ii. 99, 247 f., 264, 310 f., 355 f., 371 f.
Ashkelon, i. 25; ii. 363 ff.
Ashtart, ii. 98 f., 310, 373.
Assarhaddon, ii. 353, 379.
Asshur, Assyria, i. 148, 161; ii. 232 f., 257 ff., 289, 314, 333 ff., 361, 372 ff., 379 ff.
Assurbanipal, ii. 379.
Assurdan, ii. 295.
Assurnaṣirpal, ii. 258.
Assurnirar, ii. 295.
Athaliah, ii. 238 f., 282, 285 f.
'Aṭarot, ii. 261.
Avaris, i. 256, 258.
'Avvites, i. 23.
Azariah (Uzziah), ii. 236 ff., 295, 329 ff.
Azuri, ii. 360.

BAAL, ii. 98 ff., 201 f., 264 f., 268 f., 279 f., 282, 286, 306 f., 322 ff., 371 ff., 381, 388 ff.
Ba'al-Berîth, ii. 83 ff., 100.
—— Hazor, ii. 169.
—— Jehûda, ii. 159.
—— Peor, i. 82, 214.

Ba'alath, ii. 185.
Baba, i. 189 f.
Babel, Babylon, i. 148; ii. 232 f., 353, 361 ff., 375, 380 ff.
Baḥûrim, ii. 172.
Balak, i. 202 f., 214, 224, 229 f.
Balaam, i. 84 ff., 202 f., 214, 220.
Bamôth. *See* High-places.
Bamôth Baal, i. 214.
Ban, the, ii. 64, 117 *n.*, 199.
Barak, ii. 72.
Baruch, ii. 389.
Barzillai, ii. 172, 179, 200.
Baasha, ii. 237 f., 249 f., 254.
Bathsheba, ii. 168, 176 ff.
Be'er, i. 213; ii. 84 *n.*
Beeroth, i. 290, 301; ii. 156.
Beersheba, i. 34, 83, 146; ii. 99, 322.
Bela, i. 137.
Benaiah, ii. 178.
Benhadad, ii. 249, 261, 271 f., 279 (*see also* Hadadezer), 290 f.
Benihassan, i. 187.
Benjamin, i. 294 f.; ii. 21, 74, 111, 116, 124, 145, 174.
Bethanath, i. 270.
Bethel, i. 34, 87 f., 89 ff., 136 ff., 141 ff., 149, 164, 269 f., 275 ff., 285; ii. 64, 99, 252, 304, 322 ff., 353.
Beth-horon, i. 305; ii. 185.
Bethlehem, i. 108 *n.*; ii. 119, 151, 320.
Beth Reḥôb, ii. 161.
Beth-shean, i. 266, 269; ii. 63, 135, 138.
Beth-shemesh, i. 270; ii. 294.
Bezek, i. 266, 307.
Bidkar, ii. 270, 281.
Bilhah, i. 155.
Blood-revenge, ii. 95, 301.
Boaz, ii. 193.
Bronze, ii. 194.
Book of the Excellent, i. 92, 302; ii. 199.
Book of the Wars, i. 90 f., 213 f.; ii. 199.
Bull-worship, i. 89, 199 f., 200; ii. 202, 253 f., 304, 308, 325 ff.
Burnt-offerings, i. 113.

CALEB, i. 201 f., 211, 218, 267, 276, 299; ii. 129 f.
Canaan, Canaanites, i. 9 f., 20, 136, 147, 200 f; conquest of, i. 263 ff., 282,

INDEX

293 ff; civilisation of, ii. 61 ff., 72 ff., 75, 125 f., 187.
Caphtor, i. 25.
Carchemish, ii. 389.
Carmel, Mount, i. 13 f.; ii. 268.
—— town, ii. 128.
Carrhae, i. 180.
Centralisation of worship, i. 60, 108 ff.; ii. 377. *See* Reform.
Chaldeans. *See* Kasdim and Babylon.
Chalybes, i. 182.
Chebar, ii. 390.
Chedorlaomer, i. 137, 178 f.
Chemosh, i. 243, 246 *n*.; ii. 276 f.
Chemoshmelek, ii. 261.
Chephirah, i. 290, 301; ii. 156.
Cherith, ii. 268.
Cherubim, ii. 192.
Chronicles, ii. 224 f., 283, 360, 378.
Chronology, ii. 8, 135, 142, 234.
Circumcision, i. 195, 281, 298 f.
Climate, i. 15.
Cloud, pillar of, i. 197.
Commander-in-Chief, ii. 300.
Covenant, Book of the, i. 59, 94, 208 f., 235; ii. 96 *n*., 376.
Covenant, Ark of the. *See* Ark.
Cuneiform inscriptions, ii. 232.
Customs, ii. 94, 199, 296 ff., 321 ff.

D, D². *See* Deuteronomy.
Da = History of David, ii. 35, 40 ff., 44, 302.
Dadda-idri, ii. 270.
Dagon, ii. 98, 107.
Daibon, ii. 261.
Damascus, i. 137; ii. 163 *n*., 184, 245, 250, 258 f., 262, 271, 273, 288 ff., 290 ff., 314, 335, 346 f.
Dan, i. 89, 270; ii. 20, 69 f., 71, 92, 101, 103, 175, 201, 250, 252, 304, 322.
Dathan, i. 212, 219.
David, ii. 35 ff., 119 ff., 138, 175, 240, 241 ff., 327, 364, 365.
Debir, Holy of Holies, ii. 192.
Debir, town, i. 267, 276, 299.
Deborah, i. 79 *n*., 87; ii. 66 ff., 71 ff., 97.
Decalogue, i. 50, 72, 198 ff., 208, 235, 244.

Dejokes, ii. 379.
Delilah, ii. 91.
Deluge, i. 34 f., 147.
Deuteronomy, i. 39, 43-69, 101, 105, 115; ii. 376 f., 382 ff; Deuteronomic editor (D²), i. 46 ff., 52, 279 ff., *passim*; ii. 53 *n*., 208, 223 f., 391.
Dinah, i. 142, 156; ii. 69 *n*.
Diodorus, i. 190.
Doeg, ii. 126.
Dor, i. 269.
Dothan, i. 158.

E (E²), i. 38, 69-96, 136-147, 203-215, 274 f., 279, 281, 310; ii. 15 ff., 26 ff., 45, 306, 308.
Ebal, i. 87, 289.
Ebenha'ezer, ii. 104.
Eber, i. 148.
Edom, Edomite, i. 23, 140 ff., 154 ff., 169, 212, 220, 276; ii. 126, 163, 184, 276, 285, 288, 291, 339, 343, 366, 392.
Eglon, town, i. 305.
—— king, ii. 78.
Egypt, i. 133, 139, 144, 150, 153, 158 f., 183 ff., 215 ff.; ii. 182, 185 ff., 244 f., 293, 333 ff., 348, 360 ff., 387 ff.
Ehud, ii. 76 *n*., 78.
Ekron, ii. 363 f.
Elah, King, ii. 237 f., 255.
Elam, i. 137, 177 f.; ii. 362.
Elath, i. 24; ii. 164, 289, 329, 343.
Elders, ii. 94, 109, 112 f., 299 f.
Eleazar, i. 87.
El-elyon, i. 180.
Elhanan, ii. 120.
Eli, ii. 107, 125, 182 f., 201.
Eliakim ben Hilkiah, ii. 367.
Eliezer, i. 137.
Elijah, ii. 213 f., 266 ff., 275, 279.
Elim, i. 217.
Elisha, ii. 214 f., 268, 278, 280 ff., 290, 292 f.
Ellasar, King, i. 177.
El-Kab, i. 189.
Elon, ii. 76.
Eltekeh. *See* Altaqu.
Emim, i. 23.
Endor, ii. 134.
Ephod, ii. 34 *n*., 82, 101, 201, 305.

Ephraim, i. 15 f., 83 f., 145, 266; ii. 63, 74, 80, 90 ff., 105, 115, 138, 187 f.; forest of, ii. 173, 342.
Er, i. 158.
Eriaku, i. 178.
Esek, i. 153.
Eshba'al, ii. 139, 141-149, 366.
Etham, i. 216.
Ethba'al, ii. 263 (366).
Ethiopia, ii. 249, 338, 366 ff.
Euphrates, i. 172; ii. 387.
Exodus from Egypt, i. 196, 206, 216, 223, 256, 260.
Ezekiel, i. 105 ff., 118 f., 126 ff.; ii. 374, 390.
Ezion-Geber, i. 24; ii. 164, 184, 283.

FAMILY LIFE, ii. 298.
Festivals, i. 114 ff.; ii. 305, 309.
Flora of Palestine, i. 16.
Fortified towns, ii. 185, 297 f.

GAAL, ii. 86 f.
Gad (tribe), i. 203, 215, 221, 225, 275; ii. 98 n.
—— prophet, ii. 225, 254.
Galilee, ii. 347.
Gath, i. 25; ii. 120, 129, 152, 288.
Gaza, i. 25; ii. 360, 363.
Geba, ii. 250.
Gedaliah, ii. 394.
Gerar, i. 138, 153.
Gerizim, ii. 85.
Gershom, i. 193.
Geshur, i. 269; ii. 163, 170.
Gezer, i. 269; ii. 63, 75, 152 f., 185.
Giants, i. 201, 211, 267.
Gibbethon, ii. 255.
Gibbôrîm, ii. 164.
Gibeah, ii. 21 n., 105, 111, 113 ff., 138 f., 154, 166 f.
Gibeon, i. 290, 300 ff.; ii. 63, 75, 144, 151 f., 156, 167, 175.
Gideon (Jerubbaal), ii. 80 ff., 81 n., 96, 202.
Gihon, ii. 178, 359.
Gilboa, i. 13; ii. 134 f., 138.
Gilead, i. 143, 155 f., 215; ii. 74, 89 n., 172, 277, 280, 347, 347 n., 380.

Gilgal, i. 87 f., 270, 275 f., 281 f.; ii. 99, 114, 117, 202, 214 n.
God. *See* Yahvé.
God, Brook of, i. 213.
Goliath, ii. 37, 120, 120 n., 152.
Gomorrha, i. 137, 151.
Goshen, i. 160, 205, 222.

H = Law of Holiness, i. 107 ff., 126 ff.
H (H¹) = Heroes, stories of, ii. 79, 81 n.
Habakkuk, ii. 391.
Habor, ii. 352.
Hadad, ii. 184.
Hadadezer, ii. 162 f. (*see also* Benhadad), 270 f.
Hagar, i. 138, 151.
Hamath, ii. 163, 293, 336.
Hamor, 1, 156, 164; ii. 69 n., 83, 87.
Hanno of Gaza, ii. 349, 352, 359.
Haran, i. 148, 172 ff.
Har-heres, i. 270; ii. 63.
Harôd, i. 11; ii. 80.
Haroseth, ii. 72.
Haseroth, i. 218, 224.
Havvoth-jair, ii. 77.
Hazael, ii. 268, 279, 288, 290 f.
Hazor, i. 308; ii. 72 n., 185, 347.
Head, tribal. ii. 94 n., 111.
Heber, ii. 74.
Hebrews, origin of the, i. 172 ff., 180; in Egypt, 183 ff.; Hebrews and Jews, ii. 394.
Hebron, i. 83 f., 137 ff., 201, 267, 276, 299 ff.; ii. 64, 99, 128 ff., 142, 144, 170 f.
Helbah, i. 269.
Heliopolis, i. 258.
Herodotus, i. 190; ii. 368, 380, 387 n.
Heroes of David, ii. 164.
Heshbon, i. 213 f.
Hezekiah, i. 63; ii. 220 ff., 239 f., 355 ff., 360 ff.
High-places, i. 88 f., 108 ff., 122 f.; ii. 100 f., 201, 208 n., 248 f., 253 f., 305, 308, 322 ff., 355 ff., 383.
Hilkiah, ii. 383.
Hinnom, ii. 373.
Hiram, ii. 157, 163, 189, 335.
Hittites, i. 22 f., 26, 163, 269; ii. 61 n., 62 n., 165, 293, 339, 353.

Hivvites, i. 21, 290 n.
Hobab, i. 200, 233 n., 268.
Hobah, i. 137.
Hofra, ii. 393.
Hophni, ii. 105.
Horeb, i. 197, 200 ff., 204, 234 ; ii. 268.
Horites, i. 23 ff., 220.
Hormah, i. 202, 211, 268.
Horse, ii. 188.
Hosea, i. 81 f. ; ii. 112 n., 113 n., 323 ff., 333.
Hoshea, ii. 238 ff., 349 ff.
Host of Heaven, i. 63 ; ii. 374.
Huldah, i. 58 ; ii. 383.
Huleh (lake), i. 13, 308.
Human sacrifices, ii. 95, 116, 202, 373.
Hur, i. 207 f.
Huramabî, ii. 195.
Hushai, ii. 171 f.
Hyksos, i. 185, 257 ff.

Ibleam, i. 269.
Ibzan, ii. 76.
Ijon, ii. 347.
Ilubidi, ii. 352.
Image-worship, i. 90, 199, 221 f., 249 ; ii. 19, 71, 82, 100 f., 201 f., 219, 253, 304, 306 f., 322.
Immanuel, ii. 346.
Incense, altar of, ii. 192.
Isaac, i. 138 f., 152 ff., 163 f., 171.
Isaiah, ii. 220 f., 250, 333, 339 ff., 356 ff., 363 ff., 375.
Ishbosheth. *See* Eshba'al.
Ishmael, i. 138, 151, 158, 163, 169 ; ii. 394.
Israel, i. 18 f., 34, 85, 94. *See also* Ephraim *and* Judah.
Issachar, ii. 63, 65 n., 74.
Ishṭôb, ii. 161.
Ithra, ii. 173.
Ittai, ii. 173.
Itureans, i. 139.
Iye-abarim, i. 220.

J = Yahvist, i. 69 ff., 149-160, 190-203, 264-270, 273 f., 279 f., 281 f., 285 ; ii. 15 ff., 45, 304.
Je = Jerusalem source, ii. 46 f., 302.
Jabbok, i. 11, 156, 213, 224.

Jabesh, ii. 111, 113, 135, 141, 144, 200.
Jabin, i. 308 ; ii. 72 n.
Jachin, ii. 193.
Jael, ii. 73.
Jahaz, i. 213.
Janoah, ii. 347.
Japhet, i. 148.
Jarmuth, i. 305 f.
Jazer, i. 213.
Jebus, i. 22, 267, 299, 301 ; ii. 63, 75, 155 f.
Jeconiah. *See* Jehoiakin.
Jehoahaz, King of Israel, ii. 238 f., 277, 291 ff.
——— King of Judah, ii. 240, 388.
Jehoash, ii. 239, 291 f.
Jehoiada, ii. 286 f.
Jehoiakim, ii. 240, 390 ff.
Jehoiakin, ii. 390.
Jehoshaphat, i. 62 ; ii. 238 f., 263, 276, 282 f.
Jehosheba, ii. 286.
Jehu, King, ii. 216, 240 ff., 268 f., 280 f., 289 ff.
——— Prophet, ii. 255.
Jephthah, ii. 89 f.
Jeremiah, i. 112, 129 ; ii. 374, 385 ff.
Jericho, i. 282 f., 293 ; ii. 64.
Jeroboam (I.), ii. 187, 206, 237 f., 242, 250 ff.
——— (II.), ii. 238 f., 295 ff., 323 ff., 331, 336.
Jerubba'al. *See* Gideon.
Jerusalem, ii. 155, 245, 286, 360 n., 367 ff. *See also* Jebus.
Jesse, ii. 119.
Jethro, i. 35, 204, 209, 223.
Jezebel, ii. 263, 281.
Jezreel, i. 12 f., 266 ; ii. 132, 133, 269, 280, 297.
Joab, ii. 144, 148 f., 161 f., 168, 170, 173 ff.
Joah, ii. 367.
Joash, ii. 239 f., 287 f.
Jochebed, i. 245.
Joel, ii. 328.
Joktan, i. 149.
Jonadab, ii. 281.
Jonathan, son of Saul, ii. 38, 114, 121 ff., 124, 135, 168.

VOL. II.   2 C

Jonathan, son of Abiathar, ii. 171, 178.
Joram, King of Israel, ii. 238 f., 274 ff., 279 ff.
—— King of Judah, ii. 238 f., 282 f., 284.
Jordan, i. 10 f., 279 f. ; ii. 81, 139, 174.
Joseph, i. 34, 83, 144 ff., 156 ff., 165, 186 ff., 203, 222, 265 ff.
Josephus, i. 134, 256.
Joshua, i. 86, 201 f., 207, 209, 211, 215, 218, 221, 265 f., 269 f., 274 ff., 284 ff., 311.
Josiah, i. 49, 58, 108 ; ii. 240, 353, 376, 379 ff.
Jotham, ii. 18 n., 84.
—— King, ii. 239 f., 330 ff.
Judah, i. 83 ff., 155, 158, 266 ff., 272, 291 ; ii. 103 f., 117, 141 f., 245, 339, 365 f., 369 ff.
Judges, ii. 65 ff., 76 f., 92.
Judicial procedure, i. 210.
Jurisdiction, appellate, i. 62.
Justice, Courts of, ii. 284, 301.

K (Ki, Kj) = Redaction of A, ii. 210 ff., 377.
Kadesh-Barnea, i. 201 f., 211 f., 220, 224, 228 f., 231 f.
—— on the Orontes, ii. 165.
—— in Naphtali, ii. 347.
Kasdim, i. 181 f.
Kebir, Tell-el-, i. 253.
Kedar, i. 139, 163.
Kedeshas, ii. 248, 325, 373.
Keilah, ii. 127.
Kenath, i. 215.
Kenaz, Kenizzites, i. 267, 276 f.
Kenites, i. 200, 250, 268, 276 f. ; ii. 74, 78.
Kerioth, i. 202.
Kibroth-Hattaavah, i. 211, 218.
Kidron, i. 12.
Kinnereth, i. 13.
Kings, Monarchy, ii. 82 f., 106 f., 112 f., 146, 197, 241 ff., 300 f.
Kings, Books of, ii. 49 ff., 207 ff., 377, 391.
Kirharoseth, ii. 276.
Kiriath-arba, i. 267, 276.

Kiriath-jearim, i. 290, 301 ; ii. 71, 108, 156, 159 n.
Kiriath-sepher, i. 267 ; ii. 96 n.
Kish, ii. 111, 168.
Kishon, i. 12 ; ii. 63, 72 ff., 268, 387.
Kitron, i. 269.
Korah, i. 219.
Kreti and Pleti, ii. 153 n., 164.
Kudur-Mabug, i. 177.
—— Nanhurdi, i. 177.
Kyaxares, ii. 381, 387.

Laban, i. 142 f., 155.
Lachish, i. 305 f. ; ii. 289, 297, 367 f.
Lagamar, i. 177 f.
Lah-u-roi, i. 153.
Laish, ii. 19, 71, 92.
Language of Israel, i. 20.
Law-book, Law-giving, i. 58 f., 96, 198 f. (in J), 208 f. (in E), 218, 224, 235.
Leah, i. 142, 155.
Lebanon, ii. 187.
—— House of the Forest of, ii. 193.
Lepers (Manetho), i. 258, 261.
Leshem, i. 270.
Levi, Levites, i. 117 ff., 155, 195, 204, 209, 212, 219 f. ; ii. 35 n., 69, 101, 107 n., 203, 305.
Literature, ii. 302.
Lô-debār, ii. 166.
Lot, allotment, i. 265, 271.
—— i. 137 f., 149 f.
Luz, i. 269.

Maachah, woman, ii. 248, 310.
—— i. 269 ; ii. 161.
Maccobas, i. 88, 141, 143 ; ii. 99, 247, 264, 310, 355 f., 373.
Machir ben Ammiel, ii. 172.
—— town, i. 214, 221 ; 74, 76.
Macpelah, i. 163, 165.
Mahanaim, i. 87, 143 ; ii. 139, 142, 147 n., 173 f.
Makkedah, i. 305.
Mamre, i. 137 ff., 151 ff., 179 ff.
Manasseh, King, i. 63 ; ii. 240, 371 ff.
—— Tribe, i. 145 ff., 269 ; ii. 80.
Manetho, i. 256 ff.
Manna, i. 201, 210, 217.
Marah, i. 207.

INDEX

Mari, ii. 293.
Martu, i. 178.
Mashkuta, Tell-el, i. 253 f.
Massah, i. 197.
Matjâ, Wadi, i. 284 ff.
Mattan, ii. 287.
Mattanah, i. 213.
Mazkir, ii. 56, 198, 208.
Mazzoth, i. 196.
Medebah, i. 214; ii. 261.
Medes, ii. 379 ff.
Megiddo, i. 12, 269; ii. 63, 185, 387.
Melchizedek, i. 137, 175, 180.
Melchishua, ii. 135.
Memphis, i. 256.
Menahem, ii. 238 ff., 332 ff.
Menander, ii. 263 n., 269.
Mephibosheth. *See* Meriba'al.
Merab, ii. 167.
Merenptah, i. 256 ff., 261.
Meriba'al, ii. 149, 168, 171, 174.
Meribah, i. 197.
Merodach-Baladan, ii. 362 ff.
Merom, i. 13, 308 f.
Meroz, ii. 74.
Mêsha', ii. 231, 261 f., 276.
Messiah, ii. 319, 346.
Micah ben Jimla, ii. 216, 272, 275.
—— of Moresheth, ii. 350 f., 355 f., 388.
Michal, ii. 39, 121 ff., 146 f., 159.
Michmash, ii. 115.
Midian, i. 144, 193, 202, 220 f., 233, 250; ii. 78 f.
Milcah, i. 149.
Milcom, i. 246; ii. 162.
Millo, ii. 187.
Miriam, i. 202, 206, 211, 225.
Misphragmuthosis, i. 257.
Mizpeh, ii. 99, 109 f., 250, 394.
Moab, i. 23, 152, 202 f., 214 f., 220, 224, 228, 230 ff.; ii. 78, 139, 161 ff, 261 f., 274 ff., 295, 339, 366, 392.
Moloch, i. 246; ii. 374.
Monotheism, i. 242 f., 246; ii. 202, 318, 372.
Moses, i. 92, 192-203, 204-215, 215-222, 223 f., 259, 363; historical existence of, 239 f.; religious creation of, 241-252.
Mugheir, i. 183 ff.

Naaman, ii. 279.
Nabal, ii. 128, 141.
Nabopolassar, ii. 387 f.
Naboth, ii. 269, 278.
Nadab, King, ii. 238 f., 254.
Nahalol, i. 269.
Nahash, ii. 113.
Nahor, i. 149, 162 n.
Nahum, ii. 381.
Naphtali, i. 270; ii. 63, 74, 250, 347.
Nathan, ii. 169, 178 ff., 254.
Nations, genealogy of, i. 148.
Nature-religion, i. 243, 244, 246; ii. 99, 264, 372 f.
Nazarites, ii. 92, 298 f.
Nebaioth, i. 163.
Nebo, i. 221.
Nebuchadrezzar, ii. 389 ff.
Necho, ii. 387.
Necromancers, ii. 134.
Negeb, ii. 128.
Nimrod, i. 148.
Nineveh, ii. 378 f.
Nizir, i. 182.
Nob, ii. 125 f., 158, 201.
Nobah, i. 215.
Nobility, ii. 94.

Obed-Edom, ii. 159.
Oboth, i. 220.
Officials, ii. 198, 300.
Omri, i. 91, ii. 238 f., 255 f., 257 ff.
Onan, i. 158.
Ophir, ii. 189, 197, 283.
Ophrah, ii. 80 ff., 201 f.
Oracle, ii. 134, 142, 151, 202.
Oreb, ii. 80.
Organisation, ii. 93 f., 197, 299 f.
Osarsiph, i. 258.
Osorkon, i. 254.
Othniel, i. 267, 276, 299; ii. 77.
Overseers under Solomon, ii. 186 f.

P = Priestly Writing, i. 96-132, 161-167, 215-222, 308; ii. 22, 377.
Pr (Pr²) = Prophetical history, ii. 213 f.
Paddan-Aram, i. 164.
Padi, ii. 365 f.
Palestine, i. 9 ff.
Palms, city of, i. 268.

Paran, i. 220.
Passover, i. 61, 116; ii. 309.
Patriarchs, historical or not, i. 168.
Pekah, ii. 240 ff., 338 ff.
Pekahiah, ii. 240 ff., 337.
Peleg, i. 149.
Pentateuch, i. 27 ff., 58 f., 97 ff., 104 ff.
Penuel, i. 81 f., 87, 99, 251, 297.
People, numbering of the, i. 237; ii. 165.
Perez, i. 158.
Pestilence, ii. 165.
Pethor, i. 214.
Phicol, i. 139.
Philistines, i. 25 f.; ii. 62, 101 ff., 118 ff., 127, 129 ff., 138 ff., 150 f., 339, 342, 359, 363, 366, 369.
Phineas, i. 220.
Phœnicians, i. 25; ii. 62 n., 93, 163, 194, 195, 262, 366.
Phraortes, ii. 379.
Pilgrimage, ii. 322.
Pisgah, i. 203.
Pithom, i. 204, 253 ff.
Potiphar, i. 144 f.
Priests, Priesthood, i. 117 ff., 209 f., 212 ff.; ii. 182 f., 201 ff., 286 f., 331.
Primitive history, i. 168 ff.
Prophets, i. 239, 242; ii. 73, 109 f., 136, 265 f., 312 ff., 376, 380 ff.
Psammetich, ii. 379.
Puah, i. 204.
Pul, ii. 333 f.

QARQAR, ii. 236, 273 f., 275, 352.

R (R^d, R^h) = Redactor or editor, i. 66 f., 75, 165-167, 194, 221, 281; ii. 3, 25 n., 208 ff.
Ri (ri) = Stories of the Judges, ii. 2 f., 13, 391.
Raamses, i. 204, 216, 254.
Rabbath-Ammon, i. 24; ii. 162, 168.
Rabsaris, ii. 367 n.
Rabshakeh, ii. 367.
Rachel, i. 87, 142, 155.
Rahab, i. 283.
Ramah, ii. 99, 107, 111, 117, 249, 297, 394.
—— in Gilead, ii. 272 f., 275, 277, 280.
Rammânnirâr, ii. 293 n., 294 f.

Rameses, King, i. 255, 260 f.; ii. 61 n.
—— land of, i. 165.
Raphia, ii. 352, 360.
Ra-Saqenen, i. 189 f.
Rebeka, i. 141 ff., 153 ff.
Rechabites, ii. 281, 298.
Red Sea, i. 196, 207, 216, 223 ff., 225 f.; ii. 164, 184, 283, 329 f.
Reform, i. 58; ii. 355 ff., 386 ff.
Reformation, ii. 384.
Rehob, i. 218, 269.
Rehoboam, ii. 211 f., 237 f., 242 ff., 246 f.
Rehoboth, i. 153.
Rephaim, i. 23, 266 n.; ii. 151.
Rephidim, i. 207, 217, 234.
Representative, Philistine, ii. 105, 114 f.
Resheph, ii. 98.
Reuben, i. 144, 155, 203, 215, 221, 225, 275; ii. 70, 74.
Rezin, ii. 335 ff., 347.
Rezôn ben Eliada‘, ii. 184.
Rizpah, ii. 150, 167, 200.
Rock, Dome of the, ii. 191.
Rogel, ii. 178 n.

S = History of Saul, ii. 29 f., 33 f., 111 n., 303.
So = History of Solomon, ii. 55 ff., 303 f.
SS = History of Samuel and Saul, ii. 29 ff., 34 f., 42 ff., 111 n., 303, 376.
Sabako, ii. 349, 362.
Saba, ii. 189.
Sacrifice, i. 111 ff.; ii. 201, 305.
Safâ, i. 276.
Sais, i. 256.
Salatis, i. 256.
Salem, i. 175.
Salmanassar (II.) ii. 236, 272 ff., 275, 289 f.; (III.) ii. 295; (IV.) ii. 348 f.
Salmonah, i. 220.
Samaria, ii. 237, 260 f., 276, 281 f., 293, 348 ff.
Samaritans, ii. 354.
Samson, ii. 11, 91, 104.
Samuel, ii. 23 ff., 106 ff., 134.
Sa-ptah, i. 261.
Sarah, i. 138, 149 ff., 162 ff.
Sargon, ii. 351, 360 ff.
Saul, ii. 23 ff., 111 ff., 135, 140, 168, 240, 302.

INDEX

Scythians, ii. 386 ff.
Seir, i. 23. *See* Edom.
Sela, i. 24 ; ii. 289.
Sennacherib, ii. 238, 360 ff.
Septuagint (LXX.), ii. 36 ff., 50 ff., 120 n., 184 n., 186 n., 188 n., 205 ff., 333 f. n.
Serah, ii. 249.
Serpent-worship, i. 212 ; ii. 310, 355.
Serpent-stone, ii. 178, 180.
Serbonian Lake, i. 262.
Sesostris, i. 191 f.
Sethos, i. 260 f.
Seti, i. 260 f.
Set-nechts, i. 261.
Shaalbim, i. 270 ; ii. 63.
Shallum, ii. 238 f., 332.
Shamgar, ii. 73, 76 n., 97 n.
Shamsî, ii. 338.
Shaphan, i. 58, 64.
Sharon, i. 14 ; ii. 103.
Shashu, i. 185.
Sheba' ben Bichri, ii. 176.
Shechem, i. 88 f., 136, 143, 149, 156, 164, 311 ; ii. 65, 69, 83, 99, 243, 251, 297.
Shebna, ii. 367.
Shefēlā, i. 14 ; ii. 103, 367.
Shelah, i. 162.
Shem, i. 148.
Sheshai, i. 201, 267.
Showbread, table of, ii. 192.
Shibboleth, ii. 90.
Shiloh, ii. 101, 105, 203, 387.
Shimei, ii. 76 n., 171, 174, 179 f.
Shinar, i. 148.
Shishak, i. 254 ; ii. 188, 247, 251.
Shittim, i. 203, 214, 279 f.
Shobi, ii. 172.
Shunem, ii. 133.
Shur, i. 207.
Siddim, i. 137.
Sidon, i. 26, 269 ; ii. 197, 258, 263, 338, 363 ff., 392.
Sihon, i. 213 f., 224 f., 228 f.
Silo. *See* Shiloh.
Siloah, ii. 230, 360.
Simeon, i. 146, 155, 266 ff., 276 ; ii. 69.
Sinai, i. 193, 197 ff., 204, 207 ff., 217, 223, 233 ff., 250.
Sin, i. 217.
Sin-offering, i. 114.

Sisera, ii. 72.
Slaves, ii. 299.
Sô (Seve), ii. 349, 352.
Sodom, i. 137, 151.
Solomon, ii. 49 ff., 177 ff., 183 ff., 240.
Solomon's districts, ii. 186, 198, 299.
Song of Miriam, i. 206, 225.
—— Moses, i. 93, 210, 215 n.
—— David, ii. 137.
Spies, i. 201, 211, 218.
Star-worship, ii. 348, 372 f.
Stations, list of, i. 95, 212 f., 221, 236.
Succoth, i. 206, 216 ; ii. 81 f.
Sun-horses, ii. 348, 374.
Superstition, ii. 116, 134, 200, 202.
Suphah, i. 213.
Supplement-Hypothesis, i. 40.
Syria, i. 26 ; ii. 152 f., 260, 271, 336, 338, 342, 348, 366, 389. *See also* Damascus.
Syro-Ephraimite War, ii. 236, 237 ff.

Taanach, i. 269 ; ii. 63.
Tabernacle, the, i. 200, 209, 217, 224, 237.
Tables of the Law, i. 199 f., 208, 217 f., 238.
Tabor, ii. 80.
Tadmor, ii. 185 n.
Tahpenês, ii. 184.
Talmai, i. 201, 267.
—— ii. 163, 170.
Tamar, woman, ii. 169 f.
—— town, ii. 185.
Tarshish, ships of, ii. 189 n., 283, 341.
Tartan, ii. 361, 367 n.
Tekoa, ii. 320.
Tema, i. 163.
Temple, ii. 159, 189 ff., 245 f., 287 f., 309 f., 331, 348 f., 357.
Teraphim, i. 142 ; ii. 20 n., 34 n., 101, 123, 202 f., 306.
Terah, sons of, i. 149.
Thebez, ii. 89.
Theophany, i. 197, 208 f.
Thothmes, i. 179 ; ii. 61 n.
Thummim. *See* Urim.
Thummosis, i. 257.
Tibni, ii. 256.
Tiglathpileser (I.), ii. 257 ; (III.) ii. 335 ff.

Timaeus, i. 256.
Timnath-serah, i. 276, 292 n.
Tirhaqa, ii. 362, 368.
Tirzah, ii. 255, 332.
Tishbe, ii. 266.
To'i, ii. 163.
Tola, ii. 76.
Town life, ii. 61 f., 297 f.
Trade, ii. 61 f., 197, 296.
Trees, sacred, ii. 99.
Tyre, ii. 157, 163, 189, 335, 338, 366, 392.

URIAH, ii. 168.
Urim and Thummim, ii. 202.
Ur Kasdim, i. 149 f., 181 ff.

WADY EL-FĀRI'A, i. 11.
—— esh-sheri'a, ii. 133.
—— Modschib. *See* Arnon.
Wāhēb, i. 213.
War-chariots, ii. 62.
Waters, City of, ii. 162.
Well, Song of the, i. 92, 213.
Writing, Art of, ii. 95.

YAHVÉ, i. 204, 242, 245-252; ii. 97, 100, 110, 157 f., 371.

Yarmûk, i. 11.

ZACHARIAH, ii. 238 f., 332.
Zadok, i. 118, 124; ii. 171, 177 ff., 179, 308.
Zalmunnah, ii. 81.
Zamzummim, i. 23.
Zaphenath-paneah, i. 145.
Zarephath, ii. 268.
Zebah, ii. 81.
Zeboim, i. 137.
Zebul, ii. 84 ff.
Zebulun, i. 269; ii. 63, 74.
Zechariah, ii. 288.
Zedek, ii. 366.
Zedekiah, ii. 240, 392 ff.
Ze'eb, ii. 80.
Zephaniah, ii. 380.
Zephath, i. 268.
Zerah, i. 158.
Zerēda, ii. 187.
Ziba, ii. 166, 171.
Ziklag, ii. 129 f., 133, 140.
Zilpah, i. 155.
Zimri, ii. 238, 255.
Zion, ii. 156 ff., 191 ff., 358, 371, 386.
Zipporah, i. 193, 195, 210 f.
Zoan, i. 201.
Zobah, ii. 161, 184.

www.ingramcontent.com/pod-product-compliance
Lightning Source LLC
Chambersburg PA
CBHW030553300426
44111CB00009B/967